Complete Spanish
STEP-BY-STEP

The Fastest Way to Achieve Spanish Mastery

Barbara Bregstein

McGraw Hill Education

New York Chicago San Francisco Athens London Madrid
Mexico City Milan New Delhi Singapore Sydney Toronto

6 7 8 9 10   LCR   21 20 19

ISBN   978-1-259-64341-5
MHID   1-259-64341-7

e-ISBN 978-1-259-64342-2
e-MHID   1-259-64342-5

This title is a combination of two previously published titles: *Easy Spanish Step-by-Step* and *Advanced Spanish Step-by-Step*.

McGraw-Hill Education Language Lab
Vocabulary flashcards and audio recordings of the readings are available to support your study of this book. Go to www.mhlanguagelab.com to access the online version of this application, or to locate links to the mobile app for iOS and Android devices. More details about the features of the app are available on the inside front cover.

The audio recordings can also be downloaded from mhprofessional.com/mediacenter. Enter the ISBN of this book (9781259643415) and your email address to receive a link to download a zipped folder of mp3 files.

McGraw-Hill Education books are available at special quantity discounts to use as premiums and sales promotions or for use in corporate training programs. To contact a representative, please visit the Contact Us pages at www.mhprofessional.com.

Contents

I   Elements of a Sentence

1   Nouns, Articles, and Adjectives   3

2   *Estar, Ser,* and Subject Pronouns   14

12 Reflexive Verbs 193

13 The Present Subjunctive 206

III   Preterit Tense, Imperfect Tense, and Double Object Pronouns

IV *Ser* and *Estar*; Present, Preterit, and Imperfect Tenses; Progressive Tenses; Present Subjunctive; Commands

29 The Past Perfect Subjunctive

30 Idioms

Preface

Complete Spanish Step-by-Step is a progressive program that will help you learn Spanish—talking, reading, and writing—as quickly and as thoroughly as possible, and then lead you to mastery and fluency in the language. Written for beginner and advanced-beginner learners, it teaches grammar and conversation in the most logical order to enable you to develop your language skills naturally to the level of intermediate and advanced learners.

To take full advantage of the unique grammatical progression of the book, you should study each chapter, or step, one after another. Do not skip around. Each step you take will lead you to the next. Each chapter contains clear grammar explanations; be sure to understand every concept before moving on to the next. Notice that there are few exceptions to rules, so once you have learned a concept, it is yours.

Try to learn the vocabulary and verbs provided; they have been carefully selected on the basis of usefulness and frequency. The vocabulary lists will help enhance your communication, while complete verb conjugations are given so that you can practice pronunciation as you learn verbs. Over 300 of the most common verbs in Spanish are presented.

Varied written and oral exercises are included to check your understanding and progress. (The book has a complete answer key in the back.) It is also a good idea to write your own questions and sentences and practice them aloud. Sometimes, your own creations are more interesting and aid in learning.

Original readings are included in every chapter; they become progressively more challenging in form and content throughout the book, leading to poems and stories by acclaimed authors. Use these reading comprehension sections to learn new vocabulary and to practice reading aloud.

Complete Spanish Step-by-Step is divided into six parts. The first gives you all the fundamentals of the language in the present tense. You will notice that the word order of English and Spanish in this part is essentially the same. This makes learning in the early stages very quick. The second part explains indirect objects, direct objects, direct object pronouns, reflexive verbs, and the present subjunctive. The third part presents the two most used tenses in the past, the preterit and the imperfect. The fourth part reviews the present tense and uses of *ser* and *estar*, the preterit and imperfect tenses, the progressive tenses, the present subjunctive, and commands. The fifth part is an in-depth explanation of nouns, articles, adjectives, pronouns, and the present and past perfect tenses. The sixth part covers the future and conditional tenses, the past subjunctive, and idioms.

A student once asked me if Spanish is truly easy. It is, in comparison to any of the other languages of the world. To start with, the pronunciation is easy. Spanish is a phonetically perfect language, which means that once you learn to pronounce each vowel and consonant, you will be able to pronounce all words correctly. Before you begin, practice all the sounds outlined in the Guide to Pronunciation in the following pages. If possible, try to practice with a native speaker. Then, remember to read and answer questions aloud as much as you can to develop your pronunciation.

This book is written with a logical approach that makes it accessible, even when some concepts are difficult, whether you are a self-study learner or a student in an organized teaching program. With *Complete Spanish Step-by-Step*, you will see that everything falls quickly into place. In a few weeks, you will be able to read and write Spanish quite easily, and as you progress, you will learn to speak fluently, using all elements of Spanish. And once you learn the Spanish in this book, you will be able to get along in any Spanish-speaking country. The grammar is standard in all parts of the Spanish-speaking world, and although accents change from place to place, you will get accustomed to the sounds very quickly. Have fun and enjoy using Spanish everywhere you need it. See you in Xochicalco!

Acknowledgments

I would like to thank Nestor Rodriguez, teacher of English and Spanish at City College of New York, for his invaluable language insights, expertise and editing of both *Easy Spanish Step-by-Step* and *Advanced Spanish Step-by-Step*, upon which this book is based. I would also like to thank John Piazza for his insights, contributions, and editing of *Advanced Spanish Step-by-Step*. I gratefully acknowledge their assistance throughout the development of this book.

I would also like to thank Silvia Ballinas, teacher and director of Escuela Experiencia in Tepoztlán, Mexico, Antonio Zea, linguist and professor at Escuela Acacias in Málaga, Spain, Alonia King, Janet Odums, and Lois Shearer. I would also like to thank William Bonner for his invaluable guidance and all my students from District Council 37 in New York City.

Guide to Pronunciation

Spanish spelling is an exact reflection of the pronunciation of the language. The pronunciation of each letter is subject to precise and consistent rules, and words are pronounced by adding together the sounds of each individual letter.

Vowels

The sounds of the vowels are clear and short. Pronounce the examples.

Letter	Pronounced like	Examples
a	the *a* in *father*	la casa, la tapa, Panamá, Canadá
e	two sounds:	
	the *e* in *café* when final	elefante, come, vive, verde, que
	the *e* in *set* elsewhere	pero, es, hotel
i	the *i* in *machine*	sí, cine, comida
o	two sounds:	
	the *o* in *hope*	oso, otro, hospital
	the *o* in *for* if followed by **r**	doctor, profesor
u	the *u* in *rule*	uno, tú, puro
	written as **ü** when pronounced in **güe** and **güi**	agüero, güira
	silent in **gue** and **gui** elsewhere	guerra, guitarra
y	Spanish **i**	y, soy, hay

Consonants

b / v	the *b* in *boat* when they occur at the beginning of a breath group, or following **l**, **m**, or **n**	baño, burro, embargo, alba, el vino, el voto, invierno, vamos
	softer elsewhere, produced through slightly opened lips	Cuba, la boca, Havana, la vaca

In Spanish, the *b* and *v* have the same sound. The sound of English *v* does not exist in Spanish.

c	the *c* in *cat* before **a**, **o**, **u**, or before a consonant	camisa, color, concreto
	the *s* in *sail* before **e** or **i**	centavo, cita, cinco
ch	the *ch* in *chum*	chocolate, chorizo

Letter	Pronounced like	Examples
d	two sounds:	
	the *d* in *dog* when it occurs at the beginning of a breath group, or following **l** or **n**	donde, falda, conde
	the *th* in *other* elsewhere	boda, poder, verdad, nada, cada, estudio
f	English *f*	futuro, fila, oficina
g	the *g* in *game* before **a, o, u**, or before a consonant	gato, gusto, grande
	the *h* in *hat* before **e** or **i**	genio, generoso, gitano
h	silent	hombre, hasta, hablar
j	English *h* (It can also be given a slightly guttural sound.)	Juan, ojo, mujer
k	English *k*	kayak, kilómetro, kiwi
l	English *l*, but with the tip of the tongue touching the roof of the mouth	el, hotel, mil, palo
ll	the *y* in *beyond*, or in some countries, the *s* in *pleasure*	caballo, bello, llave
m	English *m*	menos, cama, marrón
n	English *n*	nota, nación, nariz
ñ	the *ny* in *canyon* or the *ni* in *onion*	mañana, España, señor
p	English *p*, but not explosive (without the puff of air in the English sound)	papel, persona, pobre
q	the *k* in *key* (found only in the combinations **que** and **qui**)	Quito, queso, equipo
r	the *dd* in *ladder* (a single tongue flap)	caro, barato, para, hablar
	The **r** at the beginning of a word or after **l**, **n**, or **s** is trilled like **rr**.	rosa, el río, Enrique, las rosas
rr	a trill or tongue roll (There is no equivalent sound in English.)	perro, horrible, carro

Letter	Pronounced like	Examples
s	English *s*	sopa, sala, blusa
t	English *t*, but not explosive (with the tip of the tongue against the back of the upper front teeth)	torta, talento, tesoro
v	Spanish **b** (There is no *v* sound in Spanish.)	
w	The letter **w** exists in Spanish only in words of foreign origin and is not considered part of the Spanish alphabet.	
x	English *x*	experto, examen
y	Spanish **ll** (the *y* in *beyond* or, in some countries, the *s* in *pleasure*)	papaya, papagayo, ayer
z	the *s* in *sail*	azul, brazo, luz

Stress, Written Accentuation, and Spelling

Natural Stress

Words that end in a vowel (**a**, **e**, **i**, **o**, **u**) or the consonants **n** or **s** have their natural stress on the next to last syllable.

cucaracha	volumen
mañana	examen
triste	tomates
hablo	

Words that end in any consonant other than **n** or **s** have their natural stress on the final syllable.

salud	mujer
amistad	cantar
papel	doctor
vegetal	nariz
azul	

Written Accents

When a word does not follow one of these two rules, it will have a written accent on the syllable that is stressed.

tel<u>é</u>fono	can<u>ción</u>
<u>lám</u>para	lec<u>ción</u>
<u>mú</u>sica	dif<u>í</u>cil
caf<u>é</u>	<u>fá</u>cil

If a one-syllable word has a written accent, it means that there is another word in the language that has the same spelling, but another meaning.

el	*the*	él	*he*
si	*if*	sí	*yes*
tu	*your*	tú	*you*
se	*oneself*	sé	*I know*

If a two-syllable word has a written accent that does not affect the pronunciation, it means that there is another word that has the same spelling, but a different meaning.

este	*this*	éste	*this one*
ese	*that*	ése	*that one*

Interrogative words have an accent mark that does not affect pronunciation.

¿qué?	*what?*	¿cómo?	*how?*
¿quién?	*who?*	¿por qué?	*why?*
¿dónde?	*where?*	¿cuál?	*which?*

Spelling Changes

• **z** to **c**

Nouns and adjectives that end in **z** change to **c** to form the plural.

el lápiz	los lápices
la nariz	las narices
feliz	felices

Z followed by **a** or **o** changes to **c** before an **e** or **i**. The sound of **z** and **c** are the same.

comienza	comience
empiezo	empiece

- **Other spelling changes**

  All other spelling changes occur in order to maintain a required sound.

  Tocar, for example, has a hard *c* sound that must be preserved in other forms of the verb. If you see **toque**, with **qu** replacing the **c**, it is to maintain the *k* sound.

  Llegar, for example, has a hard *g* sound, which must be preserved. If you see **llegue**, with **gu** replacing the **g**, it is to maintain the hard *g* sound.

Castilian Spanish

There are only a few differences in pronunciation between the Spanish spoken in Latin America and that spoken in Spain.

- Both the **c** that precedes **e** or **i** and the **z** have the *th* sound heard in English *thought* and *thing*.

- When **j** or **g** precedes **e** or **i**, it has a slightly more guttural sound.

Tips for Pronunciation
- While practicing, remember to keep the vowel sounds short and clear.
- Always use the Spanish **r** sound. Resist the use of the English *r*.
- Implode the sounds of **p** and **t**. Make sure there is no puff of air.
- Always pronounce **z** like the letter **s**.
- Give the syllables an almost equal emphasis, a sort of staccato sound. Pronounce every syllable clearly and precisely in order to develop an even speech pattern.

The Alphabet

El alfabeto o abecedario

Letter(s)	Name	Letter(s)	Name
A	a	**N**	ene
B	be larga / be grande	**Ñ**	eñe
C	ce	**O**	o
CH	che	**P**	pe
D	de	**Q**	cu
E	e	**R**	ere
F	efe	**RR**	erre
G	ge	**S**	ese
H (always silent)	hache	**T**	te
I	i	**U**	u
J	jota	**V**	ve corta
K	ka	**W**	doble ve / doble u
L	ele	**X**	equis
LL	elle	**Y**	i griega / ye
M	eme	**Z**	zeta

Greetings and Salutations

Hola.	*Hello.*
Buenos días.	*Good morning.*
Buenas tardes.	*Good afternoon.*
Buenas noches.	*Good evening.*
Me llamo Susana.	*My name is Susan.*
¿Cómo se llama usted?	*What's your name?*
Me llamo David.	*My name is David.*
Mucho gusto.	*Pleased to meet you.*
¿Cómo está usted?	*How are you?*
Bien, gracias, ¿y usted?	*Fine, thanks. And you?*
Regular. Más o menos.	*So-so. More or less.*
Hasta luego.	*So long.*
Hasta mañana.	*Until tomorrow.*
Hasta pronto.	*See you soon.*
Adiós.	*Good-bye.*

I

Elements of a Sentence

1

Nouns, Articles, and Adjectives

The Gender of Nouns and the Definite Article

A noun is a person, place, or thing.

In Spanish, all nouns are either *masculine* or *feminine*.

In Spanish, the definite article (English *the*) agrees with the noun in gender (masculine or feminine) and number (singular or plural): **el**, **la**, **los**, **las**.

Singular Nouns

Masculine

The masculine singular noun takes the definite article **el**.

Most nouns that end in **-o** are masculine. Pronounce the following words aloud.

el amigo	*the friend*	el libro	*the book*
el banco	*the bank*	el muchacho	*the boy*
el baño	*the bathroom*	el niño	*the little boy, the child*
el carro	*the car*	el perro	*the dog*
el gato	*the cat*	el teléfono	*the telephone*
el hermano	*the brother*	el vino	*the wine*

Many masculine nouns do not end in **-o**; therefore, it is necessary to learn each noun with its article.

el animal	*the animal*	el hospital	*the hospital*
el café	*the coffee*	el hotel	*the hotel*
el doctor	*the doctor*	el tomate	*the tomato*
el hombre	*the man*	el tren	*the train*

Some masculine nouns end in **-a** or **-ma**.

el clima	*the climate*	el planeta	*the planet*
el día	*the day*	el poema	*the poem*
el drama	*the drama*	el problema	*the problem*
el idioma	*the language*	el programa	*the program*
el mapa	*the map*	el sistema	*the system*

Feminine

The feminine singular noun takes the definite article **la**.

Most nouns that end in **-a** are feminine. Pronounce the following words aloud.

la amiga	*the friend*	la lámpara	*the lamp*
la blusa	*the blouse*	la mesa	*the table*
la bolsa	*the bag*	la muchacha	*the girl*
la cama	*the bed*	la niña	*the little girl*
la casa	*the house*	la persona	*the person*
la cerveza	*the beer*	la planta	*the plant*
la comida	*the meal*	la silla	*the chair*
la hermana	*the sister*	la tienda	*the store*
la iglesia	*the church*	la ventana	*the window*

Nouns that end in **-ción**, **-sión**, **-dad**, **-tad**, or **-tud** are feminine.

la canción	*the song*	la televisión	*the television*
la conversación	*the conversation*	la ciudad	*the city*
la invitación	*the invitation*	la verdad	*the truth*
la lección	*the lesson*	la amistad	*the friendship*
la ilusión	*the illusion*	la actitud	*the attitude*

A few nouns that end in **-o** are feminine.

la foto	*the photograph*
la mano	*the hand*
la radio	*the radio*

Many feminine nouns do not follow these patterns; therefore, it is important to learn each noun with its article.

la clase	*the class*	la mujer	*the woman*
la flor	*the flower*	la piel	*the skin*
la luz	*the light*	la suerte	*the luck*

Exercise 1.1

Write the appropriate masculine or feminine form of the definite article for each of the following nouns. As you write the answer, make sure you know the meaning of the word.

1. _____ amigo
2. _____ hombre
3. _____ casa
4. _____ luz
5. _____ hotel
6. _____ hermano
7. _____ ciudad
8. _____ carro
9. _____ tomate
10. _____ cerveza

11. _____ persona
12. _____ canción
13. _____ teléfono
14. _____ muchacho
15. _____ flor
16. _____ mujer
17. _____ baño
18. _____ vino
19. _____ comida
20. _____ conversación

A noun ending in **-ista** can be masculine or feminine, depending on whether it refers to a male or a female. The article indicates the gender of the noun.

el artista	*the (male) artist*	el pianista	*the (male) pianist*
la artista	*the (female) artist*	la pianista	*the (female) pianist*
el dentista	*the (male) dentist*	el taxista	*the (male) cabdriver*
la dentista	*the (female) dentist*	la taxista	*the (female) cabdriver*

A noun ending in **-nte** can be masculine or feminine, depending on whether it refers to a male or a female. The article indicates the gender of the noun.

el cantante	*the (male) singer*
la cantante	*the (female) singer*
el estudiante	*the (male) student*
la estudiante	*the (female) student*
el gerente	*the (male) manager*
la gerente	*the (female) manager*
el presidente	*the (male) president*
la presidente	*the (female) president*

Plural Nouns

Masculine

A masculine noun that ends in a vowel adds **-s** to form the plural; it takes the definite article **los**.

Singular	Plural
el día	los días
el hermano	los hermanos
el libro	los libros
el muchacho	los muchachos
el perro	los perros
el problema	los problemas

If the noun ends in a consonant, **el** changes to **los** and the noun adds **-es**.

el animal	los animales
el doctor	los doctores
el hospital	los hospitales
el hotel	los hoteles
el tren	los trenes

Feminine

A feminine noun that ends in a vowel adds **-s** to form the plural; it takes the definite article **las**.

la bolsa	las bolsas
la lámpara	las lámparas
la niña	las niñas
la persona	las personas
la tienda	las tiendas
la ventana	las ventanas

If the noun ends in a consonant, **la** changes to **las** and the noun adds **-es**.

la canción	las canciones
la ciudad	las ciudades
la flor	las flores
la invitación	las invitaciones
la lección	las lecciones
la mujer	las mujeres

Exercise 1.2

Write the plural form of each of the following singular nouns.

EXAMPLE   el hotel   *los hoteles*

1. el animal   los animales
2. la amistad   las amistades
3. el teléfono   los telefonos
4. el tren   los trenes
5. la ventana   las ventanas
6. el doctor   los doctores
7. la ciudad   las ciudades
8. la bolsa   las bolsas
9. la mesa   las mesas
10. el idioma   los idiomas

11. la planta   las plantas
12. la flor   las flores
13. el perro   los perros
14. la ilusión   las ilusiónes
15. la clase   las clases
16. la lección las lecciónes
17. el taxista   los taxistas
18. la lámpara   las lámparas
19. la silla   las sillas
20. la luz   las luses

The Indefinite Article

The Spanish singular indefinite article (English *a, an*) is **un** before a masculine noun and **una** before a feminine noun. Pronounce the words in the following lists aloud. By learning these nouns, you are building your vocabulary.

Singular Indefinite Articles

Masculine

un amigo	*a (male) friend*	un jardín	*a garden*
un baño	*a bathroom*	un museo	*a museum*
un carro	*a car*	un pianista	*a (male) pianist*
un espejo	*a mirror*	un sillón	*an armchair*
un gato	*a cat*	un tiquete	*a ticket*

Feminine

una amiga	*a (female) friend*	una mujer	*a woman*
una biblioteca	*a library*	una página	*a page*
una ciudad	*a city*	una persona	*a person (male or female)*
una idea	*an idea*		
una librería	*a bookstore*	una pluma	*a pen*
una maleta	*a suitcase*		

Plural Indefinite Articles

The Spanish plural indefinite article (English *some*) is **unos** before a masculine plural noun and **unas** before a feminine plural noun.

Masculine

unos barcos	*some boats*	unos idiomas	*some languages*
unos gatos	*some cats*	unos libros	*some books*

Feminine

unas artistas	*some (female) artists*
unas casas	*some houses*
unas conversaciones	*some conversations*
unas flores	*some flowers*

Exercise 1.3

Translate the following nouns into English. Remember to practice pronouncing the words.

1. el libro   the book
2. la página   the page
3. la casa   the house
4. las flores   the flowers
5. el baño   the bathroom
6. el vino   the wine
7. el muchacho   the boy
8. el hermano   the brother
9. la biblioteca   the library
10. el café   the coffee
11. el tren   the train
12. el planeta   the planet
13. el dentista   the dentist
14. el jardín   the garden
15. la flor   the flower

16. la cerveza — the beer
17. la planta — the plant
18. la amistad — the friendship
19. la verdad — the truth
20. la suerte — the luck
21. la gerente — manager
22. la tienda — store
23. la ventana — window
24. un museo — museum
25. un espejo — mirror
26. una librería — book store
27. una pluma — pen
28. una lección — lesson
29. una idea — idea
30. una maleta — suitcase
31. el sillón — armchair
32. los amigos — friends

Adjectives

An adjective is a word that describes a noun.

A Spanish adjective agrees in gender and number with the noun it modifies. In Spanish, an adjective almost always follows the noun it describes.

Singular Form of Adjectives

Adjectives that end in **-o** are *masculine* in form and agree with a masculine noun. As you pronounce the following examples aloud, note that the *adjective follows the noun* it describes.

el libro blanco	*the white book*
el gato negro	*the black cat*
el carro rojo	*the red car*
el muchacho simpático	*the nice boy*
el hombre hermoso	*the handsome man*

Adjectives that end in **-o** change the **-o** to **-a** when describing a feminine noun.

la casa blanca	*the white house*
la chaqueta negra	*the black jacket*
la lámpara roja	*the red lamp*
la muchacha simpática	*the nice girl*
la mujer hermosa	*the beautiful woman*

Adjectives that do not end in **-o** have the same form for describing both masculine and feminine nouns. It doesn't matter what letter ends the adjective, as long as it is not **-o**.

Masculine	Feminine
el libro excelente	la comida excelente
el perro horrible	la cucaracha horrible
el poema difícil	la lección difícil
el barco azul	la pluma azul
el baño verde	la cama verde
el tren gris	la mesa gris
el tema interesante	la idea interesante
el hombre fuerte	la mujer fuerte

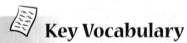 ## Key Vocabulary

Los colores (The colors)

amarillo	*yellow*	morado	*purple*
anaranjado	*orange*	moreno	*brown-skinned*
azul	*blue*	negro	*black*
blanco	*white*	rojo	*red*
gris	*gray*	rosado	*pink*
marrón, pardo	*brown*	verde	*green*

Other Adjectives

agradable	*agreeable, pleasant*	delgado	*slender*
alegre	*happy*	difícil	*difficult*
barato	*inexpensive*	estupendo	*great, terrific*
caro	*expensive*	excelente	*excellent*
débil	*weak*	fácil	*easy*

fantástico	*fantastic*	interesante	*interesting*
feliz	*happy*	joven	*young*
feo	*ugly*	maravilloso	*marvelous, wonderful*
flaco	*thin*	pequeño	*little, small*
frágil	*fragile*	pobre	*poor*
fuerte	*strong*	rico	*rich*
gordo	*fat*	simpático	*nice*
grande	*big*	sincero	*sincere*
guapo	*handsome, beautiful*	tacaño	*stingy*
		típico	*typical*
hermoso	*beautiful*	triste	*sad*
horrible	*horrible*	viejo	*old*
inteligente	*intelligent*		

Exercise 1.4

Complete the following phrases with the following Spanish adjective.

1. el hombre __viejo__ (old)
2. la situación __deficil__ (difficult)
3. el idioma __marvilloso__ (marvelous)
4. la persona __simpática__ (nice)
5. la flor __amarillo__ (yellow)
6. el jardín __bonito__ (beautiful)
7. la muchacha __delgada__ (slender)
8. el vino __blanco__ (white)
9. el apartamento __~~barato~~ caro__ (expensive)
10. el carro __barato__ (inexpensive)
11. el hotel __piqueño__ (small)
12. el clima __fantastico__ (fantastic)
13. la hermana __intelligente__ (intelligent)
14. el libro __interesante__ (interesting)
15. la ciudad __grande__ (big)
16. el hombre __rico__ (rich)
17. el dentista __joven__ (young)

18. la bolsa __roja__ (red)
19. la ventana __azul__ (blue)
20. la planta __verde__ (green)

Plural Form of Adjectives

Adjectives that end in a vowel add **-s** to form the plural.

Singular	Plural
blanco	blancos
roja	rojas
verde	verdes
excelente	excelentes

Adjectives that end in a consonant add **-es** to form the plural.

gris	grises
fácil	fáciles
joven	jóvenes
marrón	marrones

Adjectives agree in gender and number with the noun they modify. Review each singular and plural form as you pronounce the following nouns and the adjectives that describe them.

Masculine

Singular	Plural
el libro blanco	los libros blancos
el tomate rojo	los tomates rojos
el hombre hermoso	los hombres hermosos
el baño verde	los baños verdes
el barco marrón	los barcos marrones
el tren gris	los trenes grises
el tiquete caro	los tiquetes caros

Feminine

la casa blanca	las casas blancas
la persona simpática	las personas simpáticas
la mujer hermosa	las mujeres hermosas

la comida excelente las comidas excelentes
la lección fácil las lecciones fáciles
la muchacha fuerte las muchachas fuertes
la tienda vieja las tiendas viejas

Exercise 1.5

Write the plural form of each of the following noun and adjective phrases.

1. la lámpara azul las lámparas azules
2. el amigo fantástico los amigos fantásticos
3. el perro gris los perros grises
4. la cerveza negra las cervezas negras
5. el vino rosado los vinos rosados
6. la persona fuerte las personas fuertes
7. el día maravilloso los días maravillosos
8. la luz verde las luses verdes
9. la ciudad pequeña las ciudades pequeñas
10. el muchacho joven los muchachos jovenes

Exercise 1.6

Translate the following phrases into Spanish.

1. the red tomatoes los tomates rojas
2. the strong men los hombres fuertes
3. the thin women la mujer flaca
4. the yellow blouses las blusas amarillos
5. the interesting songs los cancillones intecisantes
6. the green planets las plantas verdes
7. the blue windows las ventanas azules
8. the old hotels los hoteles viejos

2

Estar, Ser, and Subject Pronouns

Subject Pronouns

Singular		Plural	
yo	*I*	**nosotros**	*we*
tú	*you*	**vosotros**	*you*

The familiar singular form **tú** is used with friends and family; its usage varies from country to country.

The familiar plural form **vosotros** is used only in Spain.

él	*he*	**ellos**	*they*

The masculine plural form **ellos** refers to a group of males or to a group that includes both males and females.

ella	*she*	**ellas**	*they*

The feminine plural form **ellas** refers to a group that includes only females.

usted	*you*	**ustedes**	*you*

Usted is more formal than **tú**. It is used when meeting people for the first time, in business situations, and with a person you might not know well. Its abbreviation is **Ud.**

The plural form **ustedes** is used to address more than one person. Latin Americans use **ustedes** for the plural of both **tú** and **Ud.** (since **vosotros** is used only in Spain). Its abbreviation is **Uds.**

There is no subject pronoun *it* in Spanish. **Él** and **ella** refer to people and sometimes to animals, but not to things.

Estar (to be)

Spanish has two verbs that are equivalent to English *to be.* Begin with the conjugation of the verb **estar**.

yo **estoy**	*I am*	nosotros **estamos**	*we are*
tú **estás**	*you are*	vosotros **estáis**	*you are*
él **está**	*he is*	ellos **están**	*they are*
ella **está**	*she is*	ellas **están**	*they are*
Ud. **está**	*you are*	Uds. **están**	*you are*

Practice the conjugations of the verb aloud. Notice that **él**, **ella**, and **Ud.** have the same form of the verb (the third-person singular). Notice also that **ellos**, **ellas**, and **Uds.** have the same form of the verb (the third-person plural).

Estar is used to express four basic concepts: location, health, changing mood or condition, and personal opinion in terms of taste or appearance.

- **Location**

  Estar is used to describe where something or someone is physically located.

Yo estoy en la clase.	*I am in the class.*
Nosotros estamos en el carro.	*We are in the car.*
El restaurante está en la ciudad.	*The restaurant is in the city.*
Ellas están en el baño.	*They are in the bathroom.*
¿Estás tú en el hospital?	*Are you in the hospital?*

The verb, which carries the action of the phrase, is the essential element of the Spanish sentence or question because of the amount of information it contains.

Verb Definitions

The **infinitive** is the unconjugated form of the verb. For example, *to be* is an infinitive in English. The **conjugations** are the forms of the verb that belong to a particular pronoun or noun subject. *I am* and *he is* are examples of conjugations of the infinitive *to be.*

- **Health**

Yo estoy bien, gracias.	*I am fine, thanks.*
Ella está enferma.	*She is sick.*
Los doctores están enfermos.	*The doctors are sick.*
¿Cómo están Uds.?	*How are you?*
Estamos bien.	*We are well.*

- **Changing Mood or Condition**

La muchacha está contenta.	*The girl is happy.*
Estoy feliz.	*I am happy.*
Los hombres están cansados.	*The men are tired.*
Estamos alegres.	*We are happy.*
¿Estás enojado?	*Are you angry?*

Often the pronouns **yo**, **tú**, and **nosotros** are omitted. This is possible because **estoy** can only mean *I am*, **estás** means *you are* whether **tú** is included or not, and **estamos** carries the meaning *we are*.

- **Personal opinion in terms of taste or appearance**

  When **estar** is used with food, the English equivalent is *taste* or *tastes*. When **estar** is used with appearance, the English equivalent is *look* or *looks*.

La comida está buena.	*The meal is (tastes) good.*
El pescado está delicioso.	*The fish is (tastes) delicious.*
La sopa está sabrosa.	*The soup is (tastes) delicious.*
Ella está hermosa hoy.	*She is (looks) pretty today.*
Él está guapo.	*He is (looks) handsome.*

A Word About Word Order

As you begin learning the basic structure of the Spanish language, you will discover that the word order of English and Spanish is essentially the same for the material covered in Part I, which includes the basic elements of a sentence.

Key Vocabulary

These words will help enhance your ability to communicate. As you learn them, remember to practice them aloud.

Interrogative Words

¿cómo?	*how?*
¿dónde?	*where?*
¿quién?	*who?*

Adverbs of Location

aquí, acá	*here*
allí, allá	*there*

Adjectives

alegre	*happy (merry)*	enojado	*angry*
bonito	*pretty*	feliz	*happy*
bueno	*good*	guapo	*beautiful, handsome*
cansado	*tired*	hermoso	*beautiful, handsome*
contento	*happy (contented)*	lindo	*pretty*
delicioso	*delicious*	sabroso	*delicious*
enfermo	*sick*		

NOTE: **Guapo** describes people only; **bonito**, **hermoso**, and **lindo** are used to describe both people and things.

Exercise 2.1

*Complete the following sentences with the correct form of **estar**. Pay attention to the meaning of each sentence. Then indicate whether the sentence expresses health, location, changing mood, or changing condition.*

EXAMPLES   Nosotros __estamos__ en la clase. (__location__)

La profesora __está__ enferma. (__health__)

1. Daniel __está__ muy cansado hoy. (~~health~~ Mood)

2. El teléfono y el libro __está__ en la mesa. (__location__)

3. La mujer __está__ bien; el hombre __está__ enfermo. (__health__)

4. ¿Cómo _está_ Uds.? (_mood_)

5. ¿Dónde _están_ ellos? (_____)

6. ¿Dónde _está_ el baño, por favor? (_____)

7. El niño _está_ enojado y la niña _esta_ triste.

   (_____)

8. Los muchachos _están_ alegres. (_____)

9. Yo _estoy_ contento. (_____)

10. ¿Quién & _está_ aquí? (_____)

Exercise 2.2

Translate the following sentences into Spanish.

1. *I am in the yellow house. Where are you?*

   Estoy en la casa amarrillo. ¿ donde estás?

2. *The red blouses are in the big store.*

   los blusas rojas está en la tienda grana.

3. *The white flower is in the window.*

   La flor blanca esta en la ventana

4. *We are in the train.*

   Nosotros estamos en el tren

5. *How are you? I am fine, thanks.*

   Como estas   yo estoy bien gracias

6. *We are tired, and we are happy.*

   Nos. estamos cansados y estamos felis

Ser (to be)

The Spanish verb **ser** is also equivalent to English *to be*.

In English, there is a single verb that means *to be*. We say, for example:

*The dog **is** here.* (location)
*The dog **is** brown.* (description)

The verb is the same in both cases. But in Spanish, there is a difference, and you have to choose the correct verb.

yo **soy**	*I am*	nosotros **somos**	*we are*
tú **eres**	*you are*	vosotros **sois**	*you are*
él **es**	*he is*	ellos **son**	*they are*
ella **es**	*she is*	ellas **son**	*they are*
Ud. **es**	*you are*	Uds. **son**	*you are*

Ser is used to express seven basic concepts: description, profession, point of origin, identification, material, possession or ownership, and where an event takes place.

- **Description**

La casa es roja.	*The house is red.*
El libro es azul.	*The book is blue.*
Los carros son viejos.	*The cars are old.*
Somos simpáticos.	*We are nice.*
¿Es la flor amarilla?	*Is the flower yellow?*

- **Profession**

Yo soy estudiante.	*I am a student.*
Él es arquitecto.	*He is an architect.*
Ellas son maestras excelentes.	*They are excellent teachers.*
Somos doctores.	*We are doctors.*
Roberto es abogado.	*Robert is a lawyer.*
¿Eres tú ingeniero?	*Are you an engineer?*

Spanish does not translate *a/an* when stating an unmodified profession.

Unmodified	José es estudiante.
Modified	José es un estudiante fantástico.

- **Point of origin**

De here means *from.*

¿De dónde es Ud.?	*Where are you from?* (sing.)
¿De dónde son Uds.?	*Where are you from?* (pl.)
Yo soy de Nueva York.	*I am from New York.*
¿De dónde es ella?	*Where is she from?*
Somos de Italia.	*We are from Italy.*
Ellos son de los Estados Unidos.	*They are from the United States.*

El vino es de Portugal.	*The wine is from Portugal.*
La cerveza es de México.	*The beer is from Mexico.*
El café es de Brazil.	*The coffee is from Brazil.*

In common English usage, we often end a sentence with a preposition, for example, *Where are you from?* This never occurs in Spanish; the preposition cannot ever end a sentence, so the preposition, in this case **de**, is placed in front of the interrogative word **dónde**.

- **Identification**

  Identification specifies characteristics such as relationship, nationality, race, or religion.

Somos amigos.	*We are friends.*
José y Eduardo son hermanos.	*Joe and Ed are brothers.*
Pablo es español.	*Paul is Spanish.*
¿Eres tú cubano?	*Are you Cuban?*
Ella es católica.	*She is Catholic.*

- **Material**

  De here means *of*.

La mesa es de madera.	*The table is of wood.*
La bolsa es de plástico.	*The bag is of plastic.*
Los zapatos son de cuero.	*The shoes are of leather.*
Las ventanas son de vidrio.	*The windows are of glass.*
La casa es de piedra.	*The house is of stone.*

- **Possession or ownership**

  De here means *of*.

La muñeca es de la niña.	*It's the child's doll.* *(The doll is of the child.)*
Los amigos son de María.	*They are María's friends.* *(The friends are of María.)*
La idea es de Pedro.	*The idea is Pedro's.* *(The idea is of Pedro.)*
El barco es del hombre rico.	*The boat belongs to the rich man.* *(The boat is of the rich man.)*
Los perros son del muchacho.	*The dogs belong to the boy.* *(The dogs are of the boy.)*

Los gatos son del niño.   The cats belong to the child.
                                          (The cats are of the child.)
El carro es de los amigos.   The car belongs to the friends.
                                          (The car is of the friends.)

NOTE: The contraction: **de** + **el** (*of* + *the*) = **del**. There are only two contractions in the Spanish language; **del** is one of them. Use **de** (English *of*) to express possession or ownership. When **de** (English *of*) is followed by the masculine **el** (English *the*), the words contract to **del**, meaning *of the*.

A Word About Possessives

You can see that the translations above are not exact. There is no apostrophe in Spanish, so when you think of *Peter's car,* for example, the Spanish structure is **el carro de Pedro** (*the car of Peter*). Make sure you understand this concept and use whichever English translation seems clearest to you.

- **Where an event takes place**

La fiesta es en la casa de José.   The party is (takes place) in Joe's
                                          house.
El concierto es en el club.   The concert is (takes place) in the club.
La protesta es en la capital.   The protest is (takes place) in the
                                          capital.

The equivalent English translation is *take* or *takes place.*

The party takes place at Joe's house.
The concert takes place at the club.
The protest takes place in the capital.

Exercise 2.3

Complete the following sentences with the appropriate form of **ser** *in each blank. Indicate whether the sentence expresses description, profession, point of origin, identification, material, or possession in parentheses.*

EXAMPLE   El hombre __es__ guapo. La mujer __es__ guapa también.
(__description__)

 1. El café __es__ de Colombia. (_____)

2. Ellos __Son__ doctores. Ella __es__ profesora.

(_____)

3. ¿De dónde __es__ los turistas? (_____)

4. Los hermanos de Pablo __Son__ simpáticos.

(_____)

5. El hotel viejo __es__ excelente. (_____)

6. Nosotros __estamos__ amigos de Raúl. (_____)

7. Los zapatos __Son__ de cuero. (_____)

8. La mujer y el hombre __Son__ de Ecuador. (_____)

9. Yo __Soy__ de Puerto Rico. ¿De dónde __es__ Ud.?

(_____)

10. El apartamento __es__ de los estudiantes jóvenes.

(_____)

11. ¿ __Eres__ tú una estudiante maravillosa? (_____)

12. Los tomates __Son__ verdes y rojos. (_____)

13. ¿Quién __es__ el presidente de los Estados Unidos?

(_____)

Exercise 2.4

A. *Complete the following sentences with the appropriate form of **ser**. Indicate the reason for your choice in parentheses.*

1. Helena __es__ de Colombia. (_____)

2. El hermano de ella __es__ católico. (_____)

3. Ellos __Son__ profesores excelentes. (_____)

4. Los carros __Son__ grises. (_____)

5. Nosotros __Somos__ estudiantes. (_____)

B. *Complete the following sentences with the appropriate form of **estar**. Indicate the reason for your choice in parentheses.*

1. San Francisco __está__ en California. (_____)

2. ¿Cómo ___está___ Ud.? Yo ___estoy___ bien.

(_____)

3. El profesor ___está___ enfermo. (_____)

4. Nosotros ___estamos___ en la clase. (_____)

5. ¿___Estás___ tú triste? (_____)

6. Los perros ___están___ en el carro. (_____)

C. *Complete the following sentences with the appropriate form of either* **ser** *or* **estar**. *Indicate the reason for each choice in parentheses.*

EXAMPLES   Yo ___soy___ español. (___identification___)

Ellos ___están___ aquí. (___location___)

1. José y Juan ___están___ enfermos. (___temp___)

2. Tú ___eres___ abogado. (___profession___)

3. La lección ___es___ fácil. (___state of being___)

4. Los estudiantes ___están___ en la ciudad. (___temp___)

5. ¿Cómo ___están___ Uds.? Nosotros ___estamos___ bien,

gracias. (_____, _____)

6. Ellas ___son___ inteligentes. (___permanent___)

7. ¿Dónde ___están___ los doctores? (___temp___)

8. El profesor ___está___ contento. (_____)

9. Los espejos en el baño ___son___ grandes. (_____)

10. La mesa, las sillas blancas y la lámpara ___están___ en la casa,

pero la casa ___es___ pequeña. (___temp___,

___perm___)

11. La amiga de Sara ___está___ enferma y Sara ___está___

triste. (_____, _____)

12. Las puertas de la casa ___son___ fuertes. (_____)

13. Los tomates ___están___ en la tienda. Los tomates verdes

___son___ de California; los tomates rojos ___son___

de Guatemala. (_____, _____,

_____)

14. ¿De dónde __es__ el vino blanco? (_____)

15. Los muchachos y las muchachas __están__ en el tren.
Ellos __están__ contentos porque __son__ amigos.
(_____, _____, _____)

16. ¿Quién __está__ en el baño? (_____)

17. ¿Dónde __está__ la familia de Fernando? (_____)

18. Nosotros __estamos__ contentos porque nosotros
__somos__ estudiantes excelentes. (_____,
_____)

19. ¿__Es__ Ud. de Suramérica? Ellos __son__
de España. (_____, _____)

20. Julia __está__ alegre porque la fiesta __es__
fantástica. (_____, _____)

Exercise 2.5

Answer the following questions aloud using the appropriate form of **ser** *or* **estar**.

1. ¿Cómo estás? Estoy bien y tú?
2. ¿Dónde está la hermana de Teresa? Ella está en casa
3. ¿De dónde es Ud.? Soy de los estados unidos
4. ¿Quién está en el carro caro? Mi padre esta....
5. ¿Dónde es el concierto? El concierto es en...
6. ¿Está Ud. alegre?
7. ¿Es fácil la lección? esto lección es my facil
8. ¿Dónde están las flores hermosas? ¿De dónde son?
9. ¿Es grande el apartamento de Tomás?
10. ¿Estás cansado?
11. ¿Están los periódicos en la casa de Alicia?
12. ¿Dónde está el restaurante barato de la ciudad?
13. ¿Es Ud. de Europa?
14. ¿Eres estudiante o profesor?

Exercise 2.6

Complete the following letter with the appropriate form of **ser** *or* **estar**.

Queridos amigos,

¿Cómo _están_ (1.) Uds.? Yo _estoy_ (2.) aquí
en Madrid. La ciudad _es_ (3.) hermosa. El museo del Prado
está (4.) en el centro de la ciudad y _es_ (5.)
muy interesante. La gente _están_ (6.) simpática y la comida
_es_ (7.) deliciosa. Hasta luego.

Reading Comprehension

La casa

Mi casa es vieja y grande, con muchas ventanas. Las cortinas en toda la
casa son gruesas. Las paredes del interior de la casa son blancas; el exterior
es gris. El patio es bonito, con flores todavía. Un espejo antiguo y una
mesa de madera fina están en el vestíbulo. El comedor es sencillo, con
una mesa y seis sillas; la alfombra es roja y azul marino. La cocina es
amplia, con paredes amarillas y gabinetes blancos.

La nevera es bastante grande, y la estufa y el horno están limpios.
Dos sillones cómodos y un piano están en la sala. Mi alcoba con un baño
privado es azul y blanca. Mis libros, mis cuadernos, mis lápices y
bolígrafos, mi colección de discos compactos, y mis videos están en
el estudio. Hoy es un día hermoso.

Nombres (Nouns)

la alcoba	*the bedroom*	el gabinete	*the cabinet*
la alfombra	*the rug*	el horno	*the oven*
el bolígrafo	*the ballpoint pen*	el lápiz	*the pencil*
la cocina	*the kitchen*	la madera	*the wood*
la colección	*the collection*	la nevera	*the refrigerator*
el comedor	*the dining room*	la pared	*the wall*
la cortina	*the curtain*	el patio	*the yard*
el cuaderno	*the notebook*	la sala	*the living room*
el espejo	*the mirror*	el sillón	*the easy chair*
el estudio	*the study*	el vestíbulo	*the entryway*
la estufa	*the stove*	el video	*the video*

Adjetivos (Adjectives)

amplio	*ample*	limpio	*clean*
antiguo	*old*	mi, mis	*my* (sing., pl.)
azul marino	*navy blue*	privado	*private*
cómodo	*comfortable*	sencillo	*simple*
fino	*fine, delicate*	todo	*all*
grueso	*thick*		

Adverbios (Adverbs)

bastante	*enough*
todavía	*still*

Preguntas (Questions)

After you have read the selection, answer the following questions in Spanish.

1. ¿Es nueva la casa? No, la casa es vieja

2. ¿Es bonito el día? _____

3. ¿Es grande la cocina? _____

4. ¿Dónde está el piano? _____

3

Hay, Interrogative Words, Days, and Months

Hay

The single Spanish word **hay** (pronounced like English *eye*) means *there is, there are, is there?*, and *are there?* in English.

Spanish sentences with **hay** and English sentences with *there is, there are* follow the same pattern with regard to the inclusion or omission of definite and indefinite articles. The Spanish definite articles **el**, **la**, **los**, and **las** (English *the*) never follow **hay**.

Hay una alfombra en la casa.	*There is a rug in the house.*
Hay un árbol en el jardín.	*There is a tree in the garden.*
Hay dos vasos en la mesa.	*There are two glasses on the table.*
Hay tres libros en el piso.	*There are three books on the floor.*

A question formed with **hay** uses the same word order as a statement. When written, it carries a question mark at the beginning and end, as all Spanish interrogative sentences do. When spoken, it should be pronounced with a rising intonation.

¿Hay una lámpara azul en la casa?	*Is there a blue lamp in the house?*
¿Hay un libro en el baño?	*Is there a book in the bathroom?*
¿Hay un hotel en la ciudad?	*Is there a hotel in the city?*
¿Hay una mesa marrón en el cuarto?	*Is there a brown table in the room?*

When **hay** is followed by a plural noun, the article is omitted.

Hay tigres en el zoológico.	*There are tigers in the zoo.*
Hay estrellas en el cielo.	*There are stars in the sky.*

¿Hay periódicos en esta tienda?	*Are there newspapers in this store?*
¿Hay tomates rojos en este mercado?	*Are there red tomatoes in this market?*

To make a sentence negative, place **no** before **hay**.

No hay luz en el baño.	*There is no light in the bathroom.*
No hay teléfonos aquí.	*There are no telephones here.*
No hay revistas en el hotel.	*There are no magazines in the hotel.*

Exercise 3.1

A. *Translate the following Spanish sentences into English.*

1. ¿Hay una lección fácil en el libro?

   <u>Is there an easy lesson in the book?</u>

2. No hay cucarachas en el restaurante.

   <u>There aren't any spoons in the restaurant</u>

3. ¿Hay blusas rojas en la tienda?

   <u>Are there red blouses in the store</u>

4. Hay flores en el balcón del apartamento.

   <u>There are flowers on the apartments balcony</u>

5. ¿Hay clase hoy?

   <u>Is there class today</u>

6. ¿Hay más preguntas de los estudiantes?

   <u>Are there more student questions</u>

B. *Translate the following English sentences into Spanish.*

1. There are many pens on the teacher's desk.

   <u>Hay mas bolígrafos en el escritorio del Maestro</u>

2. Is there a doctor in the hospital?

   <u>¿Hay un doctor en el Hospital?</u>

3. There are two women in the class.

   <u>Hay doc mujeres en clase</u>

4. *There is no beer in Lisa's house.*

No hay cervesa en la casa de Lisa

Interrogative Words

All interrogative words carry written accents; the accent marks do not affect the pronunciation of the word.

¿Cómo? *How?*

¿Cómo estás tú?	*How are you?*
¿Cómo están los muchachos?	*How are the boys?*

¿Dónde? *Where?*

¿Dónde está la casa del alcalde?	*Where is the mayor's house?*
¿Dónde estamos?	*Where are we?*

¿Quién? (sing.), **¿Quiénes?** (pl.) *Who?*

¿Quién está aquí?	*Who is here?*
¿Quién es la persona con José?	*Who is the person with Joe?*
¿Quiénes están en el carro?	*Who is in the car?*
¿Quiénes son ellos?	*Who are they?*

¿Qué? *What?*

¿Qué día es hoy?	*What day is today?*
¿Qué libro está en la mesa?	*What book is on the table?*
¿Qué hay en el menú?	*What is there on the menu?*

¿Qué? used before **ser** asks for a definition.

¿Qué es comunicación?	*What is communication?*
¿Qué es esto?	*What is this?*
¿Qué es filosofía?	*What is philosophy?*

¿Cuál? (sing.), **¿Cuáles?** (pl.) *Which, which one? Which ones?*

¿Cuál? used immediately before **ser** asks for a selection or choice from among various possibilities.

¿Cuál es la capital de Perú?	*What (which city) is the capital of Peru?*

¿Cuál es el problema?	*What (which problem) is the problem?*
¿Cuál es el nombre de la niña?	*What (which name) is the girl's name?*
¿Cuáles son los días de la semana?	*What (which days) are the days of the week?*

¿Por qué? *Why?*

¿Por qué estamos alegres?	*Why are we happy?*
¿Por qué es azul el cielo?	*Why is the sky blue?*

¿Cuánto? *How much?*

¿Cuánto es?	*How much is it?*
¿Cuánto cuesta?	*How much does it cost?*
¿Cuánto vale?	*How much is it worth?*

¿Cuántos?, **¿Cuántas?** *How many?*

¿Cuántos gatos hay en la ciudad?	*How many cats are there in the city?*
¿Cuántas estrellas hay en el cielo?	*How many stars are there in the sky?*

Cuántos and **cuántas** are adjectives and must agree in gender with the plural nouns they describe.

¿Cuándo? *When?*

¿Cuándo es la fiesta?	*When is the party?*
¿Cuándo es el concierto?	*When is the concert?*

 Exercise 3.2

Complete the following questions with the appropriate interrogative word. As you do this exercise, review **ser**, **estar**, *and* **hay**.

1. ¿_____ es la bolsa de María, la bolsa roja o la bolsa azul?

2. ¿_____ día es hoy?

3. ¿_____ están los estudiantes?

4. ¿_____ hay muchas personas en el parque hoy?

5. ¿＿＿＿＿＿＿＿ es la mujer con el perro marrón?

6. ¿＿＿＿＿＿＿＿ no hay espejos en el baño de los hombres?

7. ¿＿＿＿＿＿＿＿ libros hay en la librería?

8. ¿＿＿＿＿＿＿＿ están Uds.?

Prepositions

You have already learned three of the most common prepositions in Spanish.

en   *in, on*
de   *from, of*
con   *with*

You can combine these prepositions with an interrogative word to further your ability to ask questions.

¿En qué tienda hay muchos libros?	*In what store are there many books?*
¿En cuál parque hay animales exóticos?	*In which park are there exotic animals?*
¿De dónde es el hombre?	*Where is the man from?*
¿De qué color es la mesa?	*(Of) what color is the table?*
¿De quién es la idea fantástica?	*Whose fantastic idea is it? (Of whom is the fantastic idea?)*
¿Con quién estás?	*Whom are you with?*

Exercise 3.3

Complete the following questions with the appropriate preposition.

1. ¿＿＿＿＿ qué ciudad está la estatua de la libertad?

2. ¿＿＿＿＿ qué color es la casa grande?

3. ¿＿＿＿＿ qué material es la ventana?

4. ¿＿＿＿＿ quiénes están Uds.?

5. ¿＿＿＿＿ cuáles países hay plazas hermosas?

6. ¿＿＿＿＿ quién es el carro caro?

Days of the Week, Months, and Seasons

Los días de la semana (The days of the week)

To refer to a day of the week in English, we say *Monday* or *on Monday*. In Spanish, the article **el** is used with the name of the day to express this idea. Days of the week are not capitalized in Spanish.

el lunes	*Monday, on Monday*
el martes	*Tuesday, on Tuesday*
el miércoles	*Wednesday, on Wednesday*
el jueves	*Thursday, on Thursday*
el viernes	*Friday, on Friday*
el sábado	*Saturday, on Saturday*
el domingo	*Sunday, on Sunday*

To form the plural of the days of the week, **el** changes to **los** and **-s** is added only to **el sábado** and **el domingo**. The names of the days of the week from **el lunes** to **el viernes** already end in **-s**.

los lunes	*Mondays, on Mondays*
los martes	*Tuesdays, on Tuesdays*
los miércoles	*Wednesdays, on Wednesdays*
los jueves	*Thursdays, on Thursdays*
los viernes	*Fridays, on Fridays*
los sábados	*Saturdays, on Saturdays*
los domingos	*Sundays, on Sundays*

Hay clase los lunes.	*There is class on Mondays.*
¿Hay fiestas los sábados?	*Are there parties on Saturdays?*
¿Dónde está Tomás los domingos?	*Where is Thomas on Sundays?*
El jueves es el día de acción de gracias.	*Thursday is Thanksgiving Day.*
El martes es el día del amor y la amistad.	*Tuesday is St. Valentine's Day.*
Estamos en clase los miércoles.	*We are in class on Wednesdays.*
¿Dónde estás los viernes?	*Where are you on Fridays?*

Los meses (The months)

enero	*January*	abril	*April*
febrero	*February*	mayo	*May*
marzo	*March*	junio	*June*

julio	*July*	octubre	*October*
agosto	*August*	noviembre	*November*
septiembre	*September*	diciembre	*December*

Las estaciones (The seasons)

el verano	*the summer*
el otoño	*the autumn, the fall*
el invierno	*the winter*
la primavera	*the spring(time)*

Partes del día (Parts of the day)

la mañana	*the morning*
la tarde	*the afternoon*
la noche	*the night, the evening*

 # Reading Comprehension

Un pueblo colonial

Estoy, con unos amigos, en Guanajuato, un pueblo° colonial y antiguo° en el centro de México. Estamos aquí con los padres de Laura. Laura y yo somos estudiantes de español; la madre de ella es arqueóloga° y el padre es político.° Hay una escuela con clases de música, de guitarra, de baile y de historia. Es el verano, el clima es maravilloso y los mexicanos son muy simpáticos. Hay fiestas los viernes y los sábados. Hay muchas clases de lunes a viernes° también y somos estudiantes serios.° La madre de Laura está contenta porque hay unas ruinas de los Olmecas° en el campo. El padre de ella está contento también porque el viaje es tranquilo y relajante.° Estoy feliz en la casa de piedra en las montañas. Hay música en la mañana, una comida en la tarde y conversación durante° el día. Todo está bien.

°el pueblo *town*
°antiguo *old, ancient*
°la arqueóloga *archeologist*
°el político *politician*
°de lunes a viernes *from Monday through Friday*

°serio *serious*
°los Olmecas *an ancient people of Mexico who disappeared around 600* A.D.
°relajante *relaxing*
°durante *during*

Nombres masculinos

el año	*the year*	el lápiz	*the pencil*
el árbol	*the tree*	el mensaje	*the message*
el ascensor	*the elevator*	el mes	*the month*
el avión	*the airplane*	el niño	*the child*
el bolígrafo	*the ballpoint pen*	el país	*the country*
el bus	*the bus*	el papel	*the paper*
el campo	*the countryside*	el parque	*the park*
el coche	*the car*	el periódico	*the newspaper*
el cuarto	*the room*	el piso	*the floor*
el cumpleaños	*the birthday*	el precio	*the price*
el día	*the day*	el ruido	*the noise*
el dinero	*the money*	el salón	*the classroom*
el edificio	*the building*	el sitio	*the place*
el equipaje	*the baggage*	el sueño	*the dream*
el hogar	*the home*	el teatro	*the theater*
el jardín	*the garden*	el tema	*the theme*
el lapicero	*the ballpoint pen*	el viaje	*the trip*

Nombres femeninos

la avenida	*the avenue*	la hoja	*the leaf*
la biblioteca	*the library*	la librería	*the bookstore*
la calle	*the street*	la llave	*the key*
la camisa	*the shirt*	la medicina	*the medicine*
la carta	*the letter*	la música	*the music*
la ciudad	*the city*	la obra	*the play*
la cocina	*the kitchen*	la página	*the page*
la cuenta	*the check, the bill*	la palabra	*the word*
la ducha	*the shower*	la pared	*the wall*
la entrada	*the entrance*	la playa	*the beach*
la escalera	*the stairs*	la pregunta	*the question*
la escuela	*the school*	la puerta	*the door*
la fiesta	*the party*	la salida	*the exit*
la frase	*the sentence*	la salud	*the health*
la gente	*the people*	la semana	*the week*
la guerra	*the war*	la tarea	*the homework*
la habitación	*the room*	la tarjeta	*the postcard*

Adjetivos

alto	*tall*	flojo	*lax*
amable	*kind*	gracioso	*amusing*
amistoso	*friendly*	hondo	*deep*
ancho	*wide*	largo	*long*
bajo	*low, short* (in height)	lento	*slow*
bello	*beautiful*	libre	*free*
cariñoso	*affectionate*	nuevo	*new*
ciego	*blind*	orgulloso	*proud*
corto	*short* (in length)	peligroso	*dangerous*
dulce	*sweet*	pesado	*heavy, dull*
duro	*hard*	rápido	*rapid, fast*
elegante	*elegant*	raro	*strange*
emocionante	*exciting*	sencillo	*simple*
especial	*special*	sordo	*deaf*
estrecho	*narrow*	suave	*soft*
fiel	*faithful*	tranquilo	*tranquil*

Conjunciones (Conjunctions)

Conjunctions are words that connect words, phrases, or clauses.

mientras	*while*	porque	*because*
o	*or*	si	*if*
pero	*but*	y	*and*

Exercise 3.4

You now have a new vocabulary of nouns and adjectives; test how many you recall in the following exercises.

A. *Translate the following Spanish phrases into English.*

1. el cuarto bello   _____

2. la persona agradable   _____

3. la amistad dulce   _____

4. la obra emocionante   _____

5. el día lindo   _____

6. el edificio bajo   _____

7. el sueño raro   _____

8. la guerra larga   _____

9. la avenida ancha   _____

10. el año nuevo   _____

B. *Translate the following English phrases into Spanish. Make sure the adjective agrees with the noun.*

1. *the affectionate child*   _____

2. *the simple homework*   _____

3. *the dangerous city*   _____

4. *the short person*   _____

5. *the short month*   _____

6. *the beautiful beach*   _____

7. *the friendly woman*   _____

8. *the kind man*   _____

9. *the narrow avenue*   _____

10. *the proud people*   _____

 Exercise 3.5

Answer the following questions aloud using **hay**, **ser**, *or* **estar**.

1. ¿Hay hojas en los árboles en el verano?

2. ¿Con quiénes estás tú en la escuela?

3. ¿De qué color es la habitación de Julia?

4. ¿De quién es el jardín?

5. ¿En qué tienda hay tomates?

6. ¿Dónde están las playas bonitas de la ciudad?

7. ¿Hay perros en el campo?

8. ¿Qué hay en el agua?

9. ¿Cuál es la idea del estudiante inteligente?

10. ¿Dónde está Ud.?

11. ¿Cuál es bella, la paz o la guerra?

12. ¿Quién está aquí con Ud.?

13. ¿Dónde está el baño, por favor?

14. ¿Hay preguntas?

 Exercise 3.6

*Complete the following sentences with the appropriate form of **ser**, **estar**, or **hay**. Be sure to include accent marks when they are needed.*

EXAMPLE   Si hoy __es__ sábado, ¿por qué __están__ enojados los hombres?

1. ¿Cuál _____ la escuela de los niños?

2. ¿Quién _____ aquí?

3. ¿De qué color _____ la puerta?

4. ¿Por qué _____ cariñosa la amiga de Laura?

5. ¿_____ mucha gente en el hotel hoy?

6. La palabra _____ en la frase; la frase _____
   en la página; la página _____ en el libro.

7. ¿_____ edificios altos en Madrid?

8. Las playas y las piscinas _____ en el campo.

   ¿Qué _____ en la ciudad?

9. _____ muchos lápices y bolígrafos en la mesa de la mujer.

   ¿_____ ella la profesora de la clase?

10. En el verano, _____ plantas verdes y flores hermosas
    en los parques.

11. Los hombres _____ altos. Los niños _____ bajos.

12. Nosotros _____ estudiantes excelentes porque las lecciones

    no _____ difíciles.

13. ¿_____ ella flaca porque ella _____ enferma?

14. Yo _____ en la clase pero el maestro no _____
    aquí.

15. ¿_____ peligrosa la ciudad en la noche?

16. _____ luces en las avenidas porque es Navidad.

17. El carro negro _____ barato; el coche verde es caro.

    ¿Cuál _____ el carro del hombre rico?

18. Si Manuel y Jorge _____ estudiantes excelentes,

    ¿por qué _____ tristes en la clase?

19. ¿Quiénes _____ en la casa los miércoles en la mañana?

    ¿Dónde _____ Ud. en la noche?

20. ¿Cuál _____ la bolsa de Sara, la bolsa roja o la bolsa gris?

21. El tren gris _____ pequeño; los buses _____
    grandes.

Exercise 3.7

Translate the following Spanish sentences into English.

1. ¿Dónde están los estudiantes los domingos?

   _____

2. El sábado y el domingo son días de fiesta.

   _____

3. En la primavera, hay flores bellas en los parques.

   _____

4. En el otoño, hay hojas amarillas y rojas en los árboles.

   _____

5. ¿Qué día es hoy? Hoy es miércoles. ¿Qué mes es? Es septiembre.

   _____

6. ¿Cuántos días hay en junio? ¿Cuántos días hay en un año?

   _____

7. Las calles de México son estrechas. Las casas son bajas y bonitas.

   _____

8. ¿Por qué están los periódicos y las revistas en el piso?

   _____

9. Hay clase, pero los estudiantes están en la playa donde hay una piscina también. El profesor está enojado pero los estudiantes están alegres.

_____

10. Los edificios de las ciudades grandes son altos.

_____

11. Los niños están en la playa porque es el verano.

_____

12. Mucha gente está en los restaurantes porque es el invierno.

_____

 Reading Comprehension

El cine

Roberto Vélez es director de cine.° Él es de España y las películas°
de él son cómicas.° Rosa Morales es argentina y es directora también.
Las películas de ella son más tristes porque en la Argentina hay mucha
pobreza.° Hoy, ellos están contentos porque están en Cannes, el festival
de la Palma de Oro. Hay actores, directores, jurados° y gente importante
en la ciudad. Roberto y Rosa están emocionados.° La presentación de
los premios° es esta noche. Muchas películas son interesantes este año,
¿pero cuál es la película favorita de los jurados?

Preguntas

After you have read the selection, answer the following questions in Spanish.

1. ¿De dónde es Roberto Vélez? ¿De dónde es Rosa Morales?

_____

2. ¿Dónde están? _____

3. ¿Son ellos amigos? _____

_____

°el cine *the movies (in general)*	°el jurado *judge*
°la película *the film*	°emocionado *excited*
°cómico(a) *funny*	°el premio *award, prize*
°la pobreza *poverty*	

4

Numbers, Dates, and Time

Cardinal Numbers

A cardinal number is any number that expresses an amount, such as *one, two, three.* Here are the Spanish cardinal numbers up to 100.

0	cero				
1	uno	21	veintiuno	50	cincuenta
2	dos	22	veintidós	60	sesenta
3	tres	23	veintitrés	70	setenta
4	cuatro	24	veinticuatro	80	ochenta
5	cinco	25	veinticinco	90	noventa
6	seis	26	veintiséis		
7	siete	27	veintisiete		
8	ocho	28	veintiocho		
9	nueve	29	veintinueve		
10	diez	30	treinta		
11	once	31	treinta y uno		
12	doce	32	treinta y dos		
13	trece	33	treinta y tres		
14	catorce	34	treinta y cuatro		
15	quince	35	treinta y cinco		
16	dieciséis	36	treinta y seis		
17	diecisiete	37	treinta y siete		
18	dieciocho	38	treinta y ocho		
19	diecinueve	39	treinta y nueve		
20	veinte	40	cuarenta		

Note the following rules for the use of cardinal numbers in Spanish.

- Numbers after 15, **quince**, are formed by combining numbers: 10 + 6 = 16, **diez y seis son dieciséis**.

- The numbers from 16 to 19 and from 21 to 29 are expressed as one word: 22, **veinte y dos → veintidós**.

- Numbers after 30, **treinta**, end in **-a** and do not combine with the next number. They are expressed as individual words: 34, **treinta y cuatro**, for example. This is true for the numbers 31 to 99, **treinta y uno** to **noventa y nueve**.

- In English we say *one hundred and ten*. Spanish does not use **y** to connect hundreds and the following number: 110, **ciento diez**; 220, **doscientos veinte**; 315, **trescientos quince**.

- When a masculine noun follows the number 21, 31, 41, 51, 61, 71, 81, or 91, the **-o** is dropped from **uno**.

veintiún años	*21 years*
treinta y un libros	*31 books*
cincuenta y un gatos	*51 cats*
sesenta y un hombres	*61 men*
noventa y un amigos	*91 friends*

- When a feminine noun follows a number ending in **uno** (English *one*), the feminine form is **una**.

cuarenta y una mujeres	*41 women*
setenta y una muchachas	*71 girls*
ochenta y una amigas	*81 friends*

- The number 100 in Spanish uses the following pattern.

cien	*100*
ciento uno	*101*
ciento cincuenta	*150*
ciento noventa y nueve	*199*

  Cien becomes **ciento** if it is followed by any number less than itself. Before all nouns, masculine or feminine, it remains **cien**.

cien libros	*100 books*	cien hombres	*100 men*
cien casas	*100 houses*	cien mujeres	*100 women*

- The numbers 200 to 900 agree with the noun they modify.

200	doscientos		
	doscientos hoteles	*200 hotels*	
	doscientas puertas	*200 doors*	
300	trescientos		
	trescientos gatos	*300 cats*	
	trescientas tiendas	*300 stores*	
400	cuatrocientos		
	cuatrocientos trenes	*400 trains*	
	cuatrocientas luces	*400 lights*	
500	quinientos		
	quinientos animales	*500 animals*	
	quinientas flores	*500 flowers*	
600	seiscientos		
	seiscientos árboles	*600 trees*	
	seiscientas fiestas	*600 parties*	
700	setecientos		
	setecientos barcos	*700 boats*	
	setecientas plantas	*700 plants*	
800	ochocientos		
	ochocientos sueños	*800 dreams*	
	ochocientas mesas	*800 tables*	
900	novecientos		
	novecientos espejos	*900 mirrors*	
	novecientas siestas	*900 naps*	

- Spanish numbers beginning with 1000, **mil**, are not counted in hundreds.

1.000	mil	
	mil años	*1000 years*
	dos mil años	*2000 years*
1.000.000	un millón (de)	
	un millón de dólares	*a million dollars*
2.000.000	dos millones (de)	
	dos millones de preguntas	*two million questions*

Mil does not change (**dos mil**, **tres mil**, **cinco mil**), nor does it need the article **un** (English *a*) in front of it.

Spanish does not count in hundreds after 1,000. The number 1992 is formed by combining 1000 + 900 + 92: **mil novecientos noventa y dos**. The number 2006 is **dos mil seis**.

The plural **miles** is used only to refer to a large but inexact amount, the way English uses *tons*: **Hay miles de personas en el restaurante.** *There are tons of people in the restaurant.*

- Note that Spanish uses the period to separate thousands; the comma is used to indicate decimals: $90,25 is **noventa dólares y veinticinco centavos**.

A Word About Numbers
Numbers are an important part of everyday life. People tell you their telephone numbers or ask you to meet them at a specific address. Try to practice numbers with a partner, perhaps a native speaker.

Exercise 4.1

Complete the following sentences by writing in the Spanish numbers (in words).

1. En febrero, hay _____ (28) días; cada _____ (4) años, hay _____ (29) días.
2. ¿En qué meses hay _____ (31) días?
3. Hay _____ (7) días en una semana; _____ (52) semanas en un año.
4. Hay _____ (76) lápices en la tienda y _____ (67) plumas.
5. Hay _____ (21) muchachas en el baño, pero hay solamente _____ (1) espejo.
6. Hay _____ (135) libros de español en la librería.
7. En la biblioteca, hay _____ (2,456) libros.

8. _____ (91) y _____ (542)

   son _____ (633).

9. _____ (860) menos _____ (50)

   son _____ (810).

10. Hay _____ (100) camisas rojas en la tienda y hay

    _____ (100) pantalones.

11. Hay _____ (15) capítulos en el libro; hay

    _____ (254) páginas.

12. Hay _____ (235) restaurantes en la ciudad.

Ordinal Numbers

Ordinal numbers express position in a series, such as *first, second, third*.

primero	*first*	sexto	*sixth*
segundo	*second*	séptimo	*seventh*
tercero	*third*	octavo	*eighth*
cuarto	*fourth*	noveno	*ninth*
quinto	*fifth*	décimo	*tenth*

Note the following rules for the use of ordinal numbers in Spanish.

• Ordinal numbers in Spanish precede the noun and agree in gender with the noun they describe.

• **Primero** and **tercero** drop the **-o** before a masculine noun: **el primer piso**, **el tercer piso**.

primero *first*
   el primer hombre   *the first man*
   la primera mujer   *the first woman*

segundo *second*
   el segundo mes   *the second month*
   la segunda parte   *the second part*

tercero *third*
   el tercer día   *the third day*
   la tercera semana   *the third week*

cuarto *fourth*

    el cuarto piso   *the fourth floor*

    la cuarta lección   *the fourth lesson*

quinto *fifth*

    el quinto mes   *the fifth month*

    la quinta avenida   *Fifth Avenue (the fifth avenue)*

sexto *sixth*

    el sexto tren   *the sixth train*

    la sexta calle   *Sixth Street (the sixth street)*

séptimo *seventh*

    el séptimo capítulo   *the seventh chapter*

    la séptima página   *the seventh page*

octavo *eighth*

    el octavo libro   *the eighth book*

    la octava pregunta   *the eighth question*

noveno *ninth*

    el noveno presidente   *the ninth president*

    la novena fiesta   *the ninth party*

décimo *tenth*

    el décimo sueño   *the tenth dream*

    la décima razón   *the tenth reason*

¿Dónde está la quinta avenida?	*Where is Fifth Avenue?*
Hay una librería en la sexta calle.	*There is a bookstore on Sixth Street.*
El tercer capítulo es interesante.	*The third chapter is interesting.*
La oficina del doctor está en el sexto piso.	*The doctor's office is on the sixth floor.*
Ana y María son las primeras estudiantes en la clase.	*Ana and María are the first students in the class.*

- Ordinal numbers are used for kings, queens, popes, and centuries; in this case, they follow the noun they describe.

    el siglo segundo   *the second century*

    Carlos Quinto   *Charles the Fifth*

- Beginning with the ordinal number *eleventh*, state the noun first, then the cardinal number. Thus *Eleventh Street* is expressed as **la calle once** (English *the street eleven*).

el piso catorce	*the fourteenth floor* *(the floor fourteen)*
la calle once	*Eleventh Street* *(the street eleven)*
la lección veintitrés	*the twenty-third lesson* *(the lesson twenty-three)*
el piso ciento tres	*the one hundred and third floor* *(the floor one hundred and three)*

 ## Exercise 4.2

Complete the following sentences with the Spanish equivalent (in words) of each phrase.

EXAMPLE   Hay una feria en ___*la tercera avenida*___ *(Third Avenue)*.

1. Hay una biblioteca en _____ *(72nd Street)*.

2. El trabajo de Lola está en _____ *(the 40th floor)*.

3. Hay un restaurante en _____ *(135th Street)*.

4. _____ *(The third chapter)* es interesante.

5. _____ *(The fourth lesson)* es horrible.

6. Mayo es _____ *(the fifth month)* del año.

The Date

Spanish uses the cardinal numbers 2 to 31 to indicate all days of the month except the first.

¿Cuál es la fecha de hoy?	*What is today's date?*
Hoy es el cinco de mayo.	*Today is May 5.*
Mañana es el seis de mayo.	*Tomorrow is May 6.*
Es el veintiocho de febrero.	*It is February 28.*
Es el treinta y uno de octubre.	*It is October 31.*

Spanish uses an ordinal number only to indicate the *first of the month,* **el primero del mes**.

Hoy es el primero de junio.   *Today is June 1.*
Mañana es el primero de octubre.   *Tomorrow is October 1.*

 ## Exercise 4.3

Complete the following sentences with the Spanish term or number. Always write numbers as words.

1. Hoy es _____ (*Thursday*), el _____
   (*11th*) de mayo.

2. ¿Por qué estamos en clase _____ (*on Saturdays*)?

3. Hay _____ (*100*) personas en el restaurante nuevo.

4. La fecha del nacimiento de Sandra es _____

   _____ (*Oct. 18, 1973*).

5. Es el _____ (*14th*) de diciembre del

   _____ (*2006*).

6. ¿Quién es el _____ (*first*) hombre y la

   _____ (*first*) mujer?

Telling Time

To express *time* in the sense of *telling time,* Spanish uses **la hora**.

¿Qué hora es?   { *What hour is it?*
                       What time is it?

In order to tell time, Spanish always uses the third-person singular or plural of **ser**. Start by learning the expressions for telling exact time on the hour, from one o'clock to twelve o'clock. **La** represents **la hora**, and **las** represents **las horas**.

Es la una.   *It is one o'clock.*
Son las dos.   *It is two o'clock.*
Son las tres.   *It is three o'clock.*
Son las cuatro.   *It is four o'clock.*

Son las cinco.	*It is five o'clock.*
Son las seis.	*It is six o'clock.*
Son las siete.	*It is seven o'clock.*
Son las ocho.	*It is eight o'clock.*
Son las nueve.	*It is nine o'clock.*
Son las diez.	*It is ten o'clock.*
Son las once.	*It is eleven o'clock.*
Son las doce.	*It is twelve o'clock.*

The part of day is specified as follows.

de la mañana	*(of the) morning,* A.M.
de la tarde	*(of the) afternoon,* P.M.
de la noche	*(of the) night,* P.M.
Son las dos de la mañana.	*It is two o'clock in the morning.*
Es la una de la tarde.	*It is one o'clock in the afternoon.*
Son las ocho de la noche.	*It is eight o'clock at night.*

To indicate the exact hour or "sharp," Spanish uses **exactamente** or **en punto**.

| Son las cinco exactamente. | *It's exactly five o'clock.* |
| Son las diez en punto. | *It's ten o'clock sharp.* |

To indicate an approximate time, Spanish uses **a eso de** + the hour or the hour + **más o menos**.

| Es a eso de la una. | *It's about one o'clock.* |
| Es la una, más o menos. | *It's one o'clock, more or less.* |

To express a time *after* the hour, state the hour + **y** (English *and, plus*) + the number of minutes. This adds the minutes to the hour.

Es la una y veinte.	*It is 1:20.*
	(It is one o'clock plus twenty minutes.)
Son las cinco y diez.	*It is 5:10.*
	(It is five o'clock plus ten minutes.)
Son las dos y cinco.	*It is 2:05.*
	(It is two o'clock plus five minutes.)

When it is a *quarter* after the hour, Spanish uses **quince** (English *fifteen*) or **cuarto** (English *quarter*).

Son las tres y quince.	*It is 3:15.* *(It is three o'clock plus fifteen minutes.)*
Son las seis y cuarto.	*It is 6:15.* *(It is six o'clock plus a quarter hour.)*

When it is *half* past the hour, Spanish uses **treinta** (English *thirty*) or **media** (English *half*).

Son las nueve y treinta.	*It is 9:30.* *(It is nine o'clock plus thirty minutes.)*
Son las ocho y media.	*It is 8:30.* *(It is eight o'clock plus a half hour.)*

To express a time *before* the hour, state the hour + **menos** (English *minus*) + the number of minutes. This subtracts the minutes from the hour.

Son las tres menos diez.	*It is 2:50.* *(It is three o'clock minus ten minutes.)*
Son las once menos cinco.	*It is 10:55.* *(It is eleven o'clock minus five minutes.)*
Son las nueve menos cuarto.	*It is 8:45.* *(It is nine o'clock minus a quarter hour.)*
Son las doce menos quince.	*It is 11:45.* *(It is twelve o'clock minus fifteen minutes.)*

An alternate way to express time *before* the hour is to state the number of minutes + **para** + the hour. This expression, which closely follows English syntax, is not a full sentence.

Cinco para las tres.	*Five (minutes) to three (o'clock).*
Veinticinco para las dos.	*Twenty-five (minutes) to two (o'clock).*
Quince para las seis.	*Fifteen (minutes) to six (o'clock).*

To indicate that something is happening *at* a certain time, Spanish uses an expression with the preposition **a** (English *at*).

¿A qué hora?	{ *At what hour?* { *At what time?*
A la una.	*At one o'clock.*
A las dos.	*At two o'clock.*
A las tres.	*At three o'clock.*

The expressions for *after* the hour (the hour + **y** + the number of minutes) and *before* the hour (the hour + **menos** + the number of minutes) remain the same after **a**.

A las cuatro y diez.	*At 4:10.*
A las cinco y cuarto.	*At 5:15.*
A las seis y cinco.	*At 6:05.*
A las siete y tres.	*At 7:03.*
A las ocho y media.	*At 8:30.*
A las nueve menos quince.	*At 8:45.*
A las diez menos veinte.	*At 9:40.*
A las once menos veinticinco.	*At 10:35.*
A la una menos diez.	*At 12:50.*

 Exercise 4.4

A. *Complete the following sentences with the appropriate Spanish time. Include* **de la mañana, de la tarde,** *or* **de la noche,** *and always write numbers as words.*

1. El programa es _____ (*at 6 P.M.*).

2. _____ (*At 8 A.M.*) estoy en casa.

3. _____ (*At 1 P.M.*) estamos en la oficina.

4. _____ (*At 7:15 P.M.*) estamos en un restaurante.

5. _____ (*It is 10 P.M.*) ¿Dónde están los niños?

B. *Translate the following time expressions into Spanish. Include the appropriate expression to indicate morning, afternoon, or evening, and always write numbers as words.*

1. *It is 2:20 P.M.* _____

2. *It is 4:30 A.M.* _____

3. *It is 9:15 P.M.* _____

4. *It is 6:00 P.M. sharp.* _____

5. *It is 3:35 P.M.* _____

6. *It is 7:10 A.M.* _____

7. *At about 2:00 P.M.* _____

8. *At 9 A.M. exactly.* _____

 # Reading Comprehension

El restaurante

Es la una de la tarde y el restaurante español está lleno.° Es un restaurante popular y económico. Hay dieciocho mesas y cinco camareros excelentes. En cada mesa hay cuatro o cinco personas. El ambiente° es espectacular. La gente está alegre porque es un día de fiesta° y no hay trabajo. Hay dos pisos; en el primer piso, hay bebidas° y tapas;° en el segundo piso, hay bebidas también y el plato del día. En el menú, hay pollo, carne y mucho pescado.° En el especial del día, hay sopa, papas, vegetales, ensalada, postre,° y café o té. Todo° está sabroso hoy.

°lleno *full*
°el ambiente *the atmosphere*
°un día de fiesta *holiday*
°una bebida *a drink*
°tapas *small appetizers, Spanish style*

°pollo, carne, pescado *chicken, meat, fish*
°sopa, papas, vegetales, ensalada, postre
 soup, potatoes, vegetables, salad, dessert
°todo *everything*

Preguntas

After you have read the selection, answer the following questions in Spanish.

1. ¿Por qué está lleno el restaurante?

   _____

2. ¿Cuántos pisos hay?

   _____

3. ¿En que país está este restaurante?

   _____

4. ¿Cuántas personas hay en el restaurante?

   _____

Nombres

el agua	*the water*	el desayuno	*the breakfast*
el almuerzo	*the lunch*	el impuesto	*the tax*
el camarero	*the waiter*	el mantel	*the tablecloth*
la carta	*the menu*	el menú	*the menu*
la cena	*the supper*	el mozo	*the waiter*
el cheque	*the check*	el plato	*the plate*
la cocina	*the kitchen*	la propina	*the tip*
el comedor	*the dining room*	la servilleta	*the napkin*
la comida	*the meal*	la tarjeta de	*the credit card*
la cuchara	*the spoon*	crédito	
el cuchillo	*the knife*	el tenedor	*the fork*
la cuenta	*the check, the bill*	el vaso	*the glass*

Spanish nouns ending in **-a** that begin with a stressed **a** or **ha** are feminine, but they take the masculine article **el** in the singular and the feminine article **las** in the plural. **El agua** is the most common of these nouns: **el agua fría**, **las aguas frías**.

el águila, las águilas	*the eagle, the eagles*
el alma, las almas	*the soul, the souls*
el arma, las armas	*the weapon, the weapons*
el hacha, las hachas	*the axe, the axes*

Adjetivos

caliente	*warm, hot*	picante	*spicy*
delicioso	*delicious*	sabroso	*delicious*
fresco	*fresh*	sano	*healthy*
frío	*cold*	seco	*dry*
limpio	*clean*	sucio	*dirty*
lleno	*full*	vacío	*empty*

Expresiones de la hora en general (Expressions of time in general)

Es mediodía.	*It is midday. / It is noon.*
Es medianoche.	*It is midnight.*
Es temprano.	*It is early.*
Es tarde.	*It is late.*

Expresiones cuantitativas (Quantitative expressions)

una vez	*one time, once*
doble	*double*
dos veces	*two times, twice*
triple	*triple*
tres veces	*three times*
la mitad	*(a) half*

Exercise 4.5

Translate the following Spanish sentences into English.

1. Son las dos de la tarde y los estudiantes están en clase.

   _____

2. La cocina está sucia pero el baño está limpio.

   _____

3. ¿Dónde están los trece camareros del restaurante?

   _____

4. Hay clase los lunes y los jueves.

   _____

5. A las ocho y media, la sopa está fría y los platos están sucios.

   _____

6. ¿Cuántos vasos hay en la mesa a las siete de la mañana en la casa de Ricardo?

 Exercise 4.6

Answer the following questions aloud.

1. ¿Cuántas semanas hay en un año?

2. ¿Cuántos días hay en un año?

3. ¿Cuánto es ochenta y dos menos veintiséis?

4. ¿Cuánto es sesenta y siete y ciento treinta?

5. En la casa hay cuatro comedores y dos cocinas. ¿Es grande la casa o es pequeña?

6. ¿Por qué están Uds. contentos los miércoles en la primavera?

7. ¿Es deliciosa la comida italiana?

8. ¿A qué hora es el desayuno?

 Reading Comprehension

El oficio de la casa

Es el otoño y el aire está fresco. Son las once de la mañana y es un buen día para el oficio de la casa. Hoy, todo es un desorden.

En el dormitorio, la ropa está en el piso; las sábanas y las almohadas están sucias. La cocina es otro cuento. Hay polvo encima de la nevera y la estufa; las cucharas, los cuchillos, los tenedores y los platos están en el lavaplatos. Hay manchas feas en el piso de la cocina. El baño del primer piso está sucio pero por lo menos, es pequeño. ¿Dónde está mi esponja para la cocina y el baño? Siempre están en el gabinete. También, hay una escoba para la sala y una aspiradora para la alfombra roja del comedor.

¿Qué hora es? Son las dos ya. Es la hora del almuerzo. En la nevera, hay sopa sabrosa de pescado y vegetales, pollo y papas fritas, y hay una torta y helado para el postre. Es el veintiuno de septiembre, el día de mi cumpleaños, un día agradable para estar en la casa.

Nombres

la almohada	*the pillow*
la aspiradora	*the vacuum cleaner*
el cumpleaños	*the birthday*
un desorden	*a mess*
el dormitorio	*the bedroom*
la escoba	*the broom*
la esponja	*the sponge*
el helado	*the ice cream*
el lavaplatos	*the dishwasher*
la mancha	*the stain*
el oficio	*the work, the job*
el polvo	*the dust*
la ropa	*the clothes*
la sábana	*the sheet*

Expresiones

al principio	*at the beginning*
es otro cuento	*it's another story*
por lo menos	*at least*

Preguntas

After you have read the selection, answer the following questions in Spanish.

1. ¿Qué estación es?

   _____

2. ¿Qué hora es al principio del cuento?

   _____

3. ¿Dónde están las cucharas, los cuchillos y los tenedores?

   _____

4. ¿Está sucia o limpia la casa?

   _____

5. ¿Es hoy el día de cumpleaños?

   _____

5

Regular Verbs

All Spanish verbs belong to one of three classifications, called conjugations, depending on the ending of the infinitive.

All infinitives end in **-ar**, **-er**, or **-ir**.

Each conjugation has its own set of endings that are added to the stem of the verb.

verb stem + infinitive ending = infinitive

cant + **ar** = **cantar**
com + **er** = **comer**
viv + **ir** = **vivir**

Verbs are considered *regular* if there is *no change in the stem* when it is conjugated.

Uses of the Present Tense

The present tense is used to express the English simple present (*I sing*) and the English present progressive tense (*I am singing*).

Ella canta una canción triste.
$\begin{cases} \textit{She sings a sad song.} \\ \textit{She is singing a sad song.} \end{cases}$

Questions are formed by inverting the subject and the verb. In this case, the translation of the Spanish present tense includes the English helping verb *do*. Questions can also be indicated by rising intonation, without a change in word order.

¿Cantas tú los domingos?   *Do you sing on Sundays?*
¿Tú cantas los domingos?   *You sing on Sundays?*

The present tense can be used to express a future event if an adverbial expression of future time is included.

Ella canta con Ud. mañana.	*She'll sing with you tomorrow.*

To make a sentence negative, place **no** directly before the verb.

Yo canto en el baño.	*I sing in the bathroom.*
No canto en el tren.	*I don't sing in the train.*

-*Ar* Verbs

To conjugate a regular **-ar** verb in the present tense, drop the infinitive ending and add **-o**, **-as**, **-a**, **-amos**, **-áis**, **-an** to the stem.

cantar *to sing*

cantar	Infinitive
cant-	Stem
-ar	Ending

yo **canto**	*I sing*	nosotros **cantamos**	*we sing*
tú **cantas**	*you sing*	vosotros **cantáis**	*you* (pl.) *sing*
él **canta**	*he sings*	ellos **cantan**	*they sing*
ella **canta**	*she sings*	ellas **cantan**	*they* (f.) *sing*
Ud. **canta**	*you sing*	Uds. **cantan**	*you* (pl.) *sing*

A Word About Pronunciation

It is important to pronounce Spanish precisely and correctly. All words that end in the vowels **a**, **e**, **i**, **o**, **u**, or the consonants **n** or **s** have their natural stress on the second-to-last, or penultimate, syllable. Make sure you pronounce the verbs this way: **yo <u>can</u>to, tú <u>can</u>tas, él <u>can</u>ta, nosotros can<u>ta</u>mos, ellos <u>can</u>tan**. If a word carries an accent mark, you will stress that syllable: **vosotros can<u>táis</u>**, for example.

Frequently Used -*ar* Verbs

bailar *to dance*

yo bailo	nosotros bailamos
tú bailas	vosotros bailáis
él baila	ellos bailan
ella baila	ellas bailan
Ud. baila	Uds. bailan

bajar *to go down, to descend*

yo bajo	nosotros bajamos
tú bajas	vosotros bajáis
él baja	ellos bajan
ella baja	ellas bajan
Ud. baja	Uds. bajan

caminar *to walk*

yo camino	nosotros caminamos
tú caminas	vosotros camináis
él camina	ellos caminan
ella camina	ellas caminan
Ud. camina	Uds. caminan

comprar *to buy*

yo compro	nosotros compramos
tú compras	vosotros compráis
él compra	ellos compran
ella compra	ellas compran
Ud. compra	Uds. compran

contestar *to answer*

yo contesto	nosotros contestamos
tú contestas	vosotros contestáis
él contesta	ellos contestan
ella contesta	ellas contestan
Ud. contesta	Uds. contestan

cocinar *to cook*

yo cocino	nosotros cocinamos
tú cocinas	vosotros cocináis
él cocina	ellos cocinan
ella cocina	ellas cocinan
Ud. cocina	Uds. cocinan

A Word About Verbs

The verbs above are presented with full conjugations so that you can practice and learn them one by one. These verbs form an essential base for all future studies. All three forms of both the third-person singular and the third-person plural conjugations have the same endings. From this point forward, only one pronoun will be used for each singular or plural third-person conjugation.

descansar *to rest*

yo descanso	nosotros descansamos
tú descansas	vosotros descansáis
ella descansa	ellas descansan

entrar (en) *to enter (in)*

yo entro	nosotros entramos
tú entras	vosotros entráis
Ud. entra	Uds. entran

escuchar *to listen to*

yo escucho	nosotros escuchamos
tú escuchas	vosotros escucháis
él escucha	ellos escuchan

estudiar *to study*

yo estudio	nosotros estudiamos
tú estudias	vosotros estudiáis
ella estudia	ellas estudian

Pronunciation Reminder
The Spanish **d** is pronounced like the **d** in English *dog* when it appears at the beginning of a breath group or follows an **l** or **n**: **donde, la falda, el conde**. In all other cases, the Spanish **d** is pronounced like the soft **th** sound in English *other*. Practice **estudiar** with a **th** sound.

hablar *to speak*

yo hablo	nosotros hablamos
tú hablas	vosotros habláis
Ud. habla	Uds. hablan

limpiar *to clean*

yo limpio	nosotros limpiamos
tú limpias	vosotros limpiáis
ella limpia	ellas limpian

llegar *to arrive*

yo llego	nosotros llegamos
tú llegas	vosotros llegáis
él llega	ellos llegan

Pronunciation Reminder
The **ll** in Spanish is pronounced like the **y** in English *beyond,* or the **s** in English *pleasure.*

mirar *to look at*

yo miro	nosotros miramos
tú miras	vosotros miráis
Ud. mira	Uds. miran

nadar *to swim*

yo nado	nosotros nadamos
tú nadas	vosotros nadáis
él nada	ellos nadan

practicar *to practice*

yo practico	nosotros practicamos
tú practicas	vosotros practicáis
ella practica	ellas practican

regresar *to return*

yo regreso	nosotros regresamos
tú regresas	vosotros regresáis
Ud. regresa	Uds. regresan

trabajar *to work*

yo trabajo	nosotros trabajamos
tú trabajas	vosotros trabajáis
él trabaja	ellos trabajan

Pronunciation Reminder
Stress the penultimate syllable of the conjugated verb: **tra<u>ba</u>jo**, **tra<u>ba</u>jas**, **tra<u>ba</u>ja**, **tra<u>ba</u>jamos**, **tra<u>ba</u>jan**.

viajar *to travel*

yo viajo	nosotros viajamos
tú viajas	vosotros viajáis
ella viaja	ellas viajan

Pronunciation Reminder
The **v** in Spanish is pronounced like the **b** in English *boy*.

The Preposition *a*

The preposition **a** means *to* in English.

When **a** is followed by the masculine **el** (meaning *the*), the words contract to **al** (meaning *to the*). This is one of only two contractions in Spanish.

Caminamos **al** hotel.	*We walk **to the** hotel.*
Yo camino **al** restaurante.	*I walk **to the** restaurant.*

A contraction is *not* formed when **a** is followed by the feminine **la** or by the plural articles **los** or **las**.

Caminamos a la tienda.	*We walk to the store.*
Ellos viajan a los estados del sur.	*They travel to the Southern states.*
Ella viaja a las ciudades grandes.	*She travels to the large cities.*

Exercise 5.1

Complete the following sentences with the correct form of the appropriate verb. Choose from the verbs listed below, but don't use any verb more than once.

> bailar, bajar, caminar, cantar, cocinar, comprar, contestar, descansar, entrar, escuchar, estudiar, hablar, limpiar, llegar, mirar, nadar, practicar, regresar, trabajar, viajar

EXAMPLE   Las estudiantes __*caminan*__ a la escuela. Ellos __*regresan*__ en bus.

1. Ricardo _____ en la piscina.

2. Ella _____ mucho porque las lecciones son difíciles.

3. En la noche, si estamos cansados, _____ en la cama.

4. María siempre _____ a casa a las seis de la noche.

5. Los niños _____ y _____ en la fiesta.

6. En conversaciones, ¿quiénes _____ más, los hombres o las mujeres?

7. ¿Por qué _____ la mujer la blusa si es cara?

8. Enrique _____ en un restaurante. Él es cocinero y _____ en la cocina.

9. Los estudiantes _____ en el salón a las ocho de la mañana.

10. Yo _____ la música a las ocho de la noche los martes.

11. Ella _____ la televisión los domingos a las nueve.

12. Los músicos están contentos porque los estudiantes _____ mucho el piano.

13. Las dos amigas _____ el apartamento cuando está sucio.

14. Yo _____ en carro a la oficina. Trabajo en el piso cuarenta.

    A las cinco de la tarde _____ al primer piso.

15. Roberto _____ las preguntas en la clase.

Exercise 5.2

Answer the following questions aloud.

1. ¿Canta Ud. en la ducha?
2. ¿A qué hora escucha Ud. la música?
3. ¿Viajas tú mucho?
4. ¿Quiénes estudian más, los muchachos o las muchachas?
5. ¿Quién cocina bien en la familia de Ud.?
6. ¿Si estás en un baile, bailas mucho?

-*Er* Verbs

To conjugate a regular **-er** verb in the present tense, drop the infinitive ending and add **-o**, **-es**, **-e**, **-emos**, **-éis**, **-en** to the stem.

comer *to eat*

comer	Infinitive
com-	Stem
-er	Ending

yo **como**	nosotros **comemos**
tú **comes**	vosotros **coméis**
él **come**	ellos **comen**
ella **come**	ellas **comen**
Ud. **come**	Uds. **comen**

Frequently Used -*er* Verbs

aprender *to learn*

yo aprendo	nosotros aprendemos
tú aprendes	vosotros aprendéis
él aprende	ellos aprenden

beber *to drink*

yo bebo	nosotros bebemos
tú bebes	vosotros bebéis
ella bebe	ellas beben

comprender *to understand*

yo comprendo	nosotros comprendemos
tú comprendes	vosotros comprendéis
Ud. comprende	Uds. comprenden

correr *to run*

yo corro	nosotros corremos
tú corres	vosotros corréis
él corre	ellos corren

leer *to read*

yo leo	nosotros leemos
tú lees	vosotros leéis
ella lee	ellas leen

meter *to put in*

yo meto	nosotros metemos
tú metes	vosotros metéis
Ud. mete	Uds. meten

prender *to turn on*

yo prendo	nosotros prendemos
tú prendes	vosotros prendéis
él prende	ellos prenden

romper *to break*

yo rompo	nosotros rompemos
tú rompes	vosotros rompéis
ella rompe	ellas rompen

vender *to sell*

yo vendo	nosotros vendemos
tú vendes	vosotros vendéis
Ud. vende	Uds. venden

Exercise 5.3

Complete the following sentences with the correct form of the appropriate verb. Choose from the verbs listed below, but don't use any verb more than once.

aprender, beber, comer, comprender, correr, leer, romper, vender

1. Si ella camina, y él _____, ¿quién llega primero?

2. Mariana _____ ocho vasos de agua cada día.

3. Nosotros _____ en los restaurantes excelentes todos los jueves.

4. Las muchachas estudian bien las lecciones de violín y _____ mucho.

5. Yo _____ un libro cada semana. ¿Cuántos libros

   _____ Uds. cada año?

6. Somos buenos estudiantes y _____ las ideas difíciles.

7. El hombre y la mujer _____ el apartamento y compran una casa.

8. Los niños _____ los platos y los vasos.

-*Ir* Verbs

To conjugate a regular **-ir** verb in the present tense, drop the infinitive ending and add **-o**, **-es**, **-e**, **-imos**, **-ís**, **-en** to the stem.

vivir *to live*

vivir	Infinitive
viv-	Stem
-ir	Ending

yo **vivo**	nosotros **vivimos**
tú **vives**	vosotros **vivís**
el **vive**	ellos **viven**
ella **vive**	ellas **viven**
Ud. **vive**	Uds. **viven**

Frequently Used -*ir* Verbs

abrir *to open*

yo abro	nosotros abrimos
tú abres	vosotros abrís
él abre	ellos abren

compartir *to share*

yo comparto	nosotros compartimos
tú compartes	vosotros compartís
ella comparte	ellas comparten

decidir *to decide*

yo decido	nosotros decidimos
tú decides	vosotros decidís
Ud. decide	Uds. deciden

describir *to describe*		**discutir** *to discuss*	
yo describo	nosotros describimos	yo discuto	nosotros discutimos
tú describes	vosotros describís	tú discutes	vosotros discutís
él describe	ellos describen	ella discute	ellas discuten

escribir *to write*		**recibir** *to receive*	
yo escribo	nosotros escribimos	yo recibo	nosotros recibimos
tú escribes	vosotros escribís	tú recibes	vosotros recibís
Ud. escribe	Uds. escriben	él recibe	ellos reciben

subir *to go up, to ascend*		**sufrir** *to suffer*	
yo subo	nosotros subimos	yo sufro	nosotros sufrimos
tú subes	vosotros subís	tú sufres	vosotros sufrís
ella sube	ellas suben	Ud. sufre	Uds. sufren

Exercise 5.4

Complete the following sentences with the correct form of the appropriate verb. Choose from the verbs listed below.

abrir, compartir, decidir, discutir, escribir, recibir, subir, vivir

1. Hay mucha comida en la mesa pero el muchacho no come mucho.

   Él _____ la porción con Elena.

2. ¿Por qué _____ Ud. la puerta si hay mucho ruido afuera?

3. Ella trabaja en la ciudad, pero _____ en el campo.

4. Hablamos y _____ las noticias del día. La conversación
   es interesante.

5. ¿_____ tú frases y preguntas con una pluma o usas
   una computadora?

6. ¿Por qué _____ Uds. estudiar el español?

7. Cecilia siempre _____ muchas cartas de la familia los lunes.

8. Todos los estudiantes _____ al noveno piso para la clase
   de química.

-Ar and -er Verbs with More than One Meaning

deber *should, ought to, must* (plus infinitive), *to owe*

yo debo	nosotros debemos
tú debes	vosotros debéis
él debe	ellos deben

Ella debe comer mejor.	*She ought to eat better.*
Él debe mucho dinero.	*He owes a lot of money.*

ganar *to win, to earn*

yo gano	nosotros ganamos
tú ganas	vosotros ganáis
ella gana	ellas ganan

Cecilia siempre gana el primer premio.	*Cecilia always wins first prize.*
Raúl gana quinientos dólares cada semana.	*Ralph earns 500 dollars each week.*

llevar *to carry, to wear*

yo llevo	nosotros llevamos
tú llevas	vosotros lleváis
Ud. lleva	Uds. llevan

Llevo una bolsa de plástico a la tienda.	*I carry a plastic bag to the store.*
Ella no lleva un abrigo hoy.	*She isn't wearing a coat today.*

pasar *to pass (by), to happen, to spend* (time)

yo paso	nosotros pasamos
tú pasas	vosotros pasáis
él pasa	ellos pasan

El tiempo pasa.	*Time passes.*
¿Qué pasa?	*What's happening?*
Ella pasa mucho tiempo con los turistas.	*She spends a lot of time with the tourists.*

tocar *to touch, to play* (an instrument)

yo toco	nosotros tocamos
tú tocas	vosotros tocáis
él toca	ellos tocan

El experto toca la mesa antigua.   *The expert touches the antique table.*
María toca bien el piano.   *Maria plays the piano well.*

tomar *to take, to have* (something to drink), *to have* (breakfast, lunch, dinner)

yo tomo	nosotros tomamos
tú tomas	vosotros tomáis
ella toma	ellas toman

Tomamos el tren al trabajo.   *We take the train to work.*
Tomo café negro cada mañana.   *I drink black coffee every morning.*
Ella toma el desayuno a las ocho. *She has breakfast at eight o'clock.*
Toma el almuerzo a la una y   *She has lunch at one o'clock and*
  la cena a las siete.   *dinner at seven o'clock.*

Exercise 5.5

Complete the following sentences with the correct form of the appropriate verb. Choose from the verbs listed below; this time you can use the verbs more than once!

deber, ganar, llevar, pasar, tocar, tomar

1. ¿A qué hora _____ Uds. el almuerzo?

2. La niña está enferma porque no _____ una chaqueta en el invierno.

3. Ella _____ caminar treinta minutos cada día.

4. Victoria _____ bien el violín.

5. Nosotros _____ compartir la torta de chocolate con Jorge y con Guillermo.

6. Yo _____ dos bolígrafos y tres lápices a la clase de matemáticas.

7. El profesor _____ mucho tiempo en las montañas en el verano.

8. El muchacho _____ la mesa antigua con las manos sucias.

9. Ricardo es maestro; no _____ mucho dinero, pero está feliz.

10. ¿_____ Ud. café con leche en la mañana?

Reading Comprehension

Una escuela en México

Es el año mil novecientos sesenta y tres. Es una época° de paz en los
Estados Unidos. En la ciudad donde vivimos este verano, hay paz también
pero no estoy segura° si hay paz en el resto de México.

La ciudad es muy linda, con calles estrechas y casas del estilo español.
Hay unas plazas hermosas y muchas iglesias. Vivimos en las montañas y
estamos a tres millas de° la ciudad. Laura y yo caminamos treinta minutos
y llegamos a la escuela a las diez de la mañana; la madre de Laura pasa
el día en el campo porque estudia las civilizaciones antiguas. El padre
de Laura descansa en la casa hasta las diez. Después,° él baja a la ciudad
y pasa la mañana en un restaurante bonito donde él toma uno o dos cafés
más; lee un periódico y habla con la gente. Ellos hablan bien el español,
pero Laura y yo no hablamos mucho; estudiamos en la escuela secundaria
porque necesitamos practicar más.

Laura y yo decidimos tomar un curso de historia de México, una clase
de baile, una clase donde los estudiantes aprenden canciones mexicanas
y aprenden a tocar la guitarra. Guanajuato está ubicada° en las montañas
y la clase de baile es difícil porque es trabajoso° respirar° en las montañas.
Las clases de música son fantásticas porque hablamos y practicamos la
pronunciación.

En la noche, regresamos a la casa y discutimos las experiencias del día.
La madre cocina bien y comemos una comida saludable.° Laura y yo
lavamos° los platos y el padre escucha la conversación y descansa.

°la época *period of time*
°estar seguro(a) *to be sure*
°estar a tres millas de *to be three miles from*
°después *afterward*
°estar ubicado(a) *to be located*

°trabajoso *difficult*
°respirar *to breathe*
°saludable *healthy, healthful*
°lavar *to wash*

Preguntas

After you have read the selection, answer the following questions in Spanish.

1. ¿Cómo es Guanajuato?

   _____

2. ¿Qué estación del año es?

   _____

3. ¿Cómo pasa el día el padre de ella?

   _____

4. ¿Qué estudian Laura y la amiga de ella?

   _____

5. En la noche, ¿de qué hablan?

   _____

6

Irregular Verbs

Spanish verbs are considered *irregular* if there is a *change in the stem* when they are conjugated.

Each verb conjugation has its own set of endings that are added to the verb stem.

The **nosotros** and **vosotros** forms are *unaffected by the stem change* in the present tense.

-Ar Verbs

Irregular verbs that end in **-ar** have two possible changes in their stem. The endings are the same as those you have learned for the regular verbs: add **-o**, **-as**, **-a**, **-amos**, **-áis**, **-an** to the stem.

Stem Change e > ie

cerrar *to close*	
yo c**ie**rro	nosotros cerramos
tú c**ie**rras	vosotros cerráis
él c**ie**rra	ellos c**ie**rran

empezar *to begin*	
yo emp**ie**zo	nosotros empezamos
tú emp**ie**zas	vosotros empezáis
ella emp**ie**za	ellas emp**ie**zan

pensar *to think*	
yo p**ie**nso	nosotros pensamos
tú p**ie**nsas	vosotros pensáis
Ud. p**ie**nsa	Uds. p**ie**nsan

A Word About Irregular Verbs
It is a good idea to learn these verbs one by one. Make sure you read them aloud. Practice as much as you can.

Stem Change o > ue

almorzar *to lunch*

yo alm**ue**rzo	nosotros almorzamos
tú alm**ue**rzas	vosotros almorzáis
él alm**ue**rza	ellos alm**ue**rzan

encontrar *to find*

yo enc**ue**ntro	nosotros encontramos
tú enc**ue**ntras	vosotros encontráis
ella enc**ue**ntra	ellas enc**ue**ntran

recordar *to remember*

yo rec**ue**rdo	nosotros recordamos
tú rec**ue**rdas	vosotros recordáis
ella rec**ue**rda	ellas rec**ue**rdan

jugar *to play, to play* (a sport)

yo **jue**go	nosotros jugamos
tú **jue**gas	vosotros jugáis
Ud. **jue**ga	Uds. **jue**gan

NOTE: The stem change for **jugar** is **u** > **ue**.

Exercise 6.1

Complete the following sentences with the correct form of the appropriate verb. Choose from the verbs listed below; use each verb only once.

almorzar, cerrar, empezar, jugar, pensar, recordar

1. Yo _____ la ventana del salón porque hay mucho ruido afuera.

2. ¿Qué _____ Ud. de la situación del mundo?

3. Los muchachos y las muchachas _____ al béisbol todas las tardes a las cinco.

4. Al mediodía, nosotros _____ en un restaurante económico con los colegas del trabajo.

5. ¿_____ tú toda la letra de las canciones?

6. La maestra _____ la clase a las seis en punto.

-*Er* Verbs

Irregular verbs that end in **-er** have two possible changes in their stem. The endings are the same as those you have learned for the regular verbs: add **-o**, **-es**, **-e**, **-emos**, **-éis**, **-en** to the stem.

Stem Change e > ie

entender *to understand*

yo ent**ie**ndo	nosotros entendemos
tú ent**ie**ndes	vosotros entendéis
ella ent**ie**nde	ellas ent**ie**nden

perder *to lose*

yo p**ie**rdo	nosotros perdemos
tú p**ie**rdes	vosotros perdéis
Ud. p**ie**rde	Uds. p**ie**rden

querer *to want*

yo qu**ie**ro	nosotros queremos
tú qu**ie**res	vosotros queréis
él qu**ie**re	ellos qu**ie**ren

tener *to have*

yo **tengo**	nosotros tenemos
tú **tie**nes	vosotros tenéis
ella **tie**ne	ellas **tie**nen

NOTE: **Tener** also has an irregular **yo** form.

Stem Change o > ue

devolver *to return* (something), *to give back*

yo dev**ue**lvo	nosotros devolvemos
tú dev**ue**lves	vosotros devolvéis
ella dev**ue**lve	ellas dev**ue**lven

poder *to be able, can, may*

yo p**ue**do	nosotros podemos
tú p**ue**des	vosotros podéis
él p**ue**de	ellos p**ue**den

volver *to return*

yo v**ue**lvo	nosotros volvemos
tú v**ue**lves	vosotros volvéis
Ud. v**ue**lve	Uds. v**ue**lven

Verbs Irregular in the *yo* Form Only

hacer *to do, to make*

yo **hago**	nosotros hacemos
tú haces	vosotros hacéis
él hace	ellos hacen

poner *to put*

yo **pongo**	nosotros ponemos
tú pones	vosotros ponéis
ella pone	ellas ponen

saber *to know* (a fact), *to know how*		**ver** *to see*	
yo **sé**	nosotros sabemos	yo **veo**	nosotros vemos
tú sabes	vosotros sabéis	tú ves	vosotros veis
Ud. sabe	Uds. saben	él ve	ellos ven

Sentence Formation

You have learned to form sentences and questions with one verb.

Ella tiene un gato.	*She has a cat.*
¿Tiene ella un perro?	*Does she have a dog?*

The word order in English and Spanish is basically the same. This allows you to put two verbs together in a similar sequence. Note that the negative word **no** comes directly before the first verb.

Yo no quiero cantar.	*I don't want to sing.*
Ellos quieren leer un libro.	*They want to read a book.*
Podemos bailar bien.	*We are able to dance well.*
Sí, sabemos cantar bien también.	*Yes, we know how to sing well also.*

You can even string three verbs together in one sentence!

Susana quiere poder hablar español.	*Susan wants to be able to speak Spanish.*
Él quiere poder correr en el maratón.	*He wants to be able to run in the marathon.*

Exercise 6.2

Complete the following sentences with the correct verb form, using the infinitive provided.

1. El muchacho _____ nadar y las amigas de

   él _____ bailar. (saber)

2. No sabemos donde estamos porque siempre _____ las direcciones. (perder)

3. ¿Qué _____ Ud. durante la primavera? (hacer)

4. Yo _____ una pluma y él _____ un libro difícil. Nosotros _____ mucha tarea para la clase. (tener)

5. El gerente _____ a la casa a las ocho y media los lunes. (volver)

6. Los estudiantes _____ la pregunta. (entender)

7. Yo _____ viajar porque tengo mucho dinero. (poder)

8. Nosotros _____ los pájaros en el parque. (ver)

9. Federico _____ los libros a la biblioteca. (devolver)

10. Yo _____ los platos en la mesa. (poner)

11. La turista _____ estar en los Estados Unidos el miércoles. (querer)

Exercise 6.3

Translate the following English sentences into Spanish.

1. *I know where there is an inexpensive restaurant on Fifth Avenue.*

   _____

2. *Carlos doesn't want to make a date with the dentist.*

   _____

3. *We don't want to clean the apartment today.*

   _____

4. *I see a gray cat and a blue bird.*

   _____

5. *She understands the ideas, but she doesn't want to talk.*

   _____

6. *Who is able to sing and dance at the party?*

   _____

7. *I do the homework at eight o'clock on Mondays.*

   _____

8. *We want to return to work on Tuesday.*

   _____

-Ir Verbs

Irregular verbs that end in **-ir** have three possible changes in their stem. The endings are the same as those you have learned for the regular verbs: add **-o**, **-es**, **-e**, **-imos**, **-ís**, **-en** to the stem.

Stem Change e > ie

mentir *to lie*

yo m**ie**nto	nosotros mentimos
tú m**ie**ntes	vosotros mentís
él m**ie**nte	ellos m**ie**nten

preferir *to prefer*

yo pref**ie**ro	nosotros preferimos
tú pref**ie**res	vosotros preferís
ella pref**ie**re	ellas pref**ie**ren

venir *to come*

yo **vengo**	nosotros venimos
tú v**ie**nes	vosotros venís
Ud. v**ie**ne	Uds. v**ie**nen

NOTE: **Venir** also has an irregular **yo** form.

Stem Change e > i

pedir *to ask for, to request*

yo p**i**do	nosotros pedimos
tú p**i**des	vosotros pedís
Ud. p**i**de	Uds. p**i**den

repetir *to repeat*

yo rep**i**to	nosotros repetimos
tú rep**i**tes	vosotros repetís
él rep**i**te	ellos rep**i**ten

seguir *to follow, to continue*

yo s**i**go	nosotros seguimos
tú s**i**gues	vosotros seguís
ella s**i**gue	ellas s**i**guen

servir *to serve*

yo s**i**rvo	nosotros servimos
tú s**i**rves	vosotros servís
Ud. s**i**rve	Uds. s**i**rven

sonreír *to smile*

yo sonr**í**o	nosotros sonreímos
tú sonr**í**es	vosotros sonreís
él sonr**í**e	ellos sonr**í**en

Stem Change o > ue

dormir *to sleep*

yo d**ue**rmo	nosotros dormimos
tú d**ue**rmes	vosotros dormís
él d**ue**rme	ellos d**ue**rmen

Stem Change in the *yo* Form Only

oír *to hear*

yo o**igo**	nosotros oímos
tú oyes	vosotros oís
ella oye	ellas oyen

NOTE: **Oyes**, **oye**, and **oyen** reflect a spelling change (that clarifies the pronunciation) rather than a stem change.

salir *to leave, to exit, to go out*

yo sal**go**	nosotros salimos
tú sales	vosotros salís
Ud. sale	Uds. salen

Exercise 6.4

Complete the following sentences with the correct form of the appropriate verb. Choose from the verbs listed below; use each verb only once.

dormir, mentir, oír, preferir, repetir, salir, seguir, servir, venir

1. ¿Por qué _____ Ud. la pregunta si ellas saben la respuesta?

2. La niña _____ mucho y sus padres están enojados con ella.

3. La fiesta es horrible; hay mucho ruido y humo. Ana quiere

   _____ .

4. Nosotros _____ ocho horas cada noche y podemos trabajar bien durante el día.

5. Ella no sabe donde vive María, pero ella tiene un mapa y puede

   _____ las direcciones a la casa.

6. Ellos _____ a Nueva York a ver los museos.

7. ¿Pueden Uds. _____ bien las voces de los estudiantes?

8. ¿Qué _____ Ud. hacer, jugar al tenis o nadar?

9. A las nueve de la mañana, la cafetería abre y los camareros

   _____ el desayuno.

Exercise 6.5

Respond aloud to the following questions.

1. ¿A qué hora almuerza Ud.? ¿Come Ud. mucho?

2. ¿Duerme Ud. bien? ¿Tiene Ud. sueños dulces?

3. ¿Tienes las llaves del edificio donde trabajas?

4. ¿Cuál prefiere Ud. beber, el vino blanco o el vino tinto?

5. ¿Qué hace Ud. el fin de semana?

6. ¿Quiénes sonríen más, los hombres, las mujeres, o los niños?

7. ¿Sabe Ud. jugar al tenis?

8. ¿Dónde pones los platos, los tenedores, las cucharas y los cuchillos?

Exercise 6.6

Complete the following sentences with the correct form of the appropriate verb. Choose from the verbs listed below.

> almorzar, cerrar, dormir, empezar, encontrar, entender,
> estar, hacer, hay, jugar, poder, poner, preferir, recordar,
> saber, salir, seguir, ser, servir, tener, venir, ver, volver

1. A las ocho de la mañana, los empleados abren la puerta de la oficina

   y entran. A las ocho de la noche, ellos _____ la puerta

   y _____ .

2. Los muchachos estudian todo el día en la escuela. A las tres de la tarde,

   si hace sol, ellos _____ al béisbol.

3. A mediodía, nosotros _____ en un restaurante económico
   con los amigos del trabajo.

4. La maestra _____ las lecciones a las seis.

5. ¿Quién _____ la letra de las canciones?

6. Ella _____ la pregunta pero no _____
   la respuesta correcta.

7. Yo toco el piano pero _____ tocar la guitarra.

8. Yo _____ mil dólares en el banco y cien dólares en la mano.

9. ¿Por qué quiere él _____ presidente?

10. Nosotros _____ el camino a la casa de Sara.

11. Los dos niños _____ nueve horas cada noche.

12. No puedo _____ un hotel barato en la ciudad.

13. Laura _____ a la oficina porque quiere hablar con el jefe.

14. Nosotros _____ cansados porque tenemos que trabajar.

15. ¿_____ Ud. preparar una torta deliciosa para la fiesta?

16. En el campo, yo _____ los árboles y los pájaros;

    en la ciudad, yo _____ los edificios altos.

17. ¿Por qué no _____ manzanas rojas en el supermercado?

18. El viaje es largo y queremos _____ a casa.

19. Yo _____ las cucharas, los cuchillos y los tenedores

    en la mesa y Teresa _____ la comida.

20. Ellos prefieren _____ la tarea a las diez de la noche;

    yo _____ la tarea a las siete de la mañana.

Exercise 6.7

Translate the following Spanish sentences into English.

1. ¿En qué piso viven los amigos de Pablo? ¿Son ellos de Perú?
   ¿Hablan bien el inglés?

   _____

   _____

2. ¿De qué habla Ud.? ¿Con quién hablan Uds.?

   _____

3. Sebastián sale de la casa de Carla a las ocho de la mañana.
   Llega a la oficina a las nueve. Él trabaja ocho horas. ¿A qué hora
   puede llegar a la casa de Carla?

   _____

   _____

4. ¿Por qué hay un árbol en la casa?

   _____

5. Ser o no ser.

   _____

6. Al mediodía, entramos en el edificio y subimos al tercer piso;
   a las tres de la tarde, bajamos al primer piso y salimos.

   _____

   _____

 # Reading Comprehension

El tren

El tren llega a tiempo como siempre. Llega a las cuatro y veintiséis.
Subo al tren con algunas personas y viajo a la ciudad.

Cerca de mí, una mujer duerme. Ella descansa completamente.
Pienso que tiene sueños dulces. Un hombre lee un periódico. Las noticias
son interesantes hoy; él lee con mucho interés. ¿Qué lee? ¿Está interesado
en los deportes o los negocios o los eventos internacionales? Es imposible
saber. Un niño grita y después sonríe. Un hombre a mi lado escribe
cartas de amor. Otras personas hablan por teléfono. Hablan y hablan.
Ellos tienen muchos amigos. Trato de escuchar las conversaciones.
A veces, quiero hablar con alguien pero prefiero viajar sola con mis libros
y mis cuadernos.

El tren llega a la ciudad a las cinco y cuatro. Camino con la muchedumbre hacia las salidas. La estación del tren es grande y hermosa.
Hay restaurantes en el sótano y farmacias y tiendas en el primer piso.
Salgo de la estación. No hay mucho sol, menos mal. La gente pasa.
El tiempo pasa. ¿Qué hago ahora, con muchas posibilidades? (Prefiero
el campo donde hay menos decisiones.) ¿Qué hago yo después de mi viaje
en el tren? Hay teatro y cine, conciertos y museos. Puedo comer en un

buen restaurante o escuchar música gratis en el parque. ¿En qué dirección
camino? No, es mejor volver al tren; en el tren todo es seguro. Siempre
sale y llega a su destino. El próximo tren sale precisamente a las cinco
y veinte. Afortunadamente, hay tiempo.

　　　Es la hora pico. Corro con la muchedumbre al tren. Subimos.
Tomamos asiento. Abrimos los libros, las revistas, los periódicos
y descansamos, contentos de estar de nuevo en el tren.

Verbos (Verbs)

estar seguro	*to be sure*
hablar por teléfono	*to speak by (on the) phone*
llegar a tiempo	*to arrive on time*
pensar en	*to think about*
ser imposible	*to be impossible*
ser seguro	*to be safe*
subir al tren	*to get on the train*
tomar asiento	*to take a seat*

Nombres

la hora pico	*the rush hour*
la muchedumbre	*the crowd*
la salida	*the exit*
el sótano	*the basement*
el teatro	*the theater*

Preposiciones (Prepositions)

cerca de mí	*near me*
a mi lado	*at my side*

Adverbios

a veces	*at times*
afortunadamente	*fortunately*
completamente	*completely*
de nuevo	*again*
después de + *infinitive*	*after (doing something)*
gratis	*free* (in cost)
hacia	*toward*
menos mal	*luckily*
mejor	*better*

Preguntas

After you have read the selection, answer the following questions in Spanish.

1. ¿Es largo el viaje a la ciudad?

   _____

2. ¿Cómo son los pasajeros que viajan en el tren?

   _____

3. ¿Sabe Ud. si el personaje principal es hombre o mujer? ¿Cómo sabe Ud.?

   _____

4. Después de salir de la estación, ¿en qué piensa el personaje?

   _____

5. ¿Qué decide hacer?

   _____

6. ¿Pasa el personaje mucho tiempo en la ciudad?

   _____

7. ¿Por qué vuelve al tren?

   _____

7

Ir and the Future

Ir (to go)

The conjugation of **ir** (English *to go*) is irregular in the present tense.

yo **voy**	*I am going, I go*	nosotros **vamos**	*we are going, we go*
tú **vas**	*you are going, you go*	vosotros **vais**	*you are going, you go*
él **va**	*he is going, he goes*	ellos **van**	*they are going, they go*
ella **va**	*she is going, she goes*	ellas **van**	*they are going, they go*
Ud. **va**	*you are going, you go*	Uds. **van**	*you are going, you go*

Vamos a la ciudad.	*We are going to the city.*
¿Vas tú a la playa los domingos?	*Do you go to the beach on Sundays?*
Ellas van a la tienda.	*They are going to the store.*
¿Adónde van ellos?	*(To) where are they going?*
Voy al banco los miércoles.	*I go to the bank on Wednesdays.*
¿Quieres ir con nosotros?	*Do you want to go with us?*
Quiero ir al supermercado.	*I want to go to the supermarket.*

A Word About the Verb *ir*
Whether this verb is translated *to go* or *to be going* depends on the context of
the sentence.

Exercise 7.1

Complete the following sentences with the correct form of **ir**.

1. El hombre y la mujer _____ al trabajo a las siete de la mañana.

2. Nosotros _____ al cine los sábados.

3. ¿Quiere Ud. _____ con nosotros?

4. La estudiante _____ a la escuela los martes.

5. Los niños quieren _____ al circo porque quieren ver los elefantes.

6. Yo _____ al gimnasio porque quiero hacer ejercicio.

7. ¿_____ tú al campo los fines de semana?

8. Ernesto no quiere _____ a España pero Mariana sí quiere

    _____ .

The Future with the Verb *ir*

Ir + **a** + an infinitive is used to express future time. The English equivalent
is *to be going to (do something).*

Ellos **van a cantar** esta noche.	*They are going to sing tonight.*
Vamos a decidir más tarde.	*We are going to decide later.*

To form a question using this construction, place the subject of the sentence
either directly after the conjugated form of **ir** or after the infinitive.

¿**Van** ellos **a cantar** esta noche?	*Are they going to sing tonight?*
¿**Van a cantar** ellos esta noche?	*Are they going to sing tonight?*
¿A qué hora **va a llegar** el tren?	*At what hour is the train going to arrive?*

Often the subject pronoun is not necessary.

¿**Vas a viajar** a España?	*Are you going to travel to Spain?*
Vamos a salir ahora.	*We are going to leave now.*

 ## Key Vocabulary

The following frequently used **-ar** verbs will help enhance your ability to
communicate. As you learn them, remember to practice them aloud.

aceptar	*to accept*	cruzar	*to cross*
apagar	*to turn off*	dibujar	*to draw*
arreglar	*to arrange, to fix*	disfrutar	*to enjoy*
cambiar	*to change*	doblar	*to turn, to fold*
celebrar	*to celebrate*	explicar	*to explain*

firmar	*to sign*	pintar	*to paint*
gozar	*to enjoy*	preparar	*to prepare*
llorar	*to cry*	repasar	*to review*
manejar	*to drive*	terminar	*to finish*
marcar	*to dial, to mark*	tirar	*to throw*
necesitar	*to need*	usar	*to use*
parar	*to stop*	viajar	*to travel*

 ## Exercise 7.2

*Complete the following sentences with the appropriate form of the Spanish verb or expression. Remember that the Spanish preposition **a** follows the verb **ir**.*

EXAMPLES   Elena __va a viajar__ (*to be going to travel*) a Portugal.

Ella __necesita__ (*to need*) aprender el portugués.

1. ¿Dónde _____ (*to be going to be*) Marí y Sara
   a las diez esta noche?

2. Samuel _____ (*to be going to sign*) un documento
   mañana.

3. Mañana, yo _____ (*to be going to finish*) la tarea.

4. ¿Quién _____ (*to be going to buy*) los tiquetes
   para el viaje?

5. Nosotros _____ (*to be going to celebrate*)
   el cumpleaños de Ana el sábado.

6. Él no _____ (*to be going to accept*) la invitación.

7. Nosotros _____ (*to be going to enjoy*) el verano

   este año porque nosotros _____ (*to go*) a Chile.

8. Esta noche yo _____ (*to be going to cook*).

   No quiero _____ (*to go*) a un restaurante.

9. ¿Quién _____ (*to be going to turn off*) las luces?

10. ¿Cómo _____ (*to be going to spend*) Uds. el día
    de acción de gracias?

Idioms

Idioms are expressions that do not translate directly from one language to another. Instead of saying, for example, how old someone or something *is*, Spanish uses the verb **tener**, *to have*.

Yo tengo treinta años.   *I am thirty years old.* (literally,
                               I have thirty years.)

Idioms with the Verb *tener*

Indeed, there are many Spanish idioms that use the verb **tener**.

tener _____ años	*to be _____ years old*
tener calor	*to be hot*
tener celos	*to be jealous*
tener cuidado	*to be careful*
tener la culpa	*to be at fault*
tener dolor de (cabeza, estómago, etc.)	*to have a (head)ache, (stomach)ache, etc.*
tener envidia	*to be envious*
tener éxito	*to be successful, to have success*
tener frío	*to be cold*
tener ganas de	*to want, to desire*
tener hambre	*to be hungry*
tener la palabra	*to have the floor*
tener lugar	*to take place*
tener miedo de	*to be afraid of*
tener prisa	*to be in a hurry*
tener que ver con	*to have to do with*
tener rabia	*to be in a rage, to be very angry*
tener razón	*to be right*
tener sed	*to be thirsty*
tener sueño	*to be sleepy*
tener suerte	*to be lucky, to have luck*
tener vergüenza	*to be ashamed*

Exercise 7.3

Answer the following questions aloud in Spanish.

1. ¿Cuántos años tienes?

2. ¿Tiene Ud. frío en el invierno donde vive?

3. ¿Es necesario tener cuidado en las calles de una ciudad grande?

4. ¿Tiene Ud. dolor de cabeza ahora?

5. ¿En qué profesión tiene Ud. éxito?

6. ¿Tiene Ud. ganas de tomar una cerveza fría o prefiere el vino blanco?

7. ¿A qué hora tiene Ud. hambre?

8. ¿Tiene Ud. miedo del agua? ¿Sabe Ud. nadar?

Exercise 7.4

*Complete the following sentences with the appropriate idiom of **tener** in the correct form. Use each idiom no more than once.*

1. Si Uds. _____, ¿comen mucho?

2. Si una persona _____, bebe agua.

3. Siempre gano los premios; yo _____, ¿es verdad?

4. Los muchachos quieren mirar televisión hasta las diez, pero los padres _____ y quieren dormir.

5. En el invierno, nosotros _____ en las montañas. Vamos de vacaciones al Caribe y si _____ nadamos en el océano.

6. ¿Quién quiere hablar? Estamos listos para escuchar las nuevas ideas. Irene _____ .

7. ¿_____ tú _____ de hablar delante de mucha gente en una conferencia grande?

8. Yo _____ . ¡Quiero salir ahora!

9. Él no tiene mucho dinero pero _____ en la vida.

10. Janet _____ de cabeza y no puede ir al trabajo.

11. ¿Es importante _____ en situaciones peligrosas?

12. Irene tiene una buena respuesta. Ramón tiene una respuesta excelente.

    No sabemos quien _____ .

13. ¿Dónde _____ la fiesta?

14. Nosotros _____ de ir a la playa el sábado.

15. ¿Cuántos _____ el hermano de Rafael?

16. Es una respuesta excelente, pero ¿qué _____ la pregunta?

Other Idioms

acabar de + infinitive *to have just (done something)*

yo acabo de llegar	*I have just arrived*
tú acabas de cantar	*you have just sung*
él acaba de salir	*he has just left*
nosotros acabamos de decidir	*we have just decided*
vosotros acabáis de pagar	*you have just paid*
ellos acaban de volver	*they have just returned*

NOTE: The present tense of **acabar de** + infinitive is translated in English as the present perfect tense + *just*.

dejar de + infinitive *to stop (doing something)*

yo dejo de fumar	*I stop smoking*
tú dejas de comer	*you stop eating*
ella deja de bailar	*she stops dancing*
nosotros dejamos de trabajar	*we stop working*
vosotros dejáis de beber	*you stop drinking*
ellas dejan de estudiar	*they stop studying*

tener que + infinitive *to have to (do something)*

yo tengo que ir	*I have to go*
tú tienes que cocinar	*you have to cook*
él tiene que hablar	*he has to speak*
nosotros tenemos que caminar	*we have to walk*
vosotros tenéis que escuchar	*you have to listen*
ellos tienen que descansar	*they have to rest*

tratar de + infinitive *to try to (do something)*

yo trato de leer	*I try to read*
tú tratas de limpiar	*you try to clean*
Ud. trata de contestar	*you try to answer*
nosotros tratamos de escribir	*we try to write*
vosotros tratáis de correr	*you try to run*
Uds. tratan de nadar	*you try to swim*

volver a + infinitive *to do (something) again*

yo vuelvo a leer	*I read again*
tú vuelves a cocinar	*you cook again*
Ud. vuelve a mentir	*you lie again*
nosotros volvemos a conversar	*we speak again*
vosotros volvéis a cantar	*you sing again*
Uds. vuelven a ganar	*you win again*

Exercise 7.5

Complete the following letter with the appropriate idiomatic expression. Choose from the expressions listed below.

   acabar de, dejar de, tener que, tratar de

Queridos amigos,

Yo _____ (1.) llegar a Lisboa en Portugal. La ciudad es bonita pero no entiendo el portugués. Yo _____ (2.) aprender a hablar el idioma si quiero gozar del país. Voy a

_____ (3.) empezar las clases mañana. No debo

_____ (4.) viajar porque aprendo mucho del país y de la gente.

Hasta pronto.

Useful Words: *que* and *para*

The Relative Pronoun *que*

Spanish **que** (English *that*, *which*, or *who*) is the most common relative pronoun in everyday speech. **Que** can refer to persons or things, either singular or plural.

El programa que miro los viernes es interesante.	*The program that I watch on Fridays is interesting.*
Los platos, que acabo de comprar, son verdes.	*The plates, which I have just bought, are green.*
Ella tiene un amigo que vive en el campo.	*She has a friend who lives in the countryside.*

The relative pronoun **que** can also be used after prepositions. As the object of a preposition, **que** refers to a thing or things only. It does not refer to a person or persons.

El libro en que escribimos es viejo.	*The book in which we write is old.*
No entiendo el tema de que habla.	*I don't understand the theme of which you speak.*
Ella tiene un bastón con que caminar.	*She has a cane with which to walk.*

The Conjunction *que*

One of the uses of conjunctions is to join two sentences into a single sentence. Spanish **que** (English *that*) used as a conjunction may join a main clause and a dependent (or subordinate) clause to form a sentence or question.

El maestro sabe que los estudiantes entienden.	*The teacher knows that the students understand.*
Él piensa que la lección es fácil.	*He thinks that the lesson is easy.*
Veo que el tren viene.	*I see that the train is coming.*

A Word About *que*

The English word *that*, whether it is used as a relative pronoun or as a conjunction, is often omitted. For example, it is correct in English to say either *the program I see* or *the program **that** I see*, and to say *I think the lesson is easy* or *I think **that** the lesson is easy*. In Spanish, **que** is never omitted.

The Preposition *para*

Para has two meanings in English.

- *for*

José tiene dos libros para la clase.	*Joe has two books for the class.*
La pregunta es para María.	*The question is for María.*
Mañana, el barco sale para Cuba.	*Tomorrow the boat sails for Cuba.*
Los guantes son para el invierno.	*The gloves are for the winter.*
¿Hay una carta para nosotros?	*Is there a letter for us?*
Ella va a estudiar para el examen.	*She is going to study for the exam.*

- *in order to*

Comemos para vivir.	*We eat in order to live.*
Ella baila para estar alegre.	*She dances in order to be happy.*
Él estudia para ser doctor.	*He studies in order to be a doctor.*
Corro para llegar a tiempo.	*I run in order to arrive on time.*
Sara hace ejercicios para cantar.	*Sarah does exercises in order to sing.*

Exercise 7.6

Complete the following sentences by translating the English phrase in parentheses.

1. Ella viene a la clase _____ (*in order to learn*).

2. Yo sé _____ (*that she is here*).

3. El hombre _____ (*who lives here*) es guapo.

4. ¿Piensa Ud. _____ (*that I should go*)?

5. Él practica _____ (*in order to play*) el piano.

6. ¿_____ (*for whom*) es la pregunta?

7. Las llaves _____ (*that I need*) están en el carro.

8. ¿Tiene Ud. una habitación _____ (*for two persons*)?

Key Vocabulary

These words will help enhance your ability to communicate. As you learn them, remember to practice them aloud.

Las partes del cuerpo (Parts of the Body)

la articulación	*the joint*	la mejilla	*the cheek*
la barba	*the beard*	la muñeca	*the wrist*
la barbilla	*the chin*	el muslo	*the thigh*
la boca	*the mouth*	las nalgas	*the buttocks*
el brazo	*the arm*	la nariz	*the nose*
el cabello	*the hair*	la nuca	*the nape*
la cabeza	*the head*	el oído	*the inner ear*
la cadera	*the hip*	el ojo	*the eye*
la cara	*the face*	la oreja	*the ear*
la ceja	*the eyebrow*	el párpado	*the eyelid*
la cintura	*the waist*	el pecho	*the chest*
el codo	*the elbow*	el pelo	*the hair*
la columna	*the spine*	la pestaña	*the eyelash*
el cuello	*the neck*	el pie	*the foot*
el dedo	*the finger*	la piel	*the skin*
el dedo del pie	*the toe*	la pierna	*the leg*
el diente	*the tooth*	el pulgar	*the thumb*
las encías	*the gums*	la quijada	*the jaw*
la espalda	*the back*	la rodilla	*the knee*
la frente	*the forehead*	los senos	*the breasts*
la garganta	*the throat*	el talón	*the heel*
el hombro	*the shoulder*	el tobillo	*the ankle*
la lengua	*the tongue*	la uña	*the nail*
la mano	*the hand*		

Dentro del cuerpo (Inside the body)

las amígdalas	*the tonsils*	el hueso	*the bone*
la arteria	*the artery*	el músculo	*the muscle*
el cerebro	*the brain*	el pulmón	*the lung*
el corazón	*the heart*	el riñón	*the kidney*
las costillas	*the ribs*	la sangre	*the blood*
el estómago	*the stomach*	el tendón	*the tendon*
el hígado	*the liver*	las venas	*the veins*

In Spanish, the definite articles **el**, **la**, **los**, and **las** are used more frequently than the possessive adjective, especially with parts of the body. In English we would use a possessive adjective (*my, your, his, her, our, their*).

Ella tiene un problema en **el pie**.	She has a problem with **her foot**.
Él tiene dolor d**el tobillo** y no puede caminar bien.	He has a pain in **his toe** and can't walk well.
El niño tiene **las manos** sucias.	The boy has dirty hands. (**His hands** are dirty.)
Tenemos veinte dedos; diez en **las manos** y diez en **los pies**.	We have twenty digits: ten on **our hands** and ten on **our feet**.

La familia

As you learn the names for family members, you will see that the plural takes the masculine form when it includes more than one male or a male and female pair. For example, **el padre** means *the father*; **la madre** means *the mother*. The *father* and *mother* together are the *parents*, which in Spanish is expressed as **los padres**.

los bisabuelos	*the great-grandparents*
el bisabuelo	*the great-grandfather*
la bisabuela	*the great-grandmother*
los abuelos	*the grandparents*
el abuelo	*the grandfather*
la abuela	*the grandmother*
los padres	*the parents*
el padre	*the father*
la madre	*the mother*
los parientes	*the relatives*
el pariente	*the (male) relative*
la pariente	*the (female) relative*
el tío, la tía	*the uncle, the aunt*
el esposo / el marido, la esposa	*the husband, the wife*
el hijo, la hija	*the son, the daughter*
el hermano, la hermana	*the brother, the sister*
el nieto, la nieta	*the grandson, the granddaughter*
el primo, la prima	*the (male) cousin, the (female) cousin*
el sobrino, la sobrina	*the nephew, the niece*
el suegro, la suegra	*the father-in-law, the mother-in-law*

el yerno, la nuera	*the son-in-law, the daughter-in-law*
el cuñado, la cuñada	*the brother-in-law, the sister-in-law*
el padrastro, la madrastra	*the stepfather, the stepmother*
el padrino, la madrina	*the godfather, the godmother*
el ahijado, la ahijada	*the godson, the goddaughter*

Time Expressions with *hacer*

To ask *how long* someone has been doing something, Spanish uses the present tense. The translation of this construction is equivalent to the present perfect tense in English. The action begins in the past and continues into the present.

¿**Cuánto tiempo hace que** + verb in the present tense

¿**Cuánto tiempo hace que** Ud. vive aquí?	*How long have you been living here?* (literally, *How much time does it make that you live here?*)
¿Cuánto tiempo hace que él estudia el francés?	*How long has he been studying French?*
¿Cuánto tiempo hace que Uds. viajan?	*How long have you been traveling?*
¿Cuánto tiempo hace que la muchacha mira televisión?	*How long has the girl been watching television?*

To answer the question of *how long* someone has been doing something, Spanish uses the following expression.

Hace + length of time + **que** + verb in the present tense

Hace quince años **que** yo vivo aquí.	*I have been living here for fifteen years.* (literally, *It makes fifteen years that I live here.*)
Hace un mes que él estudia el francés.	*He has been studying French for a month.*
Hace seis semanas que viajamos.	*We have been traveling for six weeks.*
Hace una hora que ella mira televisión.	*She has been watching television for an hour.*

A Word About "How Long"
The **hace** + the length of time + **que** + the verb in the present tense construction looks complicated because the English translation uses the present perfect tense. But in Spanish, whenever you want to express *how long* someone has been doing something, just use the present tense.

Exercise 7.7

Complete the following sentences with the correct form of the appropriate verb. Choose from the infinitives listed below; use each verb no more than once.

abrir, beber, cerrar, cocinar, comer, correr, deber, dormir, empezar, estar, hacer, ir, jugar, nadar, perder, saber, salir, ser, tener que, trabajar, tratar, vivir

1. María y Tomás van a España. El viaje va a _____ fantástico.

2. Susana practica para poder _____ en el maratón.

3. ¿Vas a _____ arroz con pollo para la familia?

4. La parte de la cabeza que _____ entre el pelo y los ojos es la frente.

5. Nosotros _____ los ojos para dormir.

6. Yo _____ la boca para hablar, pero las palabras

    no _____ .

7. Enrique _____ de estudiar pero prefiere jugar al tenis.

8. Para aprender bien, los estudiantes _____ que asistir a la clase.

9. ¿Qué _____ Ud. si tiene sed? ¿_____ agua o jugo?

10. Ella quiere _____ a Sudamérica. Ella _____ en Canadá.

11. La película popular _____ a las siete. Nosotros

    _____ comprar los tiquetes a las seis.

12. Yo soy ingeniero y _____ en el décimo piso del edificio.

13. El hombre fuerte _____ ocho horas cada noche;

    él _____ vegetales y pescado; _____

en la piscina del gimnasio en el invierno, y él _____

al béisbol en el verano.

14. ¿Quién _____ la historia de los Estados Unidos?

15. Ella siempre _____ las llaves de la casa.

Exercise 7.8

Complete the following sentences with the correct form of **ir**.

1. El hombre quiere _____ al partido de béisbol.

   Él _____ siempre los domingos.

2. ¿Por qué no _____ tú al cine con Elena? Ella es una mujer simpática.

3. Nosotros _____ a comprar un carro para el cumpleaños de Pablo.

4. ¿Adónde _____ Uds.?

5. Yo _____ a la escuela los lunes y los miércoles. Los martes,

   _____ a la biblioteca para estudiar.

Exercise 7.9

Complete the following sentences with the correct form of the appropriate verb or expression. Choose from the list below; use each option no more than once.

bajar, cocinar, estar, ganar, hacer, hay, leer, llegar, perder, preferir, regresar, saber, salir, ser, subir, tener calor, tener frío, tener hambre, tener miedo, tener razón, tener sed, tener sueño, tomar, venir, volver

1. Son las doce de la noche. Carlos no puede dormir bien y

   _____ . Tomás _____ y quiere comer.

2. ¿Quiere Ud. _____ aquí a Nueva York a ver una obra de teatro?

3. Ella no quiere _____ una cita con el doctor porque

   _____ de las inyecciones.

4. Los hijos de Bernarda _____ de la casa a las siete y media

    de la mañana. Ellos _____ a casa a las cuatro.

5. El viajero _____ los periódicos y las revistas porque quiere

    _____ las noticias del día.

6. ¿Cuántas guerras _____ en el mundo?

7. El hermano de Alicia siempre _____ el bus para llegar

    al trabajo, pero Alicia _____ caminar.

8. Miguel piensa que va a _____ mucho dinero este año.

9. Yo trato de _____ a tiempo a la clase.

10. Los dos amigos _____ de Perú. El apartamento de ellos

    _____ en la calle cuarenta y dos con la avenida doce.

11. Vivo en el décimo piso. Yo _____ y _____
    en el ascensor.

12. A las seis de la noche, Elena _____ a casa y empieza

    a _____ una comida para la familia.

13. Si yo _____, llevo un suéter extra.

14. Si ella _____, va a la playa porque quiere nadar.

15. ¿Bebe Ud. mucho si _____?

16. No jugamos bien al tenis y siempre _____ el juego.

17. Julia piensa que el sol es importante. Ramón piensa que la luna es

    más importante. ¿Quién _____?

Exercise 7.10

Complete the following sentences with the appropriate part of the body in each blank.

1. Ella tiene _____ corto. Tiene _____
   azules y una sonrisa hermosa.

2. La nariz y las cejas son partes de _____.

3. Es difícil correr si tenemos dolor del _____.

4. Comemos con _____. Vamos al dentista para cuidar

   _____ .

5. Si yo tengo una infección y no puedo oír bien, la infección está

   en _____ .

6. Si una persona toma mucho alcohol, va a tener problemas

   en _____ .

7. Si una persona tiene asma, el problema está en _____ .

8. El tobillo, el pie, y la _____ son partes de la pierna.

9. Tengo dolor del _____ y no quiero comer.

10. Sonreímos con _____ .

Exercise 7.11

Review **ser** *and* **estar**, *then complete the following sentences.*

1. ¿Quién _____ aquí?

2. Los guantes del hombre _____ verdes.

3. Ella quiere _____ con su familia en Navidad.

4. ¿Cómo sabes quién _____ ella?

5. _____ o no _____ . Es la cuestión.
   (la cuestión = *the issue*)

6. El muchacho _____ contento si no tiene que ir
   a la escuela.

7. ¿Estás donde quieres _____?

8. Nosotros _____ buenos amigos.

9. Jorge _____ un buen hombre.

10. La fiesta _____ en la casa de Manuel.

11. ¿Cuál _____ la fecha de hoy? ¿Qué día _____
    hoy?

12. Yo _____ de Filadelfia. ¿De dónde _____
    Uds.?

Exercise 7.12

Complete the following sentences with the appropriate family member in Spanish.
Use each term no more than once.

1. Graciela tiene sesenta y seis años y tiene dos _____ .
   El nombre de uno es Enrique; la otra es Felicia.

2. Enrique tiene treinta años. Felicia tiene treinta y dos años. Ellos son

   _____ .

3. Enrique tiene una _____ bonita de treinta y un años.
   Ellos tienen dos hijos.

4. Felicia tiene un _____ flaco de treinta y cuatro años.
   Ellos tienen dos hijas.

5. Los hijos de Enrique y Felicia son jóvenes. Ellos son los

   _____ de Graciela.

6. Los hijos de Enrique y Felicia están contentos porque Graciela es muy

   simpática y ella es la _____ de ellos.

7. El hermano de Felicia es el _____ de los niños de ella.

8. La hermana de Enrique es la _____ de los niños de él.

9. El hermano del esposo de Felicia es el _____ de ella.

10. La hermana del esposo de Felicia es la _____ de ella.

11. El padre de la esposa de Enrique es el _____ de él.

12. La madre de la esposa de Enrique es la _____ de él.

13. El padre del padre de Felicia es el _____ de ella.

14. Todos son _____ de ellos.

Reading Comprehension

La cita

La sala de espera de este doctor es muy grande porque trabaja solo.
Debe tener mucho éxito porque tiene tres secretarias que contestan
sus llamadas, hacen las citas, dan consejos sobre los seguros médicos y
organizan su horario. Confieso que la sala de espera es común; tiene una
mesa como cualquier otra, con revistas de moda para las mujeres y revistas
de deportes para los hombres. Hay una mesita con una lámpara en cada
rincón del cuarto. Son las dos menos quince. Tomo asiento y escojo una
de las revistas.

    Un hombre amable entra. Él debe tener la primera cita de la tarde.
En seguida, una viejecita llega con su hija y toman asiento cerca de mí.
Logro escuchar su conversación. La madre tiene dolor de cabeza; su
hija no camina bien. Un hombre con el brazo roto entra; después,
un muchacho que tiene problemas con el tobillo, una mujer con dolor
del cuello y de la espalda, y un hombre simpático con dolor del estómago.
Algunos están tranquilos, pero la mayoría de ellos están inquietos. Miran
sus relojes a menudo; tratan de leer pero no pueden; tratan de hacer
conversación para pasar el tiempo. Mientras tanto, la gente llega y llega
y llega. Parece que no va a caber ninguna persona más en la sala pequeña.
Pero vienen más y más hasta llenar todo el cuarto con pacientes.

    Son las dos y media. Por fin, el doctor emerge de su oficina.
La secretaria empieza a leer los nombres que están en su lista. Al escuchar
su nombre, cada persona desaparece en la oficina por un rato, sale del
consultorio, hace otra cita antes de volver a casa. Sigue así toda la tarde.

    La secretaria ve que todavía estoy aquí. Tenemos esta conversación:

LA SECRETARIA	¿Cuál es su nombre?
YO	Me llamo Isabel.
LA SECRETARIA	¿Cuál es su apellido?
YO	Pereira. Mi apellido es Pereira.
LA SECRETARIA	Pero su nombre no aparece en la lista.
YO	No tengo una cita hoy. Estoy bien de salud.
LA SECRETARIA	¿Quiere Ud. hacer una cita?
YO	No, estoy bien, gracias.
LA SECRETARIA	La oficina cierra a las seis. Ud. tiene que salir.
YO	Está bien.

Verbos

aparecer	*to appear*	escoger	*to choose*
caber	*to fit*	lograr	*to achieve,*
confesar	*to confess*		*to succeed in* (+ infinitive)
desaparecer	*to disappear*	llenar	*to fill*
emerger	*to emerge*	ver	*to see*

Expresiones verbales

al escuchar	*upon listening, upon hearing*
dar consejos	*to give advice*
estar inquieto	*to be nervous, fidgety*
estar tranquilo	*to be calm*
parece	*it seems*
sigue así	*it continues in this way*

Nombres

el apellido	*the last name, the surname*
la cita	*the appointment*
el consultorio	*the doctor's office*
el horario	*the schedule*
la llamada	*the phone call*
la mayoría	*the majority*
la moda	*the style, the fashion*
el nombre	*the name*
el paciente	*the patient*
el personaje	*the character*
el reloj	*the watch*
el rincón	*the corner*
la sala de espera	*the waiting room*
la secretaria	*the secretary*
los seguros médicos	*medical insurance*

Adjetivos

común	*common*
roto	*broken*
solo	*alone*

Expresiones

a menudo	*frequently*
al final	*at the end*

al principio	*at the beginning*
antes de + *infinitive*	*before (doing something)*
como cualquier otra	*like any (whatever) other*
en seguida	*right away*
mientras tanto	*meanwhile*
por fin	*at last*
por un rato	*for a little while*

Preguntas

After you have read the selection, answer the following questions in Spanish.

1. ¿Cuál es el nombre del personaje principal?

   _____

2. ¿Cómo es la sala de espera?

   _____

3. ¿Cómo están los pacientes?

   _____

4. ¿Qué pasa a las dos y media?

   _____

5. ¿Cómo puede ser la sala grande al principio del cuento y pequeña al final?

   _____

6. Si Isabel no tiene una cita con el doctor y si no está enferma, ¿por qué está ella en la oficina del doctor?

   _____

8

Adjectives and Adverbs

Possessive Adjectives

Possessive adjectives in Spanish agree in gender and number with the noun they modify. Possessive adjectives precede the noun they modify.

mi, **mis** *my*

Mi hermana quiere ir a España.	*My sister wants to go to Spain.*
Mis amigos quieren ir a Portugal.	*My friends want to go to Portugal.*

tu, **tus** *your* (**tú** form)

Tu libro está en la mesa.	*Your book is on the table.*
Tus lápices están en la silla.	*Your pencils are on the chair.*

su, **sus** *your* (**Ud.** form), *his, her, their*

In Spanish, there is only one form for the third-person possessive: the **su** and **sus** form. **Su** is used before a singular noun to show possession; **sus** is used with a plural noun. Because **su/sus** can be very ambiguous, the form that you have already learned and used—the noun + **de** + the pronoun—can be used to clarify the meaning.

Pedro y Linda están aquí.	*Peter and Linda are here.*
Necesito su carro.	*I need his/her/their car.*
¿El carro de él o el carro de ella?	*His car or her car?*
Sus ideas son fantásticas.	*Your/his/her/their ideas are fantastic.*
¿Las ideas de quién?	*Whose ideas?*
Las ideas de Uds.	*Your ideas.*
Ellos viven en las montañas.	*They live in the mountains.*
Su casa es grande.	*Their house is big.*

Ella escribe mucho.	*She writes a lot.*
Sus artículos son interesantes.	*Her articles are interesting.*

nuestro, **nuestra**, **nuestros**, **nuestras** *our*

Nuestro tren viene.	*Our train is coming.*
Nuestra fiesta va a ser fantástica.	*Our party is going to be fantastic.*
Nuestros libros son viejos.	*Our books are old.*
Nuestras computadoras son nuevas.	*Our computers are new.*

vuestro, **vuestra**, **vuestros**, **vuestras** *your* (**vosotros** form)

Like **vosotros**, this form is used only in Spain. It is explained here so that you will be aware of it, but when you need a word for *your* in Spanish, use **su** or **sus**.

Vuestro amigo es de España.	*Your friend is from Spain.*
Vuestra casa está en Madrid.	*Your house is in Madrid.*
¿Son españoles vuestros maestros?	*Are your teachers Spanish?*
Vuestras amigas son españolas.	*Your friends are Spanish.*

 Exercise 8.1

Complete the sentences using **mi**, **mis**, **tu**, **tus**, **su**, **sus**, **nuestro**, **nuestros**, **nuestra**, *or* **nuestras**.

1. Soy estudiante; _____ libros están en la mesa.

2. Él es un profesor excelente; _____ ideas son interesantes.

3. Ellos son abogados; _____ clientes pueden ser culpables o inocentes.

4. Nuestro hermano es profesor; _____ padres enseñan también.

5. Ella es mi abuela; _____ casa está en Florida.

6. El cuñado de Cecilia es carpintero; _____ nombre es Manuel.

7. Uds. son estudiantes; _____ libros son nuevos.

8. Liliana está en Texas; _____ hermanas están en Arizona.

9. Vivo con cuatro amigos y dos gatos; _____ casa es grande.

10. Somos principiantes; _____ tarea no es fácil.

11. Mis primos escriben libros; _____ trabajo es interesante.

12. La hija de Beatriz es doctora; _____ hijo es arquitecto.

Demonstrative Adjectives

In Spanish, there are three demonstrative adjectives; they agree in number and gender with the nouns they modify.

	Masculine	Feminine
• Near the speaker		
this	este	esta
these	estos	estas
• Near the listener		
that	ese	esa
those	esos	esas
• Far from both speaker and listener		
that (over there)	aquel	aquella
those (over there)	aquellos	aquellas

Este periódico es interesante.	*This newspaper is interesting.*
Esta revista es interesante también.	*This magazine is interesting also.*
Estos hombres son fuertes.	*These men are strong.*
Estas mujeres son fuertes también.	*These women are strong also.*
Ese piano es viejo.	*That piano is old.*
Esa guitarra es nueva.	*That guitar is new.*
Esos libros son caros.	*Those books are expensive.*
Esas plumas son costosas.	*Those pens are costly.*
Aquel traje es feo.	*That suit (over there) is ugly.*
Aquella blusa es más bonita.	*That blouse (over there) is prettier.*
Aquellos árboles son enormes.	*Those trees (over there) are enormous.*
Aquellas casas son pequeñas.	*Those houses (over there) are small.*

Neuter Demonstrative Pronouns

Neuter demonstrative pronouns refer to an object that is not known, a statement, or a general idea.

esto	*this*
eso	*that*
aquello	*that (farther away in place or time)*

¿Qué es esto? ¿Qué es eso?	*What is this? What is that?*
Aquello no es necesario.	*That is not necessary.*

 ## Exercise 8.2

Complete the following sentences using demonstrative adjectives.

EXAMPLE   ¿Quién es __*ese*__ hombre que está con Julia? (*that*)

1. _____ revista que tú lees es interesante, pero _____ artículo tiene más información. (*this/that*)

2. ¿Piensa Ud. que _____ camisas son hermosas, o prefiere Ud. _____ camisas azules? (*these/those*)

3. ¿En qué sitio prefieren Uds. comer, en _____ restaurante o en _____ cafetería? (*that [over there]/that [over there]*)

4. _____ falda es bonita, pero voy a comprar _____ pantalones porque son más cómodos. (*this/those*)

5. _____ mujeres corren en el maratón. (*those [over there]*)

6. ¿Por qué mira Ud. _____ programas en televisión si son repeticiones? (*those*)

7. _____ mes va a ser maravilloso. (*this*)

Adjectives of Nationality

When an adjective of nationality ends in a consonant, **-a** is added to form the feminine.

español	*Spanish*
el restaurante español	*the Spanish restaurant*
la comida española	*the Spanish meal*

inglés	*English*
el hombre inglés	*the English man*
la mujer inglesa	*the English woman*
francés	*French*
el vino francés	*the French wine*
la cerveza francesa	*the French beer*
alemán	*German*
el escritor alemán	*the German writer* (m.)
la escritora alemana	*the German writer* (f.)
japonés	*Japanese*
el muchacho japonés	*the Japanese boy*
la muchacha japonesa	*the Japanese girl*
holandés	*Dutch*
el niño holandés	*the Dutch child* (m.)
la niña holandesa	*the Dutch child* (f.)

In all other cases, the adjectives of nationality will follow the rules you have already learned. Adjectives that end in **-o** change to **-a** when describing a feminine noun.

el hombre cubano	*the Cuban man*
la mujer cubana	*the Cuban woman*
el muchacho chileno	*the Chilean boy*
la muchacha chilena	*the Chilean girl*
el niño norteamericano	*the North American child* (m.)
la niña norteamericana	*the North American child* (f.)
el amigo suizo	*the Swiss friend* (m.)
la amiga suiza	*the Swiss friend* (f.)

Adjectives that end in vowels other than **-o** do not change.

el hombre canadiense	*the Canadian man*
la mujer canadiense	*the Canadian woman*
el niño hindú	*the Hindu child* (m.)
la niña hindú	*the Hindu child* (f.)
el hombre israelí	*the Israeli man*
la mujer israelí	*the Israeli woman*

Country	Nationality	Country	Nationality
Alemania	alemán	Irlanda	irlandés
Arabia Saudita	saudí/saudita	Israel	israelí
(la) Argentina	argentino	Italia	italiano
Austria	austriaco	Jamaica	jamaiquino
Bélgica	belga	Japón	japonés
Bolivia	boliviano	Marrueco	marroquí
(el) Brasil	brasileño	México	mexicano
(el) Canadá	canadiense	Nicaragua	nicaragüense
Chile	chileno	Noruega	noruego
China	chino	Nueva Zelanda	neocelandés
Colombia	colombiano	Pakistán	pakistaní
Corea	coreano	(el) Panamá	panameño
Costa Rica	costarricense	(el) Paraguay	paraguayo
Cuba	cubano	(el) Perú	peruano
Dinamarca	danés	Polonia	polaco
(el) Ecuador	ecuatoriano	Portugal	portugués
Egipto	egipcio	Puerto Rico	puertorriqueño
Escocia	escocés	(la) República	dominicano
España	español	Dominicana	
(los) Estados	norteamericano/	Rusia	ruso
Unidos	estadounidense	El Salvador	salvadoreño
Finlandia	finlandés	Siria	sirio
Francia	francés	Sudán	sudanés
Grecia	griego	Suecia	sueco
Guatemala	guatemalteco	(la) Suiza	suizo
Haití	haitiano	Tailandia	tailandés
Holanda	holandés	Taiwán	taiwanés
Honduras	hondureño	Turquía	turco
Hungría	húngaro	(el) Uruguay	uruguayo
(la) India	hindú	Venezuela	venezolano
Inglaterra	inglés	Vietnám	vietnamita
Irak/Iraq	iraquí	Yemen	yemení
Irán	iraní		

Continent		Continent	
África	africano	Australia	australiano
Antártica	antártico	Europa	europeo
el Ártico	ártico	Norteamérica	norteamericano
Asia	asiático	Sudamérica	sudamericano

Adjectives That Precede a Noun

In Chapter 1, you learned that adjectives follow the nouns they describe. Now you will learn the few adjectives that precede the noun they modify. Remember that adjectives agree in number and gender with the noun they describe.

Two frequently used adjectives, **bueno** and **malo**, drop the **-o** before a masculine singular noun.

bueno *good*

Este niño es un **buen** estudiante.	*This child is a good student.*
Su hermana es una **buena** estudiante.	*His sister is a good student.*
Ellos son **buenos** estudiantes.	*They are good students.*
Ellos tienen **buenas** maestras.	*They have good teachers.*

malo *bad*

Ella tiene un **mal** perro.	*She has a bad dog.*
Su amiga tiene una **mala** idea.	*Her friend has a bad idea.*
Ellas tienen tres **malos** gatos.	*They have three bad cats.*
Son **malas** situaciones.	*They are bad situations.*

 Bueno and **malo** can follow the noun as well as precede it. The use is less frequent, though, and the description loses intensity.

El hombre bueno.	*The (fairly) good man.*

Adjectives That Express Quantity

mucho *a lot of, much, many*

Él no tiene **mucho** dinero.	*He doesn't have a lot of money.*
Tiene **muchos** amigos.	*He has a lot of friends.*
Ellas preparan **mucha** comida para **muchas** personas.	*They prepare a lot of food for a lot of people.*

poco *a little bit, a few, not much, not many*

Hay **poco** dinero en este banco y hay **pocos** clientes.	*There is not much money in this bank and not many clients.*
Poca gente vive en esta calle y hay **pocas** casas.	*Not many people live on this street, and there are few houses.*

bastante, **suficiente** *enough*

Ellos ganan **suficiente** dinero y tienen **bastante** trabajo.	*They earn enough money and they have enough work.*

ambos *both*

España y Portugal son bellos. Los viajeros van a visitar **ambos** países.	*Spain and Portugal are beautiful. The travelers are going to visit both countries.*

cada *each*

Cada casa tiene dos baños.	*Each house has two bathrooms.*
Cada apartamento tiene una cocina.	*Each apartment has a kitchen.*

NOTE: **Cada** has the same form for both masculine and feminine.

varios *several*

Varios restaurantes sirven tacos.	*Several restaurants serve tacos.*
Varias tiendas venden burritos.	*Several stores sell burritos.*

alguno *some*

Él va a volver **algún** día.	*He is going to return some day.*
¿Hay **alguna** farmacia cerca?	*Is there some pharmacy nearby?*
Algunos pensamientos son buenos.	*Some thoughts are good.*
Algunas ideas son malas.	*Some ideas are bad.*

NOTE: **Alguno** drops the **-o** before a masculine noun.

otro *other, another*

Él quiere **otro** carro.	*He wants another car.*
Ella quiere **otra** casa.	*She wants another house.*
Él tiene **otros** problemas difíciles.	*He has other difficult problems.*
Ella va a comprar **otras** cosas.	*She is going to buy other things.*

NOTE: **Un** and **una** do not precede any form of **otro** and **otra**.

todo *all, every*

Ella lee **todo** el día.	*She reads all day.*
Todo el mundo está aquí.	*Everyone (all the world) is here.*
Leo **toda** la información.	*I read all the information.*
Él escribe **todos** los días.	*He writes every day (all the days).*
Ella hace **todas** las preguntas.	*She asks all the questions.*

Adjectives That Express *Next*, *Only*, and *Last*

próximo *next*

Vamos a viajar el **próximo** año.	*We are going to travel next year.*
La **próxima** lección es interesante.	*The next lesson is interesting.*
¿Qué va a pasar en los **próximos** años y en las **próximas** generaciones?	*What is going to happen in the next years and in the next generations?*

único *only*

Ricardo es el **único** mexicano aquí.	*Ricardo is the only Mexican here.*
Ella es la **única** española.	*She is the only Spaniard.*

último *last, final*

El **último** mes del año es diciembre.	*The last month of the year is December.*
Hoy es la **última** clase del semestre.	*Today is the last class of the semester.*

Adjectives Whose Meaning Depends on Position

Some adjectives have different meanings depending on whether they precede or follow the noun they modify.

Preceding the Noun	Following the Noun
antiguo	
su antiguo novio *her former boyfriend*	una civilización antigua *an ancient civilization*
cierto	
cierto día *a certain day*	una cosa cierta *a sure thing*
grande	
el gran hombre *the great man*	el hombre grande *the big man*
la gran mujer *the great woman*	la mujer grande *the big woman*

NOTE: **Grande** shortens to **gran** before any singular noun.

pobre	
el pobre niño *the poor, unfortunate little boy*	el hombre pobre *the poor man (without money)*

mismo

el mismo libro *the same book*   el profesor mismo
la misma idea *the same idea*   *the professor himself*

viejo

los viejos amigos   los amigos viejos
   the longtime friends   *the old friends (in years)*

 When **mismo** *follows* a noun or pronoun, it *intensifies* the word it describes. For example:

esta casa misma *this very house*
yo mismo *I myself*
el doctor mismo está enfermo *the doctor himself is sick*
ahora mismo *right now*

Exercise 8.3

Complete the following sentences by using the appropriate adjective of nationality.

1. Micaela es de España y habla español porque su padre es español;

   ella habla francés porque su madre es _____ .

2. Pensamos que la comida _____ es deliciosa.
   El sushi y el sashimi son platos típicos.

3. Hay mucha arte en Guatemala. ¿Son artistas _____?

4. Para entrar en los Estados Unidos, el ciudadano _____
   tiene que cruzar la frontera entre el Canadá y los Estados Unidos.

5. _____ tienen la reputación de ser poetas.
   La gente de Nicaragua trabaja duro y escribe poesía.

6. Costa Rica es un país con muchos parques nacionales.

   _____ visitan los parques todo el año.

7. Este hombre de India es _____ . Su esposa es

   _____ también.

8. Soy portuguesa. Mi hermano es _____ también.

Exercise 8.4

Complete the following sentences using the adjectives from the list below. Use each adjective only one time. Answers may vary.

> alguno, ambos, bastante, bueno, cada, malo, mucho, otro,
> poco, próximo, suficiente, todo, último, único, varios

1. Carlos lee todo el día; quiere leer _____ los libros de la biblioteca.

2. Ella es la _____ persona en la clase que no tiene una computadora.

3. Es necesario tomar _____ agua para estar bien.

4. Hay dos películas que ella quiere comprar, pero no tiene

   _____ dinero para comprar _____ videos.

5. El _____ mes del año es diciembre.

6. El pianista practica el piano dos horas _____ día.

7. Queremos ir a un _____ restaurante para comer bien.

8. No es una _____ idea pasar el día en la playa.

9. Hay _____ revistas y _____ periódicos en la librería.

10. La librería tiene _____ libros sobre la historia de los aztecas, pero tiene más libros sobre la historia de los incas.

11. El _____ tren sale a las nueve y veinte de la mañana.

12. Loreta no está contenta porque el bus no viene y su carro viejo no

    es bueno. Ella quiere comprar _____ carro nuevo.

13. Hay _____ palabras en este artículo que puedo entender.

 Exercise 8.5

In each sentence, place one of the following adjectives either before or after the noun, according to the meaning of the sentence: **antiguo, cierto, grande, pobre, mismo, viejo**.

1. Mi amiga y yo asistimos a la _____ clase _____ .

2. Atenas y Roma son _____ ciudades _____ .

3. El _____ hombre _____ no tiene dinero.

4. La _____ niña _____ está triste porque no tiene amigos.

5. ¿Quién es una _____ mujer _____ de nuestra generación?

6. Somos _____ amigas _____ . Pasamos mucho tiempo juntas.

Comparative Adjectives

The comparative structure expresses *more than, less than,* or *the same as.*

- More than

  más + adjetivo + **que**

  Julia es **más** fuerte **que** Juan.
  La revista es **más** interesante **que** el libro.

  more + adjective + ***than***

  Julia is stronger than John.
  The magazine is more interesting than the book.

- Less than

  menos + adjetivo + **que**

  El libro es **menos** interesante **que** la revista.
  Las camisas son **menos** caras **que** los vestidos.

  less + adjective + ***than***

  The book is less interesting than the magazine.
  The shirts are less expensive than the dresses.

- The same as

  tan + adjetivo + **como**

  Estas tortas son **tan** dulces **como** esos pasteles.
  ¿Es el perro **tan** inteligente **como** el gato?

  as + adjective + ***as***

  These cakes are as sweet as those pastries.
  Is the dog as intelligent as the cat?

Superlative Adjectives

- The most/the least

el (la) **más** + adjetivo + **de**	(**the**) **most** + adjective + **of**
el (la) **menos** + adjetivo + **de**	(**the**) **least** + adjective + **of**

NOTE: In the superlative structure, Spanish **de** can be translated as *in*.

¿Quién es la persona **más** fuerte **de** su familia?	*Who is the strongest person in your family?*
¿Cuál es la clase **menos** interesante **de** la escuela?	*Which is the least interesting class in the school?*

Irregular Comparatives and Superlatives

bueno	*good*
mejor	*better*
el mejor, la mejor	*the best* (sing.)
los mejores, las mejores	*the best* (pl.)

Esta torta es buena.	*This cake is good.*
El pastel que Ud. tiene es mejor.	*The pastry that you have is better.*
Estos postres son los mejores de todos.	*These desserts are the best of all.*

malo	*bad*
peor	*worse*
el peor, la peor	*the worst* (sing.)
los peores, las peores	*the worst* (pl.)

Él es malo.	*He is bad.*
Ella es peor.	*She is worse.*
Ella es la peor de su escuela.	*She is the worst in her school.*

joven	*young*
menor	*younger*
el menor, la menor	*the youngest* (sing.)
los menores, las menores	*the youngest* (pl.)

NOTE: **Menor** refers only to people: **mi hermano menor**. If you want to compare *trees*, for example, just use the regular comparative structure: **Estos árboles son menos viejos que aquellos árboles.**

El niño es joven.	*The child is young.*
Su hermano es menor.	*His brother is younger.*

Su hermana es la menor de
  su familia.

*His sister is the youngest in their
  family.*

viejo	*old*
mayor	*older*
el mayor, la mayor	*the oldest* (sing.)
los mayores, las mayores	*the oldest* (pl.)

NOTE: **Mayor** refers only to people: **mi hermana mayor**. If you want to compare *buildings*, for example, just use the regular comparative structure: **Estos edificios son más viejos que aquellos edificios.**

Ella es vieja.

She is old.

Su madre es mayor.

Her mother is older.

Su abuela es la mayor de todas.

*Her grandmother is the oldest
  of all.*

Comparing Nouns

- **más** + nombre + **que**   *more* + noun + *than*
  menos + nombre + **que**   *less* + noun + *than*

  Tengo **más** lápices **que** María.   *I have more pencils than Maria.*
  Ella tiene **menos** libros **que** yo. *She has fewer books than I.*

- **tanto** + nombre + **como**   *as much* + noun + *as*
                                     as many + noun + *as*

NOTE: **Tanto** is an adjective and agrees with the noun it modifies.

Él corre **tantos** metros **como**
  su hijo.

*He runs as many meters as his
  son.*

Ella trabaja **tantas** horas **como** Ud.   *She works as many hours as you.*
José tiene **tanta** música **como** Sara.   *Joe has as much music as Sarah.*
Él tiene **tanto** pelo **como** su tío.   *He has as much hair as his uncle.*

Comparing Verbs

más que	*more than*
menos que	*less than*
tanto como	*as much as*

Yo estudio **más que** tú.   *I study more than you.*
Tú lees **menos que** yo.   *You read less than I.*
Ella aprende **tanto como** él. *She learns as much as he.*

Exercise 8.6

Complete the following sentences, using the words in parentheses.

1. Esta película es buena; es _____ de todas. (*the best*)

2. Su carro es caro, pero no es _____ como mi carro.
   (*as expensive*)

3. El apartamento de María es _____ del edificio.
   (*the biggest*)

4. Nuestra clase de matemáticas es _____ que la clase
   de historia. (*more interesting*)

5. Uds. tienen _____ exámenes como nosotros. (*as many*)

6. Su casa es _____ que mi apartamento. (*smaller*)

7. Ella es _____ que él, pero él no es el estudiante

   _____ de la clase. (*taller/tallest*)

8. Estas películas son _____ que los programas de
   televisión. (*more exciting*)

9. Mi hermana _____ está _____

   que mi hermano _____ . (*younger/happier/older*)

10. Las calles son _____ que las avenidas. (*less wide*)

11. ¿Piensa Ud. que los caballos son _____ como
    los perros? (*as intelligent*)

12. Esa casa roja es _____ que la casa amarilla. (*older*)

13. Yo leo _____ tú. (*more than*)

14. Él sabe _____ nosotros. (*less than*)

15. Ellos viven en el sitio _____ del país. (*most beautiful*)

16. Este restaurante sirve _____ comida de la ciudad.
    (*the best*)

17. Pienso que Mónica es _____ que Martina. (*older*)

18. Anita tiene dos años. Ella es _____ de su familia.
    (*the youngest*)

19. La comida hindú es _____ que la comida china. (*spicier*)

20. El baño está _____ que el comedor. (*cleaner*)

21. Somos _____ que nuestros vecinos. (*more affectionate*)

22. ¿Quién es _____ político de los Estados Unidos?

    ¿Quién es _____? (*the best/the worst*)

23. Isabel piensa que el sol es _____ que la luna.

    Ramón piensa que la luna es _____. (*more important*)

24. Estoy _____ que ellos. (*sadder*)

25. Los padres están _____ que sus hijos. (*more tired*)

26. Ella tiene _____ energía como sus estudiantes. (*as much*)

27. Las muchachas juegan _____ deportes como los muchachos. (*as many*)

28. Ellas cantan _____ que sus hermanos. (*better*)

29. Vendo _____ cigarrillos que compro. (*less*)

30. Ellos ganan _____ dinero que Pedro. (*more*)

Adverbs

Adverbs describe verbs or adjectives. In Spanish, adverbs are formed by adding **-mente** to the *feminine form* of the adjective. The suffix **-mente** corresponds to the English suffix *-ly*.

To change the adjective **perfecto** to an adverb, use the feminine form **perfecta** and add **-mente**. The result is the adverb **perfectamente**.

Adjective		Adverb	
claro	*clear*	claramente	*clearly*
rápido	*rapid*	rápidamente	*rapidly*
lento	*slow*	lentamente	*slowly*
franco	*frank*	francamente	*frankly*
honesto	*honest*	honestamente	*honestly*
íntimo	*intimate*	íntimamente	*intimately*
último	*last*	últimamente	*lastly*

If an adjective does not end in **-o**, it has only one form for both masculine and feminine. To form an adverb from these adjectives, simply add **-mente** to the adjective.

Adjective		Adverb	
alegre	*happy*	alegremente	*happily*
feliz	*happy*	felizmente	*happily*
triste	*sad*	tristemente	*sadly*
fácil	*easy*	fácilmente	*easily*
frecuente	*frequent*	frecuentemente	*frequently*

If there are two adverbs in a series, only the final one will add **-mente**. The first one in the series takes the feminine form of the adjective.

Él camina frecuente y alegremente.	*He walks frequently and happily.*
Él corre lenta y tristemente.	*He runs slowly and sadly.*
Hablo clara y concisamente.	*I speak clearly and concisely.*
Ella vive tranquila y libremente.	*She lives calmly and freely.*

 ## Exercise 8.7

Change the following adjectives to their corresponding adverbial form.

1. sincero (*sincere*)   _____ (*sincerely*)

2. loco (*crazy*)   _____ (*crazily*)

3. total (*total*)   _____ (*totally*)

4. verdadero (*true*)   _____ (*truly*)

5. inocente (*innocent*)   _____ (*innocently*)

6. cariñoso (*affectionate*)   _____ (*affectionately*)

7. completo (*complete*)   _____ (*completely*)

8. normal (*normal*)   _____ (*normally*)

Adverbs That Do Not Take the Suffix -*mente*

Adverbs of Quantity

mucho	*a lot*	más	*more*
tanto	*so much*	menos	*less*
poco	*a little bit*	demasiado	*too much*
casi	*almost*		

Adverbs That Tell How Something Is Done

bien	*well*	mejor	*better*
mal	*badly*	peor	*worse*

Adverbs of Time and Place

a veces	*sometimes*	cerca	*nearby*
ahora	*now*	en lo alto	*up, up there*
ahora mismo	*right now*	lejos	*far off*
siempre	*always*	adelante	*in front*
todavía	*still, yet; no, not yet*	al fondo	*in back,*
ya	*already*		*at the bottom*
ya no	*no longer*	atrás	*in back*
temprano	*early*	arriba	*up, upstairs*
tarde	*late*	abajo	*down, downstairs*
aquí, allí	*here, there*	adentro	*inside*
acá, allá	*here, there*	afuera	*outside*

NOTE: **Acá** and **allá** are usually used with verbs of motion.

Adverbs of Direction

a la derecha	*to the right*
a la izquierda	*to the left*
derecho, recto	*straight ahead*

Ya sé que ella está **aquí**.	*I already know that she is here.*
Él **siempre** hace bien su tarea.	*He always does his homework well.*
Los niños cocinan **poco**.	*The children cook a little bit.*
¿Por qué no vienes **acá**?	*Why don't you come here?*
María llega **temprano**.	*María arrives early.*
Su amiga llega **tarde**.	*Her friend arrives late.*
A la derecha, hay una iglesia.	*To the right, there is a church.*
A la izquierda, hay un banco.	*To the left, there is a bank.*

Exercise 8.8

Complete the following sentences with the adverb in parentheses.

1. Llego al trabajo a las siete de la mañana; _____ llego

   _____ . (*always/early*)

2. Para hablar _____ el español, tengo que pronunciar

   _____ . (*well/clearly*)

3. ¿Corre ella _____? (*slowly*)

4. Todo el mundo quiere vivir _____ . (*happily*)

5. Simón y Teresa viajan cada mes. Viajan _____ .
   (*frequently*)

6. ¿Puede Ud. comer después de su operación? _____ .
   (*not yet*)

7. ¿Necesita Ud. ayuda con sus problemas? _____ .
   (*no longer*)

8. ¿Dónde están los niños? ¿Están _____ o

   _____? (*upstairs/downstairs*)

9. El hombre camina _____ y _____ .
   (*quickly/happily*)

10. La muchacha _____ firma sus cartas

    _____ . (*always/affectionately*)

11. Los adolescentes comen _____ . (*a lot*)

12. _____ , hay un río. (*straight ahead*)

13. ¿A que hora llegamos _____? (*there*)

14. Hablo _____ y _____ . (*honestly/sincerely*)

Some adverbs can be replaced by **con** or **sin** + the corresponding noun. The most common such adverbs are the following.

con cuidado	*with care* (instead of *carefully*)
sin cuidado	*without care* (instead of *carelessly*)
con cariño	*with affection* (instead of *affectionately*)
con dificultad	*with difficulty*
sin dificultad	*without difficulty*
con inteligencia	*with intelligence* (instead of *intelligently*)

Exercise 8.9

Translate the following sentences into Spanish.

1. *My younger brother is ten years old.*

   _____

2. *He understands this chapter, but he doesn't want to learn all the words.*

   _____

   _____

3. *I know why his sister wants to go to Spain. Her relatives are there.*

   _____

4. *Every year at Thanksgiving, we cook too much.*

   _____

5. *Juan always loses his gloves.*

   _____

6. *His grandmother is older than his grandfather.*

   _____

7. *The last month of the year is December; the first month is January.*

   _____

8. *We have a good class; we learn a lot.*

   _____

9. *Your book has just arrived.*

   _____

10. *I know that my cat is smarter than your dog.*

    _____

11. *These trees are older than those trees over there.*

    _____

12. *We listen to the same sad songs every day.*

    _____

13. *Do you think that the president of the United States is a great man?*

    _____

14. *Are you coming to our party on Friday? It begins at nine o'clock at night.*

_____

_____

15. *Carolina is as tall as Enrique; her sister is the tallest of all.*

_____

16. *This book is the most interesting book in the library.*

_____

17. *Which is the most dangerous animal in the world?*

_____

18. *I am the only person in the family who knows how to play tennis.
Sometimes I win; sometimes I lose.*

_____

_____

Exercise 8.10

Translate the following sentences into English.

1. El señor Gómez hace su trabajo con dificultad.

_____

2. Ella habla sinceramente, y su amigo responde humildemente.

_____

3. Esta mujer siempre explica todo claramente.

_____

4. Francamente, no quiero salir esta noche. Prefiero leer y escribir
tranquilamente.

_____

_____

5. Bernardo va siempre al mismo restaurante. Él piensa que es el mejor
restaurante de la ciudad.

_____

_____

Reading Comprehension

La fiesta

Esta noche hay una fiesta en la casa de una conocida. Tengo la invitación encima del piano que ya no toco. No sé si quiero ir. La fiesta empieza a las ocho. Pienso que los invitados van a llegar a las nueve. (No sé porque las invitaciones siempre llevan la hora equivocada. Si ella sabe que vamos a llegar después de las nueve, ¿por qué escribe que empieza a las ocho?)

¿Cómo imagino la fiesta? Primero hay música. Con mucho cuidado, los anfitriones ponen música alegre. La casa está limpia y hay entremeses y bocadillos en la mesa. Hay mucho que beber también: vino y cerveza, vodka y tequila. Hay soda y gaseosa, agua mineral y jugo para la gente que no quiere tomar alcohol. Después de mucha preparación, todo está listo.

Al entrar, los invitados sonríen y ponen las botellas de vino que llevan consigo en la mesa. La gente empieza a hablar, un poquito al principio, y mientras que toman, hablan más y más y en voz más y más alta. Ponen la música en alto volumen y algunas parejas empiezan a bailar. Las personas que saben la letra de las canciones cantan. Todo el mundo está muy alegre. Pasan unas horas y la anfitriona va a la cocina. Apagan las luces; ella vuelve con una torta de chocolate con velas y todos los amigos cantan 'Cumpleaños Feliz'.

Voy a mi alcoba a mirar mi vestuario. Mi cuarto es muy tranquilo, con una brisa que viene del mar. Las paredes son de un color azul celeste que produce calma. El ambiente es relajante, un ambiente de quietud. Es una habitación cómoda donde descanso, leo y miro la televisión todas las noches. Son las ocho ya. Va a empezar mi programa favorito en media hora.

Verbos

apagar	*to turn off*	imaginar	*to imagine*
al entrar	*upon entering*	sonreír	*to smile*

Nombres

el ambiente	*the atmosphere*	la brisa	*the breeze*
el anfitrión/	*the host/*	la conocida	*the acquaintance*
la anfitriona	*the hostess*	el entremés	*the appetizer*
el bocadillo	*the snack*	el invitado	*the guest*
la botella	*the bottle*	la letra	*the words* (of a song)

la pareja	*the couple*	el vestuario	*the closet,*
la soda, la gaseosa	*the soda*		*the wardrobe*
la vela	*the candle*		

Preposiciones

| acerca de | *about* |
| encima de | *on top of* |

Expresiones

la hora equivocada	*the wrong hour*
consigo	*with themselves*
en alto volumen	*loudly*

Preguntas

After you have read the selection, answer the following questions in Spanish.

1. ¿A qué hora empieza la fiesta?

   _____

2. ¿Cuál es la actitud de Isabel acerca de la fiesta después de recibir la invitación?

   _____

3. ¿Toca ella su piano?

   _____

4. ¿Dónde tiene lugar la fiesta?

   _____

5. ¿Qué hace la gente en la fiesta?

   _____

6. ¿Piensa Ud. que ella va a ir a la fiesta?

   _____

9

Negatives and Prepositions

Negatives

You already know how to make a sentence negative by placing **no** directly before the first verb.

Yo canto.	*I sing.*
Yo **no** canto.	*I don't sing.*
Yo **no** quiero cantar.	*I don't want to sing.*

The following list of negative words adds to this base.

nada	*nothing*
nadie	*no one*
nunca	*never*
jamás	*never*
ninguno	*not one*

Learn the affirmative words also.

algo	*something*
alguien	*someone*
a veces, algunas veces	*sometimes*
siempre	*always*
alguno	*some*

nada *nothing*

To form a negative sentence, **no** precedes the first verb and **nada** follows it.

No tengo **nada** en mi bolsa.	*I have nothing in my bag.*
Ella **no** entiende **nada**.	*She doesn't understand anything.*

¿Tienen Uds. algo para ella?   *Do you have something for her?*
No, **no** tenemos **nada**.   *No, we have nothing.*

If you have two verbs in the sentence, **no** precedes the first verb and **nada** follows the second verb.

Ella **no** quiere hacer **nada**.   *She doesn't want to do anything.*
No vamos a escribir **nada**.   *We are not going to write anything.*

A Word About Negatives

You can see that Spanish, unlike English, uses a double negative. In fact, a Spanish sentence can include three or four negatives. The more negatives you use, the more negative the sentence becomes.

Algo can sometimes be used as an adverb to mean *somewhat.*

El libro es algo interesante.   *The book is somewhat interesting.*

Nada can be used as an adverb to mean *not at all.*

El libro no es nada interesante.   *The book is not interesting at all.*

nadie *no one*

No precedes the verb and **nadie** follows it.

¿Hay alguien aquí?   *Is there someone here?*
No, **no** hay **nadie**.   *No, there is no one.*
No viene **nadie** a mi fiesta. *No one is coming to my party.*

Nadie can also be placed directly before the first verb. In this case, **no** is not used.

Nadie quiere cocinar esta noche. *No one wants to cook tonight.*
Nadie sabe donde está el tren.   *No one knows where the train is.*

nunca, **jamás** *never*

No precedes the verb and **nunca** or **jamás** follows it. Both **nunca** and **jamás** mean *never.*

Ella **no** habla **nunca**; es muy   *She never talks; she is very shy.*
   tímida.
Él **no** baila **jamás**.   *He never dances.*

Nunca and **jamás** can also be placed directly before the first verb with no change in the meaning.

El niño **nunca** practica el piano.   *The boy never practices the piano.*

Jamás bebo café con azúcar.   *I never drink coffee with sugar.*

ninguno *not one, no*

No precedes the verb and **ninguno** follows it.

Ninguno is the only negative expression in the list above that is an adjective. This means that it must agree in number and gender with the noun it modifies. **Ninguno** shortens to **ningún** before a masculine singular noun. **Ninguno** is not used in the plural unless the noun it modifies is always used in the plural, such as **vacaciones**.

No hay **ningún** hotel en esta ciudad.   *There is no hotel in this city.*

No tenemos **ninguna** idea.   *We have no (not one) idea.*

No tenemos **ningunas** vacaciones en agosto.   *We don't have any vacation in August.*

Ninguno may also precede the noun. In this case, **no** is not used.

Ningún muchacho va a la playa.   *Not one boy is going to the beach.*

Ninguna persona llega tarde para la clase.   *Not one person arrives late for the class.*

Exercise 9.1

Answer the following questions in the negative.

EXAMPLE   ¿Entiende ella todo? No, ___*ella no entiende nada.*___

1. ¿Aprenden Uds. algo en México? No, _____

2. ¿Cuántas personas van a su fiesta? _____

3. ¿Escuchas siempre las noticias? No, _____

4. ¿Tienen ellos muchos enemigos? No, _____

5. ¿Hay un hospital aquí? No, _____

6. ¿Vas a viajar? No, _____

7. ¿Es la película algo cómica? No, _____

8. ¿Bailas a veces? No, _____

More Negative Expressions

no... ni... ni... *neither . . . nor . . .*

Él **no** fuma **ni** cigarrillos **ni** cigarros.	*He smokes neither cigarettes nor cigars.*
Ella **no** compra **ni** revistas **ni** periódicos.	*She buys neither magazines nor newspapers.*

no más que *not more than* (with numbers)

Él **no** tiene **más que** cien dólares en el banco.	*He doesn't have more than one hundred dollars in the bank.*

NOTE: In an affirmative sentence, **más de** is used.

Él tiene **más de** cien dólares en el banco.	*He has more than 100 dollars in the bank.*

tampoco *neither, either*

Ella nunca va al cine.	*She never goes to the movies.*
Yo **no** voy **tampoco**.	*I don't go either.*

ni... tampoco *not . . . either*

Él no entiende la lección.	*He doesn't understand the lesson.*
Ni yo **tampoco**.	*Neither do I.*

sino *but rather*

Sino is used in the second clause of a sentence in which the first clause is negative.

Yo no soy profesor, **sino** estudiante.	*I am not a teacher, but rather a student.*
Ellos no son cubanos, **sino** españoles.	*They are not Cubans, but rather Spaniards.*
No vendemos, **sino** compramos.	*We don't sell, but rather we buy.*

de nada, **por nada** *you're welcome, think nothing of it*
no hay de que *you're welcome, don't mention it*

Gracias por el regalo.	*Thanks for the gift.*
De nada./No hay de que.	*You're welcome.*

ya no *no longer*

Ella **ya no** quiere trabajar.	*She no longer wants to work.*

ahora no *not now*

> ¿Puede Ud. pagar la cuenta? *Can you pay the bill?*
> **Ahora no.** *Not now.*

todavía no *not yet*

> ¿Están Uds. listos? *Are you ready?*
> **Todavía no.** *Not yet.*

ni siquiera *not even*

> Él **ni siquiera** sabe escribir. *He doesn't even know how to write.*

sin + infinitive + **nada** *without* + gerund + *anything*

> Él contesta **sin** saber **nada**. *He answers without knowing anything.*

no es para tanto *it's not such a big deal*

> Elena no cocina bien, pero su esposo piensa que **no es para tanto**. *Elena doesn't cook well, but her husband thinks that it's not such a big deal.*

casi nunca *almost never, hardly ever*

> María toca el piano, pero **casi nunca** practica. *María plays the piano, but she almost never practices.*

más que nada *more than anything*

> Silvia quiere viajar **más que nada**. *Sylvia wants to travel more than anything.*

nada más *nothing more, that's all*

> Paula tiene una casa en las montañas, **nada más**. *Paula has a house in the mountains, nothing more.*

In Spanish, unlike English, the more negatives you use, the more negative the sentence becomes.

> **No** recibo **nunca ninguna** carta de **nadie**. *I never receive any letter from anybody.*
> Él **jamás** pide **nada** a **nadie**. *He never asks anything of anybody.*
> Ellos **no** quieren viajar **nunca jamás**. *They don't want to travel ever again.*

Exercise 9.2

Rewrite the following sentences in the negative.

EXAMPLE   Yo como siempre.
            Yo no como nunca.

1. Yo tengo más de treinta dólares en mi cartera.

_____

2. Siempre estamos contentos.

_____

3. Hago mucho hoy.

_____

4. Quiero ir también.

_____

5. Este programa es algo interesante.

_____

6. ¿Quieres tomar algo?

_____

7. ¿Hay alguna farmacia aquí? [Write a negative response.]

_____

8. ¿Tiene ella muchas amigas? [Write a negative response.]

_____

9. El novio siempre limpia el apartamento.

_____

10. Ella estudia todo el tiempo.

_____

11. Muchas mujeres quieren bailar con él.

_____

12. Alguien vive en la casa blanca.

_____

Exercise 9.3

Answer the following questions aloud, using a negative expression.

1. No quiero ir al cine con Luisa. ¿Quieres ir tú?
2. ¿Quién cocina para Ud.?
3. ¿Es el programa algo interesante?
4. Ellos siempre van de vacaciones en el verano. ¿Y Ud.?
5. ¿Con quién hablas a las seis de la mañana?
6. ¿Por qué siempre corres al tren?

Prepositions

A preposition shows the relationship of a noun or a pronoun to some other word in a sentence, clause, or phrase. You already know the most commonly used prepositions.

a	*at, to*	en	*in, on*
con	*with*	para	*for, in order to*
de	*of, from, about*	sin	*without*

In general, prepositions are followed by verbs in the infinitive form, nouns, or pronouns.

- Followed by an infinitive of a verb

  Ella estudia **para aprender**.   *She studies in order to learn.*
  Él habla **sin pensar**.   *He speaks without thinking.*

  An infinitive that follows a preposition in Spanish is often translated with the English gerund (*thinking*, for example). In Spanish, the verb is always the infinitive (for example, **pensar**, *to think*).

- Followed by a noun

  Él tiene un libro **para la clase**.   *He has a book for the class.*

- Followed by a pronoun

  El libro es **para ella**.   *The book is for her.*

Prepositions Followed by Verbs or Nouns

antes de *before*

Antes de nadar, ella quiere comer.	*Before swimming, she wants to eat.*
Antes de la clase, ellos estudian.	*Before the class, they study.*

después de *after*

Después de correr, ellos tienen sed.	*After running, they are thirsty.*
Después de la comida, él va a casa.	*After the meal, he goes home.*

en vez de *instead of*

En vez de correr, él prefiere caminar.	*Instead of running, he prefers to walk.*

además de *in addition to*

Además de ser valiente, ella es simpática.	*In addition to being brave, she is nice.*

a pesar de *in spite of*

A pesar de estar enfermo, él va al trabajo.	*In spite of being sick, he goes to work.*

Prepositions Followed by Nouns or Pronouns

contra	*against*	según	*according to*
durante	*during*	sobre	*above, on top of,*
entre	*between, among*		*about* (a theme or topic)
excepto	*except*	hasta	*until*
hacia	*toward*	desde	*since; from* (a point of
salvo	*except*		departure in place or time)

Hacia can be combined with an adverb with the following meanings.

hacia atrás	*toward the rear*
hacia adelante	*toward the front*
hacia arriba	*upward*
hacia abajo	*downward*

Sobre means *on top of, about* a theme or topic. It can also mean *about* in the sense of *approximately.*

El sartén está sobre la estufa.	*The pan is on top of the stove.*
El autor escribe sobre la historia.	*The author writes about history.*
Vamos al cine sobre las ocho.	*We are going to the movies about eight o'clock.*

Desde means *from* if you have a specific point of departure in terms of place or time.

Veo el río desde mi ventana.	*I see the river from my window.*
Ella trabaja desde las siete de la mañana hasta las tres de la tarde.	*She works from seven o'clock in the morning until three in the afternoon.*

In addition to simple prepositions, there are many compound prepositions that are followed by nouns or pronouns. The list below includes both types.

al lado de	*next to*
alrededor de	*around*
cerca de	*near*
debajo de	*underneath*
bajo	*under* (more figurative than **debajo de**)
delante de	*before, in front of* (physical location)
ante	*before, in front of, in the presence of*
dentro de	*inside of*
detrás de	*behind*
tras	*after* (in a set of expressions)
encima de	*on top of*
enfrente de, frente a	*in front of, opposite, facing, across from*
fuera de	*outside of*
junto a, pegado a	*close to, right next to*
lejos de	*far from*

Pronouns That Follow Prepositions

You have already learned that subject pronouns follow prepositions.

para él	*for him*	para Ud.	*for you* (sing.)
para ella	*for her*	para Uds.	*for you* (pl.)
para ellos	*for them* (m.)	para nosotros	*for us*
para ellas	*for them* (f.)	para vosotros	*for you*

The only exceptions appear in the first-person and second-person singular.

para **mí**	*for me*
para **ti**	*for you*

There are a few situations, however, where the subject pronouns **tú** and **yo** are used after prepositions. Note the following expressions.

entre tú y yo	*between you and me*
menos tú y yo	*except you and me*
excepto tú y yo	*except you and me*
según tú	*according to you*
incluso yo	*including me*
salvo yo	*except me*

The only preposition that combines with a pronoun is **con**.

conmigo	*with me*
contigo	*with you*
consigo	*with yourself, with himself, with herself, with themselves*

The Preposition *por*

Por has the following meanings.

- *through, by*

El ladrón sale por la ventana.	*The robber leaves through the window.*
Preferimos viajar por avión.	*We prefer to travel by plane.*
Él manda mensajes por correo electrónico.	*He sends messages by e-mail.*

- *because of, on account of, for the sake of, out of*

La planta es verde por la clorofila.	*The plant is green because of the chlorophyll.*
Él está triste por el mal clima.	*He is sad because of the bad weather.*
Ella no quiere hablar por miedo.	*She doesn't want to talk out of fear.*
Ellas aprenden bien por ti.	*They learn well because of you.*

- *in exchange for; in place of* (suggests a substitution)

Pago diez dólares por este vestido.	*I pay $10 (in exchange) for this dress.*

El estudiante enseña por el profesor.

The student teaches for (instead of) the teacher.

- *per*

Él gana quinientos dólares por semana.

He earns $500 per week.

Recibe mil doscientos dólares por mes.

He receives $1,200 per month.

- *for* (before a period of time)

Cada día, corro por una hora.   *Each day, I run for an hour.*
Cada noche, leo por media hora.   *Each night, I read for a half hour.*
Ella tiene ganas de estudiar el español por dos años.

She wants to study Spanish for two years.

Por adds the idea of motion to prepositions of location.

El niño corre por debajo de la mesa.

The child runs under the table.

El gato salta por encima del sofá.   *The cat jumps over the sofa.*

Por appears in some common expressions.

por acá, por aquí	*around here*
por allá, por allí	*around there*
por ahora	*for now*
por casualidad	*by chance*
por lo común	*usually*
por costumbre	*usually*
por ejemplo	*for example*
por eso	*therefore, for this reason*
por favor	*please*
por fin	*finally*
por lo menos	*at least*
por poco	*almost*
por primera vez	*for the first time*
por supuesto	*of course*
por todas partes	*everywhere*
por la mañana	*in the morning* (imprecise time)
por la tarde	*in the afternoon*
por la noche	*in the evening*

Por and *para* Compared

Remember that **para** means *for.*

El regalo es para su hijo.   *The gift is for her son.*
Tengo una pregunta para ella.   *I have a question for her.*

Para is also used to express a specific time limit or deadline in the future. In this context, it can be translated as *for, by, on,* or *before.*

Necesito la blusa para el viernes.   *I need the blouse for Friday.*

Por is translated as simple *for* only when **por** precedes a quantity of time.

Voy a viajar por varios meses.   *I am going to travel for several months.*

Ella mira televisión por una hora.   *She watches television for an hour.*
Dormimos por ocho horas cada   *We sleep for eight hours every noche.*   *night.*

With the exception of their English translations as *for,* the meanings of **por** and **para** do not overlap. Again, **por** means *for* only when it precedes a period of time. **Para** means *for* in almost all other cases.

Queremos una habitación para   *We want a room for two persons dos personas por una noche.*   *for one night.*
El tren sale para el Canadá.   *The train is leaving for Canada.*

 Exercise 9.4

Complete the following sentences with the correct prepositions and pronouns.

1. ¿Quieres salir _____ a las cinco? (*with me*)

2. No quiero salir _____. (*without you*)

3. ¿Tiene Ud. confianza _____? (*in him*)

4. Ella lleva su bolsa _____. (*with her*)

5. Este regalo es _____. (*for them*)

6. _____, ¿quién cocina mejor? (*between him and her*)

7. _____, esta película es horrible. (*between you and me*)

8. Los niños corren _____. (*toward us*)

9. El hombre quiere hablar _____, pero yo no quiero hablar

   _____. (*with me/with him*)

10. Hay una estatua _____. (*near him*)

11. Julia no quiere tocar el piano _____. (*in front of them*)

12. Primero, ella quiere practicar _____. (*in front of us*)

13. Este hombre siempre está sentado _____. (*behind her*)

14. La familia de Pedro vive _____ pero vive _____.
    (*far from him/near me*)

Exercise 9.5

Complete the following sentences with the Spanish for the words in parentheses.

1. _____, las muchachas van a practicar el piano.
   (*before lunch*)

2. _____, quieren mirar televisión. (*after dinner*)

3. _____, vamos a la playa. (*after eating*)

4. _____ a su trabajo, ella toma su desayuno.
   (*before going*)

5. _____ temprano, ella llega tarde. (*in spite of
   leaving*)

6. El muchacho baila _____ la música. (*without
   listening to*)

7. Ella estudia _____. (*in order to learn*)

8. ¿Están las llaves _____ la ventana o _____
   la puerta? (*underneath/on top of*)

9. Vamos al teatro que está _____ la tercera avenida. (*near*)

10. El padre corre _____ su hija. (*toward*)

11. ¿Cuándo sale el tren _____ Madrid? (*for*)

12. Hay muchos árboles _____ la casa lujosa. (*behind*)

13. La radio habla _____ la situación mundial. (*about*)

14. Tomás va a estar de viaje _____ seis meses. (*for*)

15. No quiero hablar _____ la clase. (*in front of*)

16. Vamos al cine una vez _____ semana. (*per*)

17. Ellos prefieren viajar _____ tren _____ tres horas. (*by/for*)

18. El rió está _____ las montañas. (*far from*)

19. Ella no quiere ir a Alaska _____ el frío. (*because of*)

20. Practico el piano _____ tocar bien. (*in order to*)

Exercise 9.6

Translate the following sentences into English.

1. Ella nunca habla contra sus amigos.

   _____

2. Los zapatos de Sara están debajo de su cama.

   _____

3. Australia está lejos de los Estados Unidos.

   _____

4. La escuela está entre la iglesia y el banco.

   _____

5. Puedo ver el río desde mi ventana.

   _____

6. Ella duerme ocho horas cada noche. Ella duerme desde las once hasta las siete.

   _____

7. Bajo la ley, ¿quién tiene protección?

   _____

8. Pongo un libro encima del otro.

   _____

9. Antonio nunca canta sin nosotros.

   _____

10. El testigo tiene que aparecer ante el juez.

    _____

11. Los niños hablan mucho de la película.

_____

12. El autor escribe sobre la historia y los derechos humanos.

_____

13. El cine está lejos del mercado.

_____

 Exercise 9.7

Translate the following sentences into Spanish.

1. _I enter the store through the door._

_____

2. _Everyone wants to go except Samuel._

_____

3. _All the men dance except Pablo._

_____

4. _My garden is next to my neighbor's garden._

_____

5. _We walk toward the park._

_____

6. _There is a bus stop in front of Laura's house._

_____

7. _According to the news, a lot of people are not going to vote._

_____

8. _There are comfortable chairs around the swimming pool._

_____

9. _Day after day, they work a lot._

_____

10. _James' house is behind the school._

_____

11. *Are you going to study for the test?*

_____

12. *She doesn't want to travel out of fear.*

_____

 Reading Comprehension

El circo

Aunque ella tiene cuarenta años, mi amiga Leonora quiere trabajar
en un circo. Es verdad que ella es soltera y maestra y tiene el verano libre
pero no entiendo por qué ella no quiere ir al Caribe o a cualquier sitio
relajante. Ella piensa que va a ser una gran aventura. Hay una gira del
circo por el noreste de los Estados Unidos y ella va a pasar todo el verano
con ellos.

Yo soy soltera también y tengo el verano libre, pero no tengo el menor
interés en el circo. ¡Es absurdo! ¿Qué hay que hacer en un circo? Según
Leonora, ella va a vender tiquetes por la mañana. Después de almorzar,
va a mirar algunos ensayos y a hablar con los trapecistas. Desde las dos
de la tarde hasta las siete, ella y sus colegas van a vender más tiquetes por
teléfono y en persona. A eso de las ocho de la noche, al escuchar la música
que indica que el circo va a empezar, Leonora va a cerrar la oficina y salir
para ir a ver la función. El colmo es que va a ganar solamente trescientos
dólares por semana. Ella sale mañana. Por mi parte, prefiero pasar el
verano aquí. Es bonito, hace buen tiempo y tengo otras amigas. De todos
modos, ella va a volver pronto.

Vocabulario

aunque	*although*	libre	*free* (as in time)
el circo	*the circus*	el noreste	*the northeast*
el colega	*the colleague*	qué hay que hacer	*what is there to do*
el colmo	*the limit*	el sitio	*the place*
el ensayo	*the rehearsal*	soltera	*single*
la gira	*the tour*	el tiquete	*the ticket*
indicar	*to indicate*	de todos modos	*anyway*
el interés	*the interest*	el trapecista	*the trapeze artist*

Nombres

la caja	*the box*	las noticias	*the news*
el correo	*the post office*	la parada	*the bus stop*
los derechos humanos	*the human rights*	la película	*the film*
		el/la testigo	*the witness*
el/la juez	*the judge*	el vecino	*the neighbor*
la ley	*the law*		

Preguntas

After you have read the selection, answer the following questions in Spanish.

1. ¿Cuántos años tiene Leonora?

_____

2. ¿Por qué quiere ir al circo?

_____

3. ¿Qué va a hacer Leonora durante el día?

_____

4. ¿Cuánto va a ganar ella por semana en el circo?

_____

 ## Key Vocabulary

These words will help enhance your ability to communicate. As you learn them, remember to practice them aloud.

Nature

el alba *(f.)*	*the dawn*	el mar	*the sea*
el cielo	*the sky*	las montañas	*the mountains*
la colina	*the hill*	el monte	*the hill*
el desierto	*the desert*	la nieve	*the snow*
la estrella	*the star*	las nubes	*the clouds*
la inundación	*the flood*	el ocaso	*the sunset*
el lago	*the lake*	el océano	*the ocean*
la lluvia	*the rain*	la puesta del sol	*the sunset*
la luna	*the moon*	el relámpago	*the lightning*
la madrugada	*the dawn, early morning*	el río	*the river*
		el sol	*the sun*

el temblor	*the tremor*	la tormenta	*the storm*
la tempestad	*the storm*	el trueno	*the thunder*
el terremoto	*the earthquake*	el viento	*the wind*
la tierra	*the earth*		

Weather

¿Qué tiempo hace?	*What's the weather like?*
Hace buen tiempo.	*The weather is good.*
Hace mal tiempo.	*The weather is bad.*

Hace calor.	*It's hot.*	Hay estrellas.	*The stars are out.*
Hace frío.	*It's cold.*	Hay luna.	*The moon is out.*
Hace fresco.	*It's cool.*	Hay neblina.	*It's foggy.*
Hace sol.	*It's sunny.*	Hay nubes.	*It's cloudy.*
Hace viento.	*It's windy.*	Hay polvo.	*It's dusty.*
		Hay lodo.	*It's muddy.*

 Exercise 9.8

Answer the following questions aloud in Spanish.

1. No comemos a las siete. ¿A qué hora comen Uds.?

2. Los libros no están en la mesa, sino en el piso. ¿Por qué están los libros en el piso?

3. ¿Qué haces por costumbre los sábados por la noche?

4. Después de hacer ejercicio, ¿en qué parte del cuerpo tienes dolor?

5. ¿Vive Ud. en un apartamento o en una casa? ¿En qué piso vive?

6. ¿Quiere Ud. viajar o prefiere Ud. ahorrar su dinero?

7. Si Ud. tiene hambre, ¿qué come? Si Ud. tiene sed, ¿qué bebe?

8. Enrique tiene ocho años. Su hermano tiene diez años y su hermana tiene doce. ¿Quién es el mayor de su familia?

9. ¿Va Ud. a la playa en el verano?

10. ¿Qué haces tú si tu amigo quiere ir a un restaurante en particular y quieres ir a otro?

Exercise 9.9

Regular and irregular verbs. *Complete the following sentences with the correct conjugation of the verbs in parentheses.*

1. Él no _____ jugo de naranja; _____ jugo de manzana. (*to drink/to drink*)

2. El niño no _____ bien el piano, porque no _____ nunca. (*to play/to practice*)

3. No _____ ningún buen hotel en la ciudad. (*there is*)

4. ¿_____ Uds. al campo con sus primos el domingo? (*to go*)

5. Yo _____ que él va a _____ un buen abogado si él estudia. (*to know/to be*)

6. Fernando _____ a Nueva York. ¿Cuántos amigos de él _____ en la ciudad? (*to want to go/to live*)

7. Yo _____ mi casa casi todos los días. No _____ limpiar mi casa los sábados. (*to clean/have to*)

8. Los dos amigos quieren _____ de fumar. (*to stop*)

9. ¿Cuál _____ su número de teléfono? (*to be*)

10. Nosotros _____ que el primo de Carlos _____ con nuestro hermano. (*to know/to be*)

11. La clase _____ a las seis. Nosotros _____ de la clase a las ocho. (*to begin/to leave*)

12. En la clase, estudiamos mucho y _____ la lección. (*to understand*)

13. ¿Dónde _____ las llaves que tú siempre pierdes? (*to be*)

14. ¿Quién _____ contestar las preguntas? (*to be able*)

15. La verdad es que ella _____ bien, pero nunca _____. (*to try to cook/to have success*)

16. ¿Qué _____ Ud. durante el día? (*to do*)

17. Toda la familia _____ a España todos los años. (*to travel*)

18. Ella _____ el piano y él _____ la flauta.

    Los domingos _____ al béisbol. (*to play/to play/to play*)

19. ¿Quién _____ la cuenta? (*to be going to pay*)

20. Mi amiga está en Portugal y no quiere _____ a los Estados Unidos. (*to return*)

21. Mi amiga _____ dolor de estómago. ¿Piensa Ud. que

    _____ a un médico? (*to have/ought to go*)

22. El carro de Juan es viejo. Él va a _____ otro. (*to buy*)

23. _____ a mi casa el sábado? ¿Qué quieres

    _____ para el desayuno? (*to come/to have*)

24. Si nadie quiere _____, ¿por qué tanta gente va a la playa? (*to swim*)

25. Ellos _____ en el maratón cada año en Boston. (*to run*)

Exercise 9.10

Prepositions and verbs. *Complete the following sentences with the Spanish for the words in parentheses.*

1. _____, las muchachas van a practicar la canción.
   (*before singing*)

2. _____, Raúl quiere ir al cine. (*after resting*)

3. _____ a las ocho, salimos a las seis y media.
   (*in order to arrive*)

4. _____, vamos a la playa. (*after eating*)

5. ¿Va ella a la fiesta _____ enferma todo el día?
   (*after being*)

6. Enrique baila _____ la música. (*without listening to*)

7. _____ duro, este hombre no tiene éxito.
   (*in spite of working*)

8. Ellos leen el periódico _____ al trabajo.
   (*before going*)

9. _____ algunas cervezas, Uds. deben comer algo.
   (*before having*)

10. _____ su tarea, el estudiante decide jugar.
    (*instead of doing*)

11. Ella quiere viajar _____ seis meses. (*for*)

12. Voy a pasar _____ la ciudad antigua en mayo. (*through*)

13. Necesito una habitación _____ una persona

    _____ tres días. (*for/for*)

14. El tren sale _____ México mañana, pero ella prefiere viajar

    _____ avión. (*for/by*)

Exercise 9.11

Numbers, telling time, adverbs, prepositions, and comparisons. *Complete the following sentences with the Spanish for the words in parentheses.*

1. Mi primo vive entre la _____ y

   la _____ avenida. (*sixth/seventh*)

2. Él llega _____ si camina _____ .
   (*rapidly/to the left*)

3. ¿Por qué vive ella en el _____ piso? (*eighth*)

4. _____ el _____ tren llega de
   Los Angeles. (*at 10:45/third*)

5. Hay un buen restaurante en la calle _____ con

   la _____ avenida. (*34th/third*)

6. Ella siempre pierde sus llaves. _____ están

   _____ su mesa. _____ están

   _____ el carro. (*at times/underneath/frequently/in*)

7. Su hermana _____ nunca lee el periódico y nunca
   sabe nada. (*older*)

8. Mi hermano _____ está feliz porque nuestra tía viene
   de Texas. (*younger*)

9. Si estoy en la _____ avenida,

   ¿debo ir _____ , _____ ,

   o _____ para llegar a la librería? (*seventh/to the right/
   to the left/straight ahead*)

10. Los domingos, mi amiga duerme _____.
    (*until 11:00* A.M.)

11. Mi amigo no trabaja los domingos, pero su trabajo empieza

    _____ los lunes. (*at 8:00* A.M.)

12. La película empieza _____ esta noche. (*at 7:45*)

13. Ella es _____ mujer de la familia que va a una
    universidad. (*the first*)

14. Las calles de México son _____ que las calles
    de España. (*narrower*)

15. Carla es _____ su hermano, pero su hermano

    es _____ ella. (*taller than/older than*)

16. El doctor piensa que el pollo es bueno, pero el pescado

    es _____ para la salud del paciente. (*better*)

17. El niño está triste pero su madre está _____ él.
    (*sadder than*)

18. Ella vive con sus tres hermanos _____. (*younger*)

19. Sara va al gimnasio porque quiere ser _____

    su _____ amiga. (*stronger than/best*)

20. ¿Cuál es la _____ película del año? (*worst*)

Exercise 9.12

Translate the following sentences into Spanish.

1. *My niece is going to be 13 years old next week.*

   _____

2. *The girls are hungry and thirsty, and no one knows how to cook.*

   _____

3. *Not one child wants to go to the dentist. I don't know why everyone
   is afraid to go.*

   _____

   _____

4. *The film begins at eight o'clock. We have to arrive at seven thirty.*

    _____

5. *She thinks that he ought to try to run every day in order to be stronger.*

    _____

    _____

6. *She always goes to Las Vegas in the winter. She loses frequently.*
   But today she is lucky and wins one hundred dollars.

    _____

    _____

7. *That church is old. It is much older than this temple.*

    _____

8. *I try to speak with my friends in Spanish. I have a lot to learn. I should*
   study every morning.

    _____

    _____

9. *Carla spends a lot of time in the store. She looks at the clothes, but she*
   leaves without buying anything.

    _____

    _____

10. *How many earthquakes are there in California each year?*

    _____

11. *Who is here? It is I.*

    _____

12. *George is a good man.*

    _____

13. *Elena and her friends are intelligent.*

    _____

14. *His grandmother and grandfather are happy because their grandchildren*
    are well.

    _____

    _____

Exercise 9.13

On a separate sheet of paper, write the English translation of the following infinitives from Part I.

1. abrir	28. dejar de	55. llegar	82. repasar
2. acabar de	29. descansar	56. llenar	83. repetir
3. aceptar	30. describir	57. llevar	84. romper
4. ahorrar	31. devolver	58. llorar	85. saber
5. almorzar	32. dibujar	59. manejar	86. salir
6. apagar	33. disfrutar	60. marcar	87. seguir
7. aparecer	34. doblar	61. mentir	88. ser
8. aprender	35. dormir	62. meter	89. servir
9. arreglar	36. empezar	63. mirar	90. sonreír
10. bailar	37. encontrar	64. nadar	91. subir
11. bajar	38. entender	65. necesitar	92. tener que
12. beber	39. entrar	66. oír	93. tener
13. cambiar	40. escribir	67. parar	94. terminar
14. caminar	41. escuchar	68. pasar	95. tirar
15. cantar	42. estar	69. pensar	96. tocar
16. celebrar	43. estudiar	70. perder	97. tomar
17. cerrar	44. explicar	71. pintar	98. trabajar
18. cocinar	45. firmar	72. poder	99. tratar de
19. comer	46. fumar	73. poner	100. usar
20. compartir	47. ganar	74. practicar	101. vender
21. comprar	48. gozar	75. preferir	102. venir
22. comprender	49. hablar	76. prender	103. ver
23. contestar	50. hacer	77. preparar	104. viajar
24. correr	51. ir	78. querer	105. vivir
25. cruzar	52. jugar	79. recibir	106. volver
26. deber	53. leer	80. recordar	107. votar
27. decidir	54. limpiar	81. regresar	

Reading Comprehension

El trabajo

No voy al trabajo hoy, ni mañana, ni pasado mañana. No tengo ganas.
Mi oficina es demasiado oscura. Cuando entro, finjo que estoy bien y que
entiendo como funcionan todas las máquinas que están allí, pero en
realidad, no entiendo nada. El cambio de un año a otro es impresionante.
Ahora no hay espacio ni para mis plantas ni para mis fotos. Hay una
computadora encima de la mesa y una impresora entre la máquina de
facsímile y la contestadora. El papel está debajo de la mesa; mis plumas y
mis lápices están al lado de la computadora. Yo sé que tengo que aprender
a usar todo para tener éxito en este nuevo mundo de la tecnología.

Durante el día, si mi jefe quiere hablar conmigo, él no sale de su
oficina. (Él está a solo veinte pasos de mi oficina.) Ya no habla conmigo
cara a cara. ¡No! Él manda un correo electrónico desde su oficina. Ya no
escucho su voz bella y expresiva. Ya no viene a mi cuartito para conversar
conmigo, ni discutimos las noticias del día, ni tomamos un café juntos.
Ahora él no busca razones para venir a mi oficina.

Son las doce. Ahora él prepara las facturas y los depósitos para la
semana. Almuerza rápidamente para volver a su computadora. Casi no
descansa. Todos los empleados salen a las cinco, pero él siempre trabaja
hasta las seis. Tengo mucho que hacer en la casa, pero si hago un gran
esfuerzo, puedo terminar antes de las cinco. Al fin y al cabo, no voy a
llamar a la oficina; es mejor ir a saludar a mis colegas.

Verbos

buscar	*to look for*	llamar	*to call*
conversar	*to converse*	mandar	*to send*
discutir	*to discuss*	saludar	*to greet*
fingir	*to pretend*		
funcionar	*to function, to work*		

Nombres

el cambio	*the change*	el correo electrónico	*e-mail*
la computadora	*the computer*		
la contestadora	*the answering machine*	el cuartito	*the little room* (**-ito** makes the room smaller)

el depósito	*the deposit*	la máquina	*the fax machine*
el empleado	*the worker*	de facsímile	
el esfuerzo	*the effort*	el mundo	*the world*
el espacio	*the space*	las noticias	*the news*
la factura	*the invoice, bill*	la razón	*the reason*
la impresora	*the printer*	la voz	*the voice*
el jefe	*the boss*		

Adjetivos

impresionante	*impressive*
oscuro	*dark*

Expresiones

al fin y al cabo	*after all*
cara a cara	*face to face, in person*
está a sólo veinte pasos	*he is only twenty steps away*
pasado mañana	*the day after tomorrow*
tengo mucho que hacer	*I have a lot to do*
todo lo necesario	*all that is necessary*

Preguntas

After you have read the selection, answer the following questions in Spanish.

1. ¿Dónde está Isabel al empezar este cuento? ¿Por qué no quiere ir al trabajo?

   _____

2. ¿Quiere ella aprender todo lo necesario de la tecnología?

   _____

3. ¿Cómo es su relación con su jefe?

   _____

4. ¿En qué piensa Isabel durante el día?

   _____

5. ¿Qué va a hacer a las cinco?

   _____

6. ¿Piensa Ud. que Isabel está contenta?

   _____

II

Objects, Reflexive Verbs, and the Present Subjunctive

10

The Indirect Object

Gustar and the Indirect Object

Gustar means *to be pleasing to* and is used to express the idea of *liking* in Spanish.

Me gusta and me gustan

Me is the indirect object pronoun that means *to me*. In Spanish, there is no exact translation of *I like*. Compare the English construction with the Spanish construction.

Singular Noun as the Subject

English Construction	*I like this class.*
Spanish Construction	**Me gusta** esta clase.
	To me is pleasing this class.

Esta clase is a singular noun—the subject.
Gusta is the verb and agrees with the singular subject.
Me is the indirect object pronoun—the person to whom the action is occurring.

Me gusta la música.	*The music is pleasing to me.*
Me gusta el libro.	*The book is pleasing to me.*
Me gusta esta idea.	*This idea is pleasing to me.*
Me gusta la cerveza.	*The beer is pleasing to me.*
Me gusta el chocolate.	*Chocolate is pleasing to me.*

NOTE: In the Spanish construction, subjects retain their articles (**el**, **la**, **los**, **las**) even when the English translation doesn't include them (for example, **el chocolate**, English *Chocolate*—not *The chocolate*—in the example above).

A Word About Practicing Orally
It is essential to practice orally **me gusta** and all the forms to follow. The more
you practice, the more natural it becomes.

Plural Noun as the Subject

If the subject of the sentence is a plural noun, **gusta** becomes **gustan** to
agree with the plural subject.

English Construction	*I like the books.*
Spanish Construction	**Me gustan** los libros.
	To me are pleasing the books.

Los libros is the plural noun—the subject.
Gustan is the verb and agrees with the plural subject.
Me is the indirect object pronoun—the person to whom the action is
    occurring.

Me gustan las fiestas.	*The parties are pleasing to me.*
Me gustan los deportes.	*Sports are pleasing to me.*
Me gustan los perros.	*Dogs are pleasing to me.*

Verb as the Subject

Me gusta is also used when the subject is a verb. The verb form is the infinitive, no matter what the English translation is. When an infinitive is the
subject, the singular **gusta** is used.

English Construction	*I like to swim.*
Spanish Construction	**Me gusta** nadar.
	To me is pleasing to swim.

Me gusta comer.	*To eat is pleasing to me.*
Me gusta bailar.	*To dance is pleasing to me.*
Me gusta ir al cine.	*To go to the movies is pleasing to me.*
Me gusta escribir y leer.	*To write and to read are pleasing to me.*

NOTE: **Gusta** remains singular even if it is followed by a series of verbs.

The only forms of **gustar** that you will need are the third-person singular,
gusta, and the third-person plural, **gustan**.

To make a sentence negative, simply place **no** before the indirect object.

No me gustan las cucarachas.   *Cockroaches are not pleasing to me.*
No me gusta cocinar.   *To cook is not pleasing to me.*

Review

- If the subject of the sentence is a singular noun or a verb, use **gusta**.

  Me gusta el hotel.
  Me gusta viajar.

- If the subject is a plural noun, use **gustan**.

  Me gustan las vacaciones.

- If the sentence is negative, place **no** before the indirect object.

  No me gustan los ratones.

Te gusta and *te gustan*

Te is the indirect object pronoun that means *to you*. When you use **te**, you are speaking in the familiar **tú** form.

English Construction   *You like his car.*
Spanish Construction   **Te gusta** su carro.
                         To you is pleasing his car.

Singular Noun as the Subject

Te gusta mi idea.   *My idea is pleasing to you.*
¿Te gusta la puesta del sol?   *Is the sunset pleasing to you?*
¿Te gusta el teatro?   *Is theater pleasing to you?*
¿Te gusta España?   *Is Spain pleasing to you?*

Plural Noun as the Subject

Te gustan las flores rojas.   *Red flowers are pleasing to you.*
¿Te gustan las lecciones?   *Are the lessons pleasing to you?*
¿Te gustan tus cursos?   *Are your courses pleasing to you?*

Verb as the Subject

Te gusta viajar.   *To travel is pleasing to you.*
Te gusta descansar.   *To rest is pleasing to you.*
Te gusta cantar y bailar.   *To sing and dance is pleasing to you.*

Le gusta and *le gustan*

Le is the indirect object pronoun that means *to him* (**a él**), *to her* (**a ella**), or *to you* (**a Ud.**).

English Construction	*He likes the wine.*
Spanish Construction	**Le gusta** el vino.
	To him is pleasing the wine.

Because **le** means *to him, to her,* and *to you*, it can have any of the following meanings.

The wine is pleasing to him.
The wine is pleasing to her.
The wine is pleasing to you.

To clarify this ambiguity, the sentence must begin with a prepositional phrase that clarifies the meaning of the indirect object pronoun **le**.

A él le gusta el vino.	*The wine is pleasing to him.*
A él le gusta cantar.	*Singing is pleasing to him.*
A él le gustan los libros.	*Books are pleasing to him.*
A ella le gusta el vino rosado.	*Rosé wine is pleasing to her.*
A ella le gusta escribir cartas.	*Writing letters is pleasing to her.*
A ella le gustan las montañas.	*The mountains are pleasing to her.*
A Ud. le gusta la cerveza.	*The beer is pleasing to you.*
A Ud. le gusta tomar un descanso.	*To take a break is pleasing to you.*
A Ud. le gustan las playas.	*Beaches are pleasing to you.*

You can also insert proper names and nouns in the prepositional phrase.

A Fernando le gusta la verdad.	*The truth is pleasing to Fernando.*
A María le gusta bailar.	*To dance is pleasing to Maria.*
A Roberto le gustan los carros nuevos.	*New cars are pleasing to Robert.*

Singular nouns can be inserted in the prepositional phrases.

A la mujer le gusta leer.	*To read is pleasing to the woman.*
Al hombre le gusta cocinar.	*To cook is pleasing to the man.*

Nos gusta and *nos gustan*

Nos is the indirect object pronoun that means *to us*.

English Construction   *We like to speak Spanish.*
Spanish Construction   **Nos gusta** hablar español.
                           To us is pleasing to speak Spanish.

Nos gusta la torta de chocolate.   *Chocolate cake is pleasing to us.*
Nos gusta comer en el parque.   *To eat in the park is pleasing to us.*
Nos gustan nuestros maestros.   *Our teachers are pleasing to us.*

Les gusta and *les gustan*

Les is the indirect object pronoun that means *to them* (**a ellos**, **a ellas**) and *to you* (**a Uds.**).

English Construction   *They like the film.*
Spanish Construction   **Les gusta** la película.
                           To them is pleasing the film.

Because **les** means both *to them* and *to you*, the meaning of this sentence can be either of the following.

The film is pleasing to them.
The film is pleasing to you (pl.).

To clarify this ambiguity, the sentence must begin with a prepositional phrase that clarifies the meaning of **les**.

¿**A Uds. les gusta** el café negro?   *Is black coffee pleasing to you?*
¿**A Uds. les gusta** el presidente?   *Is the president pleasing to you?*
A ellas les gustan los hoteles.   *Hotels are pleasing to them.*
A ellos les gusta dormir bien.   *To sleep well is pleasing to them.*

Nouns and proper names can be inserted in the prepositional phrases.

A Sara y Enrique les gusta nadar.   *To swim is pleasing to Sara and Henry.*
A los niños les gustan los juguetes.   *Toys are pleasing to the children.*
A las niñas les gustan las lecciones.   *The lessons are pleasing to the girls.*

If you want to add emphasis to the constructions of **me gusta** and **te gusta**, add **a mí**, which emphasizes **me**, and **a ti**, which emphasizes **te**.

A mí me gusta el café.	*Coffee is pleasing to me.*
A ti te gusta el vino.	*Wine is pleasing to you.*

There is no ambiguity in these examples. **A mí** and **a ti** give the feeling of the emphasized pronoun in English: *I like coffee.* **You** *like wine.*

Exercise 10.1

Pronounce the examples aloud so you can become familiar with the sound.

Singular Subject	Singular Subject	Plural Subject
Me gusta el hotel.	Me gusta viajar.	Me gustan los hoteles.
Te gusta la clase.	Te gusta correr.	Te gustan las clases.
Le gusta el libro.	Le gusta escribir.	Le gustan los libros.
Nos gusta la comida.	Nos gusta comer.	Nos gustan las comidas.
Les gusta el programa.	Les gusta leer.	Les gustan los programas.

Exercise 10.2

Complete the following sentences. Choose the correct indirect object pronoun, as indicated by the prepositional phrase in parentheses, then choose either **gusta** *or* **gustan**, *depending on whether the subject is singular or plural.*

EXAMPLES   (A mí) *me gusta* el helado.

(A él) *le gustan* las galletas.

(A nosotros) *nos gusta* el postre.

1. (A mí) _____ el café con azúcar.

2. (A ella) _____ el café negro.

3. (A María) _____ el té.

4. (A mí) _____ escribir libros.

5. (A mis amigos) _____ cocinar.

6. (A Susana y a Miguel) _____ viajar.

7. (A ellos) _____ comer en buenos restaurantes.

8. (A mí) _____ ir al teatro.

9. (A ti) _____ ir al cine.

10. (A nosotros) _____ salir los sábados.

11. (A Guillermo) _____ los restaurantes japoneses.

12. (A su amiga) _____ los restaurantes hindúes.

13. (A Uds.) _____ los restaurantes franceses.

14. (A mí) _____ las playas del Caribe.

15. (A ti) _____ las piscinas grandes.

16. (A tu hermana) _____ la ciudad.

17. (Al hermano de José) _____ el campo.

18. (A nosotros) _____ viajar.

19. (A Cecilia y a su familia) _____ conversar.

20. (A los niños) _____ aprender todo.

21. (A los adolescentes) _____ jugar deportes.

22. ¿(A Uds.) _____ el alcalde de su ciudad?

Verbs like *gustar*

You have just learned a very important form, not only to express the idea of *I like,* but for other verbs as well. The following verbs are used with an indirect object.

agradar *to be pleasing to* (very close in meaning to **gustar**)

¿No te agrada nadar?	*Isn't swimming pleasing to you?*
Me agrada vivir en el campo.	*To live in the country is pleasing to me.*

convenir *to suit someone, to be convenient (for)*

¿Te conviene tomar ese trabajo?	*Does it suit you to take that job?*
No nos conviene viajar ahora.	*It does not suit us to travel now.*

doler *to be painful, to hurt*

Me duele la cabeza.	*My head hurts me.*
Te duelen los dientes.	*Your teeth hurt you.*
¿A Uds. les duelen los pies si caminan mucho?	*Do your feet hurt you if you walk a lot?*

NOTE: In Spanish, the possessive adjective is not used with parts of the body and the indirect object pronoun.

encantar *to be enchanting to, to like very much*

Le encanta viajar.	*To travel is enchanting to him. (He loves traveling.)*
Le encanta visitar España.	*To visit Spain is enchanting to him.*

NOTE: **Encantar** is much stronger than **gustar**. **Encantar** cannot be used in the negative.

faltar *to be lacking* (something), *to be missing* (something)

A ellos les falta disciplina.	*They lack discipline.*
Aquí falta luz.	*Here there is no light.*

NOTE: **Faltar** can be used without the indirect object pronoun.

fascinar *to fascinate, to be fascinating (to)*

Nos fascina el baile flamenco.	*Flamenco dance fascinates us.*
Me fascinan estos dibujos.	*These drawings are fascinating to me.*

hacer falta *to need* (something)

Me hace falta tomar unas vacaciones.	*I need to take a vacation.*

importar *to be important to, to matter*

No me importa.	*It is not important to me.*
A Sandra le importan sus amigos.	*Sandra's friends are important to her.*
No importa.	*It doesn't matter. / Never mind.*

NOTE: **Importar** can be used without the indirect object pronoun.

interesar *to be interesting (to)*

Les interesa estudiar.	*To study is interesting to them.*
Me interesa ir a museos.	*It interests me to go to museums.*

molestar *to bother, to annoy*

¿Le molesta si alguien fuma? *Does it bother you if someone smokes?*

A él no le molesta nada. *Nothing bothers him.*

parecer *to seem, to appear to be*

Me parece que es una buena escuela. *It seems to me that it is a good school.*

Parece que va a llover. *It seems that it is going to rain.*

NOTE: **Parecer** can be used without the indirect object pronoun.

quedar *to be left over, to remain*

Nos quedan veinte minutos. *We have 20 minutes left.*

No me queda mucho dinero. *I don't have much money left.*

¿Cuántas páginas nos quedan por leer? *How many pages are left for us to read?*

NOTE: **Quedar por** + an infinitive = *to remain to be.*

sobrar *to have more than enough of* (something)

Me sobra comida para mañana. *I have more than enough food for tomorrow.*

tocarle a alguien *to be someone's turn*

Cada vez que me toca a mí, gano. *Every time it's my turn, I win.*

Cada vez que le toca a él, pierde. *Every time it's his turn, he loses.*

 ## Exercise 10.3

Complete the following sentences with the correct prepositional phrase, according to the words in parentheses.

EXAMPLE ___A él___ le gusta nadar. *(to him)*

1. _____ le gusta el tenis. *(to her)*

2. ¿_____ le gustan todos los deportes? *(to you)*

3. _____ me gusta leer, pero me encanta escribir. *(to me)*

4. Yo sé que _____ te gusta estudiar, pero _____ les gusta ir a fiestas. *(to you/to them)*

5. Parece que _____ le gusta cocinar. (*to no one*)

6. ¿ _____ le gusta limpiar su apartamento? (*to whom*)

Exercise 10.4

Change the following singular sentences to plural. Make sure both the subject and the verb are plural. The indirect object pronoun will remain the same.

EXAMPLE   Me gusta su idea.   *Me gustan sus ideas.* _____

1. Les encanta ese carro rojo. _____

2. Te agrada el programa. _____

3. Me gusta la silla. _____

4. Nos importa nuestro amigo. _____

5. Le fascina esa computadora. _____

Exercise 10.5

Translate the following sentences into English.

EXAMPLE   Me gusta viajar. *Traveling / To travel is pleasing to me.*

1. A Susana le duele la cabeza. _____

2. Me falta un lápiz con que escribir. _____

3. ¿Por qué no te gusta bailar? _____

4. Nos fascinan los viajes exóticos. _____

5. A ella le interesan las noticias del día.

   _____

6. ¿A Ud. le molesta su perfume? _____

7. ¿A Uds. les importan las lecciones? _____

8. ¿Te conviene seguir tus estudios este año?

   _____

9. A él no le gusta manejar en la lluvia.

   _____

10. A ella no le gusta el clima caliente. _____

Exercise 10.6

Answer the following questions aloud in Spanish.

1. ¿A Ud. le duele la cabeza después de trabajar todo el día?

2. ¿Qué les conviene estudiar ahora?

3. ¿Cuántos libros nos quedan por leer?

4. ¿Por qué a Uds. les fascina hablar español?

5. ¿Les gustan los carros grandes que usan mucha gasolina?

6. ¿Te interesa la tecnología?

7. ¿Qué le encanta hacer?

8. En su familia, ¿a quién le gusta jugar al baloncesto? ¿A quién le gusta bailar?

9. ¿Te importa saber de la política?

10. ¿A Uds. les fascina viajar?

The Indirect Object Pronoun

Review the indirect object pronouns.

me		*to me*
te		*to you* (sing., familiar)
le	a Ud.	*to you* (sing., formal)
	a él	*to him*
	a ella	*to her*
nos		*to us*
os		*to you* (pl., familiar; used only in Spain)
les	a Uds.	*to you* (pl., formal)
	a ellos	*to them* (m.)
	a ellas	*to them* (f.)

So far, you have learned the indirect object with verbs like **gustar**. Now make sure you know what an indirect object is in other sentences as well. For example, *I give the gift **to him***. In this sentence, *to him* is the indirect object.

The indirect object receives the action of the verb indirectly. It answers questions about to whom or for whom an action is done.

In order to have an indirect object in a sentence, there must be a direct object, either real or implied. In the example above, *the gift* is the direct object.

The translation of the indirect object is *to me, to you, to him, to her, to us, to them.*

A Word About Indirect Objects

Be sure to practice the indirect object orally as much as you can. The structure of Spanish and English is quite different here, so take your time and practice.

Verbs that commonly take indirect objects follow.

cobrar *to charge* (money)

yo cobro	nosotros cobramos
tú cobras	vosotros cobráis
Ud. cobra	Uds. cobran

comprar *to buy*

yo compro	nosotros compramos
tú compras	vosotros compráis
él compra	ellos compran

contar *to relate, to tell a story, to count;* **contar con** *to count on, to rely on*

yo cuento	nosotros contamos
tú cuentas	vosotros contáis
él cuenta	ellos cuentan

contestar *to answer*

yo contesto	nosotros contestamos
tú contestas	vosotros contestáis
ella contesta	ellas contestan

dar *to give*

yo doy	nosotros damos
tú das	vosotros dais
él da	ellos dan

decir *to say, to tell*

yo digo	nosotros decimos
tú dices	vosotros decís
ella dice	ellas dicen

enseñar *to teach*

yo enseño	nosotros enseñamos
tú enseñas	vosotros enseñáis
Ud. enseña	Uds. enseñan

enviar *to send*

yo envío	nosotros enviamos
tú envías	vosotros enviáis
él envía	ellos envían

hacer *to do, to make*

yo hago	nosotros hacemos
tú haces	vosotros hacéis
Ud. hace	Uds. hacen

preguntar *to ask* (a question)

yo pregunto	nosotros preguntamos
tú preguntas	vosotros preguntáis
él pregunta	ellos preguntan

prestar *to lend*		**traer** *to bring*	
yo presto	nosotros prestamos	yo traigo	nosotros traemos
tú prestas	vosotros prestáis	tú traes	vosotros traéis
ella presta	ellas prestan	Ud. trae	Uds. traen

vender *to sell*	
yo vendo	nosotros vendemos
tú vendes	vosotros vendéis
ella vende	ellas venden

Position of the Indirect Object Pronoun

The indirect object pronoun can be placed in either of two positions in a sentence or phrase.

Indirect Object Pronoun Placed Directly Before the First Verb

In the first position, the indirect object pronoun is placed *directly before the first verb* in a sentence or question.

Carlos **me escribe** una carta.	*Charles writes a letter to me.*
Carlos **te escribe** una carta.	*Charles writes a letter to you.*
Yo **le escribo** una carta.	*I write a letter to you.* / *I write a letter to him.* / *I write a letter to her.*
Carlos **os escribe** una carta.	*Charles writes a letter to you.*
Yo **les escribo** una carta.	*I write a letter to you.* / *I write a letter to them.*

Remember that the indirect object pronoun **le** is ambiguous. It means *to him, to her, to you.* Out of context, there is no way to know what the meaning is. So a prepositional phrase is added to clarify the meaning.

María **le escribe** una carta **a Ud.**	*Maria writes a letter to you.*
María **le escribe** una carta **a él**.	*Maria writes a letter to him.*
María **le escribe** una carta **a ella**.	*Maria writes a letter to her.*

Remember also that a proper noun can be inserted in the clarifying prepositional phrase.

María **le escribe** una carta **a Juan**.	*Maria writes a letter to John.*
María **le escribe** una carta **a Susana**.	*Maria writes a letter to Susana.*

A noun can also be inserted in the prepositional phrase.

María **le escribe** una carta **a su hermana**.	*Maria writes a letter to her sister.*
María **le escribe** una carta **a mi amigo**.	*Maria writes a letter to my friend.*
Juan **le escribe** una carta **a su padre**.	*John writes a letter to his father.*
Juan **le escribe** una carta **a su primo**.	*John writes a letter to his cousin.*

Like **le**, **les** is ambiguous. It means *to you* (**a Uds.**) and *to them* (**a ellos**, **a ellas**). A prepositional phrase is added to clarify the meaning. A proper noun or a noun can also be used as a clarifier.

Juan **les escribe** una carta **a Uds.**	*John writes a letter to you.*
Juan **les escribe** una carta **a ellas.**	*John writes a letter to them.*
Él **les escribe** una carta **a sus hermanos**.	*He writes a letter to his brothers.*
Juan **les escribe** una carta **a Ana y José**.	*John writes a letter to Ana and Joseph.*

With the verbs **comprar** and **hacer**, the translation of the indirect object pronoun is *for me, for you, for him, for her, for us, for them*.

Él **me compra** flores.	*He buys flowers for me.*
Yo **le compro** flores a él.	*I buy flowers for him.*
Te hago un favor.	*I do (for) you a favor.*

 Exercise 10.7

Using the new verbs, complete the following sentences with the correct verb and indirect object pronoun. Add clarifiers when necessary.

1. Julia _____ dos tarjetas cada semana. (*to write/to me*)

2. José y Maria _____ tarjetas desde Barcelona.
   (*to write/to us*)

3. Carlos _____ la lección de hoy. (*to give/to me*)

4. Yo _____ si mi tarea está en tu casa. (*to ask/you*)

5. Él _____ que su hermana vive en Nueva York.
   (*to say/to me*)

6. Ella _____ su bolígrafo. (*to lend/to him*)

7. Nosotros _____ a hablar español. (*to teach/to Ana y José*)

8. Ellos _____ café con leche a mi oficina. (*to bring/to us*)

9. Yo _____ los resultados de la elección. (*to tell/to him*)

10. Yo _____ , "¿Cuánto _____ Ud.?" (*to ask/the cab driver, to charge/me*)

 ## Exercise 10.8

Complete the following sentences with the correct verb and indirect object pronoun. Notice that these sentences include two verbs. Practice placing the indirect object pronoun directly before the first verb.

EXAMPLES   Juan _me quiere dar_ una lámpara. (*to want to give/to me*)

Juan _me va a dar_ una lámpara. (*to be going to give/to me*)

1. Alicia _____ una alfombra.
(*to want to give/to me*)

2. El maestro _____ el francés.
(*to want to teach/to his students*)

3. Mis primos _____ un carro para mi cumpleaños. (*to be going to buy/for me*)

4. Yo _____ mi computadora vieja.
(*to want to sell/to you*)

5. ¿Tienes frío? Yo _____ una chaqueta.
(*to be able to bring/to you*)

6. Ud. _____ la verdad. (*ought to tell/him*)

7. ¿Quién _____ las lecciones de hoy?
(*to be able to teach/us*)

8. ¿_____ Ud. el favor de limpiar mi casa?
(*to be able to do/for me*)

9. Yo _____ buenas direcciones, pero no sé donde estoy. (*to want to give/to you*)

10. Ellos siempre _____ cómo estoy. (*to ask/me*)

Indirect Object Pronoun Attached to the Infinitive

In the second position, the indirect object pronoun is *attached to the infinitive* if there is an infinitive in the sentence or question.

Let us say, for example, that a sentence includes a phrase that has an infinitive but no other form of a verb. In that type of phrase, any indirect object pronoun *must* be attached to the infinitive.

Antes de prestarte dinero,...	*Before lending you money, . . .*
Después de enseñarnos el francés,...	*After teaching us French, . . .*
En vez de escribirme una carta,...	*Instead of writing a letter to me, . . .*

In other cases, sentences may include a phrase with more than one verb, one of which is an infinitive. You may also attach an indirect object pronoun to the infinitive in this type of phrase.

¿Puede Ud. **hacerme** el favor de cerrar la ventana?	*Can you do me the favor of closing the window?*
Pedro quiere **darte** un libro.	*Peter wants to give you a book.*
Vamos a **enseñarle** a pintar.	*We are going to teach him to paint.*
Ella quiere **traernos** café.	*She wants to bring coffee to us.*
El niño va a **decirles** la verdad.	*The boy is going to tell them the truth.*

Exercise 10.9

Complete the following sentences by attaching the indirect object pronoun to the infinitive. Use the words within parentheses as well as the prepositional phrases in the sentences for clarification.

1. Ella _____ un cuento esta noche.
   (*to want to tell/to me*)

2. Patricia _____ a Ud. su guitarra.
   (*to be going to lend*)

3. ¿Quién _____ a su familia?
   (*to be going to write*)

4. Nosotros _____ a sus amigos la casa.
   (*to be going to sell*)

5. Yo _____ a Uds. mi bicicleta. (*to want to lend*)

Exercise 10.10

Some of the following sentences have two verbs; some have one. Complete the sentences with the correct verb or verbs and indirect object pronoun. The verbs in this lesson are very important, so try to memorize them as you do the following exercise.

1. Si tienes frío, yo _____ un suéter.
   (*to give/to you*)

2. El camarero _____ al hombre un vaso de agua.
   (*to bring/to him*)

3. Manuel _____ a cocinar.
   (*to want to teach/to us*)

4. Nosotros _____ el viernes.
   (*to be going to write/to them*)

5. Tú _____ tus libros todo el tiempo.
   (*to lend/to me*)

 Review the positions of the indirect object pronoun.

- Directly before the first verb
- Attached to the infinitive

Whether the indirect object pronoun is placed directly before the first verb or is attached to the infinitive, the meaning is exactly the same. Practice the indirect object pronouns and the verbs aloud as much as you can.

Yo **te quiero escribir** una carta. Yo **quiero escribirte** una carta.	*I want to write you a letter.*
Él **me va a vender** un carro. Él **va a venderme** un carro.	*He is going to sell me a car.*
Ellos **nos quieren contar** un cuento. Ellos **quieren contarnos** un cuento.	*They want to tell us a story.*
Les debemos decir a Uds. la verdad. **Debemos decirles** a Uds. la verdad.	*We ought to tell you the truth.*

Exercise 10.11

Translate the following sentences into English.

1. Me puede decir, ¿por qué a Sandra no le gusta tocar la guitarra?

   _____

2. El amigo de Elena le presta a Ud. sus libros.

   _____

3. Elena le da a su hermano los bolígrafos que él necesita.

   _____

4. Las lecciones de música no son caras. El maestro les cobra a sus estudiantes quince dólares por hora.

   _____

   _____

5. Me fascina jugar al tenis, pero más me conviene nadar.

   _____

6. El doctor no está en su consultorio. No sé si quiere hablar conmigo.

   _____

7. Entre tú y yo, tenemos que decidir quien va a contarles a los niños el cuento.

   _____

   _____

8. ¿Por qué el abogado les hace preguntas a los testigos si ya sabe las respuestas?

   _____

   _____

9. ¿Puede Ud. venderme rápidamente dos maletas? Voy a viajar mañana.

   _____

10. Ella nos quiere llamar el día de acción de gracias.

    _____

11. A ella le gusta celebrar el día del amor y la amistad.

    _____

12. ¿Les conviene tomar sopa de pollo cuando Uds. están enfermos?

_____

13. Le digo a ella que su idea es buena.

_____

14. A ella no le gusta el café; su colega siempre le trae el té.

_____

15. El camarero le trae al hombre un vaso de agua. Él les trae a los jovencitos un vaso de leche.

_____

_____

 ## Exercise 10.12

Translate the following sentences, then answer the questions orally in Spanish.

EXAMPLE   ¿Es esta lección difícil? _Is this lesson difficult?_

(Oral) _Sí, es difícil, pero me gusta aprender._

1. ¿Quiere Ud. viajar conmigo el año que viene? ¿Tiene Ud. vacaciones? ¿Adónde quiere ir?

_____

2. ¿Dónde te gusta comer? ¿Prefieres comer en un restaurante o en casa?

_____

3. ¿A Ud. le molesta la contaminación de las ciudades grandes?

_____

4. ¿Te gusta bailar? ¿A quién le gusta bailar contigo?

_____

5. A ellos no les gusta el restaurante en la calle cuarenta y dos con la novena avenida. ¿Sabe Ud. la razón?

_____

_____

6. Es el cumpleaños de Susana. ¿Le debo traer flores?

_____

7. Les decimos a los niños que es importante estudiar. ¿Por qué no nos prestan atención?

_____

_____

8. Le presto dinero a María porque ella es una buena amiga y siempre me devuelve el dinero. ¿Les presta Ud. dinero a sus amigos?

_____

_____

9. ¿Qué le contesta Ud. al muchacho si él le dice que él tiene miedo de nadar?

_____

_____

10. Ellos quieren darte un carro para celebrar el nuevo año pero tienen solamente quinientos dólares. ¿Qué deben hacer?

_____

_____

11. Tenemos hambre. ¿Quién nos va a enseñar a cocinar?

_____

12. ¿Dónde estoy? ¿Me puedes dar buenas direcciones?

_____

13. Tu mejor amigo quiere darte un buen regalo. Él quiere hacerte el favor de limpiar tu apartamento. ¿Cuántos cuartos tienes?

_____

_____

14. El niño le pregunta a Ud., "¿por qué hay nubes en el cielo?" ¿Sabe Ud. la razón?

_____

_____

Exercise 10.13

Translate the following sentences from English to Spanish.

1. *Every year he gives a gift to his girlfriend.*

   _____

2. *Carla never tells me her secrets.*

   _____

3. *Henry doesn't want to lend money to us.*

   _____

4. *Who is going to buy books for the children?*

   _____

5. *After writing to his friends, he is going to the movies.*

   _____

6. *They charge us too much. We charge them little.*

   _____

7. *Why don't you answer the students? They ask you many questions.*

   _____

8. *We are going to give a dog to Peter and Rosa.*

   _____

9. *I'll bring you coffee if you bring me tea.*

   _____

10. *I tell you that the train is coming.*

    _____

11. *Why do you teach us German if we want to learn French?*

    _____

12. *She listens to everything, but says nothing to you.*

    _____

13. *Susan's aunt tells her that she wants to go to Mexico for her vacation.
    She tells me that she wants to go to Paris.*

    _____

    _____

14. *After studying a lot, do your eyes hurt?*

_____

15. *Everyone wants to go to the football game except me.*

_____

 Reading Comprehension

Ir de compras

A mi amigo Julio y a mí nos gusta ir de compras. Nos fascina pasear
en el carro a regiones en las afueras. Durante el día, nos encanta probar
la comida típica del área. Al entrar en un restaurante, el camarero nos
dice "¿En qué puedo servirles?" y le preguntamos, "¿qué clase de comida
nos recomienda?" Él nos recomienda los mariscos y nos da unos minutos
para decidir. Después de un rato, nos dice, "Disculpe, están Uds.
listos para ordenar?" Julio le pregunta cuánto cuesta la langosta. "No hay"
nos contesta. Escogemos, pues, crema de almejas, cangrejo con ajo
y camarones. Después de la comida deliciosa, continuamos alegremente
nuestro viaje turístico.

Vocabulario

ir de compras	*to go shopping*
pasear en el carro	*to take a ride*
las afueras	*outskirts, suburbs*
probar	*to taste, to take a taste*
el área (*f.*)	*the area*
al entrar	*upon entering*
en qué puedo servirles	*how can I serve (help) you*
recomendar	*to recommend*
los mariscos	*seafood*
un rato	*a little while*
disculpe	*excuse me*
están Uds. listos para ordenar	*are you ready to order*
la langosta	*the lobster*
escoger	*to choose*
crema de almejas	*clam chowder*
el cangrejo	*crab*
el ajo	*garlic*
los camarones	*shrimp*

Preguntas

After you have read the selection, answer the following questions in Spanish.

1. ¿Por qué a los dos amigos les gusta ir de compras?

   _____

2. ¿Qué les gusta comer?

   _____

3. ¿Adónde van después de comer?

   _____

 ## Reading Comprehension

El viaje

Me gusta viajar porque cuando viajo no soy de aquí ni soy de allá.
Me fascina la idea. Pienso ir a Italia. Me dicen que es un país maravilloso,
el más bello del mundo. Me cuentan que la gente es muy amable y que
gozan de la vida cada día. Me dicen que exactamente a las siete todas las
noches en todas las ciudades y todos los pueblos, la gente sale, los jóvenes
y los viejos, salen de sus casas y dan una vuelta por la ciudad. Después
de caminar por una hora, vuelven a la casa para cenar. ¡Qué imagen más
hermosa! Me parece que me va a gustar Italia.

No me importa que hay mucho que hacer antes de viajar. Primero,
tengo que hacer las reservaciones. Voy a pedir un asiento con ventanilla
porque me encanta mirar el cielo y las nubes por la ventana. Yo sé que
a otras personas les gusta el asiento en el pasillo para poder andar por
el avión sin molestar a nadie.

La parte que me encanta más es la hora de la comida. La azafata nos
pregunta, "¿qué quieren Uds.?" Le contestamos con "pollo, por favor,"
o "pescado," o "prefiero carne, por favor." Nos dan lo que pedimos y por
un rato hay silencio en el avión mientras los pasajeros comen. Si es largo
el viaje, nos muestran una película y también podemos escuchar música
con los audífonos que nos dan. Yo misma prefiero leer o escribir pero
a muchos viajeros les gusta mirar la película mientras otros duermen.

No puedo tardar más. Primero, voy a escoger una buena fecha que
me va a traer suerte. Después voy a comprar un tiquete de ida y vuelta
y un vuelo directo. Finalmente, voy a arreglar solamente una maleta para
no cargar mucho. Yo sé que una buena experiencia me espera.

Verbos y expresiones verbales

andar	*to walk*	escoger	*to choose*
arreglar la maleta	*to pack the suitcase*	esperar	*to await*
cargar	*to carry*	gozar (de)	*to enjoy*
cenar	*to dine*	tardar	*to delay*
dar una vuelta	*to take a walk*		

Nombres

el asiento	*the seat*
los audífonos	*the headphones*
la azafata	*the stewardess, flight attendant*
la imagen	*the image*
el pasillo	*the aisle*
la ventanilla	*the window in a car, boat, or airplane*
el vuelo	*the flight*

Pronombres relativos y conjunciones

lo que	*that which,* often translated as *what*
mientras	*while*

Expresiones

hay mucho que hacer	*there is a lot to do*
ida y vuelta	*round-trip*
por un rato	*for a little while*

Preguntas

After you have read the selection, answer the following questions in Spanish.

1. ¿A Isabel le gusta viajar?

   _____

2. ¿Por qué escoge Italia?

   _____

3. ¿Qué tiene que hacer antes de viajar?

   _____

4. ¿Qué piensa hacer ella durante el viaje? ¿Qué hacen los otros pasajeros?

   _____

5. ¿Piensa Ud. que Isabel va a viajar?

   _____

11

The Direct Object

The Personal *a* and the Direct Object

The direct object receives the action of the verb directly.
The direct object can be a thing.

*I see **the tree**.*

The direct object can be a person.

*I see **the woman**.*

When the direct object is a person, an untranslated **a** is placed directly before the direct object person. This is called the *personal **a***.

Yo veo **a la mujer**.	*I see the woman.*
Vemos **a Pedro**.	*We see Peter.*
Uds. ven **a sus primos**.	*You see your cousins.*

If the direct object person is masculine and singular, the **a** combines with **el** and becomes **al**.

Yo visito **al hombre**.	*I visit the man.*
Tú visitas **al niño**.	*You visit the child.*

Personal **a** is used before **alguien** and **nadie**.

¿Quieres llamar **a alguien**?	*Do you want to call someone?*
No puedo llamar **a nadie**.	*I can't call anyone.*

Personal **a** is not used with **tener**.

Tengo dos hermanas.	*I have two sisters.*
Ella tiene cinco sobrinos.	*She has five nephews.*

Remember that if the direct object is a *thing,* there is no personal **a.**

Yo veo el árbol.	*I see the tree.*
Queremos ver una película hoy.	*We want to see a film today.*
Él espera el tren en la estación.	*He waits for the train in the station.*

Transitive Verbs

Transitive verbs are verbs that take a direct object.

The English translation for many Spanish verbs includes a preposition. That means that for this type of verb, the direct object will immediately follow the verb in Spanish, but it will follow a preposition in English. Look closely at the headings for verbs such as **buscar** *to look **for**.* Study the following examples.

Yo escucho la música.	*I **listen to** the music.*
Ella mira la casa.	*She **looks at** the house.*
Esperamos el tren.	*We **wait for** the train.*

Here is a list of frequently used transitive verbs.

abrazar *to embrace, to hug*

yo abrazo	nosotros abrazamos
tú abrazas	vosotros abrazáis
ella abraza	ellas abrazan

acompañar *to accompany*

yo acompaño	nosotros acompañamos
tú acompañas	vosotros acompañáis
él acompaña	ellos acompañan

amar *to love*

yo amo	nosotros amamos
tú amas	vosotros amáis
ella ama	ellas aman

ayudar *to help*

yo ayudo	nosotros ayudamos
tú ayudas	vosotros ayudáis
Ud. ayuda	Uds. ayudan

besar *to kiss*

yo beso	nosotros besamos
tú besas	vosotros besáis
él besa	ellos besan

buscar *to look for*

yo busco	nosotros buscamos
tú buscas	vosotros buscáis
ella busca	ellas buscan

conocer *to be acquainted with, to know* (a person or place)

yo conozco	nosotros conocemos
tú conoces	vosotros conocéis
Ud. conoce	Uds. conocen

Conocer means to know a person or place in terms of being acquainted.

Yo conozco a esta mujer.	*I know (am acquainted with) this woman.*
Él conoce Paris.	*He knows Paris.*

Compare this with **saber**, which means to know a fact or to know how to do something.

Ella sabe la verdad.	*She knows the truth.*
Yo sé nadar.	*I know how to swim.*

cuidar *to take care of*

yo cuido	nosotros cuidamos
tú cuidas	vosotros cuidáis
él cuida	ellos cuidan

dejar *to leave* (something or someone) *behind*

yo dejo	nosotros dejamos
tú dejas	vosotros dejáis
ella deja	ellas dejan

Dejar means to leave something or someone behind.

Dejo mis llaves en mi casa.	*I leave my keys in my house.*

Compare that with **salir**, which means to exit.

Salgo de mi oficina a las tres.	*I leave my office at three o'clock.*

encontrar *to find*

yo encuentro	nosotros encontramos
tú encuentras	vosotros encontráis
Ud. encuentra	Uds. encuentran

NOTE: **Encontrar** and **hallar** are synonyms and can be used interchangeably.

escuchar *to listen to*

yo escucho	nosotros escuchamos
tú escuchas	vosotros escucháis
ella escucha	ellas escuchan

esperar *to wait for*

yo espero	nosotros esperamos
tú esperas	vosotros esperáis
él espera	ellos esperan

extrañar *to miss* (a person or a place)

yo extraño	nosotros extrañamos
tú extrañas	vosotros extrañáis
ella extraña	ellas extrañan

gritar *to yell at, to scream at*

yo grito	nosotros gritamos
tú gritas	vosotros gritáis
él grita	ellos gritan

hallar *to find*

yo hallo	nosotros hallamos
tú hallas	vosotros halláis
Ud. halla	Uds. hallan

NOTE: **Hallar** and **encontrar** are synonyms and can be used interchangeably.

invitar *to invite*

yo invito	nosotros invitamos
tú invitas	vosotros invitáis
él invita	ellos invitan

llamar *to call*

yo llamo	nosotros llamamos
tú llamas	vosotros llamáis
ella llama	ellas llaman

llevar *to carry, to carry off, to carry away; to wear*

yo llevo	nosotros llevamos
tú llevas	vosotros lleváis
Ud. lleva	Uds. llevan

matar *to kill*

yo mato	nosotros matamos
tú matas	vosotros matáis
él mata	ellos matan

mirar *to look at, to watch*

yo miro	nosotros miramos
tú miras	vosotros miráis
ella mira	ellas miran

querer + **a** + person
to love a person

yo quiero	nosotros queremos
tú quieres	vosotros queréis
Ud. quiere	Uds. quieren

Querer a una persona means *to love a person*. This verb is less strong than **amar**.

Ella quiere a su amiga.   *She loves her friend.*

Compare that with **amar**, which expresses a deeper love.

Él ama a su esposa.   *He (deeply) loves his wife.*

recoger *to gather, to pick up*	
yo recojo	nosotros recogemos
tú recoges	vosotros recogéis
ella recoge	ellas recogen

saludar *to greet*	
yo saludo	nosotros saludamos
tú saludas	vosotros saludáis
él saluda	ellos saludan

ver *to see*	
yo veo	nosotros vemos
tú ves	vosotros veis
Ud. ve	Uds. ven

visitar *to visit*	
yo visito	nosotros visitamos
tú visitas	vosotros visitáis
él visita	ellos visitan

Exercise 11.1

Complete the following sentences, using the correct form of the verb and the personal **a**.

EXAMPLES   Nosotros *visitamos a Susana* cada año en España.
(*to visit Susan*)

Ella *ama a su madre*. (*to love her mother*)

1. Antes de salir de la casa, ella _____ .
   (*to kiss her husband*)

2. Carlos quiere _____ el día del amor
   y la amistad. (*to call his friends*)

3. Yo siempre _____ a la tienda.
   (*to accompany my grandmother*)

4. No puedo _____ . No sé donde está.
   (*to find my younger brother*)

5. El estudiante del primer año _____ .
   (*to miss his family*)

6. En clase, nosotros _____ , y prestamos
   atención. (*to look at the teacher*)

7. María y Sofía quieren _____ en el hospital.
    (*to help the patients*)

8. Yo _____ well. (*to know Peter*)

9. Los profesores _____ cada día en el colegio.
    (*to see their students*)

10. Los padres _____ .
    (*to take care of their children*)

11. El taxista _____ al hotel.
    (*to take the tourists*)

12. Ella no entiende la lección porque no _____ .
    (*to listen to the teacher*)

13. Jorge no puede _____ y está preocupado.
    (*to find his sister*)

14. No sé porque él _____ . (*to yell at his boss*)

15. Roberto va a _____ a la fiesta.
    (*to invite Ramona*)

16. Veinte minutos pasan y Teresa no quiere _____
    más. (*to wait for her friend*)

The Direct Object Pronoun

The direct object pronouns **me**, **te**, **nos**, and **os** have the same form as the indirect object pronouns **me**, **te**, **nos**, and **os**. The only new forms are **lo**, **los**, **la**, and **las**.

me	*me*		nos	*us*
te	*you*		os	*you* (used only in Spain)
lo	*him, it* (m., object)		los	*them* (m., persons and objects)
la	*her, it* (f., object)		las	*them* (f., persons and objects)

Make sure you know what the direct objects and direct object pronouns are in all cases. Review the following.

> *I see **the man**.*

In this sentence, *the man* is the direct object.

> *I see **the tree**.*

In this sentence, *the tree* is the direct object.

The direct object pronoun replaces the direct object.

*I see the man. I see **him**.*
*I see the tree. I see **it**.*

Review what you know about direct object pronouns.

- The direct object pronoun replaces the direct object.
- The direct object pronoun can refer to a person or a thing.
- It receives the action of the verb directly.
- It answers the question about what or who received the action.

Position of the Direct Object Pronoun

The direct object pronoun can be placed in either of two positions in a sentence or phrase.

Direct Object Pronoun Placed Directly Before the First Verb

In the first position, the direct object pronoun is placed *directly before the first verb* in a sentence or question.

Ella **me** conoce bien.	*She knows me well.*
Los niños **te** van a escuchar.	*The children are going to listen to you.*
Ellas **nos** saludan los lunes.	*They greet us on Mondays.*
¿**Os** podemos recoger a la una?	*Can we pick you up at one o'clock?*

Direct Object Pronoun Attached to the Infinitive

In the second position, the direct object pronoun is attached to the infinitive. Whether the direct object pronoun is placed before the first verb or attached to the infinitive, the meaning of the sentence is the same.

Ella quiere **visitarme** en México.	*She wants to visit me in Mexico.*
Queremos **invitarte** a la fiesta.	*We want to invite you to the party.*
Debo **llamarlo** ahora.	*I ought to call him now.*
¿Quién quiere **ayudarla**?	*Who wants to help her?*
¿Puedes **esperarnos**?	*Can you wait for us?*
Vamos a **extrañarlos** mucho.	*We are going to miss them a lot.*

The Direct Object Pronoun as a Person

The direct object pronoun needs no clarifiers, since it is clear that **lo** can only mean *him*, **la** can only mean *her*, **los** can only mean *them* (masculine, or masculine and feminine), and **las** can only mean *them* (feminine).

lo	*him*	los	*them* (m.)
la	*her*	las	*them* (f.)

María **lo** ama.	*Mary loves him.*
Jorge **la** besa.	*George kisses her.*
Los conozco de mi viaje a México.	*I know them from my trip to Mexico.*
Yo **las** debo acompañar al tren.	*I ought to accompany them to the train.*

In order to express the direct object pronoun *you* in the **Ud.** and **Uds.** form, the indirect object pronoun **le** and **les** is used in most countries.

Yo **le** conozco, ¿verdad?	*I know you, right?*
¿Puedo **ayudarle**?	*May I help you?*
Les acompañamos al parque.	*We accompany you to the park.*

To make a sentence negative, place **no** before the direct object pronoun.

No lo veo.	*I don't see him.*
Ella **no** me conoce.	*She doesn't know me.*
Ellos **no** nos quieren abrazar.	*They don't want to hug us.*

When the direct object pronoun is attached to the infinitive, place **no** before the first verb.

No quiero escucharlo.	*I don't want to listen to him.*
Él **no** quiere esperarme.	*He doesn't want to wait for me.*
No queremos buscarla.	*We don't want to look for her.*

Exercise 11.2

Complete the following sentences with the correct form of the verb and the direct object pronoun.

1. Ricardo _____ hasta las seis todas las noches.
   (*to wait for me*)

2. Él _____ , pero no recuerda de donde.
   (*to know you* [familiar])

3. Nuestros amigos _____ con la tarea.
   (*to be going to help us*)

4. Cecilia y Susana van a viajar mañana. Vamos a _____ .
   (*to miss them*)

5. Enrique es un buen estudiante, pero no está en clase hoy.

   Yo _____ , pero no _____ .

   (*to look for him/to find him*)

6. Francisca quiere a su amigo Pablo. Ella _____ mucho.
   (*to love him*)

7. ¿Quién quiere _____? (*to visit her*)

8. ¿Dónde están las muchachas? _____ Uds.? (*to see them*)

9. ¿Saludan Uds. a sus amigos todos los días? Nosotros no

   _____ nunca. (*to greet them*)

10. Su amigo es simpático. No sé por qué Ud. _____ .
    (*to be going to leave him*)

11. Cuando sus padres están ocupados y no pueden cuidar a sus hijos,

    una niñera _____ . (*to take care of them*)

12. _____ , ella va a preparar la cena. (*after calling him*)

13. ¿Conocen Uds. a mi amiga Ramona? Sí, nosotros _____
    bien. (*to know her*)

14. Ella mira a la profesora y _____ . (*to listen to her*)

15. _____ a la fiesta, él tiene que encontrar su número
    de teléfono. (*before inviting her*)

Exercise 11.3

Translate the following sentences into English.

1. Si un hombre acompaña a una mujer hermosa a la reunión, ¿la va a besar?

   _____

2. Nos parece que el muchacho está enfermo y no puede hacer su tarea.
   Decidimos ayudarlo.

   _____

3. Sara siempre llega tarde y no la queremos esperar más.

_____

4. ¿Extraña Ud. a su familia que vive lejos? ¿La quiere visitar?

_____

5. Los ingleses van a llegar a los Estados Unidos esta tarde. Vamos a llevarlos del aeropuerto a un buen hotel.

_____

_____

 Exercise 11.4

Translate the following sentences into Spanish.

1. _I see José, but he doesn't see me._

_____

2. _We don't know where the tourists are who are visiting us from Spain._

_____

3. _They are going to visit their friends in Canada after selling their boat._

_____

The Direct Object Pronoun as a Thing

lo	_it_ (m.)	los	_them_ (m.)
la	_it_ (f.)	las	_them_ (f.)

Guillermo compra **el carro**.	_Bill buys the car._
Él **lo** compra.	_He buys it._

Let's review what we know about direct object pronouns.

• The direct object pronoun replaces the direct object.
• The direct object pronoun is placed directly before the first verb or attached to the infinitive.

Guillermo vende su carro.	_Bill sells his car._
Él **lo** vende.	_He sells it._

Yo tengo la llave.	*I have the key.*
La tengo.	*I have it.*
Comemos los vegetales.	*We eat the vegetables.*
Los comemos.	*We eat them.*
Ella lee las revistas.	*She reads the magazines.*
Ella **las** lee.	*She reads them.*
Veo las flores en el jardín.	*I see the flowers in the garden.*
¿Puedes **verlas** también?	*Can you see them also?*
Él espera el tren a las nueve.	*He waits for the train at nine.*
Tiene que **esperarlo**.	*He has to wait for it.*
Ella no entiende la lección.	*She doesn't understand the lesson.*
Necesita estudiar para **entenderla**.	*She needs to study in order to understand it.*
Tengo dos buenos libros en casa.	*I have two good books at home.*
Voy a **leerlos** mañana.	*I am going to read them tomorrow.*

Exercise 11.5

Complete the following sentences with the correct form of the verb and the direct object pronoun.

1. ¿Tiene Ud. el libro rojo? Sí, yo _____, pero yo no

   _____. (*to have it/to want to read it*)

2. Su casa está sucia, pero Pedro no _____.
   (*to want to clean it*)

3. ¿Dónde están nuestros mapas de México? Nosotros siempre

   _____ en el coche, pero hoy no _____.

   (*to have them/to see them*)

4. No sé por qué él tiene tres carros; él _____ pero

   él no _____ tampoco. (*is not able to use them/*

   to want to sell them)

5. Necesitamos cuarenta tenedores, quince cuchillos y ochenta cucharas

   para la fiesta. ¿Quién tiene tiempo para _____?

   (*to buy them*)

6. En el verano, ella busca buenos libros; ella _____ en la biblioteca. (*to find them*)

7. Antes de estudiar la lección, ella está nerviosa. Después de

   _____, tiene más confianza. (*to study it*)

8. Las revistas que recibimos están en la casa pero no podemos

   _____. (*to find them*)

9. Los niños escuchan a sus padres porque sus padres

   _____. (*to love them*)

10. Este hombre tiene mucho dinero debajo de su cama, pero ¿es mejor

    _____ en el banco? (*to have it*)

Review Chart of Indirect and Direct Object Pronouns

Subject Pronoun	Indirect Object Pronoun	Direct Object Pronoun
yo	me	me
tú	te	te
él	le (a él)	lo
ella	le (a ella)	la
Ud.	le (a Ud.)	—
nosotros	nos	nos
vosotros	os	os
ellos	les (a ellos)	los
ellas	les (a ellas)	las
Uds.	les (a Uds.)	—

Notice again that there is no direct object pronoun for *you*. In order to express the direct object *you*, use **le** for the singular and use **les** for the plural.

Quiero ayudarlo.	*I want to help him.*
Quiero ayudarla.	*I want to help her.*
Quiero ayudar**le**.	*I want to help you* (sing.).
Quiero ayudarlos.	*I want to help them.*
Quiero ayudarlas.	*I want to help them.*
Quiero ayudar**les**.	*I want to help you* (pl.).

Exercise 11.6

Test your knowledge. *Complete the following sentences with the correct indirect or direct object pronoun. Place the pronoun before the first verb or attach it to the infinitive.*

1. ¿Conoce Ud. a mi amiga Sara? Sí, _____ conozco. (*her*)

2. ¿Dónde está Mario? ¿_____ ves? (*him*)

3. Ella mira a la profesora y _____ escucha bien. (*her*)

4. A ella _____ gustan las lecciones. (*to her*)

5. ¿Por qué siempre _____ dices mentiras si yo _____ digo la verdad? (*to me/to you*)

6. ¿Pedro _____ va a dar regalos a sus hijos este año? (*to them*)

7. _____ voy a ayudar a cocinar. (*them*)

8. ¿Cuánto tiempo _____ queda? (*us*)

9. ¿_____ escribes a tus padres? (*to them*)

10. Ellos quieren enviar _____ una carta desde Madrid. (*to them*)

11. ¿Por qué _____ haces preguntas si ya sabes la respuesta? (*me*)

12. Los niños quieren dar_____ a sus padres un beso. (*to them*)

13. En vez de invitar_____ al concierto, él decide ir solo. (*her*)

14. Antes de ver_____, ella va al cine. (*them*)

15. ¿Lees el periódico en la mañana o _____ lees en la tarde? (*it*)

16. La comida esta fría y no _____ queremos comer. (*it*)

17. Las lecciones son difíciles, y ella estudia mucho. Después de una hora, ella _____ entiende. (*them*)

18. La maestra repite las preguntas para los estudiantes. Ella _____ repite para practicar la pronunciación también. (*them*)

19. ¿Dónde están mis llaves? Siempre _____ pierdo. No _____ veo. (*them/them*)

20. _____ dan flores pero no _____ gustan. (*to me/to me*)

Exercise 11.7

*Review **gustar** and indirect object pronouns, and then answer the questions orally.*

1. ¿A los hombres les gusta hablar mucho?
2. ¿A los soldados les gusta luchar o prefieren vivir en paz?
3. ¿A los niños qué les gusta hacer?
4. ¿A quién le gusta trabajar mucho? ¿A quién le gusta ir de vacaciones?
5. ¿Por qué a algunas personas no les gusta nada?

Exercise 11.8

Translate the following sentences into Spanish.

1. I see my friends every Saturday. It is pleasing to us to go to the movies.

   _____

2. She looks at the teacher, she listens well, but still she understands nothing.

   _____

   _____

3. Lisa waits for her sister, who always arrives late.

   _____

4. We travel to Ecuador in order to be with our relatives.

   _____

5. The lesson is difficult and he wants to study it for the test.

   _____

6. Can you go to the post office for me? I have a letter for my friend and I want to send it today.

   _____

   _____

7. Do you want to accompany him to the party? He is shy and doesn't want to go alone.

   _____

   _____

8. *Where do you know her from? Do you see her all the time?*

_____

9. *She has new shoes but she never wears them.*

_____

10. *I hardly ever see you.*

_____

 ## Reading Comprehension

La bienvenida

¡Es increíble! Aquí estoy en Italia. Hay muchos italianos en el aeropuerto que esperan a los pasajeros. Yo los miro: un hombre besa a una mujer; tres niños corren hacia una mujer y emocionados la besan, y ella, con lágrimas en los ojos, los besa y los abraza. Una mujer le dice a su novio lo extraña cuando está lejos de ella; él le dice que la ama. Los niños, tan contentos de ver a sus padres de nuevo, saltan de alegría. Los viajeros como yo, sin familia (nadie nos espera porque no conocemos a nadie), recogemos nuestras maletas y seguimos a la aduana. No me molesta esperar un rato. Dentro de poco, sellan mi pasaporte y me dan una bienvenida cariñosa.

Salgo del aeropuerto al sol. Camino hacia los taxistas. Hace fresco y estoy bien. Tomo el primer taxi en la fila, le pregunto al conductor cuanto cobra por el viaje y me parece justo. Me lleva a la plaza central donde hay muchos hoteles interesantes. Pago la tarifa, le doy una propina, y con una sonrisa, me bajo del taxi.

Entro en el hotel que me interesa y le pregunto al dueño cuanto cobra por una noche para una persona. Le digo que quiero una habitación sencilla y tranquila con un baño privado. El dueño, muy simpático, me dice que tiene una habitación hermosa que da a la plaza. Después de verla, la tomo. Él mira mi pasaporte. Escribo mi nombre en el registro, y él me da las llaves. Estoy cansada pero estoy emocionada también. Ya es tarde. Decido comer un pasaboca e ir al cuarto para dormir. Yo sé que voy a tener sueños dulces.

Verbos

abrazar	*to embrace*	recoger	*to pick up*
bajarse de	*to get off*	saltar	*to jump*
dar a (la plaza)	*to face/overlook (the plaza)*	sellar	*to stamp*

Nombres

la aduana	*customs*	el pasaboca	*the snack*
la bienvenida	*the welcome*	la propina	*the tip*
el conductor	*the driver*	un rato	*a little while*
el dueño	*the owner*	el registro	*the register*
la fila	*the line*	la sonrisa	*the smile*
la lágrima	*the tear*	la tarifa	*the fare*
la maleta	*the suitcase*	el viajero	*the traveler*

Conjunción

e   *and*

For reasons of pronunciation, **y** meaning *and* is replaced by **e** before words beginning with **i** or **hi**.

Adjetivos

cariñoso	*affectionate*
emocionado	*excited*

Preguntas

After you have read the selection, answer the following questions in Spanish.

1. ¿Cómo está Isabel al llegar a Italia? Si Ud. piensa que está alegre, ¿por qué? Igualmente, si piensa que está triste, ¿por qué?

   _____

2. ¿Espera ella mucho tiempo en el aeropuerto?

   _____

3. ¿Qué tiempo hace?

   _____

4. ¿Escoge un hotel con cuidado?

   _____

5. ¿Quiere Isabel salir la primera noche? ¿Qué hace?

   _____

12

Reflexive Verbs

A verb is reflexive when the subject and the object refer to the same person. The purpose of the reflexive verb is to show that the action of the verb remains with the subject. This can be seen in the following sentence.

I wash myself.

Subject	Verb	Object
I	*wash*	*myself*

The Reflexive Pronouns

The reflexive pronouns are object pronouns.

me	*myself*	nos	*ourselves*
te	*yourself*	os	*yourselves*
se	*himself, herself, yourself*	se	*themselves, yourselves*

In Spanish reflexive verbs, **-se** is added to the basic infinitive.

To conjugate a reflexive verb, drop the **-se** and place the reflexive pronoun before the conjugated verb. The reflexive verb always has a reflexive pronoun.

lavarse *to wash oneself*

yo **me** lavo	*I wash myself*	nosotros **nos** lavamos	*we wash ourselves*
tú **te** lavas	*you wash yourself*	vosotros **os** laváis	*you wash yourselves*
él **se** lava	*he washes himself*	ellos **se** lavan	*they wash themselves*
ella **se** lava	*she washes herself*	ellas **se** lavan	*they wash themselves*
Ud. **se** lava	*you wash yourself*	Uds. **se** lavan	*you wash yourselves*

193

Compare the reflexive verb with the nonreflexive verb.

Reflexive	Él se lava.	*He washes **himself**.*
Nonreflexive	Él lava el carro.	*He washes **the car**.*

Some Frequently Used Reflexive Verbs

bañarse *to bathe oneself*

yo me baño	nosotros nos bañamos
tú te bañas	vosotros os bañáis
él se baña	ellos se bañan

dedicarse *to dedicate oneself*

yo me dedico	nosotros nos dedicamos
tú te dedicas	vosotros os dedicáis
ella se dedica	ellas se dedican

defenderse *to defend oneself*

yo me defiendo	nosotros nos defendemos
tú te defiendes	vosotros os defendéis
Ud. se defiende	Uds. se defienden

divertirse *to amuse oneself, to have a good time*

yo me divierto	nosotros nos divertimos
tú te diviertes	vosotros os divertís
él se divierte	ellos se divierten

expresarse *to express oneself*

yo me expreso	nosotros nos expresamos
tú te expresas	vosotros os expresáis
ella se expresa	ellas se expresan

llamarse *to call oneself*

yo me llamo	nosotros nos llamamos
tú te llamas	vosotros os llamáis
Ud. se llama	Uds. se llaman

preguntarse *to ask oneself, to wonder*

yo me pregunto	nosotros nos preguntamos
tú te preguntas	vosotros os preguntáis
él se pregunta	ellos se preguntan

A Word About Reflexive Verbs
It is not necessary to use both the subject pronoun and the reflexive pronoun with reflexive verbs, except in the third person for clarity. From now on, the subject pronouns **yo**, **tú**, **nosotros**, and **vosotros** will be omitted. Practice reflexive verbs aloud with their reflexive pronouns.

Reflexive Verbs Whose English Translations Do Not Necessarily Include *Oneself*

acostarse *to go to bed*

me acuesto	nos acostamos
te acuestas	os acostáis
él se acuesta	ellos se acuestan

despertarse *to wake up, to wake oneself*

me despierto	nos despertamos
te despiertas	os despertáis
Ud. se despierta	Uds. se despiertan

ducharse *to shower, to take a shower*

me ducho	nos duchamos
te duchas	os ducháis
él se ducha	ellos se duchan

dormirse *to fall asleep*

me duermo	nos dormimos
te duermes	os dormís
ella se duerme	ellas se duermen

enfermarse *to get sick*

me enfermo	nos enfermamos
te enfermas	os enfermáis
Ud. se enferma	Uds. se enferman

levantarse *to get up, to raise oneself*

me levanto	nos levantamos
te levantas	os levantáis
él se levanta	ellos se levantan

sentarse *to sit down, to seat oneself*

me siento	nos sentamos
te sientas	os sentáis
ella se sienta	ellas se sientan

vestirse *to get dressed*

me visto	nos vestimos
te vistes	os vestís
Ud. se viste	Uds. se visten

Position of the Reflexive Pronoun

The reflexive pronoun can be placed in either of two positions in a sentence or phrase.

In the first position, the reflexive pronoun is placed directly before the conjugated verb.

Nos despertamos a las ocho.	*We wake up at eight o'clock.*
Nos levantamos a las ocho y media.	*We get up at eight thirty.*

| Ellos **se** divierten los fines de semana. | *They have a good time on weekends.* |
| ¿A qué hora **te** acuestas? | *At what time do you go to bed?* |

In the second position, the reflexive pronoun is attached to the infinitive.

Ella va a **dedicarse** a la ley.	*She is going to dedicate herself to the law.*
Voy a **bañarme** antes de **acostarme**.	*I am going to bathe myself before going to bed.*
Queremos **expresarnos** bien en español.	*We want to express ourselves well in Spanish.*

 Exercise 12.1

Complete the following sentences with the correct form of the appropriate verb. Use each verb only one time.

acostarse, bañarse, dedicarse, despertarse, divertirse, dormirse, ducharse, expresarse, levantarse, llamarse, sentarse

1. Soy enfermera; tengo que _____ a las seis de la mañana.

2. Después de despertarme, _____ y voy a la cocina a preparar mi desayuno.

3. Antes de vestirme, _____ o _____ . Me gusta cantar en el baño.

4. A las siete, _____ en la mesa para comer.

5. Tengo dos buenos amigos; _____ Carlos y Julia.

6. Ellos son abogados y _____ a defender a la gente.

7. Trabajamos mucho durante la semana y _____ los fines de semana.

8. Practicamos la gramática de español por horas y horas en conversación y siempre tratamos de _____ bien.

9. Durante la semana, les hablo por teléfono. A mí me gusta leer hasta tarde, pero a ellos les gusta _____ a las once.

10. Me gusta acostarme a las doce. _____ rápidamente.

Reflexive Verbs with Parts of the Body and Clothing

Note that the possessive adjective is not used with reflexive verbs when you are talking about parts of the body or clothing. The definite article is typically used instead.

afeitarse *to shave*

me afeito	nos afeitamos
te afeitas	os afeitáis
él se afeita	ellos se afeitan

cepillarse (los dientes, el pelo)
to brush (one's teeth, one's hair)

me cepillo	nos cepillamos
te cepillas	os cepilláis
ella se cepilla	ellas se cepillan

maquillarse (la cara) *to put makeup on, to make up* (one's face)

me maquillo	nos maquillamos
te maquillas	os maquilláis
Ud. se maquilla	Uds. se maquillan

peinarse (el pelo)
to comb (one's hair)

me peino	nos peinamos
te peinas	os peináis
él se peina	ellos se peinan

pintarse (las uñas) *to put makeup on, to put (nail) polish on*

me pinto	nos pintamos
te pintas	os pintáis
ella se pinta	ellas se pintan

ponerse *to put on* (clothing)

me pongo	nos ponemos
te pones	os ponéis
Ud. se pone	Uds. se ponen

quitarse *to take off* (clothing)

me quito	nos quitamos
te quitas	os quitáis
él se quita	ellos se quitan

Reflexive Verbs That Express Emotion

Regular

alegrarse (de)	*to become happy, to be glad*
animarse	*to cheer up*
asustarse	*to get frightened/scared*
calmarse	*to calm down*
enfadarse (con)	*to get angry*
enojarse (con)	*to get angry*
preocuparse (de)	*to worry*
tranquilizarse	*to calm down*

Reflexive Verbs That Express Movement

Regular

quedarse   *to remain*
mudarse   *to move* (from one place to another)
pararse   *to stand up*

Irregular

caerse *to fall down*	
me caigo	nos caemos
te caes	os caéis
él se cae	ellos se caen

irse *to go away, to leave quickly*	
me voy	nos vamos
te vas	os vais
ella se va	ellas se van

moverse *to move*	
me muevo	nos movemos
te mueves	os movéis
Ud. se mueve	Uds. se mueven

Exercise 12.2

Complete the following sentences with the correct form of the appropriate verb. Use each verb only one time.

afeitarse, alegrarse, caerse, cepillarse, enojarse, mudarse, peinarse, pintarse, ponerse, preocuparse, quedarse, quitarse, tranquilizarse

1. El niño alegre está en el árbol. No tiene miedo de _____ .

2. El esposo _____ la barba mientras su esposa

   _____ las uñas.

3. No entiendo por qué _____ tú si alguien te critica.

4. Al entrar en el apartamento lujoso, nosotros _____ los zapatos.

5. Hace frío y ellos _____ un suéter y una chaqueta.

6. Es un buen hotel, pero no quiero _____ en esta ciudad.

7. El estudiante _____ mucho porque tiene un examen mañana.

8. Voy a _____ a San Francisco; me dicen que es un sitio hermoso.

9. Ella está nerviosa; para _____ ella toma leche caliente.

10. Nosotros _____ mucho de escuchar las buenas noticias.

11. Antes de dormirme, siempre _____ los dientes.

12. Después de despertarse, ellos _____ el cabello.

Reflexive Verbs That Express "To Become"

Ponerse + adjective

Ponerse is the most common expression for *to become*; it is used for physical or emotional changes.

Me pongo brava al escuchar las noticias.	*I become angry upon hearing the news.*
Ella se pone roja porque es tímida.	*She gets red (blushes) because she is shy.*

Volverse + adjective

Volverse is used to express a sudden, involuntary change.

Hasta los psicólogos se vuelven locos.	*Even the psychologists go crazy.*

Hacerse, llegar a ser

Both **hacerse** and **llegar a ser** are used with nouns expressing profession; they imply effort on the part of the subject.

Ella se hace doctora.	*She is becoming a doctor.*
Él llega a ser doctor también.	*He is becoming a doctor also.*

Most Frequently Used Reflexive Verbs

Regular

arreglarse	*to get ready to go out, to fix oneself up*
aprovecharse (de)	*to take advantage of*
atreverse (a)	*to dare to*
burlarse (de)	*to make fun of*
callarse	*to become quiet*
demorarse	*to delay*
desayunarse	*to have breakfast*
enamorarse (de)	*to fall in love with*
equivocarse	*to make a mistake*

fiarse (en)	*to trust, to have trust in*
fijarse (en)	*to notice*
lastimarse	*to hurt oneself*
llevarse (bien) (con)	*to get along (well) with*
mejorarse	*to get better*
meterse (en)	*to get involved in, to meddle*
portarse (bien/mal)	*to behave oneself (well/badly)*
quejarse (de)	*to complain about*
quemarse	*to burn oneself, to get burned*
reunirse (con)	*to meet with*

Irregular

acordarse (de) *to remember*

me acuerdo	nos acordamos
te acuerdas	os acordáis
él se acuerda	ellos se acuerdan

darse cuenta (de) *to realize*

me doy cuenta	nos damos cuenta
te das cuenta	os dais cuenta
ella se da cuenta	ellas se dan cuenta

encontrarse (con) *to meet*

me encuentro	nos encontramos
te encuentras	os encontráis
Ud. se encuentra	Uds. se encuentran

A Word About Prepositions That Follow Reflexive Verbs
The prepositions that follow certain reflexive verbs in Spanish cannot be omitted even if the English translation does not include them.

Me fijo mucho **en** los detalles.	*I notice the details a lot.*
Él se acuerda **de** ella.	*He remembers her.*

morirse *to die*

me muero	nos morimos
te mueres	os morís
él se muere	ellos se mueren

parecerse (a) *to resemble, to look like*

me parezco	nos parecemos
te pareces	os parecéis
Ud. se parece	Uds. se parecen

reírse *to laugh*

me río	nos reímos
te ríes	os reís
él se ríe	ellos se ríen

sentirse (bien/mal) *to feel (well/ill)* (or any emotion or health condition)

me siento	nos sentimos
te sientes	os sentís
ella se siente	ellas se sienten

Exercise 12.3

Complete the following sentences with the correct form of the appropriate reflexive verb. Use each verb only one time. Be sure to include prepositions when you need them.

> acordarse, aprovecharse, atreverse, burlarse, callarse, demorarse, desayunarse, enamorarse, encontrarse, equivocarse, fiarse, fijarse, meterse, parecerse, ponerse, portarse, quejarse, reírse

1. A la familia le gusta comer juntos en la mañana. Siempre

   _____ con cereal y jugo antes de salir de la casa.

2. A los adolescentes les gusta ir a la escuela secundaria porque

   _____ sus amigos todos los días.

3. Muchas personas _____ nerviosas antes de tener
   un examen.

4. La niña feliz piensa que todo es gracioso; ella _____
   todo el tiempo.

5. Él _____ mucho porque habla sin saber nada.

6. Yo no _____ nunca del número de teléfono de mi tío.

7. ¿_____ Ud. de una buena situación?

8. Ella _____ sus vecinos porque hacen mucho ruido.

9. La obra de teatro es interesante; el tiempo pasa rápidamente y la audiencia

   no _____ la hora.

10. Nadie debe _____ nadie.

11. La hija tiene la misma nariz que su mamá. _____ mucho.

12. No me gusta _____ los problemas de otros.

13. Ella llega tarde porque _____ los trenes durante la hora
    pico.

14. El hombre soltero _____ locamente de la mujer hermosa.

15. Nosotros _____ para escuchar hablar al experto que
    habla en voz baja.

16. Carla tiene miedo del agua y no _____ viajar en barco.

17. ¿Piensan Uds. que los adolescentes _____ bien o mal?

18. Él no tiene amigos porque no _____ nadie.

Review Chart of Indirect and Direct Object Pronouns and Reflexive Pronouns

Subject Pronoun	Indirect Object Pronoun	Direct Object Pronoun	Reflexive Pronoun
yo	me	me	me
tú	te	te	te
él	le	lo	se
ella	le	la	se
Ud.	le	le	se
nosotros	nos	nos	nos
vosotros	os	os	os
ellos	les	los	se
ellas	les	las	se
Uds.	les	les	se

Reflexive Verbs with Reciprocal Meanings

The plural forms of reflexive verbs are sometimes used to express the idea of *each other*. If the meaning is unclear, Spanish uses **el uno al otro**, **la una a la otra**, **los unos a los otros**, and **las unas a las otras** for clarification.

ayudarse	*to help each other*
conocerse	*to know each other*
entenderse	*to understand each other*
escribirse	*to write to each other*
hablarse	*to speak to each other*
quererse	*to love each other*
verse	*to see each other*

Elena y Paula se ayudan mucho.	*Helen and Paula help each other a lot.*
Mis amigos se ayudan el uno al otro.	*My friends help each other.*
Nos conocemos bien.	*We know each other well.*
¿Se conocen Uds.?	*Do you know each other?*
Las dos hermanas se entienden bien.	*The two sisters understand each other well.*
Roberto y Sonia se quieren.	*Robert and Sonia love each other.*
Ellos se ven todos los días.	*They see each other every day.*

Se and Impersonal Expressions

In impersonal expressions with **se**, the verb has no personal subject. In English these sentences are translated by subjects such as *one, you, they, people* (in general), or by the passive voice.

The third-person singular or plural of the verb is used in these expressions.

English Construction *How do you say "hello" in Spanish?*
Spanish Construction ¿Cómo **se dice** "hello" en español?

Se vive bien en este país. *One lives well in this country.*
Se cree que los italianos son *It is believed (one believes / people* románticos. *believe) that Italians are romantic.*
Se sabe que él es un buen *It is known that he is a good worker.* trabajador.

Aquí **se habla** español. { *One speaks Spanish here.*
 Spanish is spoken here.

No **se permite** nadar aquí. *It is not permitted to swim here.*
¿Dónde **se puede** estacionar *Where can one park in New York?* en Nueva York?
Se prohíbe fumar. *It is prohibited to smoke.*

Exercise 12.4

Complete the story by filling in the blanks with the verbs in parentheses.

Ricardo _____ (1. *wakes up*) a las seis todos los días.

Él _____ (2. *takes a shower*) antes de _____

(3. *to get dressed*). Le gusta _____ (4. *to have breakfast*)

en casa antes de salir para su trabajo. Ricardo _____

(5. *meets with*) sus colegas a las siete y media de la mañana. Todos son

bomberos y _____ (6. *dedicate themselves*) a apagar

incendios. _____ (7. *They help each other*).

_____ (8. *One says*) que los bomberos son héroes;

_____ (9. *they dare to*) a entrar en edificios peligrosos

sin _____ (10. *to worry*). Ellos ayudan a la gente a

_____ (11. *calm down*) y _____ (12. *to feel*)

mejor. De vez en cuando, _____ (13. *they delay*) en apagar

el incendio y el edificio _____ (14. *gets burned*). Ricardo

_____ (15. *stays*) en la estación de bomberos por tres días.

Al regresar a casa, él come algo, _____ (16. *takes a bath*),

_____ (17. *goes to bed*) temprano y _____

(18. *falls asleep*) rápidamente.

 ## Reading Comprehension

El encuentro

Me despierto bien. Me gustan las cortinas delgadas porque dejan entrar
la luz de la mañana. Más allá de mi ventana, veo las plantas exuberantes
de verde radiante. Después de ducharme largamente, me pongo un vestido
sencillo pero elegante y salgo del hotel con el libro de turismo en mi bolsa.
Busco un restaurante acogedor para tomar el primer café del día. Entro
en uno que tiene un ambiente agradable y miro todos los pasteles.
No puedo escoger entre el de nata y la torta con crema y fruta; pues,
pido dos pasteles y un café solo, y me los da. Me siento en una mesa
hermosa para dos.

El café está fuerte y delicioso. No hay razón para apresurarme y como
los pasteles tranquilamente. El restaurante se llena; se ve que la gente
es muy amable y habladora. Conversan con todo el cuerpo, sobre todo
con las manos. ¿De qué hablan, tan animados, a esta hora tan temprano
de la mañana?

No conozco a nadie. Pero me parece posible encontrarme a alguien,
a una persona con quien pueda tener una conversación interesante. (Este
restaurante es un buen sitio; no me muevo de aquí por un rato.) Alguien
va a verme, aquí sentada, y en vez de pasar por mi mesa sin decir nada,
me va a decir; "Señorita, está ocupada esta silla?" Yo le voy a contestar con
una sonrisa, "No, Ud. puede sentarse." Y él se sienta complacido. Dentro
de poco somos amigos, y después de tomar otro café y otro pastel, él me
invita a acompañarlo a un museo y tomar un vino con él. Charlamos y nos
reímos y nos divertimos mucho durante nuestra cena de pescado y
camarones. A lo lejos, en la distancia, lo veo venir.

Verbos

apresurarse	*to rush*	escoger	*to choose*
charlar	*to chat*	llenarse	*to fill up*
conversar	*to converse*	moverse	*to move*
dejar	*to let*	pedir	*to ask for, to request*

Nombres

los camarones	*the shrimp*
la nata	*the cream*
el pastel	*the pastry*

Adjetivos

acogedor	*cozy*	hablador(-a)	*talkative*
animado	*energetic, excited*	ocupado	*busy*
complacido	*satisfied*	radiante	*radiant*
delgado	*thin, slim*	sentado	*seated*

Expresiones

a lo lejos	*far away*
más allá de mi ventana	*outside my window*
sobre todo	*above all*

Preguntas

After you have read the selection, answer the following questions in Spanish.

1. ¿Cómo se despierta?

   _____

2. Después de vestirse, ¿adónde va?

   _____

3. ¿Por qué escoge ella una mesa para dos?

   _____

4. Mientras ella come los pasteles, ¿lee Isabel su libro?

   _____

5. ¿Dónde tiene lugar la conversación que ella tiene con el hombre?

   _____

6. Al final de este cuento, ¿está ella sola o acompañada?

   _____

13

The Present Subjunctive

The present subjunctive is a mood in the present tense, widely used in Spanish but rarely used in English. So far you have studied the present tense in the indicative mood, the most frequently used mood in the language. This chapter introduces the present subjunctive. It is important to learn it now so that you can express yourself confidently and freely in the present tense.

The present subjunctive cannot exist alone. Another element in the sentence always causes it to be used. The subjunctive is often needed after the following elements.

- Certain impersonal expressions
- Certain verbs
- Certain conjunctions
- Certain dependent adjective clauses
- Certain expressions

Formation of the Present Subjunctive

- Almost all verbs form the present subjunctive from the first-person singular **yo** form of the present indicative. Drop the **-o** to get the stem for the present subjunctive.

- Verbs that are irregular in the present indicative are irregular in the present subjunctive in the same way.

- There are only six verbs that do not form the present subjunctive from the **yo** form of the present indicative.

-Ar **Verbs**

In order to conjugate both regular and irregular **-ar** verbs in the present subjunctive, you start with the **yo** form of the present indicative. Drop the **-o** and add **-e**, **-es**, **-e**, **-emos**, **-éis**, **-en** to the stem.

Infinitive	**yo** Form	Present Subjunctive	
cantar	canto	yo cante	nosotros cantemos
		tú cantes	vosotros cantéis
		él cante	ellos canten
bailar	bailo	yo baile	nosotros bailemos
		tú bailes	vosotros bailéis
		ella baile	ellas bailen
cerrar	cierro	yo cierre	nosotros cerremos
		tú cierres	vosotros cerréis
		Ud. cierre	Uds. cierren
pensar	pienso	yo piense	nosotros pensemos
		tú pienses	vosotros penséis
		ella piense	ellas piensen
recordar	recuerdo	yo recuerde	nosotros recordemos
		tú recuerdes	vosotros recordéis
		él recuerde	ellos recuerden

Note that the first-person singular and the third-personal singular are identical in the present subjunctive.

The first two examples, **cantar** and **bailar**, are regular. The last three, **cerrar**, **pensar**, and **recordar**, are irregular in the present indicative. Note that their stem changes in the present indicative are also present in the present subjunctive, except in the **nosotros** and **vosotros** forms, which are unaffected by stem changes.

A Word About the Present Subjunctive

The formation of the subjunctive comes from the conjugation of the *first-person singular* of the present indicative. Any irregularity that the verb has in the present indicative **yo** form also occurs in the present subjunctive. To learn the subjunctive well, practice the **yo** form of the verbs, because that will be the stem of the present subjunctive.

-*Er* and -*ir* Verbs

In order to conjugate both regular and irregular **-er** and **-ir** verbs in the present subjunctive, you drop the **-o** from the first-person singular of the present indicative and add **-a**, **-as**, **-a**, **-amos**, **-áis**, **-an** to the stem.

-*Er* Verbs

Infinitive	**yo** Form	Present Subjunctive	
comer	como	yo coma	nosotros comamos
		tú comas	vosotros comáis
		él coma	ellos coman
querer	quiero	yo quiera	nosotros queramos
		tú quieras	vosotros queráis
		ella quiera	ellas quieran
poder	puedo	yo pueda	nosotros podamos
		tú puedas	vosotros podáis
		Ud. pueda	Uds. puedan
ver	veo	yo vea	nosotros veamos
		tú veas	vosotros veáis
		él vea	ellos vean

-*Ir* Verbs

Infinitive	**yo** Form	Present Subjunctive	
vivir	vivo	yo viva	nosotros vivamos
		tú vivas	vosotros viváis
		él viva	ellos vivan
mentir	miento	yo mienta	nosotros mintamos
		tú mientas	vosotros mintáis
		ella mienta	ellas mientan
pedir	pido	yo pida	nosotros pidamos
		tú pidas	vosotros pidáis
		Ud. pida	Uds. pidan
dormir	duermo	yo duerma	nosotros durmamos
		tú duermas	vosotros durmáis
		él duerma	ellos duerman

NOTE: In the irregular **-ir** verbs, there is an additional irregularity in the **nosotros** and **vosotros** forms. The stem change **e** > **ie** or **e** > **i** has an **-i-** in the **nosotros** and **vosotros** forms. The stem change **o** > **ue** has a **-u-** in the **nosotros** and **vosotros** forms.

-Er and *-ir* Verbs with *-g-* or *-zc-* in the *yo* Form

In the present subjunctive, certain **-er** and **-ir** verbs carry the irregularity of the first-person singular throughout the conjugation. There are no **-ar** verbs that have this irregularity.

Infinitive	**yo** Form	Present Subjunctive	
conocer	conozco	yo conozca	nosotros conozcamos
		tú conozcas	vosotros conozcáis
		él conozca	ellos conozcan
decir	digo	yo diga	nosotros digamos
		tú digas	vosotros digáis
		ella diga	ellas digan
hacer	hago	yo haga	nosotros hagamos
		tú hagas	vosotros hagáis
		Ud. haga	Uds. hagan
poner	pongo	yo ponga	nosotros pongamos
		tú pongas	vosotros pongáis
		él ponga	ellos pongan
salir	salgo	yo salga	nosotros salgamos
		tú salgas	vosotros salgáis
		ella salga	ellas salgan
tener	tengo	yo tenga	nosotros tengamos
		tú tengas	vosotros tengáis
		Ud. tenga	Uds. tengan
traer	traigo	yo traiga	nosotros traigamos
		tú traigas	vosotros traigáis
		él traiga	ellos traigan
venir	vengo	yo venga	nosotros vengamos
		tú vengas	vosotros vengáis
		ella venga	ellas vengan

Irregular Verbs

There are only six verbs that have a present subjunctive that is not formed from the first-person singular. They are irregular in that they cannot be formed from the **yo** form.

Infinitive	**yo** Form	Present Subjunctive	
dar	doy	yo dé	nosotros demos
		tú des	vosotros deis
		él dé	ellos den
estar	estoy	yo esté	nosotros estemos
		tú estés	vosotros estéis
		ella esté	ellas estén
ir	voy	yo vaya	nosotros vayamos
		tú vayas	vosotros vayáis
		Ud. vaya	Uds. vayan
saber	sé	yo sepa	nosotros sepamos
		tú sepas	vosotros sepáis
		él sepa	ellos sepan
ser	soy	yo sea	nosotros seamos
		tú seas	vosotros seáis
		ella sea	ellas sean
haber	he	yo haya	nosotros hayamos
		tú hayas	vosotros hayáis
		Ud. haya	Uds. hayan

NOTES: **Dé** (the form for both the first- and third-person singular of **dar**) has a written accent to distinguish it from **de** (*of*).

The word **hay** comes from the infinitive **haber**. You will not need this form for any other use at this time.

Verbs with Orthographic Changes

Verbs with orthographic changes are not irregular. The spelling changes simply maintain the sound of the **yo** form. Some of the most common spelling changes are the following.

- Verbs that end in **-gar** change **g** to **gu**.
- Verbs that end in **-car** change **c** to **qu**.
- Verbs that end in **-zar** change **z** to **c**.

Infinitive	**yo** Form	Present Subjunctive	
apagar	apago	yo apague	nosotros apaguemos
		tú apagues	vosotros apaguéis
		él apague	ellos apaguen
buscar	busco	yo busque	nosotros busquemos
		tú busques	vosotros busquéis
		Ud. busque	Uds. busquen
comenzar	comienzo	yo comience	nosotros comencemos
		tú comiences	vosotros comencéis
		ella comience	ellas comiencen
empezar	empiezo	yo empiece	nosotros empecemos
		tú empieces	vosotros empecéis
		él empiece	ellos empiecen
explicar	explico	yo explique	nosotros expliquemos
		tú expliques	vosotros expliquéis
		Ud. explique	Uds. expliquen
llegar	llego	yo llegue	nosotros lleguemos
		tú llegues	vosotros lleguéis
		ella llegue	ellas lleguen
tocar	toco	yo toque	nosotros toquemos
		tú toques	vosotros toquéis
		Ud. toque	Uds. toquen

NOTE: The change **z** > **c** occurs before the vowel **e** without affecting the sound. The consonants **c** (before **i** and **e**), **s**, and **z** all have the same sound.

A Word About Pronunciation of the Present Subjunctive

Like the present indicative, the stress in the present subjunctive tense is on the second to last syllable. As you practice, make sure you pronounce the verbs in this way: **yo can̲te, tú can̲tes, él can̲te, nosotros cantem̲os, ellos can̲ten.** If a word carries an accent mark, stress the accented syllable: **vosotros cant̲éis.**

Uses of the Present Subjunctive

Remember that the subjunctive mood cannot exist alone; it must always be caused by some other element in the sentence. This is a mood that expresses wishes, doubts, and what is possible, rather than what is certain. Following are the specific uses of the present subjunctive.

After Certain Impersonal Expressions

A sentence or question may consist of a main clause and a dependent or subordinate clause connected by the Spanish conjunction **que**.

Here is a sentence with a main clause and a subordinate clause in the indicative mood.

Él sabe   = the main clause
que yo cocino bien.   = the dependent clause

However, suppose that the main clause has an impersonal expression, such as **Es dudoso**. This causes the subjunctive to be used in the dependent clause.

Es dudoso que yo **cocine** bien.   *It is doubtful that I cook well.*

Frequently used impersonal expressions are the following.

es bueno (que)	*it is good (that)*
es difícil (que)	*it is difficult (that)*
es dudoso (que)	*it is doubtful (that)*
es fácil (que)	*it is easy (that)*
es imposible (que)	*it is impossible (that)*
es importante (que)	*it is important (that)*
es malo (que)	*it is bad (that)*
es mejor (que)	*it is better (that)*
es necesario (que)	*it is necessary (that)*
es posible (que)	*it is possible (that)*
es probable (que)	*it is probable (that)*
es preciso (que)	*it is extremely necessary (that)*
es una lástima (que)	*it is a pity (that)*
es urgente (que)	*it is urgent (that)*

Es importante que ella **coma** bien.   *It is important that she eat well.*
Es necesario que **estudiemos**   *It is necessary that we study for*
   para el examen.   *the test.*

Es imposible que él **tenga** razón.	*It is impossible that he is right.*
¿Es posible que ella **venga** mañana?	*Is it possible that she will come tomorrow?*
Es probable que mi amiga me **vea** en el restaurante.	*It is probable that my friend will see me in the restaurant.*
Es un lástima que Pedro no lo **quiera** hacer.	*It is a pity that Peter doesn't want to do it.*
Es dudoso que **viajemos** a España.	*It is doubtful that we will travel to Spain.*

Once you begin a sentence with one of the impersonal expressions above, it is mandatory to use the subjunctive in the dependent clause. You do not have to make any decisions, nor do you have a choice about whether or not to use it. These impersonal expressions in the main clause always trigger the subjunctive in the subordinate clause.

Notice that some of the example sentences and questions above are translated with the future in English. This is because the present subjunctive carries with it a feeling of the future and doubt.

If you wish to make a general statement with an impersonal expression, you need neither a dependent clause nor a subjunctive. You simply use the structure you have already learned, which follows English word order.

Es importante comer bien.	*It is important to eat well.*
¿Es necesario trabajar mucho?	*Is it necessary to work a lot?*
Es posible salir temprano.	*It is possible to leave early.*
Es bueno nadar cada día.	*It is good to swim every day.*

 ## Exercise 13.1

Complete the following sentences with the correct form of the verb in parentheses.

EXAMPLE   Es importante que nuestros amigos __*vengan*__ a la fiesta. (venir)

1. Es posible que él me _____ la verdad. (decir)

2. Es una lástima que Sara no lo _____. (hacer)

3. ¿Es posible que Uds. _____ a mi amigo Raúl? (conocer)

4. Es necesario que nosotros _____ bien. (dormir)

5. Es importante que ella _____ bien las direcciones. (saber)

6. Es necesario que nosotros _____ mucha agua fría en el verano. (tomar)

7. Es dudoso que ellos _____ temprano. (levantarse)

8. ¿Es posible que ella _____ a tiempo? (llegar)

9. Es posible que yo _____ en Francia. (quedarse)

10. Es probable que mucha gente importante _____ en la conferencia. (estar)

11. Es difícil que yo te _____ una buena respuesta. (dar)

12. Es urgente que tú _____ al doctor hoy. (ir)

13. Es dudoso que ellos _____ ricos. (ser)

14. Es importante que los padres les _____ a sus hijos. (leer)

15. La niña acaba de comer. Es imposible que _____ hambre. (tener)

16. Es probable que nosotros le _____ flores al profesor. (traer)

17. Es bueno que Uds. _____ mejor. (sentirse)

After Certain Verbs

Expressing Wishes or Preferences

Verbs that express wishes or preferences *with regard to other people* in the main clause will cause the subjunctive mood in the dependent clause. The subject in the main clause must be different from the subject in the dependent clause.

querer	*to want*
desear	*to desire, to want*
preferir	*to prefer*

Here is a sentence with a main clause and a subordinate clause in the indicative mood.

Él sabe	= the main clause
que yo canto.	= the dependent clause

However, suppose that the main clause has one of the verbs above, such as **Él quiere**. This causes the subjunctive to be used in the dependent clause.

Él quiere que yo **cante**.
{ *He wants that I sing.*
{ *He wants me to sing.*

The English equivalent does not always show the distinction in moods like Spanish does. But even in the English translation of the above example, it is clear that the person in the main clause, *he*, wants the other person, *me*, to do something.

Quiero que él **baile**.	*I want him to dance.*
Deseamos que ella **esté** bien.	*We want her to be well.*
Ella prefiere que su hijo **juegue** al béisbol.	*She prefers that her son play baseball.*

If there is only one subject for the two verbs in a sentence, there is neither a dependent clause nor a subjunctive.

Yo quiero cantar.	*I want to sing.*
Deseamos descansar.	*We want to rest.*
Ella prefiere dormir.	*She prefers to sleep.*

Expressing Hope, Happiness, Sadness, or Regret

Verbs that express hope, happiness, sadness, or regret with regard to other people in the main clause will cause the subjunctive mood in the dependent clause.

alegrarse de	*to be glad*
esperar	*to hope*
estar contento de	*to be happy*
estar triste de	*to be sad*
gustarle a uno	*to be pleasing*
sentir	*to regret*
tener miedo de, temer	*to be afraid of, to fear*

Me alegro de que Uds. **estén** bien.	*I am glad that you are well.*
Esperamos que Ud. **tenga** un buen fin de semana.	*We hope that you have a good weekend.*
La maestra está contenta de que **hagamos** la tarea.	*The teacher is happy that we do the homework.*
¿Estás triste de que no **podamos** aceptar tu invitación?	*Are you sad that we cannot accept your invitation?*
Me gusta que mi familia **venga** a verme.	*It pleases me that my family is coming to see me.*
Lo siento que Ud. nunca se **gane** la lotería.	*I am sorry that you never win the lottery.*

El líder tiene miedo de que el grupo no **resuelva** el problema.	*The leader fears that the group will not resolve the problem.*
Los padres temen que sus hijos no **quieran** estudiar.	*The parents fear that their children don't want to study.*

If there is only one subject for the two verbs in a sentence, the sentence follows the basic structure that you have learned.

Me alegro de estar aquí.	*I am glad to be here.*
Él espera salir dentro de una hora.	*He hopes to leave within the hour.*
Me gusta ir al cine.	*It pleases me to go to the movies.*
Ella tiene miedo de volar.	*She is afraid of flying.*

Expressing Orders, Requests, or Advice

Verbs that express orders, requests, or advice in the main clause will cause the subjunctive mood in the dependent clause.

aconsejar	*to advise*
decir	*to tell* (someone to do something)
dejar	*to permit, to let*
insistir en	*to insist*
pedir	*to request, to ask for*
permitir	*to permit*
prohibir	*to prohibit*
mandar	*to order*
sugerir	*to suggest*

Te aconsejo que **tomes** el tren.	*I advise you to take the train.*
Ella insiste en que yo **me quede**.	*She insists that I stay.*
Les pedimos que **vayan** de vacaciones.	*We ask them to go on vacation.*
Le sugiero que Ud. **lea** este artículo.	*I suggest that you read this article.*

Dejar, **permitir**, **prohibir**, and **mandar** can be used in two ways.

Les dejo que **entren.** Les dejo entrar.	*I let them enter.*
Te permito que **nades** aquí. Te permito nadar aquí.	*I permit you to swim here.*
Te prohíbo que **fumes** en la casa. Te prohíbo fumar en la casa.	*I prohibit you to smoke in the house.*

El capitán les manda que los soldados **descansen**. Les manda descansar.	*The captain orders the soldiers to rest. He orders them to rest.*

Decir is used, as you have learned, to relate a fact. This idea is expressed with the indicative.

José nos dice que el tren viene.	*Joe tells us that the train is coming.*
Ella me dice que le gusta viajar.	*She tells me that she likes to travel.*

However, when **decir** is used to give an *order*, the subjunctive is used in the dependent clause.

Yo te digo que **vayas** al doctor.	*I tell you to go to the doctor.*
Ud. me dice que yo **me quede.**	*You tell me to stay.*
Les decimos que **se acuesten** ahora.	*We tell them to go to bed now.*
Él nos dice que **tengamos** cuidado.	*He tells us to be careful.*
¿Puede Ud. decirle que me **llame**?	*Can you tell her to call me?*

Notice that when English *to tell* is being used to order someone to do something, the command form is always the conjugation of the verb *to tell* + the infinitive.

An English command is expressed as follows: *He tells me to go.*

Compare that to simply relating a fact: *He tells me that the bus is here.*

Expressing Doubt or Uncertainty

Verbs that express doubt or uncertainty in the main clause will cause the subjunctive mood in the dependent clause.

dudar	*to doubt*
no creer	*not to believe*
no pensar	*not to think*

Ella duda que yo **sepa** tocar el piano.	*She doubts that I know how to play the piano.*
La gente no cree que **sea** la verdad.	*The people don't believe that it is the truth.*
No pensamos que Daniel nos **invite** a la fiesta.	*We don't think that Daniel will invite us to the party.*

Exercise 13.2

Complete the following sentences with the correct form of the present subjunctive.

1. ¿Qué quieres que yo te _____? (decir)
2. Él quiere que su amiga _____ la cuenta. (pagar)
3. Espero que Uds. _____ bien. (sentirse)
4. Ellos se alegran de que el bebé _____. (dejar de llorar)
5. Ellos nos piden que _____ mejor la idea. (explicar)
6. A él no le gusta que yo siempre _____ razón. (tener)
7. Rosa insiste en que su jefe le _____ más dinero. (dar)
8. No creo que Alicia _____ la fecha. (saber)
9. Ellas dudan que _____ mucho tráfico hoy. (haber)
10. Les sugiero a sus padres que _____ de vacaciones. (ir)
11. Me alegro de que no _____ nada grave. (ser)
12. Los expertos nos aconsejan que _____ ejercicio. (hacer)
13. Paula espera que su hermana _____ bien. (estar)
14. Yo dudo que Uds. me _____ en la reunión. (ver)

Exercise 13.3

Rewrite the following indicative sentences so that the subjunctive is required. Choose any appropriate verb that causes the subjunctive to be needed in the dependent clause.

EXAMPLE   A mis padres les gusta viajar. _Quiero que ellos viajen._

1. Mi amigo tiene malos sueños. _____
2. Ella no se divierte mucho. _____
3. Nosotros somos buenos estudiantes.

   _____

4. No vamos a volver a los Estados Unidos.

   _____

5. Sara me trae flores a mi casa. _____

6. ¿Conoce Ud. a mi tío? [Write a response.]

_____

7. Mi hermano y yo no nos vemos mucho.

_____

8. ¿Hay clase los lunes? _____

9. Carla es de Polonia. _____

✎ Exercise 13.4

Indicative or subjunctive? _Complete the following sentences with the correct form of the verb in parentheses._

EXAMPLES   Espero que Uds. ___*tengan*___ un buen fin de semana. (tener)

               Yo sé que Uds. ___*tienen*___ muchos amigos. (tener)

1. Ricardo prefiere que yo lo _____ en febrero. (visitar)

2. Él quiere que nosotros le _____ recuerdos. (traer)

3. Nos gusta que él nos _____. (amar)

4. Es importante que nos _____ cada año. (ver)

5. ¿Sabe Ud. que ellos _____ aquí? (estar)

6. Yo pienso que Rosario _____ poco. (quejarse)

7. Dudo que ella _____. (entender)

8. Lo sentimos que tú no _____ acompañarnos. (poder)

9. Espero que ella _____ de las instrucciones. (acordarse)

10. ¿No crees que aquellas tortas _____ deliciosas? (estar)

✎ Exercise 13.5

Complete the story with the correct form (subjunctive, indicative, or infinitive) of each verb in parentheses.

Mariana _____ (1. levantarse) temprano porque hoy

sus nietos quieren _____ (2. ir) al circo. Ella insiste

en que ellos _____ (3. desayunarse) bien antes

de _____ (4. salir). Ella espera que

_____ (5. divertirse) mucho porque el circo

_____ (6. venir) raras veces a su pueblo. Hace frío y ella

les aconseja que _____ (7. ponerse) la chaqueta para

el invierno. Ellos están contentos de que su abuela _____

(8. ser) tan simpática.

After Certain Conjunctions

A subjunctive form follows directly after one of the following conjunctions
if the main clause has a different subject than the dependent clause.

a pesar de que	*in spite of*
antes de que	*before*
después de que	*after*
en caso de que	*in case*
hasta que	*until*
para que	*in order that, so that*
sin que	*without*

Here is a sentence in which there is only one subject.

Ella practica el piano **antes de cantar**.	*She practices the piano before singing.*

In the following sentence, there are two subjects connected by the conjunction **que**.

Ella practica el piano **antes de que** él **cante**.	*She practices the piano before he sings.*

The English equivalent does not show the distinction in moods the way
Spanish does. However, there are clearly two subjects in the example above:
she and *he*.

Él enseña **para que** los estudiantes **aprendan**.	*He teaches so that the students learn.*
Voy a esperar **hasta que** tú **llegues**.	*I am going to wait until you arrive.*
Lo voy a hacer **sin que** Ud. me **ayude**.	*I'm going to do it without your helping me.*

If there is only one subject in the sentence, an infinitive will follow the preposition.

Ella estudia para aprender.	*She studies in order to learn.*
Después de trabajar, ella descansa.	*After working, she rests.*
Él habla sin pensar.	*He speaks without thinking.*

Some conjunctions of time always cause a subjunctive, whether there are two subjects or only one in the sentence. Such conjunctions are the following.

a menos que	*unless*
luego que	*as soon as*
tan pronto como	*as soon as*

Vamos a bailar **a menos que** no **haya** música.	*We are going to dance unless there is no music.*
Voy a llegar **tan pronto como** yo **pueda**.	*I am going to arrive as soon as I can.*

After *cuando*

The subjunctive form directly follows **cuando** if the future is implied.

Vamos a viajar **cuando tengamos** tiempo y dinero.	*We are going to travel when we have time and money.*
¿Me puedes llamar **cuando llegues** a casa?	*Can you call me when you arrive home?*
El niño quiere ser bombero **cuando sea** grande.	*The child wants to be a fireman when he grows up.*

When **cuando** introduces a question, the indicative form is used.

¿Cuándo vas a estar en casa?	*When are you going to be home?*
¿Cuándo quieren Uds. viajar?	*When do you want to travel?*

When **cuando** introduces a sentence that involves either a repeated action or a general statement in the present, the indicative mood is used.

Cuando hace frío, los niños juegan en la nieve.	*When it is cold, the children play in the snow.*
Ella se siente alegre cuando baila.	*She feels happy when she dances.*
Cuando voy a la playa, siempre me divierto.	*When I go to the beach, I always have a good time.*

Exercise 13.6

Complete the following sentences, using the verbs and conjunctions in parentheses.

EXAMPLE   Él va a limpiar su apartamento ___*antes de que*___ (*before*) su

familia lo __*visite*__ . (*to visit*)

1. _____ (*after*) yo _____ (*to bathe myself*), voy a vestirme.

2. No voy _____ (*unless*) Uds. _____ (*to go*) también.

3. Él va a invitar a su amiga a la fiesta _____ (*as soon as*)

   él _____ (*to have*) confianza.

4. Les doy las instrucciones _____ (*so that*) ellos

   _____ (*to know how*) llegar.

5. Uds. pueden jugar al baloncesto _____ (*as soon as*)

   Uds. _____ (*to finish*) su tarea.

6. _____ (*before*) su novio _____ (*to come*) a verla, Rosa va a arreglarse.

7. Te presto el dinero _____ (*so that*) tú

   _____ (*to be able to*) comprar un carro usado.

8. Vamos a estar aquí _____ (*until*) ellos

   _____ . (*to arrive*)

9. _____ (*in case*) Uds. no _____ (*to have*) nada que hacer mañana, ¿podemos ir al cine?

10. A Ricardo no le gusta estudiar. Pero va a estudiar _____

    (*so that*) sus padres _____ (*to be*) contentos.

11. _____ (*in spite of*) ellos _____ (*to be*) frío, ellos quieren dar una vuelta.

12. Tú puedes venir a mi casa _____ (*without*) yo te

    _____ . (*to invite*)

13. Graciela va a descansar _____ (*after*) sus nietos

    _____ . (*to go away*)

14. Cuando Ud. _____ (*to be able*), ¿me puede acompañar al tren?

15. Elena me va a ver cuando nosotros _____ (*to meet*) en México.

16. Cuando ellos _____ (*to return*) a los Estados Unidos, van a comprar una casa pequeña.

17. El hombre va a estar contento cuando _____ (*to learn*) a manejar.

In Certain Dependent Adjective Clauses

The subjunctive mood is used in the dependent clause if the object or person described in the main clause is indefinite or nonexistent. In the following examples, the objects and persons described in the main clause are not known.

Busco **un apartamento** que **sea** grande y barato.	*I am looking for an apartment that is big and cheap.*
¿Conoce Ud. a **alguien** que **sepa** hablar alemán?	*Do you know anyone who knows how to speak German?*
¿Hay **alguien** aquí que **baile** bien?	*Is there anyone here who dances well?*
No hay **nadie** que siempre **tenga** razón.	*There is no one who is always right.*

After the Expressions *por más que* and *por mucho que*

Por más que ella **limpie**, su casa está siempre desordenada.	*No matter how much she cleans, her house is always a mess.*
Por mucho que él **coma**, no se engorda.	*No matter how much he eats, he doesn't get fat.*

After *ojalá*

An interjection of Arabic origin, **ojalá** means *would to God that* or *may God grant* and expresses great desire. It can also be translated as *I hope*.

Ojalá que ella **tenga** suerte.	*Would to God that she has luck.*
Ojalá que Uds. **reciban** el cheque.	*I hope you receive the check.*
Ojalá que él **se quede**.	*Would to God that he stays.*

After *acaso*, *quizás*, and *tal vez*

Acaso él me **visite** mañana.   *Perhaps he will visit me tomorrow.*
Quizás ellos me **digan** la verdad.   *Perhaps they will tell me the truth.*
Tal vez me **digan** mentiras.   *Perhaps they will tell me lies.*

After *aunque*

The subjunctive mood is used if the action has not yet occurred.

Voy al cine **aunque** no **vayan**   *I am going to the movies although*
mis amigos.   *my friends may not go.*
Aunque Pedro **se quede** esta   *Although Peter may stay tonight,*
noche, yo voy a salir.   *I am going to leave.*
Aunque sea difícil, él lo puede   *Although it may be difficult,*
hacer.   *he can do it.*

After Compounds of -*quiera*

Quienquiera que **esté** aquí,   *Whoever is here can leave with us.*
puede salir con nosotros.
Cualquiera que **sea** sincero,   *Whichever (one) is sincere can be*
puede ser un buen amigo.   *a good friend.*
Adondequiera que **vayas**,   *Wherever you go, I wish you the*
te deseo lo mejor.   *best.*
Dondequiera que **estén ellos**,   *Wherever they are, I am going to*
los voy a buscar.   *look for them.*

After *como*

The subjunctive mood is used after **como** if the meaning is *however.*

Ellas van a preparar la comida   *They are going to prepare the meal*
como tú **quieras**.   *however you want.*

 ## Exercise 13.7

Complete the following sentences with the correct form of the verb in parentheses.

1. Tal vez ellos _____ por la comida. (enfermarse)

2. Ojalá que nosotros _____ hoy. (descansar)

3. Aunque él _____ mañana, no quiero lavar el baño. (llegar)

4. Por mucho que ellas _____, no van a hacer nada. (quejarse)

5. Quienquiera que _____ bien, puede ser experto. (cocinar)

6. Ojalá que tú _____ bien esta noche. (dormir)

7. Aunque _____ mucho tráfico, queremos viajar. (haber)

8. Mi amiga busca un apartamento que _____ tres cuartos. (tener)

9. Carlos necesita una casa que _____ en el campo. (estar)

10. El hombre quiere hacer el proyecto como Ud. lo _____. (querer)

11. No conozco a nadie que me _____ a la playa. (acompañar)

12. Ella busca un novio que _____ inteligente. (ser)

13. Quizás él _____ la semana que viene. (venir)

14. Por más que Tomás _____, no sabe nada. (hablar)

Exercise 13.8

Subjunctive or indicative? *Complete the following sentences with the correct form of the verb in parentheses.*

1. Es importante que yo _____ temprano. (acostarse)

2. Esperamos que ella _____. (mejorarse)

3. Yo sé que las lecciones _____ difíciles. (ser)

4. ¿Quiere Ud. que Leopoldo _____ la historia? (estudiar)

5. No pienso que Loreta _____ bien el violín. (tocar)

6. Sabemos que a ella no le _____ practicar. (gustar)

7. Lo sentimos que Uds. no _____ a la conferencia mañana. (ir)

8. Es posible que _____ mucha gente interesante. (haber)

9. Espero que ellos _____ en su casa cuando yo

   _____ . (estar/llegar)

10. Cuando Linda _____ de vacaciones, ella se relaja siempre. (ir)

11. María quiere que Pedro _____ a sus padres. (conocer)

12. Por mucho que yo _____ , no pierdo peso. (nadar)

13. Ojalá que Uds. _____ pronto. (volver)

14. Ella quiere que tú la _____ el primero de mayo. (visitar)

15. ¿Conoce Ud. a alguien que _____ hacer todo lo que
    quiere hacer? (poder)

16. La madre quiere que los niños _____ la mesa. (poner)

17. Ella insiste en que ellos _____ la tarea antes de jugar.
    (hacer)

18. Se alegran de que Uds. _____ mejor. Esperan que Uds.

    _____ bien y contentos. (sentirse/estar)

19. ¿Por qué dudas que Rosa y Reinaldo _____
    en noviembre? (casarse)

20. Te aconsejo que _____ al dentista tres veces por año. (ir)

21. Pensamos que tú _____ despertarte más temprano para
    llegar a tiempo. (deber)

22. Carmen piensa que su amigo _____ un buen carro.
    (necesitar)

Exercise 13.9

Subjunctive, indicative, or infinitive? *Complete the following sentences with the correct form of the verb in parentheses.*

1. José y Susana están enamorados y _____ casarse. (querer)

2. Es difícil que yo te _____ la respuesta correcta. (dar)

3. ¿Es importante _____ honesto en este mundo? (ser)

4. Después de _____ ocho horas, me siento bien. (dormir)

5. Hablo despacio para que mis estudiantes me _____ .
   (entender)

6. A Francisco le gusta _____ mucho. (leer)

7. A los amigos de Julia les gusta que ella _____ mucho. (reírse)

8. Te pido que _____ tu oficio. (hacer)

9. Yo sé que el restaurante que nos gusta _____ lejos de tu oficina. ¿Quieres que yo _____ otro? (estar/escoger)

10. ¿Es posible que nosotros _____ cenar juntos? (poder)

11. Es importante que Uds. _____ del edificio rápida y tranquilamente. (salir)

12. ¿Es importante _____ bien para _____ bien? (comer/vivir)

13. Carla tiene la bolsa que me _____ . (gustar)

14. Ella me dice que los guantes _____ de cuero. (ser)

15. ¿Quieren ellos que nosotros _____ los artículos sobre la contaminación de las ciudades grandes? (buscar)

16. ¿Sabe Ud. por qué Irene no _____ nunca la chaqueta cuando _____ frío? (ponerse/hacer)

17. Me alegro de _____ aquí. Me alegro de que Uds. _____ aquí también. (estar/estar)

18. ¿Es necesario _____ para _____ otro idioma? (viajar/aprender)

19. Les muestro a Uds. las fotos luego que _____ . (llegar)

20. Él se alegra de que su esposa _____ abogada. (ser)

21. Ella prefiere _____ hasta las nueve, pero su jefe prefiere que ella _____ más temprano. (dormir/despertarse)

22. Es preciso que Uds. no le _____ que su hermana está en la ciudad. Es una sorpresa y ella quiere _____ sin que él lo _____ . (decir/llegar/saber)

23. Nos gusta _____ todo. (compartir)

24. Los padres le prohíben a Guillermo que _____ chocolates. (comer)

25. Quiero que Uds. _____ éxito en todo que hagan. (tener)

26. Ojalá que tú _____ . (quedarse)

27. Te espero hasta que tú _____ . (regresar)

✎ Exercise 13.10

Change the following sentences to the subjunctive mood if necessary.

EXAMPLE   Ricardo no cocina. (Es una lástima)
            Es una lástima que no cocine.

1. Enrique se va. (No me gusta)

   _____

2. Ella le da flores a su esposo. (Él se alegra)

   _____

3. Ella sabe la fecha. (Es importante)

   _____

4. Mis amigos están bien. (Me alegro)

   _____

5. Paula conoce a Raúl. (Es dudoso)

   _____

6. Yo soy una buena estudiante. (Es posible)

   _____

7. La película empieza a las dos. (Esperamos)

   _____

8. Hace buen tiempo hoy. (Ojalá)

   _____

9. El tren llega a tiempo. (Tal vez)

   _____

10. Rosa tiene mucha suerte. (Quiero)

    _____

11. Nos vemos mucho. (Me alegro)

    _____

Exercise 13.11

Translate the following sentences into Spanish.

1. *Peter doesn't think that the trip will be good.*

   _____

2. *I am glad to know you.*

   _____

3. *We hope that you are feeling better.*

   _____

4. *Can you call me when you arrive home?*

   _____

5. *Laura insists that the children put on their jackets.*

   _____

6. *Roberto hopes that Julia will dance with him tonight.*

   _____

Exercise 13.12

On a separate sheet of paper, write the English translation of the following infinitives from Part II.

1. abrazar	12. animarse	23. burlarse	34. contar
2. acompañar	13. apresurarse	24. buscar	35. convenir
3. aconsejar	14. aprovecharse	25. caerse	36. conversar
4. acordarse	15. arreglarse	26. callarse	37. cuidar
5. acostarse	16. asistir	27. calmarse	38. dar
6. afeitarse	17. asustarse	28. cargar	39. darse cuenta
7. agradar	18. atreverse	29. cepillarse	40. decir
8. agradecer	19. ayudar	30. charlar	41. dedicarse
9. alegrarse	20. bajarse	31. cobrar	42. defenderse
10. amar	21. bañarse	32. comenzar	43. dejar
11. andar	22. besar	33. conocer	44. demorarse

45. desayunarse	66. extrañar	87. matar	108. quedarse
46. desear	67. faltar	88. mejorarse	109. quejarse
47. despedirse	68. fascinar	89. meterse	110. quemarse
48. despertarse	69. fiarse	90. molestar	111. quitarse
49. divertirse	70. fijarse	91. morirse	112. recoger
50. doler	71. gritar	92. moverse	113. reírse
51. dormirse	72. haber	93. mudarse	114. reunirse
52. ducharse	73. hacerse	94. pararse	115. saltar
53. dudar	74. hallar	95. parecer	116. saludar
54. enamorarse	75. importar	96. parecerse	117. sentarse
55. encantar	76. insistir	97. pedir	118. sentirse
56. encontrarse	77. interesar	98. peinarse	119. sugerir
57. enfadarse	78. invitar	99. permitir	120. tardar
58. enfermarse	79. irse	100. pintarse	121. traer
59. enojarse	80. lastimarse	101. ponerse	122. tranquilizarse
60. enseñar	81. lavarse	102. portarse	123. ver
61. enviar	82. levantarse	103. preguntar	124. vestirse
62. equivocarse	83. llamar	104. preguntarse	125. visitar
63. escoger	84. llamarse	105. preocuparse	126. volverse
64. esperar	85. mandar	106. prestar	
65. expresarse	86. maquillarse	107. prohibir	

Reading Comprehension

La despedida

Esta noche, cuando me acueste, va a ser mi última noche en Italia.
Es una lástima que ya no pueda pasar las mañanas en pura tranquilidad
en ese restaurante acogedor donde tomo mi café.

La soledad es diferente aquí que allí, quizás por el calor humano de
los italianos. Mi amiga Beatriz quiere que me quede. Nos llevamos bien.
A ella le gusta mostrarme lo histórico de las ciudades y la verdad es que
me fascina lo antiguo. Realmente, no me importa mucho adonde vamos,
si vamos a un sitio u otro, porque siempre nos divertimos juntas.

Cuando yo esté en los Estados Unidos (no lo puedo imaginar) quiero
que ella me escriba desde Italia. La voy a extrañar. Pero es el fin de mi
viaje.

A todas las personas con quienes me reúno, les deseo lo mejor y les
agradezco por todo. Voy a despedirme de ellos con un abrazo y mucho
cariño cuando les diga "adiós".

Verbos

agradecer	*to thank*
despedirse	*to take one's leave*

Nombres

el abrazo	*the embrace*	la despedida	*the farewell*
el calor humano	*human warmth*	el fin	*the end*
el cariño	*affection*	la soledad	*the solitude*

Adverbio

realmente	*actually*

The Spanish word **actualmente** means *nowadays* or *at the present time*.

Expresiones

The neuter article **lo** is used before masculine adjectives to make them into
nouns.

lo antiguo	*the ancient*
lo histórico	*the historic*
lo mejor	*the best*

Conjunción

u   *or*

For reasons of pronunciation, **o** is replaced by **u** before words beginning with **o** or **ho**.

Preguntas

After you have read the selection, answer the following questions in Spanish.

1. ¿Piensa Ud. que Isabel debe quedarse en Italia o es mejor que regrese a los Estados Unidos?

    _____

2. ¿Se da cuenta ella que es la primera vez que menciona el nombre de una amiga o un amigo?

    _____

3. ¿Que parte de su viaje le gusta más a Isabel?

    _____

4. ¿Piensa Ud. que hay un cambio en Isabel desde el primer cuento hasta el último?

    _____

III

Preterit Tense, Imperfect Tense, and Double Object Pronouns

14

The Preterit Tense

The preterit expresses an action or actions completed in the past. The English translation is usually the simple past (for example, *I sang*). The preterit is used to express the following.

- Actions completed in the past
- A series of completed actions in the past
- Conditions no longer in effect

Formation of the Preterit

Verbs are considered regular if there is no change in the stem. Most verbs are regular in the preterit. This tense is formed by adding the preterit endings to the stem of the infinitive of **-ar**, **-er**, and **-ir** verbs.

There are only 17 basic irregular verbs in the preterit. Compound forms of these verbs are conjugated in the same way as the main verb.

Some **-ir** verbs have a stem change in the third person of the preterit, but these verbs are not considered irregular.

Regular *-ar* Verbs

In order to conjugate a regular **-ar** verb in the preterit tense, drop the ending and add **-é**, **-aste**, **-ó**, **-amos**, **-asteis**, **-aron** to the stem. All **-ar** verbs except **andar**, **dar**, and **estar** are regular in the preterit.

ayudar	
yo ayudé	nosotros ayudamos
tú ayudaste	vosotros ayudasteis
Ud. ayudó	Uds. ayudaron

cantar	
yo canté	nosotros cantamos
tú cantaste	vosotros cantasteis
él cantó	ellos cantaron

pensar		recordar	
yo pensé	nosotros pensamos	yo recordé	nosotros recordamos
tú pensaste	vosotros pensasteis	tú recordaste	vosotros recordasteis
ella pensó	ellas pensaron	ella recordó	ellas recordaron

trabajar		viajar	
yo trabajé	nosotros trabajamos	yo viajé	nosotros viajamos
tú trabajaste	vosotros trabajasteis	tú viajaste	vosotros viajasteis
Ud. trabajó	Uds. trabajaron	Ud. viajó	Uds. viajaron

In **-ar** verbs, the first-person plural preterit **nosotros** form is identical to the present indicative **nosotros** form. Whether a particular verb is in the present or the past becomes clear in context.

A Word About Pronunciation
Notice that the first- and third-person singular forms carry written accents. It is very important to practice the pronunciation and to stress the accented syllable. Pronounce the verbs in this way: **yo cant<u>é</u>, tú can<u>tas</u>te, el can<u>tó</u>, nosotros can<u>ta</u>mos, vosotros can<u>tas</u>teis, ellos can<u>ta</u>ron**. Review the basic pronunciation rules: All words that end in **n**, **s**, or any vowel have the stress on the second to last, or penultimate, syllable.

Regular *-er* and *-ir* Verbs

In order to conjugate regular **-er** and **-ir** verbs, drop the ending and add **-í**, **-iste**, **-ió**, **-imos**, **-isteis**, **-ieron** to the stem. The endings are the same for both **-er** and **-ir** verbs.

-Er Verbs

comer		entender	
yo comí	nosotros comimos	yo entendí	nosotros entendimos
tú comiste	vosotros comisteis	tú entendiste	vosotros entendisteis
él comió	ellos comieron	ella entendió	ellas entendieron

ver	
yo vi	nosotros vimos
tú viste	vosotros visteis
Ud. vio	Uds. vieron

Notice that the verb **ver** is regular. It does not carry an accent mark on the third-person singular, **vio**, because the form has only one syllable.

-Ir Verbs

compartir

yo compartí	nosotros compartimos
tú compartiste	vosotros compartisteis
él compartió	ellos compartieron

descubrir

yo descubrí	nosotros descubrimos
tú descubriste	vosotros descubristeis
Ud. descubrió	Uds. descubrieron

salir

yo salí	nosotros salimos
tú saliste	vosotros salisteis
ella salió	ellas salieron

In **-ir** verbs, the **nosotros** form of the preterit is identical to the present indicative **nosotros** form. Its meaning becomes clear in context.

 ## Key Vocabulary

These words will help enhance your ability to communicate. As you learn them, remember to practice them aloud.

anoche	*last night*
ayer	*yesterday*
anteayer	*the day before yesterday*
hace	*ago* (when it is used before a period of time in the past)
hace (dos días)	*(two days) ago*
pasado	*past, last*
la semana pasada	*last week*
el mes pasado	*last month*
el año pasado	*last year*

 ## Exercise 14.1

Complete the following sentences with the correct preterit form of the verb in parentheses.

1. Ella _____ la puerta. (abrir)

2. Yo _____ la ventana. (cerrar)

3. Nosotros _____ a México hace ocho meses. (viajar)

4. Anoche, el niño _____ televisión por dos horas. (mirar)

5. Ayer, yo _____ a mi amigo, y lo _____ a tomar unas cervezas conmigo. (visitar/invitar)

6. Anteayer, _____ a llover y _____ hasta las nueve de la noche. (empezar/llover)

7. Ellas _____ a casa y _____ las canciones de Celia Cruz. (regresar/escuchar)

8. A ellos les _____ la película. (gustar)

9. ¿A qué hora _____ Ud. anoche? (acostarse)

10. Esta mañana a las once _____ el teléfono. (sonar)

11. Anoche, ella _____ con un hombre elegante. (soñar)

12. Yo _____ un elefante en la calle. (ver)

13. Nosotros _____ mucho en la fiesta anoche. (divertirse)

14. Ella le _____ al hombre un vaso de agua. (ofrecer)

15. Ellos me _____ con la pronunciación. (ayudar)

Uses of the Preterit

Always keep in mind that the action or actions expressed by the preterit are over. It doesn't make any difference how long the action went on before; the action has a definite end.

To Express an Action Completed in the Past

Anoche, ella cantó una canción triste.	*Last night, she sang a sad song.*
Ayer, yo estudié por dos horas.	*Yesterday, I studied for two hours.*
Anteayer, escribimos dos cartas.	*The day before yesterday, we wrote two letters.*
La semana pasada, él me llamó por teléfono.	*Last week, he called me on the phone.*
El año pasado, ¿compró Ud. una casa nueva?	*Last year, did you buy a new house?*
¿Perdiste tus llaves esta mañana?	*Did you lose your keys this morning?*
¿Por qué no cocinaron Uds. anoche?	*Why didn't you cook last night?*
Ellos salieron hace tres horas.	*They left three hours ago.*

No vimos a nadie.	*We didn't see anyone.*
No me prestaron dinero.	*They didn't lend me money.*
Yo no les enseñé a los estudiantes a nadar.	*I didn't teach the students to swim.*
Samuel jugó al tenis.	*Samuel played tennis.*
Ella lo amó mucho, ¿verdad?	*She loved him a lot, right?*

To Express a Series of Completed Actions in the Past

Anoche en la fiesta, bailamos, cantamos y hablamos.	*Last night at the party, we danced, we sang, and we talked.*
El domingo pasado, ellos corrieron en el maratón, descansaron y comieron.	*Last Sunday, they ran in the marathon, rested, and ate.*
Él se despertó, se lavó y se afeitó.	*He got up, washed, and shaved.*
Caminé a la tienda, compré lechuga y tomates, saludé a los dueños y salí.	*I walked to the store, bought lettuce and tomatoes, greeted the owners, and left.*

To Express a Condition That Is No Longer in Effect

¿Te sentiste mal la semana pasada?	*Did you feel ill last week?*
Me sentí bien la semana pasada, pero me siento mal hoy.	*I felt well last week, but I feel bad today.*
A Miguel le dolió todo el cuerpo ayer, pero hoy está bien.	*Yesterday, Michael had pain in his whole body, but today he is fine.*

 Exercise 14.2

Rewrite each of the following sentences in the preterit.

1. Me gusta viajar. _____

2. Cada mañana, leo un periódico. Ayer, yo _____

3. Ellos cierran la puerta del apartamento. Anoche, ellos _____

   _____

4. Les ofrezco ayuda. _____

5. ¿Por qué vuelves tú tarde? ¿Por qué _____

6. Los niños no se callan. Anoche, ellos _____

7. Leonora no se acuerda de la idea. La semana pasada _____

    _____

8. La película empieza a las ocho. Anoche, _____

    _____

Irregular Verbs

It is important to memorize all the irregular verbs. Once you do, you will be able to use any verb you wish in the preterit.

Irregular verbs in the preterit have an irregular stem and a special set of endings. Note that the endings do not carry accent marks. In order to conjugate an irregular verb in the preterit, add the endings **-e**, **-iste**, **-o**, **-imos**, **-isteis**, **-ieron** to the irregular stems.

andar

yo anduve	nosotros anduvimos
tú anduviste	vosotros anduvisteis
él anduvo	ellos anduvieron

caber

yo cupe	nosotros cupimos
tú cupiste	vosotros cupisteis
ella cupo	ellas cupieron

estar

yo estuve	nosotros estuvimos
tú estuviste	vosotros estuvisteis
Ud. estuvo	Uds. estuvieron

hacer

yo hice	nosotros hicimos
tú hiciste	vosotros hicisteis
él hizo	ellos hicieron

poder

yo pude	nosotros pudimos
tú pudiste	vosotros pudisteis
Ud. pudo	Uds. pudieron

poner

yo puse	nosotros pusimos
tú pusiste	vosotros pusisteis
él puso	ellos pusieron

querer

yo quise	nosotros quisimos
tú quisiste	vosotros quisisteis
ella quiso	ellas quisieron

saber

yo supe	nosotros supimos
tú supiste	vosotros supisteis
Ud. supo	Uds. supieron

tener

yo tuve	nosotros tuvimos
tú tuviste	vosotros tuvisteis
él tuvo	ellos tuvieron

venir

yo vine	nosotros vinimos
tú viniste	vosotros vinisteis
él vino	ellos vinieron

decir

yo dije	nosotros dijimos
tú dijiste	vosotros dijisteis
ella dijo	ellas dijeron

producir

yo produje	nosotros produjimos
tú produjiste	vosotros produjisteis
Ud. produjo	Uds. produjeron

traer

yo traje	nosotros trajimos
tú trajiste	vosotros trajisteis
él trajo	ellos trajeron

Dar, **ir**, and **ser** have slightly different endings.

dar

yo di	nosotros dimos
tú diste	vosotros disteis
ella dio	ellas dieron

ir

yo fui	nosotros fuimos
tú fuiste	vosotros fuisteis
Ud. fue	Uds. fueron

ser

yo fui	nosotros fuimos
tú fuiste	vosotros fuisteis
él fue	ellos fueron

The conjugations for **ir** and **ser** are identical in the preterit. The meaning is clarified in context, as in the following examples.

Ella fue doctora.	*She was a doctor.*
Ella fue a la tienda.	*She went to the store.*

Haber is used to express English *there was, there were, was there?, were there?* The third-person singular preterit form **hubo** is used with both singular and plural subjects.

Note the following about the irregular preterit verbs above.

- **Hizo** (the third-person singular of **hacer**) shows the spelling change **c** > **z** to maintain the sound of /s/.

- Irregular preterits whose stem ends in **j** have **-eron**, not **-ieron**, in the third-person plural, for example, **dijeron**, **trajeron**.

Compound forms of verbs are conjugated in the same way as the main verb.

decir

contradecir	*to contradict*	contradije, *etc.*

hacer

deshacer	*to undo*	deshice, *etc.*

poner

componer	*to compose*	compuse, *etc.*
proponer	*to propose*	propuse, *etc.*

tener

contener	*to contain*	contuve, *etc.*
detener	*to detain*	detuve, *etc.*
mantener	*to maintain*	mantuve, *etc.*

producir

conducir	*to drive*	conduje, *etc.*
traducir	*to translate*	traduje, *etc.*

traer

atraer	*to attract*	atraje, *etc.*
distraer	*to distract*	distraje, *etc.*

venir

prevenir	*to prevent*	previne, *etc.*

Here are some examples of irregular verbs in the preterit.

Pedro y Jorge anduvieron en las montañas por dos días.	*Peter and George walked in the mountains for two days.*
¿Hicieron Ud. su tarea para hoy?	*Did you do your homework for today?*
Tuve una cita con el dentista, pero no fui.	*I had an appointment with the dentist, but I didn't go.*
¿Por qué no vino Ud. a mi fiesta anoche?	*Why didn't you come to my party last night?*
¿Quién le dijo a Sofía la verdad?	*Who told Sophie the truth?*
Los estudiantes produjeron su propia obra de teatro.	*The students produced their own play.*
Le trajimos una bicicleta al niño.	*We brought the child a bicycle.*
Miguel le dio a su novia un anillo.	*Michael gave a ring to his girlfriend.*

En mil novecientos ochenta,
  Nestor fue músico. Ahora él
  es maestro.

*In 1980, Nestor was a musician.
  Now he is a teacher.*

 Exercise 14.3

*Complete the following sentences with the preterit form of the verb. Try to memorize
the irregular verbs as you do the exercise.*

1. ¿Qué me _____ Ud. anoche? No le _____
   nada. (decir/decir)

2. Nosotros no _____ nada ayer. ¿Qué _____
   Uds.? (hacer/hacer)

3. ¿Por qué me _____ tú tantos regalos. No tengo nada para
   _____ a ti. (dar/dar)

4. _____ una fiesta ayer. (haber)

5. Yo _____ vino a la fiesta. Mis amigos no _____
   nada. (traer/traer)

6. Los niños _____ los platos sucios en el horno. Su mamá los
   sacó del horno y los _____ en el lavaplatos. (poner/poner)

7. Yo _____ en el banco a las nueve esta mañana. ¿Dónde
   _____ Uds.? (estar/estar)

8. Él _____ un accidente en carro ayer. Yo no
   _____ nunca un accidente. (tener/tener)

9. ¿A qué hora _____ Uds. a la biblioteca? Nosotros
   _____ a las cuatro. (ir/ir)

10. Él _____ pintor; ahora es abogado. Yo _____
    camarera; ahora soy actriz. (ser/ser)

11. ¿Por qué _____ Uds. a mi casa en tren? ¿Cómo
    _____ Beatriz? (venir/venir)

12. Nosotros _____ lentamente a la escuela. Nuestros maestros
    _____ rápidamente. (andar/andar)

13. Yo _____ una obra de teatro hace un año. (producir)

14. Once payasos _____ en el carro del circo esta mañana. (caber)

Exercise 14.4

Review the conjugations for the irregular verbs, and complete the following sentences with the correct form of the appropriate verb. Use each irregular verb only one time.

andar, caber, dar, decir, estar, haber, hacer, ir, poder,
poner, producir, querer, saber, ser, tener, traer, venir

1. El hombre trató de meter todos sus libros en su carro, pero no

   _____ en el carro pequeño.

2. Empezó a llover y la hija le _____ a su madre un paraguas.

3. Ayer _____ un día de mucha lluvia; hace buen tiempo
   hoy.

4. Los viajeros no _____ salir del país sin su pasaporte;
   se quedaron en los Estados Unidos.

5. Ella no _____ subir la pirámide. Sus amigos subieron
   sin ella.

6. Nosotros _____ a ver una película popular pero no nos
   gustó.

7. Nosotros _____ hacia el parque. Miramos la puesta del sol
   y salimos.

8. El paciente _____ en la oficina del doctor precisamente
   a las siete y media de la mañana.

9. Yo _____ mis llaves en el carro en vez de ponerlas en
   mi bolsillo.

10. La muchacha se despertó y le _____ a su hermana,

    "_____ un mal sueño."

11. ¿Por qué no _____ tú una cita con tu dentista la semana
    pasada?

12. Hubo un ataque terrorista ayer. Nosotros lo _____ hoy.

13. El papá les _____ muchos regalos a sus hijos porque
    los quiere mucho.

14. ¿Quién _____ aquella obra de arte? Es horrible.

15. Mis primos y mis sobrinos _____ a verme hace dos días.

16. El sábado pasado, _____ una fiesta en el club.

Exercise 14.5

Complete the following sentences, using only **ser**, **ir**, **irse**, *and* **estar** *in the preterit, according to the context of the sentence.*

1. Ella es profesora hoy, pero antes _____ azafata.

2. Yo _____ gerente por dos años.

3. Nosotros _____ muy contentos ayer porque nos ganamos la lotería.

4. ¿Por qué _____ tan rápido sin despedirte de nosotros?

5. Ellos _____ al supermercado hoy a comprar alimentos.

6. La semana pasada, Raúl _____ en México. Regresó a casa ayer.

7. Los muchachos _____ enfermos anteayer, pero están bien hoy.

8. _____ una buena idea.

9. ¿Dónde _____ la familia de Federico esta tarde?

10. ¿Quién _____ a la librería a las nueve y media esta mañana?

Exercise 14.6

Answer the following questions orally in Spanish.

1. Yo no hice nada anoche. ¿Qué hicieron Uds.?

2. ¿Le gusta comer? ¿Cocinó anoche?

3. ¿A qué hora te acostaste anoche? ¿A qué hora te despertaste esta mañana?

4. ¿Quién fue el presidente en el año mil novecientos noventa y seis?

5. ¿Vio Ud. a sus amigos ayer?

6. ¿Piensa Ud. que Cristóbal Colón descubrió América?

7. ¿Hizo sol ayer?

8. ¿Por qué decidieron Uds. asistir a clases de español?

9. ¿Dónde nació Ud.?

10. ¿Quién bailó contigo la semana pasada?

-Ir Verbs with Stem Changes in the Third Person

-Ir verbs that are irregular in the present indicative have a stem change in the preterit. This stem change occurs only in the third-person singular and plural forms of the preterit.

e > ie in the present indicative
e > i in the preterit

Infinitive	Present Indicative	Preterit	
divertirse	me divierto	me divertí	nos divertimos
		te divertiste	os divertisteis
		se divirtió	se divirtieron
mentir	yo miento	yo mentí	nosotros mentimos
		tú mentiste	vosotros mentisteis
		él mintió	ellos mintieron
preferir	yo prefiero	yo preferí	nosotros preferimos
		tú preferiste	vosotros preferisteis
		Ud. prefirió	Uds. prefirieron
sentirse	me siento	me sentí	nos sentimos
		te sentiste	os sentisteis
		se sintió	se sintieron
sugerir	yo sugiero	yo sugerí	nosotros sugerimos
		tú sugeriste	vosotros sugeristeis
		ella sugirió	ellas sugirieron

e > i in the present indicative
e > i in the preterit

Infinitive	Present Indicative	Preterit	
corregir	yo corrijo	yo corregí	nosotros corregimos
		tú corregiste	vosotros corregisteis
		ella corrigió	ellas corrigieron
despedirse	me despido	me despedí	nos despedimos
		te despediste	os despedisteis
		se despidió	se despidieron
pedir	yo pido	yo pedí	nosotros pedimos
		tú pediste	vosotros pedisteis
		Ud. pidió	Uds. pidieron

Infinitive	Present Indicative	Preterit	
reírse	me río	me reí	nos reímos
		te reíste	os reísteis
		se rió	se rieron
repetir	yo repito	yo repetí	nosotros repetimos
		tú repetiste	vosotros repetisteis
		Ud. repitió	Uds. repitieron
seguir	yo sigo	yo seguí	nosotros seguimos
		tú seguiste	vosotros seguisteis
		él siguió	ellos siguieron
servir	yo sirvo	yo serví	nosotros servimos
		tú serviste	vosotros servisteis
		Ud. sirvió	Uds. sirvieron
sonreír	yo sonrío	yo sonreí	nosotros sonreímos
		tú sonreíste	vosotros sonreísteis
		él sonrió	ellos sonrieron
vestirse	me visto	me vestí	nos vestimos
		te vestiste	os vestisteis
		se vistió	se vistieron

o > ue in the present indicative
o > u in the preterit

Infinitive	Present Indicative	Preterit	
dormir	yo duermo	yo dormí	nosotros dormimos
		tú dormiste	vosotros dormisteis
		ella durmió	ellas durmieron
morir	yo muero	yo morí	nosotros morimos
		tú moriste	vosotros moristeis
		él murió	ellos murieron

 ## Exercise 14.7

Complete the following sentences with the correct form of the preterit.

1. Anoche, el niño _____ nueve horas. (dormir)

2. ¿Por qué no _____ Uds. las instrucciones? (seguir)

3. Yo ＿＿＿＿＿＿ quedarme en un hotel de lujo; ella

＿＿＿＿＿＿ quedarse también; él ＿＿＿＿＿＿ irse.
(preferir/preferir/preferir)

4. Anoche, su novio ＿＿＿＿＿＿ de ella por última vez. (despedirse)

5. Nosotros ＿＿＿＿＿＿ mucho en la fiesta. Nuestros amigos no

＿＿＿＿＿＿ nada y se fueron. (divertirse/divertirse)

6. Siempre la mujer elegante se viste bien, pero ayer ella no

＿＿＿＿＿＿ bien y ＿＿＿＿＿＿ mal. (sentirse/vestirse)

7. Su sobrino ＿＿＿＿＿＿ ayer. Él lo supo hoy. (morirse)

8. Anoche fuimos a un buen restaurante. Nos ＿＿＿＿＿＿
una mariscada en salsa verde. (servir)

9. Casi nunca miento. Pero ayer, ＿＿＿＿＿＿. Estuve con unas

amigas y ellas ＿＿＿＿＿＿ también. (mentir/mentir)

10. La niña ＿＿＿＿＿＿; con su sonrisa el mundo se alegró. (sonreír)

11. No sé porque el hombre ＿＿＿＿＿＿. Yo no vi nada cómico.
(reírse)

12. La estudiante aplicada ＿＿＿＿＿＿ la lección para entenderla bien.
(repetir)

13. Sus maestros les ＿＿＿＿＿＿ la gramática. (corregir)

14. Yo ＿＿＿＿＿＿ bien ayer. ¿Cómo ＿＿＿＿＿＿ Uds.?
(sentirse/sentirse)

Verbs with Orthographic Changes

-Ar Verbs

Verbs with orthographic changes are not irregular. The spelling changes simply maintain the necessary sound. Only verbs in the **yo** form are affected by the spelling changes in the preterit of **-ar** verbs.

- Verbs that end in **-gar** change **g** to **gu**.
- Verbs that end in **-car** change **c** to **qu**.
- Verbs that end in **-zar** change **z** to **c**.

apagar	yo apa**gué**	nosotros apagamos
	tú apagaste	vosotros apagasteis
	él apagó	ellos apagaron

buscar	yo bus**qué**	nosotros buscamos
	tú buscaste	vosotros buscasteis
	ella buscó	ellas buscaron
comenzar	yo comen**cé**	nosotros comenzamos
	tú comenzaste	vosotros comenzasteis
	Ud. comenzó	Uds. comenzaron
explicar	yo expli**qué**	nosotros explicamos
	tú explicaste	vosotros explicasteis
	él explicó	ellos explicaron
llegar	yo lle**gué**	nosotros llegamos
	tú llegaste	vosotros llegasteis
	ella llegó	ellas llegaron
tocar	yo to**qué**	nosotros tocamos
	tú tocaste	vosotros tocasteis
	Ud. tocó	Uds. tocaron

Note that the spelling change **z** > **c** occurs before the vowel **e** without affecting the sound, as in **comenzar**, **comencé**.

A Word About Pronunciation

Make sure to stress the final sound of the first-person singular (**yo** form) and the third-person singular (**él, ella, Ud.** form). Spanish pronunciation is precise, and the tense you use depends on the correct pronunciation. So continue to practice in this way: **yo apagué, tú apagaste, él apagó, nosotros apagamos, vosotros apagasteis, ellos apagaron**.

Here are more **-ar** verbs with spelling changes.

-gar

ahogarse	*to drown*
cargar	*to carry, to load*
castigar	*to punish*
colgar	*to hang*
entregar	*to hand in, to deliver*
madrugar	*to get up early*
pegar	*to hit, to glue*
tragar	*to swallow*
vagar	*to wander*

-car

acercarse	*to approach*
arrancar	*to pull out, to root out*
colocar	*to put, to place*
destacar	*to stick out*
justificar	*to justify*
mascar	*to chew*
pescar	*to fish*
publicar	*to publish*
sacar	*to take out*
suplicar	*to beg*

-zar

alcanzar	*to reach, to overtake*
amenazar	*to threaten*
lanzar	*to throw, to shoot*
realizar	*to fulfill*
rezar	*to pray*
tropezarse (con)	*to bump into*

 Exercise 14.8

Complete the following sentences with the correct form of the preterit.

1. Me desperté con vértigo y _____ con la pared. (tropezarse)

2. Hace una semana, Laura pagó la cuenta, pero ayer yo la

   _____ . (pagar)

3. El estudiante orgulloso le _____ su tarea a la profesora. (entregar)

4. Nosotros _____ de un lado a otro el año pasado. (vagar)

5. Anoche, yo _____ una pintura en la pared. (colgar)

6. Su papá se enojó anteayer y _____ a sus hijos. (castigar)

-Er and *-ir* Verbs

Verbs with spelling changes are not irregular. The spelling changes shown for **-er** and **-ir** verbs with stems ending in a vowel avoid the use of three vowels in a row.

Verbs with a vowel immediately preceding the infinitive ending change **i** to **y** in the third-person singular and plural. In these verbs, there is a written accent over the letter **i** on the **yo**, **tú**, **nosotros**, and **vosotros** endings.

caer	yo caí	nosotros caímos
	tú caíste	vosotros caísteis
	él ca**yó**	ellos ca**yeron**
leer	yo leí	nosotros leímos
	tú leíste	vosotros leísteis
	ella le**yó**	ellas le**yeron**
oír	yo oí	nosotros oímos
	tú oíste	vosotros oísteis
	Ud. o**yó**	Uds. o**yeron**

Note, for example, that the third-person singular of **caer** is **cayó** rather than **caió**.

Verbs that end in **-uir** change **i** to **y**; the accent over the **i** appears only over the first-person singular.

construir	yo construí	nosotros construimos
	tú construiste	vosotros construisteis
	él constru**yó**	ellos constru**yeron**
destruir	yo destruí	nosotros destruimos
	tú destruiste	vosotros destruisteis
	ella destru**yó**	ellas destru**yeron**

Here are more **-er** and **-ir** verbs with spelling changes.

creer	*to believe*	huir	*to flee*
concluir	*to conclude*	incluir	*to include*
contribuir	*to contribute*	influir	*to influence*
distribuir	*to distribute*	poseer	*to possess*
fluir	*to flow*		

Exercise 14.9

Complete the following sentences with the correct preterit form of the verb in parentheses.

1. El hombre tacaño se puso feliz la primera vez que él _____ con dinero. (contribuir)

2. El niño _____ del árbol pero no se lesionó. (caerse)

3. Mi maestro de la escuela secundaria _____ mucho en mi educación. (influir)

4. Hubo un incendio y todas las personas en la ciudad _____. (huir)

5. Los carpinteros _____ dos casas el año pasado. (construir)

6. ¿Por qué _____ tú la bicicleta de Susana? (destruir)

 Exercise 14.10

Translate the following sentences into Spanish.

1. *I worked a lot yesterday. Last night, I rested.*

   _____

2. *Last night, we watched television instead of studying.*

   _____

3. *I gave him my dog; he gave me nothing.*

   _____

4. *She read her friend's letter a month ago.*

   _____

5. *We received the package a week ago.*

   _____

6. *What did you say to her? I told you that he died last year.*

   _____

7. *The children went to bed at nine o'clock last night.*

   _____

8. *I saw your sister yesterday.*

   _____

Verbs with Special Meanings in the Preterit

Meaning in the Preterit

conocer *to know, to be acquainted with*

¿Dónde conociste a tu novio?	*Where did you **meet** your boyfriend?*
Lo conocí en España.	*I **met** him in Spain.*
¿Cuándo conocieron Uds. a Paulina?	*When did you **meet** Pauline?*
La conocimos hace tres años.	*We **met** her three years ago.*

saber *to know a fact, to know how to do something*

Ella tuvo un accidente ayer. Lo supe hoy.	*She had an accident yesterday. I **found out** today.*
No nos dijeron nada pero supimos la verdad.	*They didn't tell us anything but we **found out** the truth.*

no querer *not to want*

Ella no quiso bajar en el ascensor.	*She **refused** to go down in the elevator.*
El niño no quiso comer.	*The child **refused** to eat.*

no poder *not to be able*

Hubo un incendio y la gente no pudo salir.	*There was a fire and the people **failed** to leave.*

A Word About Translations

The preterit expresses an action completed in the past. These translations are as close as possible to transmitting the idea of the sentence. **No querer** means *not to want.* But in the preterit, the action is over, so the concept is stronger than she didn't want to go down in the elevator. She didn't want to, and she didn't; therefore, she refused. Similarly, **no poder** means *not to be able.* But in the preterit, the people were not able to leave, and the action is completed; therefore, they didn't manage to leave, or failed to leave.

Exercise 14.11

Complete the following sentences with the correct form of the preterit.

1. Yo _____ en el apartamento a las ocho anoche. (entrar)

2. Nosotros _____ un chocolate caliente. (tomar)

3. Ellos _____ a las once. Yo _____ a la una.
   (dormirse/dormirse)

4. ¿Me _____ Uds. ayer? Yo no los _____.
   (ver/ver)

5. _____ a nevar a las siete esta mañana. (empezar)

6. _____ mucho sol ayer. (hacer)

7. El taxista le _____ a mi primo veinte pesos. ¿Cuánto

   te _____ a ti? (cobrar/cobrar)

8. Nosotros les _____ a nuestros parientes dos tarjetas,

   pero ellos no las _____. (escribir/recibir)

9. El trabajador _____ temprano esta mañana. (despertarse)

10. ¿_____ tú las llaves? (encontrar)

11. Yo no _____ bajar en el ascensor. (querer)

12. Cuando él _____ joven, él _____ un buen
    deportista. (ser/ser)

13. ¿Por qué no me _____ Ud. la verdad? (decir)

14. La tarea fue difícil, pero los estudiantes la _____ hacer.
    (poder)

A Word About the Preterit
Practice and study. Learn the irregular verbs and the regular verbs. Pronounce all regular **-ar**, **-er**, and **-ir** verbs aloud as much as you can. Use the verb lists in this chapter as reference, and use the verbs as you need them. Spend at least a week on the preterit to learn the form and the concept.

Reading Comprehension

Estimados lectores,

Espero que a Uds. les guste la siguiente historia. Está en forma
de diálogo y basada en acontecimientos de la vida real. Intenten adivinar
quien es el personaje principal según las claves que aparecen en esta
escena. Para que gocen de lo lindo y para que aprendan de la historia,
es necesario que Uds. lean con cuidado.

En la corte (primera escena)

*La escena tiene lugar en 399 B.C. en la corte griega ante una asamblea
de 501 ciudadanos. El acusado entra y empieza a hablar.*

ACUSADO   Tengo setenta años y es la primera vez que me ven en la corte.
¿Cuál es la primera acusación contra mí?

ACUSADOR   Ud. es culpable de investigar bajo la tierra y en el cielo y
de enseñarles a otros las mismas cosas.

ACUSADO   No tengo nada que ver con estas acusaciones y nada de esto
es verdad.

ACUSADOR   Pero, ¿cuál es el problema, entonces? ¿Por qué hay tantos
prejuicios contra Ud. si dice que no hace nada diferente de los demás?
Nos puede decir Ud. lo que es, para que le demos un veredicto justo.

ACUSADO   Bueno. Voy a decirles toda la verdad. Me dan esta reputación
por cierta sabiduría que tengo. Menciono el dios de Delfos para que
él sea mi testigo. ¿Se acuerdan Uds. de Querefón? Él fue al dios de
Delfos y le preguntó si hay una persona más sabia que yo. El dios
contestó que no hay nadie. Pero, ¿qué significa la idea de que yo soy
el hombre más sagaz de todos? Me tocó investigar la cuestión. Yo fui
a ver a un hombre que tiene la reputación de ser sagaz. Lo examiné.
No es necesario que les diga su nombre, él es un político, y esto es
el resultado.

Verbos

adivinar	*to guess*
intentar	*to intend, to try*

Nombres

los acontecimientos	*the events*
el ciudadano	*the citizen*
la clave	*the key, the code*

la corte	the court
la cuestión	the issue
los demás	the rest
el diálogo	the dialogue
el dios de Delfos	the god of Delphi
la escena	the scene
el personaje	the character
el político	the politician
el prejuicio	the prejudice
la sabiduría	the knowledge
el veredicto	the verdict

Adjetivos

justo	fair, just
principal	main, principal
sabio	wise
sagaz	wise, clever
siguiente	following

Preguntas

After you have read the selection, answer the following questions in Spanish.

1. ¿En que sitio empieza la acción?

   _____

2. ¿Cuántos años tiene el acusado?

   _____

3. ¿Cuál es la acusación contra él?

   _____

4. ¿Qué hizo el acusado después de escuchar que él es el más sabio de todos?

   _____

15

The Imperfect Tense

The imperfect tense expresses an action or actions in the past that are not seen as completed. The imperfect is used in the following ways.

- To "set the stage" in the past; to express a narration, situation, or background in the past
- To express habitual, customary, or repeated actions in the past
- To express continuous actions or actions in progress in the past
- To express a description in the past
- To express point of origin in the past
- To express time in the past
- To express one's age in the past

Formation of the Imperfect

Almost all verbs are regular in the imperfect tense. The tense is formed by adding the imperfect endings to the stem of the **-ar**, **-er**, and **-ir** verbs. There are only three irregular verbs in the imperfect.

Regular *-ar* Verbs

To conjugate an **-ar** verb in the imperfect tense, drop the ending and add **-aba**, **-abas**, **-aba**, **-ábamos**, **-abais**, **-aban** to the stem. Note that the first- and third-person singular forms (**yo**, **él/ella/Ud.**) are identical in the imperfect. There are no irregular **-ar** verbs.

acompañar

yo acompañaba	nosotros acompañábamos
tú acompañabas	vosotros acompañabais
él acompañaba	ellos acompañaban

dar

yo daba	nosotros dábamos
tú dabas	vosotros dabais
ella daba	ellas daban

estar

yo estaba	nosotros estábamos
tú estabas	vosotros estabais
Ud. estaba	Uds. estaban

hablar

yo hablaba	nosotros hablábamos
tú hablabas	vosotros hablabais
él hablaba	ellos hablaban

recordar

yo recordaba	nosotros recordábamos
tú recordabas	vosotros recordabais
ella recordaba	ellas recordaban

trabajar

yo trabajaba	nosotros trabajábamos
tú trabajabas	vosotros trabajabais
Ud. trabajaba	Uds. trabajaban

A Word About the Imperfect

Practice the pronunciation of the imperfect **-ar** verbs. There are one-syllable, two-syllable, three-syllable, and four-syllable verbs. Be sure to pronounce the imperfect in this way: **yo trabajaba, tú trabajabas, él trabajaba, nosotros trabajábamos, vosotros trabajabais, ellos trabajaban.**

Regular *-er* and *-ir* Verbs

To conjugate regular **-er** and **-ir** verbs in the imperfect, drop the ending and add **-ía**, **-ías**, **-ía**, **-íamos**, **-íais**, **-ían** to the stem. The endings are the same for both **-er** and **-ir** verbs.

-*Er* Verbs

entender

yo entendía	nosotros entendíamos
tú entendías	vosotros entendíais
él entendía	ellos entendían

hacer

yo hacía	nosotros hacíamos
tú hacías	vosotros hacíais
ella hacía	ellas hacían

poder

yo podía	nosotros podíamos
tú podías	vosotros podíais
Ud. podía	Uds. podían

querer

yo quería	nosotros queríamos
tú querías	vosotros queríais
él quería	ellos querían

saber

yo sabía	nosotros sabíamos
tú sabías	vosotros sabíais
ella sabía	ellas sabían

tener

yo tenía	nosotros teníamos
tú tenías	vosotros teníais
Ud. tenía	Uds. tenían

Haber is used to express English *there was, there were, was there?, were there?* The third-person singular imperfect form **había** is used with both singular and plural subjects.

-*Ir* Verbs

decir

yo decía	nosotros decíamos
tú decías	vosotros decíais
él decía	ellos decían

divertirse

me divertía	nos divertíamos
te divertías	os divertíais
ella se divertía	ellas se divertían

sentirse

me sentía	nos sentíamos
te sentías	os sentíais
Ud. se sentía	Uds. se sentían

venir

yo venía	nosotros veníamos
tú venías	vosotros veníais
él venía	ellos venían

Irregular Verbs

ir

yo iba	nosotros íbamos
tú ibas	vosotros ibais
él iba	ellos iban

ser

yo era	nosotros éramos
tú eras	vosotros erais
ella era	ellas eran

ver

yo veía	nosotros veíamos
tú veías	vosotros veíais
Ud. veía	Uds. veían

The translation of **ir** in the imperfect is *was going, were going.*

Yo iba a hablar.	*I was going to speak.*
Nosotros íbamos a comprar un carro nuevo.	*We were going to buy a new car.*

Uses of the Imperfect

The imperfect tense expresses actions in the past that are not seen as completed. It is used to indicate situations or actions in the past with no specific reference to their beginning or end.

To "Set the Stage" in the Past; to Express a Narration, Situation, or Background

El sol brillaba y los pájaros cantaban.	*The sun was shining and the birds were singing.*
La luna alumbraba el río y los pescadores lanzaban sus redes.	*The moon lit up the river and the fishermen were throwing out their nets.*
Había un silencio profundo en el bosque; ya caía la noche.	*There was a profound silence in the forest; night was already falling.*
No había nadie en la casa. Los ladrones esperaban afuera.	*There was no one in the house. The thieves were waiting outside.*

To Express Habitual, Customary, or Repeated Actions in the Past

Todos los veranos, yo jugaba al tenis con mis amigos.	*Every summer, I used to play tennis with my friends.*
Todos los días, Paulina y yo almorzábamos a la una de la tarde.	*Every day, Pauline and I used to have lunch at one o'clock in the afternoon.*
Cada noche, antes de dormirse, el viejo ponía sus dientes en un vaso de agua.	*Each night, before going to sleep, the old man put his teeth in a glass of water.*

A Word About the Translations

Read the example sentences again, and try to understand the concepts without the translations. Try to imagine these examples as scenes: they are situations, narrations in the past; they are backgrounds; they "set the stage." The English translations are not precise or consistent in the imperfect. Make sure you understand this important concept and choose whichever translation or idea is clearest for you.

To Express Continuous Actions in the Past

Marisol cuidaba su jardín mientras sus nietos jugaban.	*Marisol was taking care of her garden while her grandchildren were playing.*
Eduardo bailaba y su novia cantaba.	*Ed was dancing and his girlfriend was singing.*
Ella buscaba sus llaves cuando el teléfono sonó.	*She was looking for her keys when the telephone rang.*
Ella iba a contestar pero escuchó un sonido en la puerta.	*She was going to answer but she heard a sound at the door.*
Yo hablaba cuando mi profesor me interrumpió.	*I was speaking when my professor interrupted me.*

Note that in the last three example sentences above, both the imperfect and the preterit tenses are used. The first part of the sentence is the ongoing action, the action in progress. The second part of the sentence, which requires the preterit, is a completed action. Here, the imperfect is used as a continuous action that is interrupted by another action.

To Express a Description in the Past

La casa era blanca.	*The house was white.*
La comida estaba buena.	*The meal was good.*
Nuestro vecino era viejo, pero tenía el pelo negro.	*Our neighbor was old, but he had black hair.*

To Express Point of Origin in the Past

El hombre era de Perú.	*The man was from Peru.*
Sus amigos eran de Chile.	*His friends were from Chile.*
Las flores rojas eran de Bolivia.	*The red flowers were from Bolivia.*

To Express Time in the Past

Eran las cinco y Federico iba a la tienda por última vez.	*It was five o'clock and Fred was going to the store for the last time.*
¿Qué hora era? Eran las dos de la tarde.	*What time was it? It was two in the afternoon.*
Eran las nueve de la noche y los niños dormían.	*It was nine at night and the children were sleeping.*

To Express One's Age in the Past

Ella tenía veinte años cuando se graduó de la universidad.	*She was 20 years old when she graduated from the university.*
Mi abuelo tenía noventa y cinco años cuando se murió.	*My grandfather was 95 years old when he died.*
El presidente tenía cincuenta y cinco años cuando lo elegimos.	*The president was 55 years old when we elected him.*

 Exercise 15.1

Complete the following sentences with the correct form of the imperfect. In the parentheses, write your reason for choosing the imperfect.

EXAMPLES   Todas las noches, Teodoro __llamaba__ a Elena. (llamar)

(__repeated action__)

Su hijo __tenía__ dos años cuando empezó a correr. (tener)

(__age__)

1. De niña, Loreta _____ pasta cada noche. (comer)

   (_____)

2. Ella _____ alta y bonita como su madre. (ser)

   (_____)

3. ¿Por qué _____ los niños a la escuela los sábados? (ir)

   (_____)

4. La mujer y su esposo _____ de España. (ser)

   (_____)

5. Nosotros _____ todos los días. (verse) (_____)

6. ¿De dónde _____ sus abuelos? (ser) (_____)

7. El tren _____ todos los días precisamente a las nueve.

   (llegar) (_____)

8. Nosotros siempre _____ a casa a las seis de la tarde. (volver)

   (_____)

9. _____ una fiesta en la casa de un conocido. (haber)

   (_____)

10. Ella _____ el piano cuando su hermano gritó. (practicar)

    (_____)

11. ¿Por qué _____ a vender tu casa? (ir) (_____)

12. Me di cuenta que yo _____ a tener éxito. (ir)

    (_____)

13. La estudiante _____ veintiún años al graduarse. (tener)

    (_____)

14. Los niños _____ pollo y sus padres _____

    pescado en el restaurante. (comer/comer) (_____,

    _____)

15. Los amigos de Pedro lo _____ en Hawai cada año. (visitar)

    (_____)

16. En el pasado, ellos _____ vino todos los fines de semana;

    ahora beben mucha agua. (beber) (_____)

17. La gente _____ muy valiente. (ser) (_____)

18. El adolescente _____ el pelo largo; yo _____

    el pelo corto. (tener/tener) (_____, _____)

19. _____ las doce y el sol _____. (ser/brillar)

    (_____, _____)

20. Él _____ su libro cuando su amigo lo llamó. (leer)

    (_____)

21. Ana _____ su tarea cuando sonó el teléfono. (hacer)

    (_____)

22. Nosotros _____ cansadas de trabajar. (estar)

    (_____)

23. La película _____ cómica; todo el mundo

    _____. (ser/reírse) (_____, _____)

24. ¿Qué me _____ cuando él me distrajo? (decir)

    (_____)

25. ¿Qué _____ Uds. cuando empezó a nevar? (hacer)

    (_____)

26. Mi amigo me dijo que _____ a verme. (venir)

    (_____)

27. _____ buen tiempo. _____ viento y sol.

    Los pájaros _____ en los árboles y todo el mundo

    _____ feliz. (hacer/hacer/estar/estar) (_____,

    _____, _____, _____)

28. Antes, yo _____ mucho. Ahora prefiero comer

    en restaurantes. (cocinar) (_____)

Exercise 15.2

Review **ser** *and* **estar** *in the imperfect, and then rewrite the following sentences in the imperfect.*

EXAMPLE   Yo soy de Venezuela.   *Yo era de Venezuela.*

1. Ellos son de España. _____

2. ¿Qué hora es? _____

3. Nosotros estamos bien. _____

4. Mi jardín es el más hermoso de la ciudad.

    _____

5. Los tres amigos están aquí. _____

6. No estoy cansada. _____

7. Somos cantantes. _____

8. ¿Dónde estás? _____

9. Yo estoy en la casa con mi perro.

    _____

Preterit and Imperfect Compared

Compare the differences in meaning between the following sentence pairs (preterit followed by imperfect).

Ella llegó ayer.	*She arrived yesterday.*
Ella llegaba a la cinco todos los días.	*She arrived at five o'clock every day.*
La semana pasada, leí un buen libro.	*Last week, I read a good book.*
Antes, yo leía mucho.	*Before, I used to read a lot.*
Beatriz vino a verme.	*Beatriz came to see me.*
Él me dijo que Beatriz venía a verme.	*He told me that Beatriz was coming to see me.*
Me levanté a las seis esta mañana.	*I got up at six o'clock this morning.*
Me levantaba tarde.	*I used to get up late.*
Fui a la tienda.	*I went to the store.*
Yo iba a la tienda cuando vi a José.	*I was going to the store when I saw Joe.*
Fuimos a la playa hoy.	*We went to the beach today.*
Íbamos a la playa todos los veranos.	*We used to go the beach every summer.*
¿Qué me dijiste hace dos minutos?	*What did you tell me two minutes ago?*
¿Qué me decías cuando el perro ladró?	*What were you saying to me when the dog barked?*
Marta comió temprano esta mañana.	*Martha ate early this morning.*
Marta siempre comía temprano.	*Martha always ate early.*
Mi papá pagó la cuenta ayer.	*My father paid the bill yesterday.*
Mi papá siempre pagaba la cuenta.	*My father always paid the bill.*
Eduardo hizo su tarea.	*Edward did his homework.*
Eduardo hacía su tarea todos los lunes.	*Edward did his homework every Monday.*
¿Qué compró Ud. ayer?	*What did you buy yesterday?*
¿Qué compraba Ud. cuando le llamé?	*What were you buying when I called you?*

Caminamos al parque hoy.	*We walked to the park today.*
Caminábamos al parque todos los días.	*We used to walk to the park every day.*
Recibimos un cheque esta tarde.	*We received a check this afternoon.*
Recibíamos cheques cada semana.	*We used to receive checks every week.*
Ella tuvo una operación anoche.	*She had an operation last night.*
Él no tenía tiempo para verla.	*He didn't have time to see her.*
Anoche, ella durmió hasta las ocho.	*Last night, she slept until eight o'clock.*
Todos los días, ella dormía hasta tarde.	*Every day, she slept until late.*
Conocimos a Silvia en Colombia.	*We met Sylvia in Colombia.*
No la conocíamos por mucho tiempo.	*We didn't know her for very long.*

Querer, poder, saber

Affirmative

Yo quise ir al circo.	*I wanted to go to the circus.*
Yo quería ir al circo.	*I wanted to go to the circus.*
Pudimos entender la lección.	*We were able to understand the lesson.*
Podíamos entender la lección.	*We were able to understand the lesson.*
Ella supo que él tuvo un accidente.	*She found out that he had an accident.*
Ella sabía que él iba a estar bien.	*She knew that he was going to be well.*

For the verbs **querer** and **poder**, the English translations of the example sentences above showing the preterit and the imperfect are the same. However, the preterit **pudimos** from **poder** indicates that the action is over. The idea is that we were able to understand the lesson; the action is completed, so we succeeded in understanding the lesson.

Negative

¿Por qué no quiso Ud. ir conmigo?	*Why did you refuse to go with me?*
¿Por qué no quería Ud. ir conmigo?	*Why didn't you want to go with me?*
No pude hacer mi tarea.	*I failed to do my homework.*
Yo no podía hacer mi tarea ayer.	*I wasn't able to (couldn't) do my homework yesterday.*
No lo supe hoy.	*I didn't find it out today.*
Yo no sabía que él estaba enfermo.	*I didn't know that he was sick.*

 Exercise 15.3

Preterit and imperfect. *Translate the following sentences into Spanish.*

1. *It was one o'clock and it was raining.*

   _____

2. *I knew it.* _____

3. *He was able to do it well.* _____

4. *The children wanted to eat hamburgers.*

   _____

5. *We were studying when the teacher entered.*

   _____

6. *The man was fleeing when the police caught him.*

   _____

7. *Every night for many years, she had the same dream.*

   _____

8. *What were you saying to me?* _____

9. *What was I going to say to you?*

   _____

10. *Why did he call her?* _____

11. *What time was it when you fell asleep last night?*

   _____

12. *Who got sick yesterday?* _____

13. *We were going to travel to Cuba, but we had no money.*

   _____

14. *I met your friend in Mexico.* _____

15. *He left without saying anything to us.*

   _____

16. *Who gave him the good news today?*

   _____

17. *The man was in the bank when the thief entered. Everyone was afraid.*

   _____

18. *Last year, we went to Spain. We had a good time.*

   _____

Exercise 15.4

Complete the following sentences with **ir** *in either the preterit or the imperfect.*

1. ¿Por qué _____ Ud. al museo ayer?

2. En julio, Graciela _____ a California a ver a sus nietos.

3. Yo _____ a llamarla, pero no tenía su número de teléfono.

4. Nosotros _____ al circo todos los veranos en el pasado.

5. Nosotros _____ al cine anoche; nos gustó la película.

6. Mis amigos _____ a vender su carro antes de ganarse la lotería.

7. Carmen _____ al banco los viernes e _____ a la playa los sábados.

8. ¿_____ tú al campo los fines de semana?

9. Isabel _____ a Italia y no regresó.

10. Marisol y su esposo _____ a Portugal.

Exercise 15.5

Translate the following sentences into English.

1. La madre del hijo le dijo que todo iba a estar bien.

   _____

2. ¿Te dolían los pies durante tu viaje?

   _____

3. Hubo un tiempo cuando yo visitaba museos.

   _____

4. Vine, vi y vencí. _____

5. Entre el primero y segundo piso, me di cuenta de que iba a caerme.

   _____

6. Nos divertíamos mucho cada día hace mucho tiempo.

   _____

7. Yo no sabía qué hacer. _____

8. Tenían una buena relación. Él siempre cocinaba y ella siempre lavaba los platos.

   _____

Exercise 15.6

Preterit or imperfect. *Complete the sentences with the correct form of the verb in parentheses.*

1. ¿Por que no _____ tú la comida ayer? (comprar)

2. Anoche, yo _____ el vino a la fiesta. (traer)

3. _____ mediodía y el niño _____ hambre. (ser/tener)

4. _____ a llover y yo _____ la ventana. (empezar/cerrar)

5. La muchacha _____ la calle cuando su mamá

   la _____ . (cruzar/llamar)

6. ¿Dónde _____ Uds. esta mañana precisamente a las nueve? (estar)

7. Nosotros _____ en el parque cuando _____ el animal exótico. (andar/ver)

8. El taxista nos _____ veinte dólares. ¿Cuánto te _____ a ti? (cobrar/cobrar)

9. Nosotros les _____ cartas a nuestros parientes desde Bolivia, pero ellos no las _____. (escribir/recibir)

10. Yo _____ por la calle equivocada cuando _____ que no _____ donde _____. (caminar/darse cuenta de/saber/estar).

11. Me agrada su amigo. ¿Dónde lo _____ Ud.? (conocer)

12. Pedro y sus amigos _____ todas las noches antes de acostarse. (divertirse)

13. Melisa _____ al cine cada domingo durante su juventud. (ir)

14. Los viajeros de Inglaterra _____ a mi casa la semana pasada y _____ conmigo hasta hoy. (llegar/quedarse)

Double Object Pronouns

In Spanish, two object pronouns can appear together with a verb.

- Double object pronouns cannot be separated from each other.

- In a negative sentence, the word **no** (or any other word of negation) comes directly before the first pronoun.

- Positions of the double object pronouns are the same as single object pronouns: The pronouns are placed directly before the first verb *or* they are attached to the infinitive.

Indirect Object Pronoun with Direct Object Pronoun

An indirect object pronoun precedes a direct object pronoun when they occur together. In the first position, the object pronouns are placed directly before the first verb.

Me lo / me la / me los / me las

Necesito tu carro esta noche.	*I need your car tonight.*
¿**Me lo** prestas?	*Will you lend it to me?*
Él tiene una revista interesante.	*He has an interesting magazine.*
Él **me la** va a dar.	*He is going to give it to me.*
Ella tiene dos secretos.	*She has two secrets.*
Ella no **me los** quería decir.	*She didn't want to tell them to me.*
El maestro explicó las nuevas lecciones.	*The teacher explained the new lessons.*
Él **me las** explicó.	*He explained them to me.*

In the second position, the object pronouns are attached to the infinitive and become one word. A written accent is added to maintain the natural stress of the infinitive. Whether the object pronouns are placed in front of the first verb or attached to the infinitive, the meaning of the sentence is the same.

Necesito tu carro esta noche.	*I need your car tonight.*
¿Puedes prestár**melo?**	*Can you lend it to me?*
Él tiene una revista interesante.	*He has an interesting magazine.*
Él va a dár**mela**.	*He is going to give it to me.*
Ella tiene dos secretos.	*She has two secrets.*
Ella no quería decír**melos**.	*She didn't want to tell them to me.*
Él trató de explicar las nuevas lecciones.	*He tried to explain the new lessons.*
Él trató de explicár**melas**.	*He tried to explain them to me.*

 ## Exercise 15.7

Translate the following sentences into English. Practice the use of the double object pronouns along with the tenses you have learned: present indicative, present subjunctive, preterit, and imperfect.

1. Yo quería tomar un café esta mañana. Mi colega me lo trajo.

   _____

2. Los niños tienen muchos regalos. Sus abuelos quieren que me los den.

   _____

3. Ella me compró una chaqueta. Después de comprármela, se puso feliz.

4. Mi papá no quiso darme su carro. En vez de dármelo, me lo vendió.

5. Aprendí bien las direcciones porque mis parientes me las dieron con mucho cuidado.

6. Ella quiere darme tres maletas para mi viaje. Prefiero que ella me las preste.

7. Cada mañana, los vendedores me vendían vegetales. Hoy no me vendieron nada.

8. Necesito dos buenos libros. Tengo que comprarlos porque mi amiga no quiere prestármelos.

A Word About Pronunciation

Practice all these examples aloud. The more you get used to the sound, the easier it becomes.

Te lo / te la / te los / te las

Te doy mi abrigo porque hace frío.	*I'll give you my coat because it is cold.*
Te lo doy esta noche.	*I'll give it to you tonight.*
¿Por qué no me dijiste la verdad?	*Why didn't you tell me the truth?*
Te la dije, pero no me escuchaste.	*I told it to you, but you didn't listen to me.*
José tuvo que leer dos cuentos anoche.	*Joe had to read two stories last night.*
Él tuvo que leér**telos** antes de las nueve.	*He had to read them to you before nine.*
Queremos mandar cartas desde Madrid.	*We want to send letters from Madrid.*
Queremos mandár**telas** esta noche.	*We want to send them to you tonight.*

Exercise 15.8

Translate the following sentences into English.

1. Ella no te da agua; ella te la vende.

   _____

2. Debemos regalarte el anillo que quieres este año. Debemos regalártelo.

   _____

3. Anoche, mi hermano mayor me trajo una manzana. Me la trajo porque yo tenía hambre.

   _____

4. Todavía tienes mis discos compactos. Quiero que me los devuelvas.

   _____

5. Me gusta la langosta en este restaurante. Espero que el camarero me la sirva rápidamente.

   _____

6. Te di el dinero porque eres un buen amigo. Te lo di porque tengo confianza en ti.

   _____

7. No sé por qué ella no quiso mostrarte sus lámparas. A mí me las mostró ayer.

   _____

8. Al principio, no queríamos darte una bicicleta, pero por fin te la dimos.

   _____

Se lo / se la / se los / se las

For reasons of pronunciation, **se** replaces the indirect object pronouns **le** and **les** when they are followed by a direct object pronoun.

le lo	→ **se lo**	les lo	→ **se lo**
le la	→ **se la**	les la	→ **se la**
le los	→ **se los**	les los	→ **se los**
le las	→ **se las**	les las	→ **se las**

Se lo traigo.
{
I bring it to him.
I bring it to her.
I bring it to you. (sing.)
I bring it to them.
I bring it to you. (pl.)
}

Out of context, there is no way to know what the meaning of the indirect object pronoun is. To clarify the ambiguity, a prepositional phrase is added.

Se lo traigo **a Ud.**	*I bring it to you.*
Se lo traigo **a ellas**.	*I bring it to them.*

In context, however, the meaning is clear without an additional prepositional phrase.

Le doy a Enrique el periódico.	*I give the newspaper to Henry.*
Se lo doy.	*I give it to him.*
Ella quiere comprar una camisa.	*She wants to buy a shirt.*
Nosotros **se la** vendemos.	*We'll sell it to her.*
Les enviamos dinero a los estudiantes.	*We send money to the students.*
Se lo enviamos.	*We send it to them.*
Ana les trae dos pasteles a sus amigas.	*Ana brings two pastries to her friends.*
Ana **se los** trae.	*Ana brings them to them.*
Yo les quiero escribir a Uds. tres cartas.	*I want to write you three letters.*
Yo quiero escribír**selas**.	*I want to write them to you.*
Él les muestra las fotos a Juan y a Ana.	*He shows the photos to John and Ana.*
Él trata de mostrár**selas**.	*He tries to show them to them.*

A Word About Double Object Pronouns

Try to practice the **se lo / se la / se los / se las** combination without going through two steps. Every time you think of *to her, to him, to you, to them* followed by a direct object pronoun, use **se**. Note also that the intransitive verbs you learned in Chapter 10 are used over and over. These are the most frequently used verbs that take indirect objects.

Exercise 15.9

Complete the following sentences with the correct double object pronoun, according to the context of the sentence.

EXAMPLE   Les trajimos las flores. ___*Se las*___ trajimos.

1. Yo quería comprarte el carro, pero no tenía bastante dinero. Al fin y al cabo, no _____ pude comprar.

2. Él no me dio el libro. No sé dónde está. ¿Él _____ dio a Ud.?

3. Necesito tu lápiz. ¿_____ prestas?

4. ¿Por qué no les dijeron Uds. a los muchachos la verdad? ¿Por qué no _____ dijeron?

5. Los hombres querían leer los periódicos de hoy. El vendedor _____ vendió.

6. Yo les traje una torta a Uds. Yo _____ traje anoche.

7. Tratamos de hacerles muchas preguntas. Tratamos de [hacer] _____ porque no sabemos nada.

8. Loreta y Roberto me mandaron dos paquetes. _____ mandaron ayer.

9. Te dimos la respuesta ya. _____ dimos hace dos horas.

10. ¿Por qué les prestaste dinero? ¿_____ prestaste porque necesitan ayuda?

11. Vamos a enseñarle la lección. _____ vamos a enseñar.

12. ¿Tienen Uds. frío? ¿Necesitan otra chaqueta? _____ puedo traer.

13. Ella no sabe que decirte. ¿Por qué no le cuentas el cuento? Es mejor [contar] _____ .

14. Nadie quería decirle los resultados de las elecciones. Nadie _____ quería decir.

Nos lo / nos la / nos los / nos las

Él va a devolvernos el suéter.	*He is going to return the sweater to us.*
Él va a devolvér**noslo**.	*He is going to return it to us.*
La mujer nos trajo una flor.	*The woman brought us a flower.*
Ella **nos la** trajo.	*She brought it to us.*
Nuestros amigos nos dan regalos cada año.	*Our friends give us gifts every year.*
Nuestros amigos **nos los** dan.	*Our friends give them to us.*
Ud. nos traía tortas los domingos.	*You used to bring us cakes on Sundays.*
Ahora Ud. nunca **nos las** trae.	*Now you never bring them to us.*

Os lo / os la / os los / os las

Vuestra tía os lee un libro en la noche.	*Your aunt reads a book to you at night.*
Ella **os lo** lee.	*She reads it to you.*
Él no quiere escribiros una carta.	*He doesn't want to write a letter to you.*
Él no quiere escribír**osla**.	*He doesn't want to write it to you.*
Ana no os mandó recuerdos.	*Ana didn't send you souvenirs.*
Ella debe mandár**oslos**.	*She should send them to you.*
El doctor no os dio las pastillas.	*The doctor didn't give you the pills.*
El farmacista **os las** vendió.	*The pharmacist sold them to you.*

Note that **os** means *to you* in the plural familiar **vosotros** form. It is used only in Spain.

 ## Exercise 15.10

Translate the following sentences into Spanish. Practice indirect objects, direct objects, and double object pronouns, as well as the tenses.

1. *I told you everything. You said nothing to me.*

———————————————————————————

2. *We were going to give two notebooks to the students.*

    _____

3. *Lisa doesn't have anything to write with. I have two pens and decide to give them to her.*

    _____

4. *I gave a violin to my nephew. I gave it to him.*

    _____

5. *He was going to give the guitar to Hector. He decided to give it to me.*

    _____

6. *Who can show us the new coats? Who wants to show them to us?*

    _____

7. *The birds were singing and the children were playing.*

    _____

8. *Carmen read a good book two weeks ago. She gave it to me yesterday.*

    _____

9. *I returned the book to her today. I returned it to her at ten o'clock in the morning.*

    _____

10. *Elena had bad dreams last night. She told them to me this morning.*

    _____

11. *We like to share everything.*

    _____

12. *Your grandmother wants you to read the article to her.*

    _____

13. *We hope that he knows how to swim so that he can teach us.*

    _____

14. *Joe lent Michael the money. He lent it to him yesterday.*

    _____

15. *Your cousin did you a favor. He did it for you because he is a good friend.*

    _____

16. *After bringing her coffee, I went to my office. She called me later.*

_____

17. *She was buying a guitar when her friend offered her a piano.*

_____

18. *We saw the sofa that she had in her house. She gave it to us.*

_____

Reflexive Pronoun with Direct Object Pronoun

This combination does not occur with many verbs. It is most common with the action of putting on or taking off clothes (**ponerse la ropa**, **quitarse la ropa**), with verbs that are used with parts of the body (**lavarse**, **cepillarse**, **lesionarse**, **peinarse**, **secarse**), and with some idiomatic verbs (**comerse**). A reflexive object pronoun precedes a direct object pronoun when they occur together.

The objects are either placed directly before the first verb or attached to the infinitive.

Me pongo un abrigo en el invierno.	*I put on a coat in the winter.*
Me lo quito en el apartamento.	*I take it off in the apartment.*
¿Te lavaste la cara hoy?	*Did you wash your face today?*
¿**Te la** lavaste hoy?	*Did you wash it today?*
Nos cepillamos los dientes cada noche.	*We brush our teeth every night.*
Nos los cepillamos en la mañana también.	*We brush them in the morning, too.*
Ellos se peinaron el pelo.	*They combed their hair.*
Ellos **se lo** peinaron.	*They combed it.*
Me comí todo el pescado.	*I ate up all the fish.*
Me lo comí.	*I ate it all up.*
Él se puso los zapatos.	*He put on his shoes.*
Él **se los** puso.	*He put them on.*
Ella se quitó la gorra.	*She took off her hat.*
Ella **se la** quitó.	*She took it off.*
¿Por qué se quitó Ud. la chaqueta?	*Why did you take off your jacket?*
¿Por qué **se la** quitó Ud.?	*Why did you take it off?*

Yo no quería cortarme el pelo.	*I didn't want to cut my hair.*
No quería cortár**melo**.	*I didn't want to cut it.*
Ella no pudo lavarse las manos anoche.	*She couldn't wash her hands last night.*
Ella no pudo lavár**selas**.	*She couldn't wash them.*
El niño trató de ponerse los calcetines.	*The child tried to put on his socks.*
Él trató de ponér**selos**.	*He tried to put them on.*

A Reminder

When reflexive verbs are used with clothes and parts of the body, the possessive adjective is not used.

Se Plus the Indirect Object Pronoun and Unplanned Occurrences

Se + the indirect object pronoun + the verb express the concept of an action that just seemed to happen—an unplanned occurrence. The indirect object pronoun indicates the person or persons *responsible for* or *affected by* the action.

This construction occurs only in the third person because the subject is a thing or things. It usually occurs in the preterit because the action has already happened.

Yo rompí el vaso.	*I broke the glass. (It was not an accident; I broke the glass on purpose.)*
Se rompió el vaso.	*The glass broke. (It was an accident, and no one is responsible.)*
Se **me** rompió el vaso.	*I broke the glass by accident. (The glass broke by accident, but I am responsible.)*
El gato se murió.	*The cat died. (No one is responsible.)*
El gato se **me** murió. {	*The cat died. (The cat died because I did not take care of it properly and I am responsible.)*
	The cat died. (I took care of the cat, but it died anyway, and I am affected.)

El niño se cayó.	*The child fell. (No one is responsible or affected.)*
El niño se **nos** cayó.	*The child fell. (The child fell because we were inattentive, and we are responsible.)* *The child fell. (We took care of the child, but he fell anyway. It is not our fault, but we are affected.)*

Here are other verbs that often express this concept.

acabarse	*to run out of*
irse	*to go away, to leave quickly*
ocurrirse	*to get the idea of, to occur to*
olvidarse	*to forget*
perderse	*to lose*

No pudiste hacer los sándwiches; se **te** acabó el pan.	*You couldn't make the sandwiches; you ran out of bread. (It wasn't your fault.)*
No se **me** ocurrió trabajar ayer.	*It didn't occur to me to work yesterday.*
Se **le** olvidó la fecha de tu cumpleaños.	*He forgot the date of your birthday by accident.*
Se **me** perdieron mis gafas.	*I lost my glasses by accident.*

 Exercise 15.11

Complete the following sentences with the correct verb form and object pronouns.

EXAMPLE   Me lastimé el tobillo. Yo _____me lo lastimé_____ .

1. ¿Por qué no te secas el pelo? ¿Por qué no _____?

2. Vamos a quitarnos el vestido. Vamos a _____ .

3. Ellos se cepillaron los dientes. Ellos _____ .

4. Él se puso las medias. Él _____ .

5. Me corté el dedo. Yo _____ .

6. Los niños se van a lavar las manos. Ellos _____ .

7. Ella se peina el pelo bonito cada día. Ella _____ .

Exercise 15.12

Translate the following sentences into English.

1. A él le gustó el pollo y se lo comió.

   _____

2. Miguel no pudo entrar en su casa porque se le perdieron las llaves.

   _____

3. Se me cayó la cuchara en la mesa y me puse furiosa.

   _____

4. Ellos se dieron cuenta de que sus amigos no venían a verlos.

   _____

5. ¿Cómo se les ocurrió escribir un libro juntos?

   _____

6. Se me olvidó hacer mi tarea. Se me acabó la paciencia.

   _____

7. ¡Cuidado! Se les van a caer los vasos. Ya se nos rompieron dos.

   _____

8. Después de ponerse las medias, ellos se pusieron los zapatos y se fueron.

   _____

 Exercise 15.13

On a separate sheet of paper, write the English translation of the following infinitives from Part III.

1. acercarse	8. castigar	15. contener	22. destruir
2. ahogarse	9. colgar	16. contradecir	23. detener
3. alcanzar	10. colocar	17. contribuir	24. distraer
4. amenazar	11. componer	18. corregir	25. distribuir
5. arrancar	12. concluir	19. creer	26. entregar
6. atraer	13. conducir	20. deshacer	27. fluir
7. caber	14. construir	21. destacar	28. huir

29. incluir	35. mascar	41. proponer	47. traducir
30. influir	36. pegar	42. publicar	48. tragar
31. justificar	37. pescar	43. realizar	49. tropezarse
32. lanzar	38. poseer	44. rezar	50. vagar
33. madrugar	39. prevenir	45. sacar	
34. mantener	40. producir	46. suplicar	

 # Reading Comprehension

El juicio (segunda escena)

ACUSADO   Cuando yo hablé con él, me di cuenta de que él no era sabio. Cuando me fui, pensaba, "Yo soy más sabio que este hombre; ninguno de nosotros no sabe nada que valga la pena saber, pero él piensa que él tiene sabiduría cuando él no la tiene, y yo, sin saber nada, no pienso que yo sea sagaz. No pienso que sé lo que no sé." Después, fui a ver a los poetas, pensando que ellos iban a ser más sagaces que yo.

Pero averigüé que no es por la sabiduría que los poetas crean sus poemas sino por una inspiración divina. Por fin, fui a ver a los artesanos. Ellos sabían lo que yo no sabía y por eso eran más sabios que yo. Pero me pareció que cada uno se creía extremadamente sagaz en cuestiones importantes porque eran hábiles en su propio arte.

Mucho prejuicio contra mi resultó de mi investigación. Y yo sigo con mi tarea de investigar y examinar a cada persona que pienso que es sagaz y si él no es sagaz yo se lo digo. Estoy tan ocupado en mi investigación que no he tenido tiempo ni para servir en posiciones del estado ni de ganar dinero. Como resultado, yo soy pobre. Es verdad lo que les dije. Y yo sé que por esta investigación de la gente hay mucha rabia contra mí. Pero lo que Uds. escuchan es mi defensa contra estas primeras acusaciones.

Verbos

averiguar	*to check out, to verify*
darse cuenta (de)	*to realize*
he tenido	*I have had* (present perfect tense)
valer	*to value*

Nombre

el arte   *the art*

NOTE: **El arte** is masculine in the singular but feminine in the plural.

el arte español   *Spanish art*
las bellas artes   *fine arts*

Adjetivos

hábil   *skillful, capable*
propio   *own*

Preguntas

After you have finished reading the selection, answer the following questions in Spanish.

1. ¿Con quiénes habló?

_____

2. ¿Qué es lo que el acusado siempre busca?

_____

3. ¿Se defendió bien el acusado?

_____

4. ¿Quién es el acusado?

_____

IV

Ser and *Estar*;
Present, Preterit,
and Imperfect Tenses;
Progressive Tenses;
Present Subjunctive;
Commands

16

Ser and *Estar*
and the Present Tense

Estar (to be)

Spanish has two verbs that are equivalent to English *to be*. Begin with the conjugation of **estar** in the present tense.

yo **estoy**	*I am*	nosotros **estamos**	*we are*
tú **estás**	*you are*	vosotros **estáis**	*you are*
él **está**	*he is*	ellos **están**	*they are*
ella **está**	*she is*	ellas **están**	*they are*
Ud. **está**	*you are*	Uds. **están**	*you are*

There is no subject pronoun *it* in Spanish. **Él** and **ella** refer to people and sometimes to animals, but not to things.

Practice the conjugation of the verb aloud. Notice that **él**, **ella**, **Ud.** (the third-person singular) have the same form of the verb. Notice also that **ellos**, **ellas**, **Uds.** (the third-person plural) have the same form of the verb.

Estar is used to express four basic concepts: location, health, changing mood or condition, and personal opinion in terms of taste or appearance.

- **Location** (where someone or something is physically located)

Nosotros estamos en el tren.	*We are on the train.*
La quinta avenida está en la ciudad.	*Fifth Avenue is in the city.*
¿Dónde están las pirámides de los Mayas?	*Where are the Mayan pyramids?*
Las mujeres están en la biblioteca.	*The women are in the library.*

Remember

The verb, which carries the action of the phrase, is the essential element of the Spanish sentence or question because of the amount of information it carries.

- **Health**

Yo estoy bien, gracias.	*I am fine, thanks.*
Ella está enferma.	*She is sick.*
Los doctores están enfermos.	*The doctors are sick.*
¿Cómo están Uds.?	*How are you?*
Estamos bien.	*We are well.*

- **Changing mood or condition**

La muchacha está contenta.	*The girl is happy.*
Estoy feliz.	*I am happy.*
Los hombres están cansados.	*The men are tired.*
Estamos alegres.	*We are happy.*
¿Estás enojado?	*Are you angry?*

- **Personal opinion in terms of taste or appearance**
  (English equivalents: *taste/tastes* with food and *look/looks* with appearance)

La comida está buena.	*The meal tastes good.*
El pescado está delicioso.	*The fish tastes delicious.*
La sopa está sabrosa.	*The soup tastes delicious.*
Ella está hermosa hoy.	*She looks pretty today.*
Él está guapo.	*He looks handsome.*

Remember

Often, the pronouns **yo**, **nosotros**, and **tú** are omitted. This is possible because the verb form **estamos** carries the meaning *we are*; **estoy** can only mean *I am*. The same is true of **tú estás**, which means *you are* whether **tú** is omitted or not.

Key Vocabulary

These words will help enhance your ability to communicate. As you learn them, remember to practice them aloud.

Interrogative Words

¿cómo?	*how?*
¿cuál?, ¿cuáles?	*which one?, which ones?*
¿cuándo?	*when?*
¿cuánto?, ¿cuántos?	*how much?, how many?*
¿dónde?	*where?*
¿por qué?	*why?*
¿qué?	*what?*
¿quién?, ¿quiénes?	*who?*

Adverbs of Location

aquí, acá	*here*
allí, allá	*there*

Adverbs of Direction

a la derecha	*to the right*
a la izquierda	*to the left*
derecho, recto	*straight ahead*

Prepositions of Location

al lado de	*next to*
alrededor de	*around*
ante	*before, in front of, in the presence of*
bajo	*under* (more figurative than **debajo de**)
cerca de	*near*
debajo de	*underneath*
delante de	*before, in front of* (physical location)
dentro de	*inside of*
detrás de	*behind*
encima de	*on top of*
enfrente de, frente a	*in front of, opposite, facing, across from*
entre	*between*
fuera de	*outside of*
junto a, pegado a	*close to, right next to*

| lejos de | *far from* |
| tras | *after* (in a set of expressions) |

Adjectives

alegre	*happy, glad*
bonito	*pretty*
bueno	*good*
cansado	*tired*
contento	*happy (contented)*
delicioso	*delicious*
enfermo	*sick*
enojado	*angry*
feliz	*happy*
guapo	*beautiful, handsome*
hermoso	*beautiful, handsome*
lindo	*pretty*
sabroso	*delicious*

NOTE **Guapo** describes people only; **bonito**, **hermoso**, and **lindo** are used to describe both people and things.

Exercise 16.1

Complete the following sentences with the correct form of **estar**. *Indicate whether the sentence expresses health, location, or changing mood.*

EXAMPLES   Nosotros _estamos_ en la clase. (_location_)

La profesora _está_ aquí. (_location_)

1. El teléfono y el libro _____ en la mesa. (_____)

2. La mujer _____ bien; el hombre _____ enfermo.

   (_____, _____)

3. ¿Cómo _____ Uds.? (_____)

4. ¿Dónde _____ ellos? (_____)

5. ¿Dónde _____ el baño, por favor? (_____)

6. El niño _____ enojado y la niña _____ triste.

   (_____, _____)

7. Los muchachos _____ alegres. (_____)

8. Yo _____ contento. (_____)

9. ¿Quién _____ aquí? (_____)

10. ¿Por qué _____ el perro en la piscina? (_____)

Exercise 16.2

Translate the following sentences into Spanish.

1. The river is near my house.

   _____

2. Australia is far from Canada.

   _____

3. The white flower is on top of the table.

   _____

4. The children are right next to their parents.

   _____

5. The school is between the church and the bank.

   _____

6. Julia's house is behind the post office.

   _____

7. Paula is here with her brothers.

   _____

8. Your shoes are underneath my chair.

   _____

9. Our problem is under control.

   _____

10. Helen's relatives are in Spain. Their suitcases are in the United States.

    _____

Ser (to be)

Ser is also equivalent to English *to be*. In English, there is only a single verb that means *to be*. We say, for example:

The dog is here.
The dog is brown.

The verb is the same in both cases. But in Spanish, there is a difference, and you have to choose which verb to use.

Following is the conjugation of **ser** in the present tense.

yo **soy**	*I am*	nosotros **somos**	*we are*
tú **eres**	*you are*	vosotros **sois**	*you are*
él **es**	*he is*	ellos **son**	*they are*
ella **es**	*she is*	ellas **son**	*they are*
Ud. **es**	*you are*	Uds. **son**	*you are*

Ser is used to express seven basic concepts: description, profession, point of origin, identification, material, possession or ownership, and where an event takes place.

- **Description**

La casa es roja.	*The house is red.*
El libro es interesante.	*The book is interesting.*
Estas corbatas son feas.	*These ties are ugly.*
Somos fuertes.	*We are strong.*
Estos zapatos son más caros que esas medias.	*These shoes are more expensive than those socks.*

- **Profession**

Yo soy abogado.	*I am a lawyer.*
Él es arquitecto.	*He is an architect.*
Ellas son maestras excelentes.	*They are excellent teachers.*
Somos doctores.	*We are doctors.*
¿Eres tú ingeniero?	*Are you an engineer?*

Spanish does not translate *a/an* when stating an unmodified profession.

UNMODIFIED	Juan es bailarín.	*Juan is a dancer.*
MODIFIED	Juan es un buen bailarín.	*Juan is a good dancer.*

- **Point of origin** (where someone or something is from)

¿De dónde es Ud.?	*Where are you from?*
¿De dónde son Uds.?	*Where are you from?*
Yo soy de Nueva York.	*I am from New York.*
¿De dónde es ella?	*Where is she from?*
Somos de Italia.	*We are from Italy.*
Ellos son de los Estados Unidos.	*They are from the United States.*
El vino es de Portugal.	*The wine is from Portugal.*
La cerveza es de México.	*The beer is from Mexico.*
El café es de Brazil.	*The coffee is from Brazil.*

Remember

In common English usage, we often end a sentence with a preposition, for example, *Where are you from?* This never occurs in Spanish; the preposition can never end a sentence. The preposition, in this case **de**, is placed in front of the interrogative word, which in this case is **dónde**.

- **Identification** (relationship, nationality, or religion)

Somos amigos.	*We are friends.*
José y Eduardo son hermanos.	*Joe and Ed are brothers.*
Pablo es español.	*Paul is Spanish.*
Ella es católica.	*She is Catholic.*

- **Material** (what something is made of)

La mesa es de madera.	*The table is of wood.*
La bolsa es de plástico.	*The bag is of plastic.*
Los zapatos son de cuero.	*The shoes are of leather.*
Las ventanas son de vidrio.	*The windows are of glass.*
La casa es de piedra.	*The house is of stone.*

- **Possession or ownership**

La muñeca es de la niña.	*It's the child's doll. /*
	The doll is the child's.
	(The doll is of the child.)
Los amigos son de María.	*They are María's friends. /*
	The friends are María's.
	(The friends are of María.)

La idea es de Pedro.	*It's Pedro's idea. /*
	The idea is Pedro's.
	(The idea is of Pedro.)
El barco es del hombre rico.	*The boat belongs to the rich man.*
	(The boat is of the rich man.)
Los perros son del muchacho.	*The dogs belong to the boy.*
	(The dogs are of the boy.)
Los gatos son del niño.	*The cats belong to the child.*
	(The cats are of the child.)
El carro es de los amigos.	*The car belongs to the friends.*
	(The car is of the friends.)

De + **el** (*of* + *the*) = **del**. There are only two contractions in the Spanish language; **del** is one of them. When **de** is followed by the masculine article **el**, meaning *the*, the words contract to **del**, meaning *of the*.

A Word About Possessives

You can see that these translations are not exact. There is no apostrophe in Spanish, so when you think of *Peter's car*, for example, the Spanish structure is *el carro de Pedro*. Make sure you understand this concept, and use whichever English translation is clearest to you.

- **Where an event takes place**

La fiesta es en la casa de José.	*The party is at Joe's house.*
El concierto es en el club.	*The concert is at the club.*
La protesta es en la capital.	*The protest is in the capital.*
La huelga es en la universidad.	*The strike is at the university.*

An equivalent English translation for *is* in the examples above is *take/takes place*:

The party takes place at Joe's house.
The concert takes place at the club.
The protest takes place in the capital.

Ser is also used to tell time and in impersonal expressions.

- **Telling time**

  Spanish uses the third-person singular or plural of **ser** for telling time. **La** refers to **la hora**.

Es la una.	*It is one o'clock.*
Son las dos.	*It is two o'clock.*
Son las tres.	*It is three o'clock.*
Son las cuatro.	*It is four o'clock.*
Son las cinco.	*It is five o'clock.*
Son las seis.	*It is six o'clock.*
Son las siete.	*It is seven o'clock.*
Son las ocho.	*It is eight o'clock.*
Son las nueve.	*It is nine o'clock.*
Son las diez.	*It is ten o'clock.*
Son las once.	*It is eleven o'clock.*
Son las doce.	*It is twelve o'clock.*

- **In impersonal expressions**

Es bueno.	*It is good.*
Es difícil.	*It is difficult.*
Es fácil.	*It is easy.*
Es imposible.	*It is impossible.*
Es importante.	*It is important.*
Es malo.	*It is bad.*
Es mejor.	*It is better.*
Es necesario.	*It is necessary.*
Es posible.	*It is possible.*
Es preciso.	*It is necessary.*
Es probable.	*It is probable.*
Es una lástima.	*It's a shame. / It's a pity.*
Es urgente.	*It is urgent.*

Exercise 16.3

*Complete the following sentences with the correct form of **ser**. Indicate whether the sentence expresses description, profession, point of origin, identification, material, possession, or an impersonal expression.*

EXAMPLE   _Es_ la una. (telling time)

1. El hombre _____ director. Él _____ de Chile.

   (_____ , _____)

2. Ellos _____ doctores. Ella _____ profesora.

   (_____ , _____)

3. ¿De dónde _____ los turistas? (_____)

4. Los hermanos de Pablo _____ simpáticos. (_____)

5. El hotel viejo _____ excelente. (_____)

6. Nosotros _____ amigos de Raúl. (_____)

7. Los guantes _____ de cuero. (_____)

8. La mujer y el hombre _____ de Ecuador. (_____)

9. Yo _____ de Puerto Rico. ¿De dónde _____ Ud.?

   (_____ , _____)

10. El apartamento _____ de los estudiantes jóvenes.

    (_____)

11. ¿ _____ tú una estudiante maravillosa? (_____)

12. Los pantalones _____ verdes y rojos. (_____)

13. El café _____ de Colombia. (_____)

14. ¿Quién _____ el presidente de los Estados Unidos?

    (_____)

15. _____ preciso comer bien. (_____)

Exercise 16.4

*Complete the following sentences with the correct form of **ser**.*

1. Helena _____ de Colombia.

2. El hermano de ella _____ católico.

3. Ellos _____ profesores excelentes.

4. Los carros _____ grises.

5. Nosotros _____ estudiantes.

*Complete the following sentences with the correct form of **estar**.*

6. San Francisco _____ en California.

7. ¿Cómo está Ud.? Yo _____ bien.

8. El profesor _____ enfermo.

9. Nosotros _____ en la clase.

10. ¿_____ tú triste?

11. Los perros _____ en el carro.

Exercise 16.5

*Complete the following sentences with the correct form of either **ser** or **estar**.*

1. Yo _____ español.

2. Ellos _____ aquí.

3. José y Juan _____ enfermos.

4. Tú _____ abogado.

5. La lección no _____ fácil.

6. Los estudiantes _____ en la ciudad.

7. ¿Cómo _____ Uds.? Nosotros _____ bien, gracias.

8. Hoy _____ miércoles. ¿Dónde _____ los doctores?

9. El profesor _____ contento.

10. Los espejos en el baño _____ grandes.

11. La mesa, las sillas blancas y la lámpara _____ en la casa, pero la casa _____ pequeña.

12. La amiga de Sara _____ enferma y Sara _____ triste.

13. ¿De dónde _____ el vino blanco?

14. Los muchachos y las muchachas _____ en el tren. Ellos _____ contentos porque _____ amigos.

15. ¿Quién _____ en el parque?

16. ¿Dónde _____ la sobrina de Fernando?

17. ¿Qué hora _____?

18. _____ las cuatro y media.

19. La presentación _____ a las siete de la noche.

20. ¿De qué color _____ la falda?

Exercise 16.6

Translate the following sentences into Spanish.

1. *The dentists are in their offices.*

   _____

2. *Everyone is sick. Even the doctors are sick.*

   _____

3. *The soup is hot. The meal is delicious.*

   _____

4. *It is necessary to study.*

   _____

5. *Is it possible to learn everything?*

   _____

Common Expressions with *estar*

está bien	*okay, fine*
estar a salvo	*to be safe*
estar bien	*to be fine*
estar con	*to be with*
estar de acuerdo con	*to be in agreement with*
estar de buen genio	*to be in a good mood*
estar de buen humor	*to be in a good mood*
estar de mal genio	*to be in a bad mood*
estar de mal humor	*to be in a bad mood*
estar de pie	*to be standing up*
estar de rodillas	*to be on one's knees*
estar de vacaciones	*to be on vacation*
estar de vuelta	*to be returning*
estar en peligro	*to be in danger*
estar entre la vida y la muerte	*to be between life and death*
estar listo	*to be ready*
estar mal	*to be bad* (adverb)
estar para	*to be about to*
estar por	*to be in favor of*
estar seguro	*to be sure*
estar sin	*to be without*

In general, **estar** is used with the adjectives **frío**, **caliente**, **sucio**, and **limpio**.

El agua está fría.	*The water is cold.*
La sopa está caliente.	*The soup is hot.*
Mi apartamento está sucio.	*My apartment is dirty.*
La casa de María está limpia.	*María's house is clean.*

Common Expressions with *ser*

ser bueno	*to be good*
ser malo	*to be bad*
ser listo	*to be clever*
ser todo oídos	*to be all ears*

Ser and *estar* and Description

You have learned that **ser** is used for basic description, as in the following examples:

> *The dog is white.*
> *The floor is gray.*
> *We are intelligent.*

However, there are specific situations with description in which **estar** is used. Following are examples of typical uses of **ser** for description, contrasted with related specific uses of **estar**.

- **Food**

  When talking about food in general, use **ser**.

El pescado es bueno para la salud.	*Fish is good for health.*
La carne es mala para la presión.	*Meat is bad for the blood pressure.*

  When giving an opinion about food, use **estar**.

Esta comida está mala.	*This meal is bad.*
El pescado está bueno.	*The fish is good.*
La sopa está sabrosa.	*The soup is delicious.*
Las papas están deliciosas.	*The potatoes are delicious.*

- **Appearance**

  When stating an inherent characteristic, use **ser**.

Ella es hermosa.	*She is beautiful.*
Él es gordo.	*He is fat.*
La actriz es vieja.	*The actress is old.*
Mis amigas son delgadas.	*My friends are slender.*

  When giving an opinion about appearance, use **estar**.

Ella está hermosa.	*She looks beautiful.*
Él está gordo.	*He looks fat to me.*
	(He has gotten fat.)
La actriz está vieja.	*The actress looks old.*

- **Classification**

  When an adjective applies to something that exists without exception, use **ser**.

  Los seres humanos son mortales. *Human beings are mortal.*
  La sangre es roja. *Blood is red.*
  El agua es necesaria para la vida. *Water is necessary for life.*
  El oxígeno es indispensable para *Oxygen is indispensable for living*
  los seres vivos. *beings.*
  La nieve es blanca. *Snow is white.*
  El cielo es azul. *The sky is blue.*

  When the description is outside the known or cultural norm, use **estar**.

  La nieve está roja por la sangre. *The snow is red because of*
  the blood.
  El cielo está anaranjado y amarillo *The sky is orange and yellow*
  por la puesta del sol. *because of the sunset.*
  La puerta está azul marino por *The door looks navy blue because*
  el sol fuerte. *of the strong sun.*
  Los labios del niño están azules *The child's lips are blue because*
  porque está congelado. *he is freezing.*

Exercise 16.7

*Complete the following sentences with the correct form of **ser** or **estar**, according to the meaning of the sentence.*

1. El niño _____ de mal genio hoy. Su mamá no sabe que hacer.

2. _____ o no _____; es la cuestión.

3. La reunión _____ en el segundo piso.

4. Las flores que los estudiantes me regalan _____ en el salón.

5. ¿Dónde _____ yo?

6. ¿Cómo sabes quien _____ (tú)?

7. ¿Qué hora _____? _____ las dos.

8. ¿Cuál _____ la fecha de hoy?

9. _____ las once de la noche. Ya _____ tarde.

10. _____ demasiado temprano para levantarse.

11. Hoy _____ lunes, el cinco de mayo.

12. El estudiante trabaja mucho para _____ doctor.

13. La muchacha llora sin _____ triste.

14. El agua _____ fría.

15. Esta comida de tu madre _____ sabrosa.

16. Con los problemas que él tiene, no me explico como este hombre

    _____ tan contento.

17. Tu rival _____ más listo que tú en esta ocasión.

18. La comida que sirven aquí _____ caliente.

19. Luis y su familia _____ muy alegres de haberse ganado la lotería.

20. Este cuarto _____ la habitación más bonita de la casa.

21. ¿Quién _____ en peligro en una ciudad grande?

22. No hay cupo en el tren y yo tengo que _____ de pie.

23. La mujer _____ muy enferma; _____ entre la vida
    y la muerte.

24. La profesora tiene una opinión pero sus estudiantes no _____
    de acuerdo con ella.

25. Siempre escucho las noticias. Yo _____ todo oídos.

26. El agua _____ necesaria para la vida.

27. La clase _____ para terminar y todo el mundo

    _____ para salir.

28. El cielo _____ gris.

29. Nosotros _____ sin un paraguas.

30. Esta lección _____ difícil.

Reading Comprehension

Machu Picchu
Ancient Mountain

Machu Picchu es uno de los sitios más impresionantes del mundo.
La ciudad antigua de los incas, construida en 1450 de piedras enormes
y jardines maravillosos, está en Perú a 120 kilómetros de Cuzco, un pueblo
colonial.

Es el año 1979. Estoy en Cuzco con un grupo turístico. Al principio,
somos un buen grupo. Pero con en el calor insoportable del verano,
el grupo cambia y somos todos contra uno y uno contra todos. En este
sitio tan espiritual, en la cumbre de las montañas de los incas, bajo una
vista majestuosa de las montañas, donde uno está cerca de los dioses
de los incas y lejos de la civilización conocida, somos enemigos mortales.

El bus de regreso está lleno de pasajeros. Son las cuatro de la tarde
y estamos de vuelta. Estoy sola ahora y según el refrán "es mejor estar
sola que mal acompañada".

Verbos

cambiar	*to change*
estar	*to be*
ser	*to be*

Preposiciones

contra	*against*
según	*according to*

Adjetivos

conocido	*known*
construido	*constructed*
insoportable	*unbearable*
lleno	*full*

Expresiones

al principio	*at the beginning*
en la cumbre	*on the top* (of a mountain)

Preguntas

After you have read the selection, answer the following questions in Spanish.

1. ¿Es el/la protagonista mujer u hombre? ¿Cómo sabe Ud.?

   _____

2. ¿Cómo es Machu Picchu?

   _____

3. ¿Es una buena experiencia para el grupo?

   _____

4. ¿Cuál estación es? ¿Cómo es el clima?

   _____

Ser and Estar in the Preterit and Imperfect Tenses

Preterit Tense

The preterit expresses action completed in the past. The English translation is usually the simple past. The preterit is used to express the following:

- An action completed in the past (action with a definite end)
- A series of actions completed in the past
- A condition that is no longer in effect

 ## Key Vocabulary

This list of words is often used when referring to past actions.

Adverbios y Adjetivos

anoche	*last night*
ayer	*yesterday*
anteayer	*the day before yesterday*
hace	*ago* (when it is used before a period of time in the past)
hace dos días	*two days ago*
pasado	*past, last*
la semana pasada	*last week*
el mes pasado	*last month*
el año pasado	*last year*

Keep in mind that the action or actions expressed by the preterit have been completed. It doesn't make any difference how long the action went on before; the action has a definite end.

Estar in the Preterit

The conjugation of **estar** in the preterit follows. Remember the three primary uses of **estar**: location, health, and changing mood or condition.

estar *to be*	
yo **estuve**	nosotros **estuvimos**
tú **estuviste**	vosotros **estuvisteis**
él **estuvo**	ellos **estuvieron**
ella **estuvo**	ellas **estuvieron**
Ud. **estuvo**	Uds. **estuvieron**

- **Location**

Estuvimos en la escuela a las once esta mañana.	*We were at school at eleven o'clock this morning.*
¿Dónde estuviste anoche?	*Where were you last night?*
Mis estudiantes estuvieron en clase ayer a las tres.	*My students were in class yesterday at three o'clock.*

- **Health**

Mi amigo estuvo con gripe el mes pasado, pero está bien hoy.	*My friend had the flu last month, but he is fine today.*
Isabel y su hermana estuvieron enfermas el martes, pero están mucho mejor hoy.	*Isabel and her sister were sick on Tuesday, but they are much better today.*
¿Cómo estuviste tú esta mañana?	*How were you this morning?*

- **Changing mood or condition**

¿Estuviste de mal humor ayer?	*Were you in a bad mood yesterday?*
Las mujeres estuvieron alegres hasta las dos.	*The women were happy until two o'clock.*
Estuvimos tristes por una hora.	*We were sad for an hour.*

Ser in the Preterit

ser *to be*

yo **fui**	nosotros **fuimos**
tú **fuiste**	vosotros **fuisteis**
él **fue**	ellos **fueron**
ella **fue**	ellas **fueron**
Ud. **fue**	Uds. **fueron**

The preterit of **ser** is used most often for profession and identification.

- **Profession**

Antonio fue médico de nuestro pueblo.	*Tony was the doctor of our town.*
Fui cantante hace mucho tiempo.	*I was a singer a long time ago.*
¿Fue Ud. la maestra de la clase?	*Were you the teacher of the class?*

- **Identification**

Fue un buen hombre.	*He was a good man.*
Fuimos amigos.	*We were friends.*
Las negociaciones fueron a favor de la paz.	*The negotiations were in favor of peace.*

 Exercise 17.1

Complete the following sentences with the correct preterit form of **ser** *or* **estar**, *according to the context of the sentence.*

1. Ella es profesora hoy, pero antes _____ azafata.

2. Yo _____ gerente por dos años.

3. Nosotros _____ muy contentos ayer porque nos ganamos la lotería.

4. ¿Por qué _____ Manuel en la cárcel sin decirnos nada?

5. Ellos _____ en el supermercado hoy para comprar alimentos.

6. La semana pasada, Raúl _____ en México. Regresó a casa ayer.

7. Los muchachos _____ enfermos anteayer, pero están bien hoy.

8. _____ una buena idea.

9. ¿Dónde _____ la familia de Federico esta tarde?

10. ¿Quiénes _____ en la librería a las nueve y media esta mañana?

11. Yo _____ por irme de vacaciones, pero me faltó valor.

12. Nosotros _____ de pie la mayor parte del concierto.

Ser and *estar* with Description in the Preterit

On an advanced level, there are situations in which the speaker can decide whether to use **ser** or **estar** in the preterit tense with adjectives. A Spanish speaker can say, for example:

El concierto **fue** fantástico.   *The concert **was** fantastic.*

With this sentence, the speaker transmits a "categorical" judgment, a completed absolute fact.

However, a Spanish speaker may choose to say:

El concierto **estuvo** fantástico.   *The concert **was** fantastic.*

This sentence is more descriptive and represents a "circumstantial" judgment.

A Word About Descriptive Judgments

When examples such as these are presented to native speakers, all generally opine that both are correct, and the majority do not find any perceptible difference between the two. Those who do find some difference are not always able to articulate exactly what this difference is.

La cantante fue maravillosa.	*The singer was marvelous.* (statement of fact)
La cantante estuvo maravillosa.	*The singer was marvelous.* (opinion indicating that the concertgoer enjoyed the performance)
Me gustó la clase. Fue buena.	*I liked the class. It was good.* (statement of fact; a categorical statement about the class)
Me gustó la clase. Estuvo buena.	*I liked the class. It was good.* (circumstantial judgment)

Imperfect Tense

The imperfect tense expresses action in the past that is not seen as completed. The imperfect is used to express the following:

- An action that "sets the stage" for another past action
- An action that expresses a narration, background, or situation in the past
- Repeated, habitual, and customary actions in the past
- Continuous actions or actions in progress in the past
- Description in the past
- Point of origin in the past
- Telling time in the past
- Telling one's age (with **tener**) in the past

Estar in the Imperfect

estar *to be*

yo **estaba**	nosotros **estábamos**
tú **estabas**	vosotros **estabais**
él **estaba**	ellos **estaban**
ella **estaba**	ellas **estaban**
Ud. **estaba**	Uds. **estaban**

- **Location**

Los enamorados estaban a la sombra de un árbol.	*The lovers were in the shade of a tree.*
El bolígrafo estaba debajo de la mesa.	*The pen was under the table.*
¿Dónde estaban Uds. anoche?	*Where were you last night?*
Estábamos en el teatro.	*We were in the theater.*

- **Health**

El hombre estaba cansado, pero siguió con su trabajo.	*The man was tired, but he continued with his work.*
Las pacientes estaban en el hospital porque estaban enfermas.	*The patients were in the hospital because they were sick.*

- **Changing mood or condition**

¿Por qué estaba triste la mujer?	*Why was the woman sad?*
Los niños estaban alegres por no tener clases.	*The children were happy because of not having class.*

- **Personal opinion about food or appearance**

La comida estaba buena.	*The meal was good.*
El pescado estaba delicioso.	*The fish tasted delicious.*
Las mujeres estaban bonitas.	*The women looked pretty.*

Ser in the Imperfect

ser *to be*

yo **era**	nosotros **éramos**
tú **eras**	vosotros **erais**
él **era**	ellos **eran**
ella **era**	ellas **eran**
Ud. **era**	Uds. **eran**

You learned that **ser** can be used in the preterit for profession and identification. The other uses of **ser** are best served by the imperfect.

- **Description in the past**

La casa era blanca.	*The house was white.*
Nuestro vecino era viejo, pero tenía el pelo negro.	*Our neighbor was old, but he had black hair.*
Era un caluroso día del mes de julio cuando nos vimos.	*It was a hot day in the month of July when we saw each other.*
Era agosto, lo recuerdo bien.	*It was August, I remember it well.*

- **Point of origin in the past**

El hombre era de Perú.	*The man was from Peru.*
Sus amigos eran de Chile.	*His friends were from Chile.*
Las flores rojas eran de Bolivia.	*The red flowers were from Bolivia.*

- **Telling time in the past**

  Eran las cinco y Federico iba a la tienda por última vez.

  It was five o'clock, and Fred was going to the store for the last time.

  ¿Qué hora era? Eran las dos de la tarde.

  What time was it? It was two in the afternoon.

  Eran las nueve de la noche y los niños dormían.

  It was nine at night and the children were sleeping.

  Eran las tres menos diez de la tarde cuando el profesor llegó.

  It was ten to three in the afternoon when the professor arrived.

- **Identification in the past**

  Era un buen hombre.

  He was a good man.

  Mi tío siempre era más alto que yo.

  My uncle was always taller than I.

  Éramos siempre buenos amigos.

  We were always good friends.

Preterit or Imperfect Determined by the Speaker

You can use both the preterit and imperfect tenses in expressing relationships and in impersonal expressions.

- **Relationships**

  Fuimos buenos amigos.   *We were good friends.*
  Éramos buenos amigos.   *We were good friends.*

  In this example, the English translations are the same, but when you use the preterit in Spanish, it means that the action is completed; the friendship is over.

- **Impersonal expressions**

  Fue bueno.   *It was good.*
  Era bueno.   *It was good.*

  The use of the preterit or imperfect in these situations is a choice made by the speaker; the speaker decides whether the action is completed.

Exercise 17.2

Review **ser** *and* **estar** *in the imperfect, then rewrite the following sentences, changing the verb from the present tense to the imperfect.*

EXAMPLE   Mi padre es de Polonia. *Mi padre era de Polonia.*

1. Yo soy de Venezuela. _____

2. Ellos son de España. _____

3. ¿Qué hora es? _____

4. Nosotros estamos bien. _____

5. Mi jardín es el más hermoso de la ciudad.

   _____

6. Los tres amigos están aquí. _____

7. No estoy cansada. _____

8. Somos cantantes. _____

9. ¿Dónde estás? _____

10. Yo estoy en la casa con mi hermana.

   _____

Exercise 17.3

Complete the following sentences with the correct form of **ser** *or* **estar** *in the preterit or imperfect, according to the meaning of the sentence.*

EXAMPLE   Lorenzo ___*fue*___ escritor. Ahora es bombero.

1. Yo _____ camarero. Ahora soy maestro.

2. Nosotros _____ en el banco precisamente a las nueve esta mañana.

3. Ayer, _____ un día de mucha lluvia. Hace buen tiempo hoy.

4. El paciente _____ en la oficina del doctor a las siete de la mañana para su operación.

5. Carlos _____ gerente por dos años.

6. _____ la última vez que yo _____ a la playa.

7. ¿Quién _____ el presidente en el año mil novecientos noventa y dos?

8. La situación no _____ tan grave.

9. _____ las dos cuando sonó el despertador.

10. El hombre _____ de Perú.

11. ¿Qué día _____ cuando ella se graduó?

12. Me gustó la obra de teatro. _____ buena.

13. Nosotros _____ enfermos ayer, pero nos sentimos bien hoy.

14. _____ difícil recordar todo.

15. _____ una buena idea, pero no vamos a usarla.

Regular Verbs in the Preterit

Most verbs are regular in the preterit tense.

Regular *-ar* Verbs

To conjugate a regular **-ar** verb in the preterit, drop the ending and add **-é**, **-aste**, **-ó**, **-amos**, **-asteis**, **-aron** to the stem.

ayudar *to help*		**cantar** *to sing*	
yo ayudé	nosotros ayudamos	yo canté	nosotros cantamos
tú ayudaste	vosotros ayudasteis	tú cantaste	vosotros cantasteis
Ud. ayudó	Uds. ayudaron	él cantó	ellos cantaron

pensar *to think*		**recordar** *to remember*	
yo pensé	nosotros pensamos	yo recordé	nosotros recordamos
tú pensaste	vosotros pensasteis	tú recordaste	vosotros recordasteis
ella pensó	ellas pensaron	ella recordó	ellas recordaron

A Word About Pronunciation

Notice that the first- and third-person singular forms carry written accents. It is very important to practice the pronunciation, stressing the accented syllable. Pronounce the verbs in this way: **yo canté, tú cantaste, Ud. cantó, nosotros cantamos, vosotros cantasteis, ellos cantaron**. Review the basic pronunciation rules: All words that end in **n, s,** or a vowel have the stress on the second-to-last (penultimate) syllable.

The preterit first-person plural **nosotros** form is identical to the present indicative form. Context clarifies whether the verb is in the present or preterit tense.

Regular -er and -ir Verbs

To conjugate regular **-er** and **-ir** verbs in the preterit, drop the ending and add **-í, -iste, -ió, -imos, -isteis, -ieron** to the stem. The endings are the same for both **-er** and **-ir** verbs.

-Er Verbs

comer *to eat*

yo comí	nosotros comimos
tú comiste	vosotros comisteis
él comió	ellos comieron

entender *to understand*

yo entendí	nosotros entendimos
tú entendiste	vosotros entendisteis
ella entendió	ellas entendieron

ver *to see*

yo vi	nosotros vimos
tú viste	vosotros visteis
Ud. vio	Uds. vieron

-Ir Verbs

compartir *to share*

yo compartí	nosotros compartimos
tú compartiste	vosotros compartisteis
él compartió	ellos compartieron

descubrir *to discover*

yo descubrí	nosotros descubrimos
tú descubriste	vosotros descubristeis
Ud. descubrió	Uds. descubrieron

salir *to leave, to go out*

yo salí	nosotros salimos
tú saliste	vosotros salisteis
ella salió	ellas salieron

 Notice that the verb **ver** is regular. It does not carry an accent mark on the third-person singular form **vio**, because the form has only one syllable. The **nosotros** form of **-ir** verbs in the preterit is identical to the present indicative form. Its meaning becomes clear in context.

-Ir Verbs with Stem Changes in the Third Person

The following verbs have a stem change in the preterit. This stem change occurs only in the third-person singular and plural forms of the preterit.

mentir *to lie*

yo mentí	nosotros mentimos
tú mentiste	vosotros mentisteis
Ud. mintió	Uds. mintieron

pedir *to request, to ask for*

yo pedí	nosotros pedimos
tú pediste	vosotros pedisteis
él pidió	ellos pidieron

dormir *to sleep*

yo dormí	nosotros dormimos
tú dormiste	vosotros dormisteis
ella durmió	ellas durmieron

Irregular Verbs in the Preterit

Verbs that are irregular in the preterit have an irregular stem and a special set of endings. Note that the endings do not carry accent marks. To conjugate an irregular verb in the preterit, add the endings **-e**, **-iste**, **-o**, **-imos**, **-isteis**, **-ieron** to the irregular stems.

andar *to walk, to stroll*

yo anduve	nosotros anduvimos
tú anduviste	vosotros anduvisteis
él anduvo	ellos anduvieron

caber *to fit* (one thing inside another)

yo cupe	nosotros cupimos
tú cupiste	vosotros cupisteis
ella cupo	ellas cupieron

estar *to be*

yo estuve	nosotros estuvimos
tú estuviste	vosotros estuvisteis
Ud. estuvo	Uds. estuvieron

hacer *to do, to make*

yo hice	nosotros hicimos
tú hiciste	vosotros hicisteis
él hizo	ellos hicieron

poder *to be able, can*

yo pude	nosotros pudimos
tú pudiste	vosotros pudisteis
Ud. pudo	Uds. pudieron

poner *to put*

yo puse	nosotros pusimos
tú pusiste	vosotros pusisteis
él puso	ellos pusieron

querer *to want*

yo quise	nosotros quisimos
tú quisiste	vosotros quisisteis
ella quiso	ellas quisieron

saber *to know, to know how*

yo supe	nosotros supimos
tú supiste	vosotros supisteis
Ud. supo	Uds. supieron

tener *to have*

yo tuve	nosotros tuvimos
tú tuviste	vosotros tuvisteis
él tuvo	ellos tuvieron

venir *to come*

yo vine	nosotros vinimos
tú viniste	vosotros vinisteis
él vino	ellos vinieron

When the irregular preterit stem ends in **-j**, the third-person endings become **-o** and **-eron**.

decir *to say, to tell*

yo dije	nosotros dijimos
tú dijiste	vosotros dijisteis
ella dijo	ellas dijeron

producir *to produce*

yo produje	nosotros produjimos
tú produjiste	vosotros produjisteis
Ud. produjo	Uds. produjeron

traer *to bring*

yo traje	nosotros trajimos
tú trajiste	vosotros trajisteis
él trajo	ellos trajeron

Dar, **ir**, and **ser** have different sets of endings.

dar *to give*

yo di	nosotros dimos
tú diste	vosotros disteis
ella dio	ellas dieron

ir *to go*

yo fui	nosotros fuimos
tú fuiste	vosotros fuisteis
Ud. fue	Uds. fueron

ser *to be*

yo fui	nosotros fuimos
tú fuiste	vosotros fuisteis
él fue	ellos fueron

A Word About *haber*

The third-person singular form of **haber** in the preterit is **hubo**, meaning *there was, there were, was there?, were there?*

It is important to memorize the preterit forms of all the irregular verbs, so that you will be able to use any verb you wish in the preterit.

Regular Verbs in the Imperfect

Regular *-ar* Verbs

To conjugate a regular **-ar** verb in the imperfect, drop the ending and add **-aba**, **-abas**, **-aba**, **-ábamos**, **-abais**, **-aban** to the stem. The first- and third-person singular forms (**yo**, **él**, **ella**, **Ud.**) are identical.

acompañar *to accompany*

yo acompañaba	nosotros acompañábamos
tú acompañabas	vosotros acompañabais
él acompañaba	ellos acompañaban

dar *to give*

yo daba	nosotros dábamos
tú dabas	vosotros dabais
ella daba	ellas daban

trabajar *to work*

yo trabajaba	nosotros trabajábamos
tú trabajabas	vosotros trabajabais
Ud. trabajaba	Uds. trabajaban

A Word About the Imperfect

There are no irregular **-ar** verbs in the imperfect. Practice the pronunciation of the verb conjugations above. There are one-syllable, two-syllable, three-syllable, and four-syllable verbs. Be sure to pronounce the imperfect in this way: **yo trabajaba, tú trabajabas, él trabajaba, nosotros trabajábamos, vosotros trabajabais, ellos trabajaban**.

Regular -er and -ir Verbs

To conjugate regular **-er** and **-ir** verbs in the imperfect, drop the ending and add **-ía, -ías, -ía, -íamos, -íais, -ían** to the stem. The endings are the same for both **-er** and **-ir** verbs. The first- and third-person singular forms are identical.

-Er Verbs

hacer *to do, to make*

yo hacía	nosotros hacíamos
tú hacías	vosotros hacíais
ella hacía	ellas hacían

poder *to be able, can*

yo podía	nosotros podíamos
tú podías	vosotros podíais
Ud. podía	Uds. podían

querer *to want*

yo quería	nosotros queríamos
tú querías	vosotros queríais
él quería	ellos querían

saber *to know, to know how*

yo sabía	nosotros sabíamos
tú sabías	vosotros sabíais
ella sabía	ellas sabían

tener *to have*

yo tenía	nosotros teníamos
tú tenías	vosotros teníais
Ud. tenía	Uds. tenían

A Word About *haber*

The third-person singular form of **haber** in the imperfect is **había**, meaning *there was, there were, was there?, were there?*

-Ir Verbs

decir *to say, to tell*

yo decía	nosotros decíamos
tú decías	vosotros decíais
él decía	ellos decían

sentirse *to feel* (an emotion)

me sentía	nos sentíamos
te sentías	os sentíais
Ud. se sentía	Uds. se sentían

venir *to come*

yo venía	nosotros veníamos
tú venías	vosotros veníais
él venía	ellos venían

Irregular Verbs in the Imperfect

There are only three irregular verbs in the imperfect.

ir *to go*

yo iba	nosotros íbamos
tú ibas	vosotros ibais
él iba	ellos iban

ser *to be*

yo era	nosotros éramos
tú eras	vosotros erais
ella era	ellas eran

ver *to see*

yo veía	nosotros veíamos
tú veías	vosotros veíais
Ud. veía	Uds. veían

The translation of **ir** in the imperfect is *was going, were going.*

Yo iba a hablar.	*I was going to speak.*
Nosotros íbamos a comprar un carro.	*We were going to buy a car.*

Comparison of Preterit and Imperfect

Remember that the preterit is a completed action. The imperfect is often an action that was repeated in the past.

Ella llegó ayer.	*She arrived yesterday.*
Ella llegaba a la cinco todos los días.	*She arrived at five o'clock every day.*
La semana pasada, leí un buen libro.	*Last week, I read a good book.*
Antes, yo leía mucho.	*Before, I used to read a lot.*
Beatriz vino a verme.	*Beatriz came to see me.*
Él me dijo que Beatriz venía a verme.	*He told me that Beatriz was coming to see me.*

Me levanté a las seis esta mañana.	*I got up at six o'clock this morning.*
Me levantaba tarde.	*I used to get up late.*
Fui a la tienda.	*I went to the store.*
Yo iba a la tienda cuando vi a José.	*I was going to the store when I saw Joe.*
Fuimos a la playa hoy.	*We went to the beach today.*
Íbamos a la playa todos los veranos.	*We used to go the beach every summer.*
¿Qué me dijiste hace dos minutos?	*What did you tell me two minutes ago?*
¿Qué me decías cuando el perro ladró?	*What were you saying to me when the dog barked?*
Marta comió temprano esta mañana.	*Martha ate early this morning.*
Marta siempre comía temprano.	*Martha always ate early.*
Mi papá pagó la cuenta ayer.	*My father paid the bill yesterday.*
Mi papá siempre pagaba la cuenta.	*My father always paid the bill.*
Eduardo hizo su tarea.	*Edward did his homework.*
Eduardo siempre hacía su tarea los lunes.	*Edward always did his homework on Mondays.*
¿Qué compró Ud. ayer?	*What did you buy yesterday?*
¿Qué compraba Ud. cuando lo llamé?	*What were you buying when I called you?*
Caminamos al parque hoy.	*We walked to the park today.*
Caminábamos al parque todos los días.	*We used to walk to the park every day.*
Recibimos un cheque esta tarde.	*We received a check this morning.*
Recibíamos cheques cada semana.	*We used to receive checks every week.*
Ella tuvo una operación anoche.	*She had an operation last night.*
Él no tenía tiempo para verla.	*He didn't have time to see her.*
Anoche, ella durmió hasta las ocho.	*Last night, she slept until eight o'clock.*
Ella siempre dormía hasta tarde.	*She always slept late.*
Conocimos a Silvia en Colombia.	*We met Sylvia in Colombia.*
No la conocíamos bien.	*We didn't know her well.*

Exercise 17.4

Preterit or imperfect? *Complete the following sentences with the correct form of the verb in parentheses.*

1. ¿Por qué no _____ tú la comida ayer? (comprar)

2. Anoche, yo _____ el vino a la fiesta. (traer)

3. _____ mediodía y el niño _____ hambre. (ser/tener)

4. _____ a llover y yo _____ la ventana. (empezar/cerrar)

5. La muchacha _____ la calle cuando su mamá

   la _____. (cruzar/llamar)

6. ¿Dónde _____ Uds. esta mañana precisamente a las nueve? (estar)

7. Nosotros _____ en el parque cuando _____ el animal exótico. (andar/ver)

8. El taxista nos _____ veinte dólares. ¿Cuánto te

   _____ a ti? (cobrar/cobrar)

9. Nosotros les _____ cartas a nuestros parientes desde Bolivia,

   pero ellos no las _____. (escribir/recibir)

10. Yo _____ por la calle equivocada cuando _____

    que no _____ donde _____.

    (caminar/darse cuenta de/saber/estar)

11. Me agrada su amigo. ¿Dónde lo _____ Ud.? (conocer)

12. Pedro y sus amigos _____ todas las noches antes de acostarse. (divertirse)

13. Melisa _____ al cine cada domingo durante su juventud. (ir)

14. Los viajeros de Inglaterra _____ a mi casa la semana pasada

    y _____ conmigo hasta hoy. (llegar/quedarse)

Reading Comprehension

Marianela
por Benito Pérez Galdós

Pérez Galdós nació en las Islas Canarias y es mejor conocido por sus vistas de la sociedad española. Se murió en 1920 en Madrid.

Aquel día Pablo y Marianela salieron al campo. Con ellos iba Choto, su perro fiel. El día estaba hermoso. El aire era suave y fresco, y el sol calentaba sin quemar.

"¿Adónde vamos hoy?" preguntó Pablo, que era ciego de nacimiento.

"Adonde quiera Ud., señor," contestó Marianela, que era su guía.

Marianela parecía crecer y adquirir nuevas fuerzas, cuando estaba al lado de su amo y amigo. Junto a él, se sentía llena de alegría. Al apartarse de él, sentía una profunda tristeza.

Pablo participaba de los mismos sentimientos hacia Marianela. En cierta ocasión le había dicho Pablo a la joven: Antes yo creía que era de día cuando hablaba la gente; y que era de noche, cuando la gente callaba y cantaban los gallos. Ahora, no hago las mismas comparaciones. Es de día cuando estamos juntos tú y yo; es de noche, cuando nos separamos.

Después de caminar un rato, llegaron a un lugar donde había muchas flores. Ambos se detuvieron. Pablo se sentó, y Marianela se puso a recoger flores para su amo. Los dos eran muy felices.

Verbos

adquirir	*to acquire*
apartarse	*to separate*
calentar	*to warm*
callar	*to quiet*
crecer	*to grow*
detenerse	*to detain*
había dicho	*had said* (past perfect tense)
ponerse (a)	*to begin to*
quemar	*to burn*
recoger	*to pick up*

Nombres

el amo	*the boss*
los gallos	*the roosters*

Preposición

hacia   *toward*

Adjetivos

ciego   *blind*
fiel   *faithful*
juntos   *together*

Expresiones

al + *infinitive*   *upon (doing something)*
al apartarse   *upon separating*

Preguntas

After you have read the selection, answer the following questions in Spanish.

1. ¿Quiénes son los personajes en el cuento? ¿Quién los acompaña?

   _____

2. ¿Cómo se sienten juntos?

   _____

3. ¿Cómo se sienten separados?

   _____

18

The Present Progressive Tense

In Spanish, the present progressive tense expresses action that is occurring at the moment, action that is in progress. It is equivalent to the English present progressive (*The woman is singing*, for example). This tense is used to express the following:

- An action that is in progress
- An action that is occurring in the moment
- Emphasis for an action that is happening right now

A Word About the Present Indicative Tense

The present indicative tense in Spanish expresses both the English simple present (*I sing, I do sing*) and the English present progressive (*I am singing*).

Ella **canta** una canción triste.	She **sings** a sad song.
	She **does sing** a sad song.
	She **is singing** a sad song.

When you don't need to describe what is happening right now, use the simple present tense.

Toco el violín.	*I play the violin.*
Ella nada en el verano.	*She swims in the summer.*
Mis primos viven en México.	*My cousins live in Mexico.*
Siempre nos divertimos los viernes.	*We always have a good time on Fridays.*
¿Por qué te ríes todo el tiempo?	*Why do you laugh all the time?*

The present progressive is a compound tense in Spanish, as it is in English. It is formed by conjugating **estar** in the present tense and adding the present participle of the main verb. The present participle, hereafter referred to as the gerund, is the -*ing* form of a verb in English. The tense is also called the present continuous.

Gerund Formation

The gerund is formed by adding **-ando** or **-iendo** to the stem of the infinitive. In English, the gerund ends in -*ing*. Practice the following verb forms aloud.

-Ar Verbs

To form the gerund of all **-ar** verbs, drop the ending and add **-ando** to the stem.

abrazar	abraz**ando**	*embracing*
adivinar	adivin**ando**	*guessing*
alquilar	alquil**ando**	*renting*
arreglar	arregl**ando**	*arranging, repairing, fixing*
arriesgar	arriesg**ando**	*risking*
bajar	baj**ando**	*descending, going down*
comenzar	comenz**ando**	*beginning*
entregar	entreg**ando**	*delivering, handing in*
esperar	esper**ando**	*waiting*
fregar	freg**ando**	*scrubbing, washing dishes*
jugar	jug**ando**	*playing*
mostrar	mostr**ando**	*showing*
pensar	pens**ando**	*thinking*
probar	prob**ando**	*testing, proving*
recordar	record**ando**	*remembering*
sacar	sac**ando**	*taking out, getting*
soñar	soñ**ando**	*dreaming*
temblar	templ**ando**	*trembling*
volar	vol**ando**	*flying*

-Er Verbs

To form the gerund of most **-er** verbs, drop the ending and add **-iendo** to the stem.

beber	beb**iendo**	*drinking*
comer	com**iendo**	*eating*
correr	corr**iendo**	*running*
coser	cos**iendo**	*sewing*
devolver	devolv**iendo**	*returning* (an object)
hacer	hac**iendo**	*doing, making*
mover	mov**iendo**	*moving* (an object)
perder	perd**iendo**	*losing*
poner	pon**iendo**	*putting*
volver	volv**iendo**	*returning*

-Ir Verbs

To form the gerund of regular **-ir** verbs, drop the ending and add **-iendo** to the stem.

abrir	abr**iendo**	*opening*
compartir	compart**iendo**	*sharing*
decidir	decid**iendo**	*deciding*
escribir	escrib**iendo**	*writing*
insistir	insist**iendo**	*insisting*
recibir	recib**iendo**	*receiving*
subir	sub**iendo**	*ascending, going up*
sufrir	sufr**iendo**	*suffering*

Orthographic Changes in -er and -ir Verbs

-Er and **-ir** verbs whose stem ends in a vowel form the gerund using **-yendo** instead of **-iendo** in order to avoid having three vowels in a row. These are not irregular forms; it is an orthographic change.

-Er Verbs

atraer	atra**yendo**	*attracting*
caer	ca**yendo**	*falling*
creer	cre**yendo**	*believing*

leer	le**yendo**	*reading*
poseer	pose**yendo**	*possessing*
traer	tra**yendo**	*bringing*

-Ir Verbs

construir	constru**yendo**	*constructing, building*
contribuir	contribu**yendo**	*contributing*
destruir	destru**yendo**	*destroying*
huir	hu**yendo**	*fleeing*
oír	o**yendo**	*hearing*

The Gerund of Irregular *-ir* Verbs

Nearly all gerunds are formed regularly. The only verbs that show an irregularity in the gerund are the **-ir** stem-changing verbs in the present indicative tense. Learn these irregular gerunds now, and you'll be able to form all the gerunds easily.

- Forming the gerund of irregular **-ir** verbs with **o > ue** and **o > u** changes in the stem

Infinitive	Present Tense **o > ue**	Gerund **o > u**	English
dormir	d**ue**rmo	d**u**rmiendo	*sleeping*
morir	m**ue**ro	m**u**riendo	*dying*

- Forming the gerund of irregular **-ir** verbs with **e > ie** and **e > i** changes in the stem

Infinitive	Present Tense **e > ie**	Gerund **e > i**	English
advertir	adv**ie**rto	adv**i**rtiendo	*warning*
hervir	h**ie**rvo	h**i**rviendo	*boiling*
mentir	m**ie**nto	m**i**ntiendo	*lying*
preferir	pref**ie**ro	pref**i**riendo	*preferring*
referir	ref**ie**ro	ref**i**riendo	*referring*
sentir	s**ie**nto	s**i**ntiendo	*regretting*
sugerir	sug**ie**ro	sug**i**riendo	*suggesting*

Infinitive	Present Tense e > i	Gerund e > i	English
bendecir	bendigo	bendiciendo	*blessing*
competir	compito	compitiendo	*competing*
conseguir	consigo	consiguiendo	*obtaining*
corregir	corrijo	corrigiendo	*correcting*
decir	digo	diciendo	*saying, telling*
elegir	elijo	eligiendo	*electing*
freír	frío	friendo	*frying*
gemir	gimo	gimiendo	*groaning*
medir	mido	midiendo	*measuring*
pedir	pido	pidiendo	*requesting*
repetir	repito	repitiendo	*repeating*
seguir	sigo	siguiendo	*following*
servir	sirvo	sirviendo	*serving*
sonreír	sonrío	sonriendo	*smiling*

 ## Exercise 18.1

Write the gerund of the following infinitives.

1. hablar _____
2. besar _____
3. andar _____
4. viajar _____
5. limpiar _____
6. cenar _____
7. sacar _____
8. beber _____
9. comer _____
10. aprender _____
11. agradecer _____
12. escoger _____
13. ver _____

14. abrir _____
15. asistir _____
16. insistir _____
17. permitir _____
18. prohibir _____
19. creer _____
20. leer _____
21. traer _____
22. huir _____
23. oír _____
24. servir _____
25. pedir _____
26. corregir _____

27. repetir	_____	30. morir	_____
28. seguir	_____	31. decir	_____
29. dormir	_____	32. hacer	_____

Formation of the Present Progressive Tense

To form the present progressive tense, conjugate **estar** in the present tense and follow it with the gerund of the main verb.

yo estoy hablando	*I am speaking*
tú estás escuchando	*you are listening*
él está comiendo	*he is eating*
nosotros estamos bebiendo	*we are drinking*
vosotros estáis cocinando	*you are cooking*
ellos están durmiendo	*they are sleeping*

Use of the Present Progressive Tense

The action expressed by the present progressive tense must be action in progress.

Following are examples formed with **estar**.

¿Cuál libro estás leyendo?	*Which book are you reading?*
El niño está jugando en su cuarto.	*The child is playing in his room.*
Está lloviendo.	*It's raining.*
Está nevando.	*It's snowing.*
Está lloviznando.	*It's drizzling.*
¿Qué están Uds. haciendo?	*What are you doing?*
¿Qué están haciendo Uds.?	*What are you doing?*

NOTE The subject pronoun **Uds.** appears in two different positions in the example sentences above. In the first example, it comes between the helping verb **estar** and the gerund. In the second example, **Uds.** follows the gerund. Both are correct.

The negative **no** comes directly before the conjugated form of **estar**.

No estamos hablando.	*We are not talking.*
No está lloviendo.	*It is not raining.*
No estoy mintiendo.	*I am not lying.*

A Word About English

In English, the present progressive tense can be used to describe what is happening right now as well as what will happen in the future.

> *I am singing right now.*
> *I am singing next Friday.*

In Spanish, the present progressive can never be used to describe a future action. For a future action, use **ir** + **a** + *infinitive*.

Estoy cantando en este momento. *I am singing right now.* (at this moment)

Voy a cantar el viernes que viene. *I am going to sing next Friday.*

 Exercise 18.2

*Complete the following sentences with the correct form of the present progressive tense. Be sure to conjugate **estar** correctly.*

EXAMPLE Miguel _está cantando_ y su amiga _está tocando_ el piano. (cantar/tocar)

1. Nuestro profesor _____ muchos exámenes. (corregir)

2. Por fin, nosotros _____ buenas notas. (sacar)

3. Me hace el favor de no hacer ruido, yo _____. (estudiar)

4. Los adolescentes les dicen a sus padres, "no _____ nada." (hacer)

5. Los cocineros _____ la cena. (preparar)

6. ¿Qué _____ tú? (decir)

7. Está lloviendo pero no _____. (nevar)

8. Ya es tarde y los niños _____. (dormir)

9. Son las nueve de la noche y todavía los periodistas

   _____. (escribir)

10. ¿Quiénes _____ por teléfono? (hablar)

11. Tú _____ los huevos para el desayuno. (freír)

12. Son las seis y media y la familia _____. (comer)

Reminder

After a preposition, use the infinitive form of the verb, even though the translation in English might be the gerund *-ing*.

Antes de **comer**, ella se lava las manos.	*Before eating, she washes her hands.*
Después de **cocinar**, la familia disfruta la comida.	*After cooking, the family enjoys the meal.*
Al **entrar** en la clase, los estudiantes se saludan.	*Upon entering the class, the students greet each other.*
A veces, hablamos sin **pensar**.	*At times, we speak without thinking.*
En vez de **leer**, preferimos jugar.	*Instead of reading, we prefer to play.*
A pesar de **despertarme** temprano, llegué tarde a la entrevista.	*In spite of waking up early, I arrived late to the interview.*

Exercise 18.3

Complete the following sentences with the infinitive, present indicative, or present progressive of the appropriate verb. Select from the list of verbs below. Use each verb only once.

almorzar, conocer, devolver, graduarse, hacer, leer, querer, saber, salir, tener, tocar

1. En el avión, en el vuelo de África, parece que los pasajeros están

   _____ sus libros de turismo.

2. ¿Quién _____ nadar?

3. Olivia sigue _____ el violín aunque a su hermano no le gusta el sonido.

4. Antes de _____ a los padres de su novio, Amalia se maquilla la cara.

5. Después de _____ éxito en la escuela secundaria, el estudiante

   _____ ir a una universidad.

6. Los trabajadores tienen hambre a las doce de la tarde; _____

   juntos a las doce y media; _____ de la fábrica a las cinco

   de la tarde.

7. Julia acaba de _____ sus libros a la biblioteca.

8. El hombre tiene veintidós años. Después de _____

de la universidad, no sabe qué _____.

Placement of Object Pronouns

Direct Object Pronouns, Indirect Object Pronouns, and Reflexive Pronouns

Following is a review chart of pronouns: subject, direct object, indirect object, and reflexive.

Subject Pronoun	Direct Object Pronoun	Indirect Object Pronoun	Reflexive Pronoun
yo	me	me	me
tú	te	te	te
él	lo	le	se
ella	la	le	se
Ud.	lo/la/le	le	se
nosotros	nos	nos	nos
vosotros	os	os	os
ellos	los	les	se
ellas	las	les	se
Uds.	los/las/les	les	se

NOTE In English, the direct object *you* can be expressed as **la** in Spanish if the direct object person is female, or **lo** if the direct object person is male. In many countries, **le** is used as the direct object pronoun instead of **lo** or **la**. Similarly, the direct object pronoun *you* in the plural **Uds.** form can be **las**, **los**, or **les**.

La ayudo.	*I help you.* (female)
Lo ayudo.	*I help you.* (male)
Le ayudo.	*I help you.* (either male or female)

This use of **le** as direct object pronoun is called **leísmo**; **le** is borrowed from the indirect object pronoun.

The indirect object pronouns, direct object pronouns, and reflexive pronouns have two possible positions:

- The object pronouns may be placed directly before the helping verb **estar**.

- The object pronouns may be attached to the gerund.

¿Qué me estás diciendo?	*What are you saying to me?*
¿Qué estás diciéndome?	*What are you saying to me?*

The written accent retains the correct pronunciation of the verb.

The placement of the object pronouns does not affect the meaning of the sentence. They can be placed in either position, and the meaning of the sentence is exactly the same.

Yo estoy trayéndote la comida.	*I am bringing the meal to you.*
Te estoy trayendo la comida.	*I am bringing the meal to you.*
Irene no está esperando el tren.	*Irene is not waiting for the train.*
No lo está esperando.	*She is not waiting for it.*
Ella no está esperándolo.	*She is not waiting for it.*
Estamos buscando los gatos de Olivia.	*We are looking for Olivia's cats.*
Los estamos buscando.	*We are looking for them.*
Estamos buscándolos.	*We are looking for them.*

Order of Double Object Pronouns

An indirect object pronoun precedes a direct object pronoun when they occur together. The reflexive object pronoun precedes the direct object pronoun when they occur together. The double object pronouns cannot be separated from one another.

Following is a review chart of double object pronouns.

me lo, me la	*it to me*
me los, me las	*them to me*
te lo, te la	*it to you*
te los, te las	*them to you*
se lo, se la	*it to him, it to her, it to you, it to them*
se los, se las	*them to him, them to her, them to you, them to them*
nos lo, nos la	*it to us*
nos los, nos las	*them to us*
os lo, os la	*it to you*
os los, os las	*them to you*

A Reminder

Se replaces **le** or **les** as the indirect object pronoun when a direct object pronoun follows.

Por fin, la jefa tiene su sueldo.	*At last, the boss has your pay.*
Ella está mandándoselo.	*She is sending it to you.*
Ella se lo está mandando.	*She is sending it to you.*
El papá les está leyendo un cuento a sus hijos.	*The father is reading a story to his children.*
Él se lo está leyendo.	*He is reading it to them.*
Está leyéndoselo.	*He is reading it to them.*

A reflexive object pronoun precedes the direct object pronoun when they occur together.

Estoy lavándome las manos.	*I am washing my hands.*
Estoy lavándomelas.	*I am washing them.*
Me las estoy lavando.	*I am washing them.*
La mujer está peinándose el cabello rubio.	*The woman is combing her blond hair.*
Se lo está peinando.	*She is combing it.*
Está peinándoselo.	*She is combing it.*

Exercise 18.4

Complete the following sentences with the correct present progressive form of the verb in parentheses. Remember to conjugate **estar** *correctly.*

1. ¿Por qué _____ la pregunta el maestro? (repetir)

2. Los adolescentes no _____ las direcciones. (seguir)

3. Nosotros _____ el libro. (leer)

4. ¿Quiénes _____ tanto ruido? (hacer)

5. Los amigos de Juan _____ en casa hoy. (almorzar)

6. Yo _____ el agua para preparar la sopa. (hervir)

7. El hombre ama a esta mujer. La _____ con su mirada. (seguir)

8. Somos nosotros a quienes ellos _____. (esperar)

Exercise 18.5

Translate the following sentences into Spanish, using the present progressive tense.

1. *Are the women talking to the men?*

   _____

2. *What are you saying to me?*

   _____

3. *Can you (Ud.) repeat the question? The students are not paying attention to you.*

   _____

4. *We know that he is searching for an idea. He needs it to write a story.*

   _____

5. *What is happening?*

   _____

6. *The fantastic lawyer is dreaming about a trip to Italy.*

   _____

Exercise 18.6

Answer the following questions aloud, using the present progressive tense.

1. ¿Quién está estudiando ahora mismo?

2. ¿Por qué estás comiendo chocolate en el salón?

3. ¿Qué está Ud. haciendo ahora mismo?

4. ¿En qué estás pensando?

5. ¿Qué está leyendo el profesor?

6. ¿Quién está huyendo de la policía?

Uses of the Gerund with Verbs Other Than *estar*

- The gerund with **seguir** expresses *to keep/continue (doing something)*.

Los músicos siguen tocando la música y seguimos escuchándola.	*The musicians keep playing the music, and we keep listening to it.*
No hay música, pero la pareja sigue bailando.	*There is no music, but the couple keeps on dancing.*

- The gerund with **ir** expresses *gradually, little by little*.

La estudiante va aprendiendo la lección.	*The student is gradually learning the lesson.*
El paciente va mejorándose.	*The patient is getting better little by little.*
Voy conociendo Madrid.	*I'm getting to know Madrid little by little.*

- The gerund with **llevar** expresses *have been doing*.

Llevo un año estudiando el español.	*I have been studying Spanish for a year. (literally, I carry a year studying Spanish.)*
Mi amigo lleva dos años viviendo aquí.	*My friend has been living here for two years.*

After you become accustomed to using the present progressive, you will find that the gerund can sometimes be used without a helping verb.

Puedo pasar el día mirando a la gente.	*I can pass the day looking at the people.*
Los ladrones salieron corriendo.	*The thieves left running.*

Either the gerund or the infinitive can be used after **ver**, **mirar**, **escuchar**, and **oír**. The meaning is the same.

Veo a los niños **jugando**.	*I see the children playing. / I see the children play.*
Veo a los niños **jugar**.	*I see the children playing. / I see the children play.*
Escuchamos al hombre cantar.	*We listen to the man sing. / We listen to the man singing.*
Lo escuchamos cantando.	*We listen to him sing. / We listen to him singing.*
Él vio a María pasar por su casa.	*He saw María passing by his house.*
La vio pasando.	*He saw her pass by.*
Susana oyó los loros hablar.	*Susan heard the parrots speak.*
Ella los oyó hablando.	*She heard them speaking.*

Verbs not generally used in the gerund form are **ser**, **estar**, **poder**, **querer**, **saber**, **tener**, **ir**, and **venir**. These verbs use the present indicative instead of the present progressive.

¿**Puede** Ud. acompañarla?	*Can you accompany her?*
Los nietos de Victoria **quieren** visitar a su abuela.	*Victoria's grandchildren want to visit their grandmother.*
Arturo **tiene** una fiesta cada año para su hijo.	*Arthur has a party every year for his son.*
Susana **va** a la manifestación.	*Susan is going to the demonstration.*
Mucho ruido **viene** de arriba.	*A lot of noise is coming from above.*

NOTES **Poder** is the only **-er** verb with an irregularity in the stem of the gerund: **pudiendo**.

The gerund of **ir** is **yendo**.

Exercise 18.7

Complete the following sentences with the correct form of either the present indicative or the present progressive of the verb in parentheses.

1. El esposo de Elizabeth no _____ celebrar el día del amor y de la amistad. (querer)

2. ¿Por qué no _____ toda la familia a mi fiesta? (venir)

3. Sócrates _____ que no _____ nada que valga la pena saber. (saber/saber)

4. Favor de no interrumpirme ahora mismo, yo _____. (pensar)

5. Nosotros _____ hablar bien si practicamos. (poder)

6. ¿Por qué lo sigues _____? (llamar)

7. La muchacha triste nunca _____. (sonreír)

8. Los deportistas _____ al tenis todos los veranos. (jugar)

9. Los detectives están contentos ahora porque el criminal _____ su crimen. (confesar)

10. A Paulina y a su amiga no les gusta _____ temprano. (despertarse)

11. Las niñas _____ a su primera fiesta mañana. (ir)

12. La estudiante lleva una hora _____ este ejercicio. (hacer)

Exercise 18.8

Translate the following sentences into English.

1. Vamos a la casa de María porque ella está preparando arroz con pollo.

   _____

2. El mesero nos está sirviendo nuestra comida.

   _____

3. Las niñeras están cuidando a muchos niños en el parque.

   _____

4. Son las ocho de la noche y ya es tarde, pero el hombre sigue leyendo su libro favorito. Sigue leyéndolo hasta las once.

   _____

   _____

5. La muchacha está nadando en la piscina porque sus padres piensan que es peligroso nadar en el océano.

   _____

   _____

6. Los niños están poniendo los platos en el horno. Los están poniendo en el horno para molestar a sus padres.

   _____

   _____

7. ¿Por qué le están Uds. mintiendo?

   _____

8. ¿Quién está riéndose?

   _____

9. El elefante lleva cinco años viviendo en el zoológico.

   _____

10. Seguimos aprendiendo el español.

    _____

Exercise 18.9

Translate the following sentences into Spanish.

1. _Why are the people crying?_

   _____

2. _It is raining._

   _____

3. _Are you watching television now?_

   _____

4. *Why are the girls laughing?*

_____

5. *It is our turn. We are using the computers now.*

_____

6. *Teresa is waiting for the train, but she is losing patience.*

_____

7. *What are you thinking about?*

_____

8. *We are trying to fall asleep.*

_____

 # Reading Comprehension

La parada del bus

La mujer se llama Lorena. No es ni joven, ni vieja, ni delgada, ni gorda. Tiene la cara pálida, con ojos marrones y pelo oscuro. No se maquilla mucho pero se nota que le gusta llevar un poco de colorete. Se ve que es conservadora por su vestimenta: su falda que cubre las piernas y la blusa con mangas largas aunque es verano.

Ella llega siempre a la parada del bus, esperando a su esposo. Se puede pasar por la banca y verla allí sentada, hora tras hora, escribiendo en su cuaderno y dibujando el rostro de su esposo amado.

Una mañana de mucho calor, un hombre se sienta cerca de ella y conversa un poco.

Él se llama Roberto; parece ser un buen hombre. Hablan de sus dibujos y como pasa ella el día. Él se entera que ella está separada de su esposo desde hace cinco años, pero siendo católicos los dos, son todavía casados. Roberto, soltero, pasa los días trabajando en computadoras, y sus noches jugando al ajedrez en un club con otros fanáticos.

Después de veinte minutos, otro bus viene, y el hombre, un poco triste ahora de dejarla, sube al bus y se va. Ella lo sigue con los ojos con una mirada llena de soledad. La gente sube al bus; otros se bajan y se van para la casa. Lorena se queda tranquilamente, extrañando a su esposo, esperando que venga en el próximo bus.

Verbos

enterarse	*to become aware*
estar sentado	*to be seated*
irse	*to go* (compared with **ir**, **irse** expresses more immediacy)
maquillarse	*to put makeup on*
se nota	*one notices*
se ve	*one sees*

Nombres

el ajedrez	*chess*
el colorete	*the lipstick*
el fanático	*the fan*

Expresiones

aunque	*although*
hora tras hora	*hour after hour*

Preguntas

1. ¿Qué estación es?

   _____

2. ¿Cómo es el clima?

   _____

3. ¿Qué hace Lorena cada día?

   _____

4. ¿Está casada la mujer?

   _____

5. ¿Está casado Roberto?

   _____

6. ¿Está Roberto interesado en Lorena? ¿Está ella interesada en él?

   _____

7. ¿Piensa Ud. que Roberto va a volver?

   _____

8. ¿Piensa Ud. que Lorena va a seguir esperando?

   _____

19

The Past Progressive Tenses

There are two progressive tenses in the past: the imperfect progressive and the preterit progressive. Both express a past action or actions that were occurring, actions that were in progress. They are equivalent to the English past progressive: *The people were running*, for example. These tenses are used to intensify the following:

- An action that was in progress in the past
- An event that was happening in the past

If you do not want to intensify an action that was in progress in the past, use the simple imperfect tense:

El hombre trabajaba mucho.	*The man was working a lot.*
La mujer cocinaba su cena.	*The woman was cooking her supper.*
Los niños se reían.	*The children were laughing.*
Toda la familia se divertía.	*The whole family was having a good time.*

The Imperfect Progressive Tense

Formation of the Imperfect Progressive Tense

The imperfect progressive is a compound tense in Spanish, as it is in English. It is formed by conjugating **estar** in the imperfect and adding the gerund of the main verb. The tense is also called the imperfect continuous.

yo estaba jugando	*I was playing*
tú estabas bebiendo	*you were drinking*
él estaba pintando	*he was painting*
nosotros estábamos corriendo	*we were running*
vosotros estabais sonriendo	*you were smiling*
ellos estaban cenando	*they were dining*

Uses of the Imperfect Progressive Tense

The action expressed by the imperfect progressive tense must be an action that was in progress in the past.

Following are examples formed with **estar**.

El estudiante estaba durmiendo cuando el maestro empezó la clase.	*The student was sleeping when the teacher began the class.*
Yo estaba atravesando la calle cuando vi venir el carro.	*I was crossing the street when I saw the car coming.*
El portero nos estaba ayudando con la maleta.	*The doorman was helping us with the suitcase.*
El gerente estaba mostrándoles la habitación.	*The manager was showing them the room.*
Estábamos bailando cuando se apagaron las luces.	*We were dancing when the lights went out.*

The verbs **seguir**, **ir**, and **venir** can also be conjugated in the imperfect and used with the gerund to form the imperfect progressive tense.

La muchacha iba aprendiendo la lección.	*The girl was learning the lesson little by little.*
Ellas venían hacia nosotros bailando y hablando.	*They were coming toward us dancing and talking.*
Los perros seguían ladrando en la calle.	*The dogs continued barking in the street.*

Verbs not generally used in the gerund form in the past progressive are **ser**, **estar**, **poder**, **querer**, **saber**, **tener**, **ir**, and **venir**. These verbs use the simple imperfect instead of the imperfect progressive.

Hubo un tiempo cuando **podíamos** viajar mucho.	*There was a time when we were able to travel a lot.*
Ella **quería** ir a España a estudiar.	*She wanted to go to Spain to study.*
Sócrates dijo que no **sabía** lo que no **sabía**.	*Socrates said that he did not know what he did not know.*
Yo **iba** a la tienda cuando vi a mi amigo.	*I was going to the store when I saw my friend.*
Mis primos me dijeron que **venían** a verme, pero no llegaron.	*My cousins told me that they were coming to see me, but they didn't arrive.*

 ## Exercise 19.1

Translate the following sentences into Spanish, using the imperfect progressive tense.

1. *I was cleaning the house.*

   _____

2. *Rosa continued eating.*

   _____

3. *Pablo was selling medicine to his friends.*

   _____

4. *We were learning to dance.*

   _____

5. *Why was she lying to me?*

   _____

6. *What were you* (Ud.) *doing?*

   _____

7. *Who was sleeping on the train?*

   _____

8. *Everyone was leaving for the exits.*

   _____

9. *The boys and girls were throwing the ball.*

_____

10. *The politicians were beginning their campaign.*

_____

The Preterit Progressive Tense

Formation of the Preterit Progressive Tense

The preterit progressive also emphasizes action that was taking place in the past. It is formed with the preterit of the verb **estar** followed by the gerund of the main verb.

yo estuve contestando	*I was answering*
tú estuviste gritando	*you were yelling*
ella estuvo bailando	*she was dancing*
nosotros estuvimos charlando	*we were chatting*
vosotros estuvisteis leyendo	*you were reading*
ellas estuvieron explorando	*they were exploring*

Uses of the Preterit Progressive Tense

Unlike the imperfect progressive, the preterit progressive tense expresses an action completed in the past. The name of the tense might seem like a contradiction in terms, but the action, although in a progressive form, is definitely over.

Ayer, en clase de ciencias, el estudiante estuvo escuchando atentamente al profesor hasta que terminó la clase.	*Yesterday, in science class, the student was listening attentively to the professor until the class ended.* (The phrase **hasta que terminó la clase** can also be translated as *until he ended the class.*)
Estuvimos riéndonos a carcajadas hasta que salimos del teatro.	*We were laughing our heads off until we left the theater.*
Anoche, Sofía, una gran pianista, estuvo practicando hasta que su novio la llamó.	*Last night, Sofia, a great pianist, was practicing until her boyfriend called her.*

The gerund is also used with **seguir**, **venir**, and **ir** to form the preterit progressive tense.

La abuela **fue poniéndose** vieja.	*The grandmother was getting older little by little.*
A Guillermo le gusta leer; después de apagar la televisión, **siguió leyendo**.	*William likes to read; after turning off the television, he continued reading.*
Pedro **vino corriendo** a la escuela y llegó a tiempo.	*Peter came running to school and arrived on time.*

Exercise 19.2

Translate the following sentences into English.

1. Nos divertíamos hasta que la obra empezó.

   _____

2. ¿Querían Uds. darles de comer a los pájaros en el parque?

   _____

3. Sabíamos que íbamos a tener éxito.

   _____

4. Las mujeres estuvieron celebrando su jubilación hasta las once de la noche.

   _____

5. Fui conociendo México.

   _____

6. Nuestro profesor estuvo enseñando por una hora ayer.

   _____

7. Estábamos trabajando cuando nuestros amigos llegaron.

   _____

8. ¿De qué estabas hablando?

   _____

9. Ella no me estuvo escuchando.

   _____

10. El camarero no nos estaba sirviendo la comida.

    _____

11. Los maestros estuvieron repitiendo las instrucciones hasta que entendimos.

    _____

12. ¿Por qué los estabas buscando por tanto tiempo cuando sabías que tus amigos estaban escondiéndose?

    _____

    _____

13. Estuvimos bailando anoche hasta medianoche.

    _____

14. Nadie estaba andando por aquí.

    _____

Exercise 19.3

Review (Preterit tense) *Complete the following sentences with the correct preterit form of the verb in parentheses.*

EXAMPLE   Mi amigo no me _*esperó*_ . (esperar)

1. Mis amigos me _____ por una hora. (esperar)

2. Ella no le _____ nada. (decir)

3. ¿Por qué no les _____ Uds. flores? (traer)

4. Las hojas _____ de los árboles. (caerse)

5. Yo nunca les _____ dinero. (dar)

6. Octavio no _____ dormir anoche. (poder)

7. Nosotros no _____ al cine el sábado. (ir)

8. Me _____ mucho la comida. (gustar)

9. Yo sé que tú me _____ en el restaurante. (ver)

10. Ella es amable. ¿Dónde la _____ Ud.? (conocer)

Exercise 19.4

Review (Imperfect tense) *Complete the following sentences with the correct imperfect form of the verb in parentheses.*

EXAMPLE   ¿Dónde __estabas__ cuando la maestra entró? (estar)

1. ¿Qué hora _____ cuando la película empezó? (ser)

2. ¿Cuántos años _____ los gemelos cuando se graduaron? (tener)

3. La doctora no _____ ver a más pacientes. (querer)

4. Yo siempre _____ para los exámenes. (estudiar)

5. En su juventud, Patricio _____ al tenis. (jugar)

6. Antes de la época de la computadora, la gente _____ cartas. (escribir)

7. Ella nunca _____ contenta. Siempre _____. (estar/quejarse)

8. El hombre viejo _____ los dientes en un vaso de agua todas las noches antes de dormirse. (poner)

Exercise 19.5

Review (Indirect object pronouns) *Complete the following sentences with the correct indirect object pronoun, according to the cue in parentheses.*

1. Yo _____ traigo flores. (*to you*)

2. Susana _____ presta dinero. (*to them*)

3. ¿Por qué _____ hablas en voz alta? (*to her*)

4. ¿Qué _____ estás diciendo? (*to me*)

5. Nosotros no _____ estamos escribiendo ahora. (*to you*).

6. ¿Por qué _____ cobra Ud. tanto? (*to us*)

Exercise 19.6

Review (Direct object pronouns) *Translate the following sentences into English.*

1. Julia busca a su hermana. Ella está buscándola.

   _____

2. Cuidamos a los bebés. Los cuidamos.

   _____

3. Los dos hermanos ayudan a su familia. La familia aprecia su ayuda.

   _____

4. El jardinero mira los pájaros. Los mira volar.

   _____

5. Los estudiantes saludan a su maestra. La saludan todos los días.

   _____

6. ¿Por qué me llamas hoy? ¿Por qué me estás llamando a casa?

   _____

7. Manuel visita a la mujer en Perú. Él quiere casarse con ella en la primavera.

   _____

8. Todos los turistas esperan el tren. No les molesta esperarlo porque hace fresco.

   _____

   _____

Exercise 19.7

Review (Double object pronouns) *Translate the following sentences into English.*

1. Te lo juro.

   _____

2. Me pongo los guantes. Me los pongo.

   _____

3. La mujer indígena no nos vende agua; ella nos la da.

   _____

4. Me gustan los mariscos en este restaurante. El camarero me los sirve con gusto.

_____

_____

5. Ana les trae el postre a sus amigas. Ella se lo trae.

_____

Exercise 19.8

Review (Indirect object pronouns, direct object pronouns, the present tense, the present progressive tense) _Translate the following sentences into Spanish._

1. _Do you tell the truth to your friends? We tell it to you._

_____

2. _I always write letters to him. I am writing them to him now._

_____

3. _Irene gives gifts to her son every Christmas. This year she is going to give them to him on his birthday._

_____

_____

4. _We show the new shoestore to my friend. She looks at the high heels, but she doesn't buy them for us._

_____

_____

5. _Sometimes people don't understand what we say. Sometimes we have to explain it to them._

_____

_____

6. _Enrique reads a story to his children every night at eight o'clock. He is reading it to them now._

_____

_____

Exercise 19.9

Review (Double object pronouns, *se* and the indirect object, the preterit tense) *Translate the following sentences into English.*

1. Miguel no pudo entrar en su casa porque se le perdieron las llaves.

   _____

2. Se me cayó la cuchara y me puse brava.

   _____

3. ¡Cuidado! Se les van a caer los vasos. Ya se nos rompieron dos.

   _____

4. No se me ocurrió trabajar ayer.

   _____

5. No pudiste preparar la sopa de ajo anoche. Se te acabó el ajo.

   _____

6. Se me olvidó hacer mi tarea.

   _____

 ## Reading Comprehension

El hospital

La pobre mamá iba caminando para no mostrarle a su hijo que estaba preocupada. Ella sabía que no era ni catarro, ni gripe, ni pulmonía. Ella sabía que era algo grave. De repente, empezó a correr hacia un taxi para llevárselos a un hospital.

Hacía dos días que su hijo estaba quejándose de un dolor de estómago, un dolor que no lo dejaba dormir. ¿Qué tiene el hijo? Viviendo sola, Silvia no tenía nadie con quien hablar a la medianoche. El taxista los dejó en la entrada del hospital. Ella le pagó y le dio una buena propina. Estuvieron esperando solamente cinco minutos cuando los médicos llegaron. Examinaron al niño que estaba llorando. La mamá, llorando también, trató de ser valiente ante su hijo, pero no pudo. Después de un rato, que le pareció una eternidad, los médicos le ofrecieron dos opciones: operar o no. La mamá, sin duda, optó por la operación y firmó el documento de consentimiento. El niño siguió sollozando.

"Pero mamá," le dijo el niño, "no quiero que me operen."

"Yo lo sé, hijo mío, pero es necesario y vas a estar muy bien y sin dolor después. Los doctores me dijeron que es apendicitis."

Con esta última conversación, los médicos lo pusieron en la camilla de operación y ellos desaparecieron en el largo corredor del hospital. La madre se retiró a la sala de espera, sintiéndose muy desolada en su soledad.

Ella estaba allá, pensando en su hijo, cuando vinieron los doctores con las noticias.

"Todo salió bien," le dijeron, "su hijo está recuperándose en su cuarto y pronto va a estar riéndose y jugando otra vez." La mamá aliviada les agradeció profundamente.

Y dentro de poco, ella y su hijo salieron charlando, ella con la mano preciosa de su hijo en la suya. Abrazándose, entraron en la casa.

Verbos

agradecer	*to thank*
desparecerse	*to disappear*
recuperarse	*to recuperate*
retirarse	*to retire*
sollozar	*to sob*

Expresiones con Verbos

dejar + *infinitive*	*to let (do something)*
llevárselo	*to carry someone or something away*
tratar de + *infinitive*	*to try to (do something)*

Nombres

la camilla	*the stretcher*
el catarro	*the cold*
la gripe	*the flu*
la pulmonía	*pneumonia*

Adjetivos

aliviado	*relieved*
desolado	*desolate*

Pronombres

la suya	*hers* (refers to *her hand*)
hijo mío	*son of mine* (gives more emphasis than **mi hijo** (*my son*))

Expresión

de repente   *suddenly*

Preguntas

1. ¿Por qué fueron al hospital a la medianoche?

   _____

2. ¿Está Ud. de acuerdo con la primera decisión de la madre?

   _____

3. ¿Qué tiene el hijo?

   _____

4. ¿Cuidaron bien los médicos al hijo y a la madre?

   _____

5. ¿Cómo se sienten la madre y su hijo al final del cuento?

   _____

20

The Present Subjunctive

The present subjunctive is a mood in the present tense, widely used in Spanish. The present subjunctive cannot exist alone. Another element in the sentence always causes it to be used. The subjunctive is often needed after the following elements:

- Certain impersonal expressions
- Certain verbs
- Certain conjunctions
- Certain dependent adjectives
- Certain expressions

Formation of the Present Subjunctive

Most verbs form the present subjunctive from the first-person singular **yo** form of the present indicative. Drop the **-o** to get the stem for the present subjunctive.

Verbs that are irregular in the present indicative are irregular in the present subjunctive in the same way.

There are only six verbs that do not form the present subjunctive from the **yo** form of the present indicative.

-Ar Verbs

In order to conjugate both regular and irregular **-ar** verbs in the present subjunctive, start with the **yo** form of the present indicative. Drop the **-o** and add -**e**, -**es**, -**e**, -**emos**, -**éis**, -**en** to the stem.

Infinitive	**yo** Form	Present Subjunctive	
bailar	bailo	yo baile tú bailes ella baile	nosotros bailemos vosotros bailéis ellas bailen
cantar	canto	yo cante tú cantes él cante	nosotros cantemos vosotros cantéis ellos canten
cerrar	cierro	yo cierre tú cierres Ud. cierre	nosotros cerremos vosotros cerréis Uds. cierren
pensar	pienso	yo piense tú pienses ella piense	nosotros pensemos vosotros penséis ellas piensen
recordar	recuerdo	yo recuerde tú recuerdes él recuerde	nosotros recordemos vosotros recordéis ellos recuerden

Note that the first-person and third-person singular forms are identical in the present subjunctive.

The first two examples, **bailar** and **cantar**, are regular in the present indicative. The last three, **cerrar**, **pensar**, and **recordar**, show stem changes. Note that the stem changes in the present indicative are also present in the present subjunctive, except in the **nosotros** and **vosotros** forms, which are unaffected by these stem changes.

A Word About the Present Subjunctive

The formation of the subjunctive comes from the conjugation of the first-person singular of the present indicative. Any irregularity that the verb has in the present indicative **yo** form also occurs in the present subjunctive. To learn the subjunctive well, practice the **yo** form of the verbs, because that will be the stem of the present subjunctive.

-Er and *-ir* Verbs

In order to conjugate both regular and irregular **-er** and **-ir** verbs in the present subjunctive, drop the **-o** from the first-person singular of the present indicative and add **-a**, **-as**, **-a**, **-amos**, **-áis**, **-an** to the stem.

-Er Verbs

Infinitive	**yo** Form	Present Subjunctive	
comer	como	yo coma	nosotros comamos
		tú comas	vosotros comáis
		él coma	ellos coman
querer	quiero	yo quiera	nosotros queramos
		tú quieras	vosotros queráis
		ella quiera	ellas quieran
poder	puedo	yo pueda	nosotros podamos
		tú puedas	vosotros podáis
		Ud. pueda	Uds. puedan
ver	veo	yo vea	nosotros veamos
		tú veas	vosotros veáis
		él vea	ellos vean

-Ir Verbs

Infinitive	**yo** Form	Present Subjunctive	
vivir	vivo	yo viva	nosotros vivamos
		tú vivas	vosotros viváis
		él viva	ellos vivan
mentir	miento	yo mienta	nosotros mintamos
		tú mientas	vosotros mintáis
		ella mienta	ellas mientan
pedir	pido	yo pida	nosotros pidamos
		tú pidas	vosotros pidáis
		Ud. pida	Uds. pidan
dormir	duermo	yo duerma	nosotros durmamos
		tú duermas	vosotros durmáis
		él duerma	ellos duerman

NOTE In the irregular **-ir** verbs, there is an additional irregularity in the **nosotros** and **vosotros** forms. Verbs with the stem change **e > ie** or **e > i** have an **-i-** in the **nosotros** and **vosotros** forms. Verbs with the stem change **o > ue** have a -**u**- in the **nosotros** and **vosotros** forms.

Irregular -er and -ir Verbs with -g- or -zc- in the yo Form

In the present subjunctive, certain **-er** and **-ir** verbs carry the irregularity of the first-person singular of the present indicative tense throughout the present subjunctive conjugation. There are no **-ar** verbs that have this irregularity.

Infinitive	**yo** Form	Present Subjunctive	
conocer	conozco	yo conozca	nosotros conozcamos
		tú conozcas	vosotros conozcáis
		él conozca	ellos conozcan
decir	digo	yo diga	nosotros digamos
		tú digas	vosotros digáis
		ella diga	ellas digan
hacer	hago	yo haga	nosotros hagamos
		tú hagas	vosotros hagáis
		Ud. haga	Uds. hagan
poner	pongo	yo ponga	nosotros pongamos
		tú pongas	vosotros pongáis
		él ponga	ellos pongan
salir	salgo	yo salga	nosotros salgamos
		tú salgas	vosotros salgáis
		ella salga	ellas salgan
tener	tengo	yo tenga	nosotros tengamos
		tú tengas	vosotros tengáis
		Ud. tenga	Uds. tengan
traer	traigo	yo traiga	nosotros traigamos
		tú traigas	vosotros traigáis
		él traiga	ellos traigan
venir	vengo	yo venga	nosotros vengamos
		tú vengas	vosotros vengáis
		ella venga	ellas vengan

Other regular **-ar** verbs:

alcanzar	*to reach, to overtake*
anular	*to annul*
arrancar	*to pull, to root out*
cargar	*to load*
colocar	*to place*
ignorar	*to be ignorant of*
lograr	*to succeed in*
madrugar	*to get up early*
masticar	*to chew*
pagar	*to pay for*
publicar	*to publish*
rezar	*to pray*
subrayar	*to underline*
tragar	*to swallow*

Other **-er** verbs like **conocer**:

agradecer	*to thank*
amanecer	*to wake up, to brighten*
aparecer	*to appear*
crecer	*to grow*
desaparecer	*to disappear*
establecer	*to establish*
merecer	*to deserve*
nacer	*to be born*
obedecer	*to obey*
ofrecer	*to offer*
padecer	*to suffer*
parecer	*to seem*
pertenecer	*to belong*
reconocer	*to recognize*
yacer	*to lie down*

Other **-ir** verbs with **-zc-** in the **yo** form:

conducir	*to drive*
introducir	*to insert*
lucir	*to light up*
producir	*to produce*

reducir	*to reduce*
traducir	*to translate*

The Spanish equivalent of the English verb meaning *to introduce* is **presentar**.

Te presento a mi familia.	*I introduce you to my family.*

Irregular Verbs

There are only six verbs whose present subjunctive is not formed from the first-person singular of the present indicative. They are irregular in that they are not formed from the **yo** form.

Infinitive	**yo** Form	Present Subjunctive	
dar	doy	yo dé	nosotros demos
		tú des	vosotros deis
		él dé	ellos den
estar	estoy	yo esté	nosotros estemos
		tú estés	vosotros estéis
		ella esté	ellas estén
ir	voy	yo vaya	nosotros vayamos
		tú vayas	vosotros vayáis
		Ud. vaya	Uds. vayan
saber	sé	yo sepa	nosotros sepamos
		tú sepas	vosotros sepáis
		él sepa	ellos sepan
ser	soy	yo sea	nosotros seamos
		tú seas	vosotros seáis
		ella sea	ellas sean
haber	he	yo haya	nosotros hayamos
		tú hayas	vosotros hayáis
		Ud. haya	Uds. hayan

NOTES The present subjunctive form **dé** (from **dar**) has a written accent to distinguish it from **de** (*of*).

The word **hay** comes from the infinitive **haber**; you will not need this form for any other use at this time.

Verbs with Orthographic Changes

Verbs with orthographic changes are not irregular. The spelling changes simply maintain the sound of the **yo** form. Some of the most common spelling changes are the following:

- Verbs that end in **-car** change **c** to **qu**.
- Verbs that end in **-gar** change **g** to **gu**.
- Verbs that end in **-zar** change **z** to **c**.

Infinitive	**yo** Form	Present Subjunctive	
buscar	busco	yo busque	nosotros busquemos
		tú busques	vosotros busquéis
		Ud. busque	Uds. busquen
explicar	explico	yo explique	nosotros expliquemos
		tú expliques	vosotros expliquéis
		Ud. explique	Uds. expliquen
tocar	toco	yo toque	nosotros toquemos
		tú toques	vosotros toquéis
		Ud. toque	Uds. toquen
apagar	apago	yo apague	nosotros apaguemos
		tú apagues	vosotros apaguéis
		él apague	ellos apaguen
llegar	llego	yo llegue	nosotros lleguemos
		tú llegues	vosotros lleguéis
		ella llegue	ellas lleguen
comenzar	comienzo	yo comience	nosotros comencemos
		tú comiences	vosotros comencéis
		ella comience	ellas comiencen
empezar	empiezo	yo empiece	nosotros empecemos
		tú empieces	vosotros empecéis
		él empiece	ellos empiecen

NOTE The change **z** > **c** occurs before the vowel **e** without affecting the sound. The consonants **c** (before **i** and **e**), **s**, and **z** all have the same sound.

A Word About Pronunciation of the Present Subjunctive
Like the present indicative, the stress in the present subjunctive is on the second-to-last syllable. As you practice, make sure you pronounce the verbs in this way: **yo cante, tú cantes, él cante, nosotros cantemos, ellos canten**. If a word carries a written accent, stress the accented syllable: **vosotros cantéis**.

Uses of the Present Subjunctive

Remember that the subjunctive mood cannot exist alone; it must always be caused by some other element in the sentence. This is a mood that expresses wishes, doubts, and what is possible, rather than what is certain. The present subjunctive in a dependent clause is caused by the present tense in the main clause. Following are the specific uses of the present subjunctive.

After Certain Impersonal Expressions

A sentence or question may consist of a main clause and a dependent or subordinate clause connected by the Spanish conjunction **que**.

Following is a sentence with a main clause and a subordinate clause that are both in the indicative mood.

THE MAIN CLAUSE	Él sabe
THE DEPENDENT CLAUSE	que yo cocino bien.

However, suppose that the main clause has an impersonal expression, such as **Es dudoso**. This causes the subjunctive to be used in the dependent clause.

Es dudoso que yo **cocine** bien.   *It is doubtful that I cook well.*

Following are some frequently used impersonal expressions:

es bueno (que)	*it is good (that)*
es difícil (que)	*it is difficult (that)*
es dudoso (que)	*it is doubtful (that)*
es fácil (que)	*it is easy (that)*
es imposible (que)	*it is impossible (that)*
es importante (que)	*it is important (that)*
es malo (que)	*it is bad (that)*
es mejor (que)	*it is better (that)*
es necesario (que)	*it is necessary (that)*

es posible (que)	it is possible (that)
es preciso (que)	it is extremely necessary (that)
es probable (que)	it is probable (that)
es una lástima (que)	it is a pity (that)
es urgente (que)	it is urgent (that)

Es dudoso que **viajemos** a España.	It is doubtful that we will travel to Spain.
Es importante que ella **coma** bien.	It is important that she eat well.
Es imposible que él **tenga** razón.	It is impossible that he is right.
Es necesario que **estudiemos** para el examen.	It is necessary that we study for the test.
¿Es posible que ella **venga** mañana?	Is it possible that she will come tomorrow?
Es probable que mi amiga me **vea** en el restaurante.	It is probable that my friend will see me in the restaurant.
Es una lástima que Pedro no lo **quiera** hacer.	It is a pity that Peter doesn't want to do it.

When you begin a sentence with one of the impersonal expressions above, it is mandatory to use the subjunctive in the dependent clause. You do not have to make any decisions, nor do you have a choice about whether or not to use it. These impersonal expressions in the main clause always trigger the subjunctive in the subordinate clause.

Notice that some of the example sentences and questions above are translated with the future in English. This is because the present subjunctive carries with it a feeling of the future and doubt.

If you want to make a general statement with an impersonal expression, there is neither a dependent clause nor a subjunctive. You simply use the structure you have already learned, which follows English word order.

Es bueno nadar cada día.	It is good to swim every day.
Es importante comer bien.	It is important to eat well.
¿Es necesario trabajar mucho?	Is it necessary to work a lot?
Es posible salir temprano.	It is possible to leave early.

Exercise 20.1

Complete the following sentences with the correct present subjunctive form of the verb in parentheses.

EXAMPLE   Es urgente que el chofer __*conduzca*__ con cuidado. (conducir)

1. Es importante que nuestros amigos _____ a la fiesta. (venir)

2. Es posible que él me _____ la verdad. (decir)

3. Es una lástima que Sara no lo _____. (hacer)

4. ¿Es posible que Uds. _____ a mi amigo Raúl? (conocer)

5. Es necesario que nosotros _____ bien. (dormir)

6. Es importante que ella _____ bien las direcciones. (saber)

7. Es necesario que nosotros _____ mucha agua fría en el verano. (tomar)

8. Es dudoso que ellos _____ temprano. (levantarse)

9. ¿Es posible que ella _____ a tiempo? (llegar)

10. Es posible que yo _____ en Francia. (quedarse)

11. Es probable que mucha gente importante _____ en la conferencia. (estar)

12. Es difícil que yo te _____ una buena respuesta. (dar)

13. Es urgente que tú _____ al doctor hoy. (ir)

14. Es dudoso que ellos _____ ricos. (ser)

15. Es importante que los padres les _____ a sus hijos. (leer)

16. La niña acaba de comer. Es imposible que _____ hambre. (tener)

17. Es probable que nosotros le _____ flores al profesor. (traer)

18. Es bueno que Uds. _____ mejor. (sentirse)

After Certain Verbs

Expressing Wishes or Preferences

Verbs in the main clause that express wishes or preferences with regard to other people will cause the subjunctive mood in the dependent clause. The subject in the main clause must be different from the subject in the dependent clause. Following are verbs that express wishes or preferences:

desear	*to desire*
preferir	*to prefer*
querer	*to desire, to want*

Following is a sentence with a main clause and a subordinate clause that are both in the indicative mood.

THE MAIN CLAUSE	Él sabe
THE DEPENDENT CLAUSE	que yo canto.

However, suppose that the main clause has one of the verbs above, such as **Él quiere**. This causes the subjunctive to be used in the dependent clause:

Él quiere que yo **cante**.   *He wants me to sing.*
                                                      (He wants that I sing.)

The English equivalent does not always show the distinction in mood like Spanish does. But even in the English translation of the example above, it is clear that the person in the main clause, *he,* wants the other person, *me,* to do something.

Deseamos que ella **esté** bien.	*We want her to be well.*
Ella prefiere que su hijo **juegue** al béisbol.	*She prefers that her son play baseball.*
Quiero que él **baile**.	*I want him to dance.*

If there is only one subject for the two verbs in a sentence, there is neither a dependent clause nor a subjunctive verb.

Deseamos descansar.	*We want to rest.*
Ella prefiere dormir.	*She prefers to sleep.*
Yo quiero cantar.	*I want to sing.*

Expressing Hope, Happiness, Sadness, or Regret

Verbs in the main clause that express hope, happiness, sadness, or regret with regard to other people will cause the subjunctive mood in the dependent clause. Following are verbs that express hope, happiness, sadness, or regret:

alegrarse de	*to be glad*
esperar	*to hope*
estar contento de	*to be happy*
estar triste de	*to be sad*
gustarle a uno	*to be pleasing to someone*
sentir	*to regret*
temer	*to fear*
tener miedo de	*to be afraid of*

Me alegro de que Uds. **estén** bien.	*I am glad that you are well.*
Esperamos que Ud. **tenga** un buen fin de semana.	*We hope that you have a good weekend.*
La maestra está contenta de que **hagamos** la tarea.	*The teacher is happy that we do the homework.*
¿Estás triste de que no **podamos** aceptar tu invitación?	*Are you sad that we cannot accept your invitation?*
Me gusta que mi familia **venga** a verme.	*It pleases me that my family is coming to see me.*
Lo siento que Ud. nunca se **gane** la lotería.	*I am sorry that you never win the lottery.*
Los padres temen que sus hijos no **quieran** estudiar.	*The parents fear that their children don't want to study.*
El líder tiene miedo de que el grupo no **resuelva** el problema.	*The leader fears that the group will not resolve the problem.*

If there is only one subject for the two verbs in a sentence, the sentence follows the basic structure that you have learned.

Me alegro de estar aquí.	*I am glad to be here.*
Él espera salir dentro de una hora.	*He hopes to leave within the hour.*
Me gusta ir al cine.	*I like to go to the movies.*
Ella tiene miedo de volar.	*She is afraid of flying.*

Expressing Orders, Requests, or Advice

Verbs in the main clause that express orders, requests, or advice will cause the subjunctive mood in the dependent clause. Following are verbs that express orders, requests, or advice:

aconsejar	*to advise*
decir	*to tell (someone to do something)*
dejar	*to permit, to let*
insistir en	*to insist*
mandar	*to order*
pedir	*to request, to ask for*
permitir	*to permit*
prohibir	*to prohibit*
sugerir	*to suggest*

Te aconsejo que **tomes** el tren.	*I advise you to take the train.*
Ella insiste en que yo **me quede**.	*She insists that I stay.*
Les pedimos que **vayan** de vacaciones.	*We ask them to go on vacation.*
Le sugiero que Ud. **lea** este artículo.	*I suggest that you read this article.*

Dejar, **mandar**, **permitir**, and **prohibir** can be used in two ways:

Les dejo que **entren**. Les dejo entrar.	*I let them enter.*
Te permito que **nades** aquí. Te permito nadar aquí.	*I permit you to swim here.*
Te prohíbo que **fumes** en la casa. Te prohíbo fumar en la casa.	*I forbid you to smoke in the house.*
El capitán les manda que los soldados **descansen**.	*The captain orders the soldiers to rest.*
Les manda descansar.	*He orders them to rest.*

As you have learned, **decir** is used to relate a fact. This idea is expressed with the indicative.

José nos dice que el tren viene.	*Joe tells us that the train is coming.*
Ella me dice que le gusta viajar.	*She tells me that she likes to travel.*

However, when **decir** is used as an order, the subjunctive is used in the dependent clause.

Yo te digo que **vayas** al doctor.	*I tell you to go to the doctor.*
Ud. me dice que yo **me quede**.	*You tell me to stay.*
Les decimos que **se acuesten** ahora.	*We tell them to go to bed now.*
Él nos dice que **tengamos** cuidado.	*He tells us to be careful.*
¿Puede Ud. decirle que me **llame**?	*Can you tell her to call me?*

When English *to tell* is used to order someone to do something, the English command form is always the conjugation of the verb *to tell* + infinitive.

An English command is expressed as follows: *I tell him **to stay**. He tells me **to go***. Compare that to simply relating a fact: *He tells me that the bus is here*.

Expressing Doubt or Uncertainty

Verbs that express doubt or uncertainty in the main clause will cause the subjunctive mood in the dependent clause. Following are verbs that express doubt or uncertainty:

dudar	*to doubt*
no creer	*not to believe*
no pensar	*not to think*

Ella duda que yo **sepa** tocar el piano.	*She doubts that I know how to play the piano.*
La gente no cree que **sea** la verdad.	*The people don't believe that it is the truth.*
No pensamos que Daniel nos **invite** a la fiesta.	*We don't think that Daniel will invite us to the party.*

Exercise 20.2

Complete the following sentences with the correct present subjunctive form of the verb in parentheses.

1. ¿Qué quieres que yo te _____? (decir)

2. Él quiere que su amiga _____ la cuenta. (pagar)

3. Espero que Uds. _____ bien. (sentirse)

4. Ellos se alegran de que el bebé _____. (dejar de llorar)

5. Ellos nos piden que _____ mejor la idea. (explicar)

6. A él no le gusta que yo siempre _____ razón. (tener)

7. Rosa insiste en que su jefe le _____ más dinero. (dar)

8. No creo que Alicia _____ la fecha. (saber)

9. Ellas dudan que _____ mucho tráfico hoy. (haber)

10. Les sugiero a sus padres que _____ de vacaciones. (ir)

11. Me alegro de que no _____ nada grave. (ser)

12. Los expertos nos aconsejan que _____ ejercicio. (hacer)

13. Paula espera que su hermana _____ bien. (estar)

14. Yo dudo que ella lo _____ en la reunión. (besar)

Exercise 20.3

Rewrite the following indicative sentences in the subjunctive mood. Choose any appropriate verb that causes the subjunctive in the dependent clause.

EXAMPLE   Mis estudiantes están en clase.

   Me alegro de que estén en clase.

1. A mis padres les gusta viajar.

   _____

2. Mi amigo tiene malos sueños.

   _____

3. Ella no se divierte mucho.

   _____

4. Nosotros somos buenos estudiantes.

   _____

5. No vamos a volver a los Estados Unidos.

   _____

6. Sara me trae flores a mi casa.

   _____

7. ¿Conoce Ud. a mi tío? [Write a response.]

   _____

8. Mi hermano y yo no nos vemos mucho.

   _____

9. ¿Hay clase los lunes?

   _____

10. Carla es de Polonia.

   _____

Exercise 20.4

Indicative or subjunctive? *Complete the following sentences with the correct form of the verb in parentheses.*

EXAMPLES   Yo dudo que Cristina __cante__ bien. (cantar)

Yo sé que ella __canta__ bien. (cantar)

1. Espero que Uds. _____ un buen fin de semana. (tener)

2. Yo sé que Uds. _____ muchos amigos. (tener)

3. Ricardo prefiere que yo lo _____ en febrero. (visitar)

4. Él quiere que nosotros le _____ regalos. (traer)

5. Nos gusta que él nos _____. (amar)

6. Es importante que nosotros _____ nuestros errores. (corregir)

7. ¿Sabe Ud. que ellos _____ aquí? (estar)

8. Yo pienso que Rosario _____ poco. (quejarse)

9. Dudo que Enrique _____. (quedarse)

10. Sabemos que ellos _____. (irse)

11. El hombre espera que ella _____ con él. (bailar)

12. Sara no quiere que su novio la _____ antes de la boda. (ver)

13. Me alegro de que Uds. _____ aquí. (estar)

14. Es importante que nosotros _____ las direcciones antes de empezar nuestro viaje. (saber)

15. Yo pienso que este hombre _____ médico. (ser)

16. A mi hermano no le importa lo que _____ yo. (hacer)

After Certain Conjunctions

A subjunctive form follows directly after one of the following conjunctions if the main clause has a different subject than the dependent clause.

a pesar de que	*in spite of*
antes de que	*before*
después de que	*after*
en caso de que	*in case*

hasta que	*until*
para que	*in order that, so that*
sin que	*without*

Here is a sentence in which there is only one subject:

| Ella practica el piano **antes de cantar**. | *She practices the piano before singing.* |

In the following sentence, there are two subjects connected by a conjunction with **que**:

| Ella practica el piano **antes de que** él **cante**. | *She practices the piano before he sings.* |

The English equivalent does not show this distinction in mood the way Spanish does. However, there are clearly two subjects in the example above: *she* and *he*.

In the example sentences below, there are two subjects in each sentence, and the subjunctive follows the conjunction:

Voy a esperar **hasta que** tú **llegues**.	*I am going to wait until you arrive.*
Él enseña **para que** los estudiantes **aprendan**.	*He teaches so that the students learn.*
Lo voy a hacer **sin que** Ud. me **ayude**.	*I'm going to do it without your helping me.*

If there is one subject in the sentence, an infinitive follows the preposition.

Después de trabajar, ella descansa.	*After working, she rests.*
Ella estudia para aprender.	*She studies in order to learn.*
Él habla sin pensar.	*He speaks without thinking.*

Some conjunctions of time always cause the subjunctive, whether there are two subjects or only one in the sentence. Following are a few conjunctions of this type:

a menos que	*unless*
luego que	*as soon as*
tan pronto como	*as soon as*

Vamos a bailar **a menos que** no **haya** música.	*We are going to dance unless there is no music.*
Voy a llegar **tan pronto como** yo **pueda**.	*I am going to arrive as soon as I can.*

After *cuando*

The subjunctive form directly follows **cuando** if the future is implied.

Vamos a viajar **cuando tengamos** tiempo y dinero.	*We are going to travel when we have time and money.*
¿Me puedes llamar **cuando llegues** a casa?	*Can you call me when you arrive home?*
El niño quiere ser bombero **cuando sea** grande.	*The child wants to be a fireman when he grows up.*

When **cuando** introduces a question, the indicative form is used.

¿Cuándo vas a estar en casa?	*When are you going to be home?*
¿Cuándo quieren Uds. viajar?	*When do you want to travel?*

When **cuando** introduces a sentence that involves either a repeated action or a general statement in the present, the indicative mood is used.

Cuando hace frío, los niños juegan en la nieve.	*When it is cold, the children play in the snow.*
Ella se siente alegre cuando baila.	*She feels happy when she dances.*
Cuando voy a la playa, siempre me divierto.	*When I go to the beach, I always have a good time.*

 ## Exercise 20.5

Complete the following sentences with the conjunction indicated and the correct form of the verb in parentheses.

EXAMPLE   Vamos de vacaciones __*tan pronto como*__ (as soon as)

nosotros __*podamos*__ (to be able to).

1. Él va a limpiar su apartamento _____ (before) su familia

   lo _____ (to visit).

2. _____ (after) yo _____ (to bathe myself),
   voy a vestirme.

3. No voy _____ (*unless*) Uds. _____ (*to go*) también.

4. Él va a invitar a su amiga a la fiesta _____ (*as soon as*)

   él _____ (*to have*) confianza.

5. Les doy las instrucciones _____ (*so that*) ellos

   _____ (*to know how*) llegar.

6. Uds. pueden jugar al baloncesto _____ (*as soon as*)

   Uds. _____ (*to finish*) su tarea.

7. _____ (*before*) su novio _____ (*to come*)
   a verla, Rosa va a arreglarse.

8. Te presto el dinero _____ (*so that*) tú _____
   (*to be able to*) comprar un carro usado.

9. Vamos a estar aquí _____ (*until*) ellos _____
   (*to arrive*).

10. _____ (*in case*) Uds. no _____ (*to have*)
    nada que hacer mañana, ¿podemos ir al cine?

11. A Ricardo no le gusta estudiar. Pero va a estudiar _____

    (*so that*) sus padres _____ (*to be*) contentos.

12. _____ (*in spite of*) _____ (*to be*) frío,
    ellos quieren dar una vuelta.

13. Tú puedes venir a mi casa _____ (*without*) yo

    te _____ (*to invite*).

14. Graciela va a descansar _____ (*after*) sus nietos

    _____ (*to go away*).

15. _____ (*when*) Ud. _____ (*to be able*),
    ¿me puede acompañar al tren?

16. Elena me va a ver _____ (*when*) nosotros

    _____ (*to meet*) en México.

17. _____ (*when*) ellos _____ (*to return*)
    a los Estados Unidos, van a comprar una casa pequeña.

18. El hombre va a estar contento _____ (*when*)

    _____ (*to learn*) a manejar.

In Certain Dependent Adjective Clauses

The subjunctive mood is used in the dependent clause if the object or person described in the main clause is indefinite or nonexistent. In the following examples, the objects and persons described in the main clause are not known.

Busco **un apartamento** que **sea** grande y barato.	*I am looking for an apartment that is big and cheap.*
¿Conoce Ud. a **alguien** que **sepa** hablar alemán?	*Do you know anyone who knows how to speak German?*
¿Hay **alguien** aquí que **baile** bien?	*Is there anyone here who dances well?*
No hay **nadie** que siempre **tenga** razón.	*There is no one who is always right.*

After the Expressions *por más que* and *por mucho que*

Por más que ella **limpie,** su casa está siempre desordenada.	*No matter how much she cleans, her house is always a mess.*
Por mucho que él **coma**, no se engorda.	*No matter how much he eats, he doesn't get fat.*

After *ojalá*

An interjection of Arabic origin, **ojalá** means *would to God that* or *may God grant that* and expresses great desire. It can also be translated as *I hope.*

Ojalá que ella **tenga** suerte.	*Would to God that she has luck.*
Ojalá que él **se quede**.	*May God grant that he stay.*
Ojalá que Uds. **reciban** el cheque.	*I hope you receive the check.*

After *acaso, quizás,* or *tal vez*

Acaso él me **visite** mañana.	*Perhaps he will visit me tomorrow.*
Quizás ellos me **digan** la verdad.	*Perhaps they will tell me the truth.*
Tal vez me **digan** mentiras.	*Perhaps they will tell me lies.*

After *aunque*

The subjunctive mood is used if the action has not yet occurred.

Voy al cine **aunque** no **vayan** mis amigos.	*I am going to the movies, although my friends may not go.*
Aunque Pedro **se quede** esta noche, yo voy a salir.	*Although Peter may stay tonight, I am going to leave.*
Aunque sea difícil, él lo puede hacer.	*Although it may be difficult, he can do it.*

If **aunque** introduces a sentence or question that expresses a known fact, a repeated action, or a general statement in the present, the indicative mood is used.

Aunque **es** verano, la mujer siempre lleva guantes.	*Although it is summer, the woman always wears gloves.*
Aunque el doctor **está** enfermo, va al hospital.	*Although the doctor is sick, he is going to the hospital.*
Aunque le **duele** la voz, la cantante decide cantar en la ópera.	*Although her voice hurts, the singer decides to sing in the opera.*
Elena no quiere ir al parque aunque sus amigos siempre **van**.	*Elena doesn't want to go to the park, although her friends always go.*

After Compounds of *-quiera*

Compounds of **-quiera**—**adondequiera** (*wherever*), **cualquiera** (*whichever*), **dondequiera** (*wherever*), and **quienquiera** (*whoever*)—all indicate uncertainty and therefore cause the subjunctive to follow.

Adondequiera que **vayas**, te deseo lo mejor.	*Wherever you go, I wish you the best.*
Cualquiera que **sea** sincero puede ser un buen amigo.	*Whichever one is sincere can be a good friend.*
Dondequiera que **estén ellos**, los voy a buscar.	*Wherever they are, I am going to look for them.*
Quienquiera que **esté** aquí puede salir con nosotros.	*Whoever is here can leave with us.*

After *como*

The subjunctive mood is used after **como** only if the meaning is *however*.

Ellas van a preparar la comida
como tú **quieras**.

*They are going to prepare the meal
however you want.*

 ## Exercise 20.6

Complete the following sentences with the correct present subjunctive form of the verb in parentheses.

1. Tal vez ellos _____ por la comida. (enfermarse)

2. Ojalá que nosotros _____ hoy. (descansar)

3. Aunque él _____ mañana, no quiero lavar el baño. (llegar)

4. Por mucho que ellas _____, no van a hacer nada. (quejarse)

5. Quienquiera que _____ bien puede ser experto. (cocinar)

6. Ojalá que tú _____ bien esta noche. (dormir)

7. Aunque _____ mucho tráfico, queremos viajar. (haber)

8. Mi amiga busca un apartamento que _____ tres cuartos. (tener)

9. Carlos necesita una casa que _____ en el campo. (estar)

10. El hombre quiere hacer el proyecto como Ud. lo _____. (querer)

11. No conozco a nadie que me _____ a la playa. (acompañar)

12. Ella busca un novio que _____ inteligente. (ser)

13. Quizás él _____ la semana que viene. (venir)

14. Por más que Tomás _____, no sabe nada. (hablar)

Other Tenses That Cause the Present Subjunctive

You have learned so far that the present indicative in the main clause can cause the present subjunctive in the subordinate clause. This is the most common use of the subjunctive mood.

Two additional tenses, the present progressive and the future periphrastic (**ir** + **a** + *infinitive*) can cause the subjunctive mood as well.

Present Progressive as Cause for the Present Subjunctive

The present progressive in the main clause can cause the present subjunctive in the dependent clause.

La preocupada mamá está
  esperando que su hijo regrese
  a casa.

*The anxious mother is hoping
  that her son returns home.*

El papá le está diciendo a su hijo
  que juegue en el parque.

*The father is telling his son to play
  in the park.*

Los padres les están rogando que
  tengan cuidado.

*The parents are begging them
  to be careful.*

Les estamos sugiriendo que los
  niños hagan más ejercicio.

*We are suggesting to them that
  the children exercise more.*

NOTE The present tense and the present progressive are both present tenses.

Future (*ir* + *a* + infinitive) as Cause for the Present Subjunctive

The present subjunctive can also be caused by the future tense in the main clause.

Vamos a estar contentos de que
  Susana tenga éxito.

*We are going to be happy that
  Susan is successful.*

Raimundo va a pedirle a su jefe
  que le compre un carro.

*Raymond is going to ask his boss
  to buy him a car.*

Voy a insistir que mis amigos
  me acompañen al cine.

*I am going to insist that my
  friends accompany me to the
  movies.*

Marisa va a estar alegre cuando
  consiga un buen apartamento.

*Marisa is going to be happy when
  she gets a good apartment.*

Exercise 20.7

Complete the following sentences with the correct present subjunctive form of the verb in parentheses. The verb in the main clause is in the present indicative. Make sure you know why the present subjunctive is used in each case.

EXAMPLE　　　El doctor me aconseja que yo ___*haga*___ más exámenes médicos. (hacer)

1. Espero que Uds. _____ bien. (estar)

2. Nos alegramos mucho de que el sol no te _____. (picar)

3. Me gusta que mi sobrina _____ un buen trabajo. (obtener)

4. Paulina insiste en que su familia _____ a su compañero. (conocer)

5. Es imposible que Roberto _____ todo. (saber)

6. Dudamos que los inquilinos _____ contra el dueño. (ganar)

7. Ojalá que los huéspedes _____. (venir)

8. ¿Hay alguien aquí que me _____ cien dólares? (prestar)

9. Enseño para que los estudiantes _____. (aprender)

10. Presentamos la obra de teatro después de que los actores _____. (ensayar)

Exercise 20.8

Complete the following sentences with the correct present subjunctive form of the verb in parentheses. The verb in the main clause is in the present progressive.

EXAMPLE   La doctora está esperando que no __*sea*__ nada grave. (ser)

1. Catarina está aconsejándonos que _____ la puerta. (abrir)

2. Te estoy sugiriendo que _____. (irse)

3. ¿Por qué me sigues diciendo que yo te _____? (perdonar)

4. Los padres del niño le están pidiendo que no _____ en aguas peligrosas. (nadar)

5. Les estamos esperando que el tren _____ a tiempo. (llegar)

Exercise 20.9

*Complete the following sentences with the correct present subjunctive form of the verb in parentheses. The verb in the main clause is in the future periphrastic (**ir** + **a** + infinitive).*

EXAMPLE   El hombre idealista va a esperar que la mujer perfecta __*venga*__. (venir)

1. ¿Va a ser imposible que los adolescentes _____ a sus padres? (escuchar)

2. Voy a pedir que la gente no _____ más. (fumar)

3. Vamos a esperar que el piloto no _____. (perderse)

4. El paciente no va a tomar su medicina hasta que el doctor

   le _____ que se la _____. (decir/tomar)

5. La obra de teatro no se va a acabar hasta que la mujer gorda

   _____. (cantar)

 ## Reading Comprehension

Estimados lectores,

   Espero que a Uds. les guste la siguiente historia. Está en forma
de diálogo y basada en acontecimientos de la vida real. Intenten adivinar
quien es el personaje principal según las claves que aparecen en esta
escena. Para que gocen de lo lindo y para que aprendan de la historia,
es necesario que Uds. lean con cuidado.
La autora

El juicio

*La escena tiene lugar en la corte griega ante una asamblea de 501
ciudadanos.*
   El protagonista entra y empieza a hablar.

PROTAGONISTA Tengo sesenta años y es la primera vez que me ven
   en la corte. ¿Cuál es la primera acusación contra mí?
ACUSADOR Ud. es culpable de investigar bajo la tierra y en el cielo
   y de enseñarles a los otros las mismas cosas.
PROTAGONISTA No tengo nada que ver con estas acusaciones y no es
   verdad.
ACUSADOR Pero, ¿cuál es el problema, entonces? ¿Por qué hay tantos
   prejuicios contra Ud. si no hace algo diferente de los demás? Nos puede
   decir Ud. lo que es, para que le demos un veredicto justo.
PROTAGONISTA Bueno. Voy a decirles toda la verdad. Me dan esta
   reputación por cierta sabiduría que tengo. Menciono el dios de Delfos
   para que él sea mi testigo. ¿Se acuerdan Uds. de Querefón? Él fue
   al dios de Delfos y le preguntó si hay una persona más sabia que yo.
   El dios contestó que no hay nadie. Pero, ¿qué significa la idea de que
   yo soy el hombre más sagaz de todos? Me tocó investigar la cuestión.
   Yo fui a ver a un hombre que tiene la reputación de ser sagaz.

Lo examiné. No es necesario que les diga su nombre, él es un político, y esto es el resultado.

Cuando yo hablé con él, me di cuenta que él no era sabio. Cuando me fui, pensaba, "Yo soy más sabio que este hombre; ninguno de nosotros no sabe nada que valga la pena saber, pero él piensa que él tiene la sabiduría cuando él no la tiene, y yo, sin saber nada, no pienso que yo sea sagaz. No pienso que sé lo que no sé." Después, fui a ver a los poetas, pensando que ellos iban a ser más sagaces que yo. Pero averigüé que no es por la sabiduría que los poetas crean sus poemas sino por una inspiración divina. Por fin, fui a ver a los artesanos. Ellos sabían lo que yo no sabía y por eso eran más sabios que yo. Pero me pareció que cada uno se creía extremadamente sagaz en cuestiones importantes porque eran hábiles en su propio arte.

Mucho prejuicio contra mi ha resultado de mi investigación. Y yo sigo investigando y examinando a cada persona que pienso es sagaz y si él no es sagaz yo se lo digo. Estoy tan ocupado en mi investigación que no he tenido tiempo ni para servir en posiciones del estado ni de ganar dinero. Como resultado, yo soy pobre. Es verdad lo que les dije. Y yo sé que por esta investigación de la gente hay mucha rabia contra mí. Pero lo que Uds. escuchan es mi defensa contra estas primeras acusaciones.

Verbos

adivinar	*to guess*
averiguar	*to check out, to verify*
darse cuenta (de)	*to realize*
examinar	*to examine*
gozar	*to enjoy*
ha resultado	*has resulted* (present perfect tense)
he tenido	*have had* (present perfect tense)
intentar	*to intend, to try*
servir	*to serve*
tener que ver con	*to have something to do with*
valer	*to value*

Nombres

los acontecimientos	*the events*	la clave	*the key, the code*
la acusación	*the accusation*	la corte	*the court*
la asamblea	*the assembly*	la cuestión	*the issue*
el ciudadano	*the citizen*	la defensa	*the defense*

los demás	*the rest*	el personaje	*the character*
el diálogo	*the dialogue*	el político	*the politician*
el dios de Delfos	*the god of Delphi*	el prejuicio	*the prejudice*
la escena	*the scene*	la sabiduría	*the knowledge*
la investigación	*the investigation*	el/la testigo	*the witness*
el/la juez	*the judge*	el veredicto	*the verdict*
el juicio	*the judgment*		

Adjetivos

culpable	*guilty*	sabio	*wise, clever*
justo	*fair, just*	sagaz	*wise*
principal	*main, principal*	siguiente	*following*

Preguntas

1. ¿En qué sitio empieza la acción?

   _____

2. ¿Contra quién se defiende el protagonista?

   _____

3. ¿Cuántas personas hay en la asamblea griega?

   _____

4. ¿Cuál es la acusación contra él?

   _____

5. ¿Qué hizo el protagonista después de escuchar que él es el más sabio de todos?

   _____

6. ¿Qué hace el protagonista en su vida diaria?

   _____

7. Según el protagonista, ¿qué significa la sabiduría?

   _____

8. ¿Se defiende bien el protagonista?

   _____

9. ¿Es inocente o culpable el protagonista?

   _____

10. ¿Quién es el protagonista?

    _____

11. ¿Quién escribió el diálogo de la defensa?

    _____

21

Commands

The command form, also called the imperative, is used to tell someone to do or not to do something. The command form is considered a mood, and exists only in the immediate present. The Spanish affirmative command is equivalent to English commands, such as *turn here* or *follow the directions*. The Spanish negative command is equivalent to English *don't scream* or *don't drink the water*, for example. Except for the affirmative **tú** command, all the constructions use a form that is the same as the present subjunctive, so your knowledge of the subjunctive is a great help.

Even though there are other ways to request that people do things, the command form is necessary in many situations. For example, let's say you need to give someone directions:

> **Go** straight ahead, and then **turn** to the right.
> **Follow** the red line.
> **Walk** in the direction of the traffic.

Sometimes you need the command form to tell people not to do something, and you don't have very much time to do it in.

> **Don't touch** the light socket!
> **Don't jump** in the water—there are sharks!
> **Don't move**.
> **Don't worry**.

Affirmative *tú* Commands

The affirmative command form in the familiar **tú** is the same as the third-person singular of the present indicative. If the third-person indicative form is irregular, so is the command form.

-*Ar* Verbs

REGULAR IN THE PRESENT	Baila. Canta.	*Dance. Sing.*
	Mira. Escucha.	*Look. Listen.*
IRREGULAR IN THE PRESENT	Empieza. Piensa.	*Begin. Think.*

-*Er* and -*ir* Verbs

REGULAR IN THE PRESENT	Come. Bebe.	*Eat. Drink.*
	Lee. Escribe. Decide.	*Read. Write. Decide.*
IRREGULAR IN THE PRESENT	Duerme. Sonríe.	*Sleep. Smile.*

Irregular *tú* Commands

The following are the only irregular commands in the affirmative **tú** form. It is a good idea to learn these imperatives right away.

Infinitive	**tú** Command	English
decir	di	*say*
hacer	haz	*do*
ir	ve	*go*
poner	pon	*put*
salir	sal	*leave*
ser	sé	*be*
tener	ten	*have*
venir	ven	*come*

Haz tus ejercicios, por favor.	*Do your exercises, please.*
Ven acá.	*Come here.*
Pon tus zapatos en el armario.	*Put your shoes in the closet.*
Ten cuidado.	*Be careful.*

NOTE The command form can be softened by adding **por favor** (*please*).

Exercise 21.1

Translate the following regular **tú** *commands into English.*

1. Toma tu medicina y llama al doctor en la mañana.

   _____

2. Sigue a la derecha, por favor.

   _____

3. Cierra la puerta, por favor, y abre la ventana.

   _____

4. Corre a la tienda y compra la leche.

   _____

5. Prepara la comida esta noche y después, saca la basura, por favor.

   _____

6. Lee *Don Quixote* para la clase y escribe tu opinión acerca del tema principal.

   _____

7. Come más frutas y verduras.

   _____

8. Cuenta conmigo.

   _____

Exercise 21.2

Write the affirmative **tú** *command form for the following verbs.*

1. apagar   *to turn off*   _____

2. compartir   *to share*   _____

3. decidir   *to decide*   _____

4. devolver   *to return* (an object)   _____

5. doblar   *to turn*   _____

6. mirar   *to look at, to watch*   _____

7. oír   *to hear*   _____

8. regresar   *to return*   _____

9. terminar   *to end*   _____

10. tirar   *to throw*   _____

 ## Exercise 21.3

Complete the following sentences with the **tú** *command form of the verb in parentheses. Both regular and irregular commands are included.*

EXAMPLE   ¿Por qué no vienes acá? __Ven__ acá.

1. Tú nunca dices la verdad. _____ la verdad. (decir)

2. Tú debes portarte bien. _____ un buen niño. (ser)

3. _____ tu pregunta, por favor. (leer)

4. _____ el correo electrónico. (escribir)

5. Hay mucho peligro en la selva. _____ cuidado. (tener)

6. _____ la ropa en el cajón, por favor. (poner)

7. _____ acá. (venir)

8. Tú te vas a engordar si no haces ejercicios. _____ ejercicios por lo menos tres veces a la semana. (hacer)

9. Necesitamos arroz para preparar la comida. _____ el arroz, por favor. (traer)

10. _____ a tu hermanita. (esperar)

Placement of Object Pronouns with Affirmative *tú* Commands

All object pronouns are attached to the affirmative form of the imperative. When two object pronouns occur together, the indirect object pronoun precedes the direct object pronoun.

Escribe la carta.	*Write the letter.*
Escríbeme la carta.	*Write the letter to me.*
Escríbemela.	*Write it to me.*
Enseña la lección.	*Teach the lesson.*
Enséñanos la lección.	*Teach us the lesson.*
Enséñanosla.	*Teach it to us.*

Presta el dinero.	*Lend the money.*
Préstale el dinero a María.	*Lend the money to María.*
Préstaselo.	*Lend it to her.*
Tráeles las galletas a tus colegas.	*Bring the cookies to your colleagues.*
Tráeselas.	*Bring them to them.*
Dame la sartén.	*Give me the frying pan.*
Dámela.	*Give it to me.*
Dinos la idea.	*Tell us the idea.*
Dínosla.	*Tell it to us.*
Perdóname.	*Pardon me. / Excuse me.*

NOTE The written accent maintains the stress on the correct syllable in the imperative: **es<u>cri</u>be**, **es<u>crí</u>beme**, **es<u>crí</u>bemela**, for example.

In Spanish, the reflexive command form is very important. The reflexive object pronoun is attached the affirmative command form, and the written accent is again used to maintain stress on the correct syllable. Practice these examples aloud.

Infinitive	**tú** Command	English
acordarse	Acuérdate.	*Remember.*
acostarse	Acuéstate.	*Go to bed.*
despertarse	Despiértate.	*Wake up.*
dormirse	Duérmete.	*Go to sleep.*
levantarse	Levántate.	*Get up.*
sentarse	Siéntate.	*Sit down.*

When a reflexive object pronoun and a direct object pronoun occur together, the reflexive object pronoun precedes the direct object pronoun.

Lávate las manos.	*Wash your hands.*
Lávatelas.	*Wash them.*
Quítate los zapatos.	*Take off your shoes.*
Quítatelos.	*Take them off.*
Ponte el abrigo.	*Put on your coat.*
Póntelo.	*Put it on.*

Exercise 21.4

Write the affirmative **tú** *command form for the following verbs. All responses require a written accent to maintain stress on the correct syllable, except* **irse**. *Pronounce each response aloud.*

1. fijarse   *to notice*   _____

2. animarse   *to cheer up*   _____

3. callarse   *to be quiet*   _____

4. arreglarse   *to get ready*   _____

5. moverse   *to move*   _____

6. irse   *to go away*   _____

7. quedarse   *to stay*   _____

8. pararse   *to stand up*   _____

9. cepillarse   *to brush one's teeth*   _____

10. vestirse   *to get dressed*   _____

11. divertirse   *to have a good time*   _____

12. dormirse   *to fall asleep*   _____

Negative *tú* Commands

The negative **tú** command form is the same as the present subjunctive form.

To form the negative **tú** command, begin with the **yo** form of the present indicative tense. Drop the final **-o** to get the stem of the present subjunctive.

- For **-ar** verbs, add **-es** to the stem.
- For **-er** and **-ir** verbs, add **-as** to the stem.

-Ar Verbs

No grites.   *Don't yell.*
No fumes en mi casa, por favor.   *Don't smoke in my house, please.*
No juegues con fósforos.   *Don't play with matches.*
No toques el enchufe.   *Don't touch the light socket.*

-Er and *-ir* Verbs

No mientas.	*Don't lie.*
No corras con tijeras.	*Don't run with scissors.*
No comas comida rápida.	*Don't eat fast food.*
No subas la montaña solo.	*Don't climb the mountain alone.*
No bebas esa agua.	*Don't drink that water.*

Pronounce the commands listed above aloud. Take time to write down both the affirmative and negative commands you need in everyday life, pronounce them, and try to learn them by memory. The negative commands are very important.

Placement of Object Pronouns with Negative *tú* Commands

All object pronouns precede the verb in a negative command. The indirect object pronoun precedes the direct object pronoun if they appear together.

No abras la ventana.	*Don't open the window.*
No la abras.	*Don't open it.*
No cierres la puerta.	*Don't close the door.*
No la cierres.	*Don't close it.*
No lo hagas.	*Don't do it.*
No me lo digas.	*Don't say it to me.*
No me traigas las tortas.	*Don't bring me the cakes.*
No me las traigas.	*Don't bring them to me.*
No nos cuentes el mismo cuento.	*Don't tell us the same story.*
No nos lo cuentes.	*Don't tell it to us.*
No le escribas una carta a Federico.	*Don't write a letter to Fred.*
No se la escribas.	*Don't write it to him.*
No les prestes dinero.	*Don't lend them money.*
No se lo prestes.	*Don't lend it to them.*
No le des nada a Dorotea.	*Don't give anything to Dorothy.*

The reflexive object pronoun also precedes the verb in a negative **tú** command.

No te enfades.	*Don't get angry.*
No te vayas.	*Don't go.*
No te quejes.	*Don't complain.*
No te asustes.	*Don't be afraid.*

If a reflexive verb and a direct object appear in the same phrase, the reflexive object pronoun precedes the direct object pronoun.

No te pongas el abrigo en el verano.	*Don't put on your coat in the summer.*
No te lo pongas.	*Don't put it on.*
No te quites el sombrero en el invierno.	*Don't take off your hat in the winter.*
No te lo quites.	*Don't take it off.*

Review of *tú* Commands

Regular *tú* Commands

	Affirmative	Negative
cantar	canta	no cantes
beber	bebe	no bebas
abrir	abre	no abras

Irregular *tú* Commands

	Affirmative	Negative
decir	di	no digas
hacer	haz	no hagas
ir	ve	no vayas
poner	pon	no pongas
salir	sal	no salgas
ser	sé	no seas
tener	ten	no tengas
venir	ven	no vengas

Exercise 21.5

Translate the following commands into English.

1. Hazme un favor. _____

2. Dinos la verdad. _____

3. Vete. _____

4. Ponte las medias. _____

5. Sal ahora. _____

6. Sé un buen perro. _____

7. Ten cuidado. _____

8. Ven acá. _____

Exercise 21.6

Write the correct affirmative and negative **tú** *commands for the following verbs, according to the example given. Pronounce each command aloud.*

	AFFIRMATIVE	NEGATIVE
EXAMPLE cruzar	*cruza (tú)*	*no cruces*
1. correr	_____	_____
2. caminar	_____	_____
3. beber	_____	_____
4. seguir	_____	_____
5. repetir	_____	_____
6. hablar	_____	_____
7. mirar	_____	_____
8. romper	_____	_____
9. vender	_____	_____
10. abrir	_____	_____
11. subir	_____	_____
12. empezar	_____	_____

13. mentir   _____   _____

14. salir   _____   _____

15. poner   _____   _____

16. tocar   _____   _____

Exercise 21.7

*Translate the following sentences into Spanish. Use the **tú** form for commands.*

1. Don't eat the salad in Guatemala. Don't eat it.

   _____

2. Don't run; another train is coming.

   _____

3. Don't tell me the secret. Don't tell it to me.

   _____

4. Don't do it.   _____

5. Don't touch it.   _____

6. Don't be afraid. _____

7. Don't lend money to her. Don't lend it to her.

   _____

8. Don't come late to the parade.

   _____

9. Don't give us bad news.

   _____

10. Don't bring candies to the child. Don't bring them to him.

    _____

11. Don't go away.   _____

12. Don't worry.   _____

13. Don't wait for me. _____

14. Don't be jealous. _____

Ud. and *Uds.* Commands

The command forms for **Ud.** and **Uds.** are identical to the present subjunctive.

- To form the **Ud./Uds.** commands for -ar verbs, begin with the **yo** form of the present indicative. Drop the **-o** and add **-e** (**Ud.**) or **-en** (**Uds.**) to the stem.

- To form the **Ud./Uds.** commands for -er and -ir verbs, begin with the **yo** form of the present indicative. Drop the **-o** and add **-a** (**Ud.**) or **-an** (**Uds.**) to the stem.

- There are only five irregular **Ud./Uds.** command forms. All regular **Ud./Uds.** commands are formed from the **yo** form of the present indicative.

Affirmative *Ud.* Commands

-Ar Verbs

Tome una aspirina si tiene dolor de cabeza.	*Take an aspirin if you have a headache.*
Firme aquí.	*Sign here.*
Entre Ud., por favor.	*Enter, please.*
Cante. Baile. Escuche música.	*Sing. Dance. Listen to music.*
Espere Ud.	*Wait.*

NOTE The command can be softened by adding **Ud.** or **Uds.**

-Er and *-ir* Verbs

Abra la ventana, por favor.	*Open the window, please.*
Coma. Beba.	*Eat. Drink.*
Venga a mi casa a las siete.	*Come to my house at seven o'clock.*
Tenga cuidado.	*Be careful.*
Haga sus ejercicios.	*Do your exercises.*

Negative *Ud.* Commands

The verb form for negative **Ud.** commands is the same as the present subjunctive. Affirmative and negative **Ud.** command forms are identical.

No tome una aspirina.	*Don't take an aspirin.*
No entre Ud.	*Don't enter.*
No grite Ud.	*Don't yell.*
No abra la ventana.	*Don't open the window.*
No coma, no beba.	*Don't eat, don't drink.*
No venga a mi casa a las siete; sino a las ocho.	*Don't come to my house at seven, but rather at eight.*

Affirmative *Uds.* Commands

Add an **-n** to the **Ud.** form of the imperative to form the **Uds.** command.

-Ar Verbs

Compren la casa.	*Buy the house.*
Apaguen la luz.	*Turn off the light.*
Caminen Uds.	*Walk.*

-Er and *-ir* Verbs

Repitan la frase, por favor.	*Repeat the sentence, please.*
Lean el periódico.	*Read the newspaper.*

Negative *Uds.* Commands

No hablen.	*Don't talk.*
No fumen en la casa.	*Don't smoke in the house.*
No griten.	*Don't yell.*
No salgan.	*Don't leave.*
No prendan la luz.	*Don't turn on the light.*
No pongan su ropa en el piso.	*Don't put your clothes on the floor.*

Pronounce the commands listed above aloud. Now list the commands that you need in everyday life. Make your own list of commands and practice them.

Placement of Object Pronouns with Affirmative *Ud./Uds.* Commands

The reflexive, indirect, and direct object pronouns are attached to the affirmative command. When an object is added to the command form, a written accent is placed over the stressed syllable to maintain the sound of the verb.

Affirmative *Ud.* Commands

Diga. Dígame. Dígamelo.	*Tell. Tell me. Tell it to me.*
Escúcheme.	*Listen to me.*
Bésela.	*Kiss her.*
Siéntese Ud.	*Sit down, please.*
Sirva el postre, por favor.	*Serve the dessert, please.*
Sírvalo.	*Serve it.*
Créame.	*Believe me.*

Affirmative *Uds.* Commands

Ayúdenla.	*Help her.*
Denles su dinero.	*Give them their money.*
Espérenme, por favor.	*Wait for me, please.*
Siéntense Uds.	*Sit down, please.*
Quédense.	*Stay.*
Enséñennos la idea. Enséñennosla.	*Teach us the idea. Teach it to us.*

NOTE The **-nn-** combination is very rare in Spanish.

Placement of Object Pronouns with Negative *Ud./Uds.* Commands

The reflexive, indirect, and direct object pronouns precede the verb in a negative **Ud./Uds.** command. The verb forms for affirmative and negative commands are the same.

Negative *Ud.* Commands

No me traiga agua.	*Don't bring me water.*
No le diga nada a nadie.	*Don't say anything to anybody.*
No nos espere.	*Don't wait for us.*
No se caiga.	*Don't fall down.*
No se desespere.	*Don't despair.*
No se preocupe.	*Don't worry.*

Negative *Uds.* Commands

No lo toquen.	*Don't touch it.*
No se preocupen.	*Don't worry.*
No se vayan.	*Don't go.*
No se rían.	*Don't laugh.*

Review of *Ud./Uds.* Commands

Regular *Ud./Uds.* Commands

	Affirmative		Negative	
	Ud.	Uds.	Ud.	Uds.
caminar	camine	caminen	no camine	no caminen
comer	coma	coman	no coma	no coman
escribir	escriba	escriban	no escriba	no escriban

Irregular *Ud./Uds.* Commands

There are only five **Ud./Uds.** command forms that are not formed from the **yo** form of the present indicative.

	Affirmative		Negative	
	Ud.	Uds.	Ud.	Uds.
dar	dé	den	no dé	no den
estar	esté	estén	no esté	no estén
saber	sepa	sepan	no sepa	no sepan
ser	sea	sean	no sea	no sean
ir	vaya	vayan	no vaya	no vayan

NOTE Remember that commands such as **diga**, **haga**, and **tenga** are not irregular. They are formed from the **yo** form of the present indicative tense.

Other Ways of Asking People to Do Things

- **Favor de** + *infinitive* (easy to use and very polite)

Favor de abrir la ventana.	*Please open the window.*
Favor de sentarse al frente.	*Please sit in front.*
Favor de esperarnos.	*Please wait for us.*

- **Tener la bondad de** + *infinitive*

¿Tiene Ud. la bondad de acompañarme al hotel?	*Will you be kind enough to accompany me to the hotel?*
¿Tienes la bondad de regalarme el anillo?	*Will you be kind enough to give me the ring?*
¿Tienen Uds. la bondad de prestarnos su carro?	*Will you be kind enough to lend us your car?*

- **Puede Ud.** + *infinitive*

¿Puede Ud. cerrar la ventana?	*Can you close the window?*
¿Puedes ayudarme, por favor?	*Can you help me, please?*

- **Hacer el favor de** + *infinitive* with *indirect object*
  (similar to **favor de**)

¿Me hace Ud. el favor de traernos el libro?	*Will you do me the favor of bringing us the book?*
¿Nos haces el favor de escribirle?	*Will do you us the favor of writing to her?*
¿Me hace Ud. el favor de bailar conmigo?	*Will you do me the favor of dancing with me?*

- Present indicative with *indirect object pronoun*
  or *direct object pronoun*

¿Me ayudas, por favor?	*Will you help me, please?*
¿Nos acompaña Ud. al tren?	*Will you accompany us to the train?*
¿Me prestas tu carro?	*Will you lend me your car?*
¿Nos da dinero?	*Will you give us money?*
¿Nos llevan Uds. al hotel?	*Will you take us to the hotel?*

A Word About the Word "Will"

In all of the constructions mentioned above, the English translation using the word "will" does not indicate a future tense, but rather a voluntary mood.

Exercise 21.8

Translate the following sentences into English, then pronounce these commands aloud.

1. No naden en este lago.

   _____

2. No caminen en el lodo.

   _____

3. No se acueste tarde.

_____

4. No nos lo dé.

_____

5. No dejen los platos sucios en la mesa.

_____

6. No trabajen tanto.

_____

7. No venga a clase el lunes.

_____

8. No lleguen tarde.

_____

 ## Exercise 21.9

Write both the affirmative and negative **Ud.** *commands for the following verbs. Practice pronouncing all commands aloud.*

	AFFIRMATIVE	NEGATIVE
EXAMPLE cantar	*Cante.*	*No cante.*
1. decir	_____	_____
2. hacer	_____	_____
3. trabajar	_____	_____
4. entrar	_____	_____
5. leer	_____	_____
6. esperar	_____	_____
7. beber	_____	_____

Exercise 21.10

Write both the affirmative and negative **Uds.** *commands for the following reflexive verbs. Practice pronouncing all commands aloud.*

		AFFIRMATIVE	NEGATIVE
EXAMPLE	irse	*Váyanse.*	*No se vayan.*
1.	quedarse	_____	_____
2.	sentarse	_____	_____
3.	levantarse	_____	_____
4.	acostarse	_____	_____
5.	dormirse	_____	_____

Reading Comprehension

Perdida en Nicaragua

"Vaya recto hasta llegar a la iglesia. Cuando llegue a la iglesia, doble a la derecha.

"Siga recto hasta llegar al ayuntamiento; camine diez minutos más, suba una colina, cruce la calle y ya está en la universidad. Si sale ahora, va a llegar mucho antes de su primera clase a las diez."

El año era 1987. Eran las siete de una mañana caliente y húmeda como siempre era en agosto en Managua. Empecé mi caminata con mucha confianza y alegría, siendo muy independiente. Caminé con las direcciones escritas en un papelito. Después de quince minutos comencé a prestar mucha atención, buscando la iglesia blanca y grande como era la descripción de ella. La temperatura siguió subiendo. No vi a nadie para pedir direcciones. No hallé ninguna iglesia, ni grande, ni pequeña, ni blanca ni de otros colores.

Desesperada, di la vuelta y seguí la misma pista que me trajo hasta este punto y volví a la pensión. Sudada, miré al grupo, todos alegres, comiendo el desayuno y charlando.

"Nunca vi la iglesia," les relaté a los dueños. Mis colegas me miraron sin poder aguantar la risa.

"Ah," me contestaron. "Ud. no es nicaragüense y no conoce bien ni la ciudad ni esta área. Le dirigimos adonde la iglesia estaba antes de la guerra."

Verbos

aguantar la risa	*to hold back laughter*
cruzar	*to cross*
dar una vuelta	*to take a walk*
doblar	*to turn*
hallar	*to find*
relatar	*to relate*

Nombres

el ayuntamiento	*town hall*
la colina	*the hill*
la pista	*the trail*

Adjetivo

sudado	*sweaty*

Direcciones

a la derecha	*to the right*
recto	*straight ahead*

Preguntas

1. ¿A qué hora es la clase de la protagonista?

   _____

2. ¿Cómo se siente ella al empezar el camino?

   _____

3. ¿Estaba ella sola o acompañada?

   _____

4. ¿Cómo volvió a la pensión?

   _____

5. ¿Por qué se rieron sus colegas?

   _____

The *nosotros* Command: "Let us . . ."

"Let's do something," or *"Let's not* do something" expresses the **nosotros** command forms. The **nosotros** command forms are the same as the present subjunctive.

Begin with the present indicative **yo** form of the verb, and drop the **-o**. That gives you the stem for the command form.

- For **-ar verbs**, add **-emos** to the stem.

- For **-er** and **-ir** verbs, add **-amos** to the stem.

- The affirmative and negative **nosotros** commands have the same form.

-Ar Verbs

Cantemos. Bailemos.	*Let's sing. Let's dance.*
Esperemos un momento.	*Let's wait a moment.*
Tomemos un café.	*Let's have coffee.*
Empecemos la lección.	*Let's begin the lesson.*

-Er and *-ir* Verbs

Salgamos ahora.	*Let's leave now.*
Abramos el libro.	*Let's open the book.*
Leamos este capítulo en clase.	*Let's read this chapter in class.*

The indirect object pronouns and direct object pronouns are attached to the affirmative command.

Digamos la verdad.	*Let's tell the truth.*
Digámosla.	*Let's tell it.*
Hagamos la tarea.	*Let's do the homework.*
Hagámosla.	*Let's do it.*
Traigámosle las flores al maestro.	*Let's bring flowers to the teacher.*
Besemos a los niños.	*Let's kiss the children.*
Besémoslos.	*Let's kiss them.*
Crucemos la calle.	*Let's cross the street.*
Crucémosla.	*Let's cross it.*

The negative **nosotros** command form is the same as the affirmative **nosotros** command form. The object pronouns (reflexive, indirect, and direct) precede the command.

No fumemos.	*Let's not smoke.*
No le digamos nada al doctor.	*Let's not say anything to the doctor.*
No les compremos nada.	*Let's not buy them anything.*
No nos acostemos tarde.	*Let's not go to bed late.*

Vamos is used instead of **vayamos** for *let's go*. In the negative, **vayamos** is used.

Vamos al cine. No vayamos al museo.	*Let's go to the movies. Let's not go to the museum.*

In the affirmative **nosotros** command form of a reflexive verb, the final **-s** is dropped before the **-nos** is added.

irse	vamos + nos	Vámonos. *Let's go.*
sentarse	sentemos + nos	Sentémonos. *Let's sit down.*
acostarse	acostemos + nos	Acostémonos. *Let's go to bed.*
ducharse	duchemos + nos	Duchémonos. *Let's take a shower.*
levantarse	levantemos + nos	Levantémonos. *Let's get up.*

The final **-s** of the command form is dropped if the indirect object pronoun **se** is added. The **-s** is dropped before the **se** is added. This is done to eliminate the **-ss-** combination.

Ella quiere un perro. Comprémoselo. (compremos + se + lo)	*She wants a dog. Let's buy it for her.*
Gloria necesita nuestra ayuda. Démosela. (demos + se + la)	*Gloria needs our help. Let's give it to her.*

In the stem-changing **-ir** verbs, there is an irregularity in the **nosotros** command form. Verbs with the **e > ie** or **e > i** change in the stem have an **-i-** in the stem of the **nosotros** command. Verbs with the **o > u** change in the stem have a **-u-** in the stem of the **nosotros** command. This is the same stem change seen in the present subjunctive.

e > ie

Advirtamos a los otros.   *Let's warn the others.*

e > i

Repitamos la pregunta.   *Let's repeat the question.*
Sirvamos la cena.   *Let's serve supper.*
Sigamos las señales.   *Let's follow the signs.*

o > u

Durmámonos ahora. Ya es tarde.   *Let's go to sleep now. It's already late.*

Exercise 21.11

*Write the affirmative **nosotros** command for the following verbs.*

1. decir   _____
2. empezar   _____
3. seguir   _____
4. irse   _____
5. despertarse   _____
6. jugar   _____
7. esperar   _____
8. entrar   _____
9. tomar   _____
10. cruzar   _____
11. dormirse   _____
12. almorzar   _____
13. comer   _____
14. descansar   _____
15. volver   _____

Affirmative *vosotros* Commands

The **vosotros** form is used only in Spain. The affirmative, familiar plural **vosotros** command is formed by dropping the final **-r** of the infinitive and adding **-d**. There are no exceptions.

Mirad. Escuchad. Caminad.	*Look. Listen. Walk.*
Bebed. Comed. Tened cuidado.	*Drink. Eat. Be careful.*
Id. Salid. Venid. Decid.	*Go. Leave. Come. Tell.*

In the affirmative **vosotros** command, both the direct and indirect object pronouns are attached to the verb form.

Leed el libro. Leedlo.	*Read the book. Read it.*
Cerrad la puerta. Cerradla.	*Close the door. Close it.*
Abrid la ventana. Abridla.	*Open the window. Open it.*

In the affirmative **vosotros** command of a reflexive verb, the final **-d** is dropped before the **-os** is added:

despertad + os − -d- = desperta(d)os = despertaos

Desayunaos. Bañaos.	*Have breakfast. Bathe.*
Poneos la chaqueta. Ponéosla.	*Put on your jacket. Put it on.*
Divertíos en vuestras vacaciones.	*Have a good time on your vacation.*

Negative *vosotros* Commands

The negative **vosotros** command is the same as the subjunctive. The reflexive, indirect, and direct object pronouns precede the verb.

No cantéis esa canción.	*Don't sing that song.*
No bailéis aquí.	*Don't dance here.*
No comáis este pescado.	*Don't eat this fish.*
No lo comáis.	*Don't eat it.*
No bebáis el agua.	*Don't drink the water.*
No la bebáis.	*Don't drink it.*
No le traigáis el paquete a Susana.	*Don't bring the package to Susan.*
No se lo tragáis.	*Don't bring it to her.*

No cerréis aquella puerta.	*Don't close that door.*
No la cerréis.	*Don't close it.*
No os sentéis en esta silla rota.	*Don't sit down in this broken chair.*
No os vayáis.	*Don't go.*
No os caigáis.	*Don't fall.*
No os preocupéis.	*Don't worry.*

For the negative **vosotros** command, as for the affirmative **nosotros** command, stem-changing **-ir** verbs show an irregularity in the command form. Verbs with the **e** > **ie** or **e** > **i** change in the stem have an **-i-** in the stem of the **vosotros** command. Verbs with the **o** > **u** change in the stem have a **-u-** in the stem of the **vosotros** command. This is the same as is found in the present subjunctive.

No mintáis.	*Don't lie.*
No os muráis.	*Don't die.*
No me corrijáis.	*Don't correct me.*
No repitáis vuestra idea.	*Don't repeat your idea.*
No sigáis a un mal líder.	*Don't follow a bad leader.*

A Word About the *vosotros* Command

The **vosotros** command is used only in Spain. It is good to know this form, however, especially when you begin to read literature by Spanish writers, or if you are planning a trip to Spain.

Exercise 21.12

Write the Spanish translation for the following commands as quickly as you can, according to the cue in parentheses. You often you have very little time to ask someone to do or not to do something. (Try to say each of the following Spanish commands in five seconds or less.)

1. *Don't touch it.* (tú)   _____

2. *Don't say it to me.* (tú)   _____

3. *Don't do it.* (tú)   _____

4. *Help me.* (Ud.)   _____

5. *Give her the book.* (Ud.) _____

6. *Give it to her.* (Ud.) _____

7. *Don't give it to her.* (Ud.) _____

8. *Kiss me.* (tú) _____

9. *Sit down, please.* (Uds.) _____

10. *Let's begin.* (nosotros) _____

11. *Wait for us.* (Uds.) _____

12. *Go to the right.* (Uds.) _____

13. *Be careful.* (tú) _____

14. *Fill out this form, please.* (Ud.) _____

15. *Don't drink so much.* (tú) _____

16. *Take out the garbage.* (tú) _____

17. *Don't go away.* (Ud.) _____

18. *Don't worry.* (Uds.) _____

19. *Let's follow the directions.* (nosotros) _____

20. *Drive slower, please.* (Ud.) _____

21. *Please stay.* (Uds.) _____

22. *Call me.* (tú) _____

23. *Don't buy anything.* (Ud.) _____

24. *Don't laugh.* (Uds.) _____

25. *Let's go.* (nosotros) _____

 ## Exercise 21.13

Subjunctive, present indicative, or infinitive? *Complete the following sentences with the correct form of the verb in parentheses.*

1. Quiero que Ud. _____. (quedarse)

2. ¿Qué quieres que yo te _____? (decir)

3. Es importante _____ bien. (comer)

4. Esperamos que Jorge y su hermana _____. (mejorase)

5. Paulina sabe que yo la _____. (buscar)

6. Es cierto que a los niños les _____ jugar. (gustar)

7. No me gusta que ella _____ a verme. (venir)

8. Los turistas buscan un hotel que _____ cómodo. (ser)

9. No sabemos quien _____ ser presidente. (querer)

10. Ojalá que toda la familia nos _____. (visitar)

11. Helena nos dice que el tren _____. (llegar)

12. El profesor les dice a los estudiantes que _____ la tarea. (hacer)

13. Vamos a estar alegres cuando _____ un buen apartamento. (comprar)

14. Me alegro _____ aquí. Me alegro de que tú

    _____ aquí también. (estar/estar)

15. Antes de _____ al concierto, las mujeres se visten bien. (ir)

16. ¿Es verdad que a la gente le _____ usar la computadora? (gustar)

17. Espero que a Uds. les _____ esta lección. (gustar)

18. Mi amigo me va a esperar hasta que yo lo _____. (llamar)

19. Buscamos una piscina que _____ limpia. (estar)

20. ¿Conoce Ud. a alguien que _____ tocar el violín? (saber)

21. ¿Sabe ella de donde _____ tú? (ser)

22. Yo le aconsejo a Alicia que ella _____ al dentista. (ir)

23. Es imposible que la mayoría siempre _____ razón. (tener)

24. Dudo que _____ mucho tráfico hoy. (haber)

As you read the following story, underline the command forms.

 # Reading Comprehension

La Noche de Brujas

"Ven acá m'hija," dijo su padre. "Ven acá para que yo pueda verte de cerca. Qué bonita estás en tu disfraz."

"Vuelve a las nueve como nos prometiste," le pidió su madre. "Y no hables con nadie, sino con tu grupito de chicas."

"Sí, no se preocupen." Y después, le murmura a su papá para que su mamá no la oiga: "Tú sabes, papá, que mamá va a seguirme, escondiéndose, detrás de los árboles."

"Eres muy lista. Yo no sabía que tú sabías. Ten cuidado, niñita,
y no cruces la calle sin mirar en ambas direcciones."

"Sí, sí, papá." Les cantó a sus padres el canto de la Noche de Brujas:
"Triqui triqui Halloween, quiero dulces para mí," y se fue.

El papá las mira salir; primero su hija, y después su esposa. Sus dos
mujeres; una mayor, la otra menor. Él se sienta en su sillón favorito, en la
casa cómoda, entre sus libros. Pasan las nueve; pasan las diez y nadie llegó.
Empezó a oír todos los sonidos de la casa, el reloj, la radio, el viento contra
la ventana, menos el sonido que él quería oír—las voces de su esposa
e hija, llenas de cuentos de sus aventuras.

Verbos

esconderse	*to hide*
murmurar	*to mumble, to whisper*
ser listo	*to be clever* (**Estar listo** means *to be ready*.)

Nombre

el disfraz	*the disguise*

Expresiones

m'hija	*my daughter* (combination of **mi** and **hija**; a term of affection)
grupito	*small group* (When you add **-ito** or **-ita** to a word, it makes the object smaller or less.)
niñita	*dear girl* (When you add **-ito** or **-ita** to a word, it can be a term of affection.)
triqui triqui	*trick or treat* (from the sound of English *trick or treat*)

Preguntas

1. ¿Adónde van la madre e hija?

_____

2. ¿Por qué no va con ellas el papá?

_____

3. ¿Piensa Ud. que ellas van a regresar?

_____

4. ¿Es una familia feliz o infeliz?

_____

V

Nouns, Articles, Adjectives, Pronouns; Present and Past Perfect Tenses

22

Nouns, Articles, Adjectives, and Pronouns

Nouns and Articles

A noun is a person, place, or thing. In Spanish, all nouns are either masculine or feminine. The definite article (**el**, **la**, **los**, **las**), agrees with its noun in gender and number, as does the indefinite article (**uno**, **una**, **unos**, **unas**).

Most of the time, inclusion of the article in Spanish is the same as it is in English.

El carro rojo cuesta treinta mil dólares.	*The red car costs 30,000 dollars.*
La comida estaba deliciosa.	*The meal was delicious.*
Los guantes de cuero son costosos.	*The leather gloves are expensive.*
Las revistas están en la mesa.	*The magazines are on the table.*
Una muchacha fue al concierto.	*A girl went to the concert.*
Un adulto la acompañó.	*An adult accompanied her.*
Unos músicos tocaron bien.	*Some musicians played well.*
Unas personas salieron contentas.	*Some people left happy.*

Similarly, omission of the article in Spanish often corresponds to English usage.

Escuchamos música.	*We listen to music.*
Escuchamos la música clásica.	*We listen to the classical music.*
El hombre enfermo toma medicina.	*The sick man takes medicine.*
Él toma la medicina que el doctor le dio.	*He takes the medicine that the doctor gave to him.*

A Word About the Definite Article

Even without many rules, you will be able to use the articles effectively.

Inclusion and Omission of Articles

Spanish does not translate *a/an* when stating an unmodified profession. If the profession is modified, the indefinite article (**un/una**) becomes necessary.

UNMODIFIED	Juan es pintor.	*Juan is a painter.*
MODIFIED	Juan es un pintor maravilloso.	*Juan is a wonderful painter.*
UNMODIFIED	Paula es doctora.	*Paula is a doctor.*
MODIFIED	Paula es una buena doctora.	*Paula is a good doctor.*
UNMODIFIED	José es maestro.	*Joseph is a teacher.*
MODIFIED	José es un mal maestro.	*Joseph is a bad teacher.*
UNMODIFIED	Eres estudiante.	*You are a student.*
MODIFIED	Eres una estudiante fantástica.	*You are a fantastic student.*

The definite article is used with days of the week. The English word *on* is not translated.

Ella salió el martes.	*She left on Tuesday.*
Ramón va a volver el sábado.	*Ramón is going to return on Saturday.*
Tenemos clase los jueves.	*We have class on Thursdays.*

The only time the article is omitted when expressing the day of the week is following a form of **ser**.

Hoy es miércoles.	*Today is Wednesday.*
¿Qué día es? Hoy es viernes.	*What day is it? Today is Friday.*

The definite article is used with seasons of the year, even though the English equivalent may not include it.

La primavera es bonita.	*Spring is beautiful.*
El verano es ideal.	*Summer is ideal.*
Me encanta viajar en el otoño.	*To travel in the autumn enchants me.*
No nos gusta esquiar en el invierno.	*To ski in the winter is not pleasing to us.*

The definite article is used after forms of **gustar** and verbs that are used like **gustar** (for example, **doler**, **encantar**, **fascinar**, **importar**), whether the English translation includes it or not.

Me gustan los vegetales.	*Vegetables are pleasing to me.*
A Paula le encanta el cine.	*Movies are very pleasing to Paula.*
A Fernando y a sus amigos les importa la verdad.	*The truth is important to Fernando and his friends.*

The Spanish definite article never follows a form of **haber**. Nouns, adjectives, and indefinite articles can follow **haber**, but not the definite article (**el**, **la**, **los**, **las**).

Hay una persona aquí.	*There is one person here.*
Había algunos libros en la mesa, pero ahora no los veo.	*There were some books on the table, but now I don't see them.*
No hay ningún buen hotel por aquí.	*There is not one good hotel around here.*
Hay poca gente en la ciudad.	*There are few people in the city.*
Hubo mucho tráfico ayer.	*There was a lot of traffic yesterday.*
Había dos fiestas el día de las madres.	*There were two parties on Mother's Day.*

When the verb **hablar** is followed by the name of a language, the definite article is omitted.

Ella habla español, pero no habla inglés.	*She speaks Spanish, but she doesn't speak English.*
Los portugueses hablan francés y portugués.	*The Portuguese speak French and Portuguese.*

The definite article is used in front of each noun if there is more than one noun stated, as in a series.

El museo tiene el arte, la escultura y los dibujos.	*The museum has art, sculpture, and drawings.*
El estudiante tiene el lápiz, la pluma y la computadora en su cuarto.	*The student has the pencil, the pen, and the computer in his room.*

The definite article is used with the name of subject matter.

Enrique estudia la ley.	*Henry studies law.*
María escribe la historia de su país.	*María writes the history of her country.*
Platón enseñó la filosofía.	*Plato taught philosophy.*
Oscar y Fernanda escriben sobre el periodismo.	*Oscar and Fernanda write about journalism.*

The definite article is used before a noun in a general statement.

Los cigarrillos son malos.	*Cigarettes are bad.*
El agua es buena.	*Water is good.*

The definite article is used before abstract nouns.

La sinceridad es importante.	*Sincerity is important.*
La honestidad es rara.	*Honesty is rare.*

The definite article is used to refer to all members of a class.

Los delfines son inteligentes.	*Dolphins are intelligent.*
Las computadoras son necesarias.	*Computers are necessary.*
Los bebés duermen mucho.	*Babies sleep a lot.*

The definite article is used in front of a personal title in Spanish, even when it is not used in the English equivalent.

El señor Muñoz está aquí.	*Mr. Muñoz is here.*
La profesora Hernández llegó ayer.	*Professor Hernández arrived yesterday.*
La señorita López cantó anoche.	*Ms. López sang last night.*

The definite article is omitted before a personal title when the person is being addressed directly.

Hola, señorita López.	*Hello, Ms. López.*
¿Cómo está Ud., señor Rodríguez?	*How are you, Mr. Rodriguez?*

NOTE The definite article is not used in front of **don/doña** or **Santo/San/ Santa**. **Santo** is used only before words beginning with **Do-** or **To-** (**Santo Domingo** and **Santo Tomás**, for example). **Santo** becomes **San** when used before words beginning with any other letters.

Don Juan tiene una mala reputación.	*Don Juan has a bad reputation.*
Doña Barbara vive en Santo Domingo.	*Doña Barbara lives in Santo Domingo.*
Santa Clara y Santo Tomás la visitan allá.	*Saint Clara and Saint Thomas visit her there.*
San Pedro quiere ir a San Juan.	*Saint Peter wants to go to San Juan.*
Desean ver San Diego, California.	*They want to see San Diego, California.*

The definite article is used before nouns of measurement, where it carries the meaning *per.*

Pagamos cien dólares la libra.	*We pay 100 dollars per pound.*
Los bananos cuestan cincuenta centavos el kilo.	*The bananas cost 50 cents per kilo.*
Ella vendió el perfume a diez dólares la onza.	*She sold the perfume at $10 per ounce.*

When two nouns are joined by **de** to form a compound noun, the definite article is omitted before the second noun.

Ella tiene un dolor de cabeza.	*She has a headache.*
A ella le gusta la casa de vidrio.	*She likes the glass house.*
María leyó dos libros de historia.	*María read two history books.*
La novia recibió un anillo de diamantes.	*The girlfriend received a diamond ring.*

The article is omitted before ordinal numbers in the names of kings, queens, and other rulers.

Carlos V (quinto)	*Carlos the fifth*
Louis XIV (catorce)	*Louis the fourteenth*

Before an apposition, which is a noun or noun phrase that is used in the same way and describes the same thing as the noun before it, the definite article is omitted.

Cervantes, **escritor**, era de España.	*Cervantes, the writer, was from Spain.*
Hugo Chávez, **presidente** de Venezuela, fue elegido en 2000.	*Hugo Chávez, president of Venezuela, was elected in 2000.*

Baryshnikov, **bailarín**, empezó
    a bailar en Moscú.

Bogotá, **capital** de Colombia,
    tiene una población de siete
    millones de habitantes.

Baryshnikov, the dancer, began
    to dance in Moscow.

Bogotá, capital of Colombia,
    has a population of seven
    million inhabitants.

 ## Exercise 22.1

Definite article or not? *Complete the following sentences with the correct definite article where it is necessary. Mark an* **X** *where no article is needed.*

1. Quiero que mi hermano me dé _____ libro de _____ medicina.

2. Yo soy _____ abogado pero no me gusta _____ ley.

3. Francamente, yo fumo pero sé que _____ cigarrillos son malos para

    _____ salud.

4. ¿Qué quiere hacer _____ verano que viene?

5. El gobernador tuvo un accidente y le dolieron mucho _____ costillas.

6. ¿Son buenas _____ computadoras?

7. Hugo Chávez, _____ presidente de Venezuela, le da gasolina

    a _____ gente pobre.

8. A _____ familia le encantan _____ vacaciones.

9. Sinceramente, el mesero no sabe si _____ comida está buena en este
    restaurante.

Possessive Adjectives

A possessive adjective agrees in gender and number with the noun it modifies.

Short-Form Possessive Adjectives

A short-form possessive adjective precedes the noun it modifies.

mi, **mis** *my*

Mi cumpleaños es bueno.   *My birthday is good.*
Mis regalos son malos.   *My gifts are bad.*

tu, **tus** *your* (**tú** form)

Tu jardín tiene muchas flores.	*Your garden has many flowers.*
Tus hijos siembran las semillas.	*Your children sow the seeds.*

su, **sus** *your* (**Ud./Uds.** forms), *his, her, their*

Su hermano tiene varias casas.	*Your brother has several houses.* (also possible: *His/Her/Their brother*)
Sus amigos lo visitan.	*His friends visit him.* (also possible: *Your/Her/Their friends*)

In Spanish, a single form (**su/sus**) expresses the third-person possessive for *your* (**Ud./Uds.** forms), *his, her,* and *their.* This means that **su/sus** can be ambiguous, so the construction noun + **de** + pronoun is often used to clarify the meaning.

El hermano de Ud. tiene varias casas.	*Your brother has several houses.*
Los amigos de él lo visitan.	*His friends visit him.*

nuestro, **nuestra**, **nuestros**, **nuestras** *our*

Nuestro abuelo es viejo.	*Our grandfather is old.*
Nuestra abuela es mayor.	*Our grandmother is older.*
Nuestros hermanos son jóvenes.	*Our siblings are young.*
Nuestras hijas son menores.	*Our daughters are younger.*

vuestro, **vuestra**, **vuestros**, **vuestras** *your* (**vosotros** form)

Like **vosotros**, this form is used only in Spain. It is explained here so that you will be aware of it, but when you need the word for *your* in Spanish, use **su/sus**.

Vuestro sobrino tiene suficiente dinero.	*Your nephew has enough money.*
Vuestra sobrina vive en Portugal.	*Your niece lives in Portugal.*
Vuestros tíos viven en España.	*Your uncles and aunts live in Spain.*
Vuestras parientes van a viajar a ambos países.	*Your (female) relatives are going to travel to both countries.*

Exercise 22.2

Complete the following sentences with the most appropriate possessive adjective from the list below.

mi, mis, tu, tus, su, sus, nuestro, nuestra, nuestros, nuestras

1. Soy estudiante: _____ libros están en la mesa.

2. Él es un buen profesor; _____ cursos son interesantes.

3. Ellos son abogados; _____ clientes pueden ser culpables o inocentes.

4. Nuestra amiga es maestra; _____ padres enseñan también.

5. Ella es mi suegra; _____ casa está en México.

6. El cuñado de Cecilia es carpintero: _____ nombre es Manuel.

7. Liliana está en Texas; _____ familia vive en Arizona.

8. Vivo con cuatro amigos, un gato y un conejo; _____ casa es grande.

9. Somos principiantes; _____ tarea es difícil.

10. La hija de Beatriz es doctora; _____ hijo es arquitecto.

Long-Form Possessive Adjectives

Spanish also has a set of long-form possessive adjectives that are used to stress one possessor over another:

*This is **my** car, not **your** car.*

They are used less frequently than the short-form possessive adjectives.

- Long-form possessive adjectives are placed after the noun, and they agree in gender and number with the noun they modify. All have four forms that indicate both gender and number.

- Long-form possessive adjectives are used to emphasize the possessor, and they are the equivalent of the English *of mine, of yours, of his, of hers, of theirs, of ours.*

- Long-form possessive adjectives are used in direct address and exclamations: **¡Dios mío!** for example.

mío, mía, míos, mías *my, of mine*

Tu carro es viejo. El carro **mío** es nuevo.	*Your car is old. **My** car is new.*
Tu casa es azul. La casa **mía** es blanca.	*Your house is blue. **My** house is white.*
Queridos amigo **míos**, ¿cómo están Uds.?	*Dear friends **of mine**, how are you?*

tuyo, tuya, tuyos, tuyas *your (**tú** form), of yours*

No me gusta mi apartamento. Prefiero el apartamento **tuyo**.	*I don't like my apartment. I prefer **your** apartment.*
Mis plumas no tienen tinta. ¿Me puedes prestar las plumas **tuyas**?	*My pens have no ink. Can you lend me **your** pens?*

suyo, suya, suyos, suyas *your (**Ud./Uds.** forms), of yours; his, of his; her, of hers; their, of theirs*

Tomás y Helena están aquí. Necesito el carro **suyo**.	*Thomas and Helen are here. I need his car.* (also possible: *her/their car*)
¿El carro de él o el carro de ella?	*His car or her car?*

Remember that in Spanish there is only one form for the third-person possessive adjective. This means that **suyo/suya/suyos/suyas** can be ambiguous. The construction noun + **de** + pronoun or noun is used to clarify the meaning.

Sara y José escriben cuentos. Los artículos de ella son aburridos, pero los artículos **suyos** son interesantes.	*Sara and Joe write short stories. Her articles are boring, but **his** articles are interesting.*
A Ana le agrada David. Ana es una amiga **suya**. A David le agrada Ana. David es un amigo **suyo**.	*Ana likes David. Ana is a friend **of his**. David likes Ana. David is a friend **of hers**.*
Las ideas **suyas** son estupendas.	*The ideas of **yours/his/her/theirs** are great.*
¿Las ideas de quiénes? Las ideas de Uds.	*The ideas of whom? Your ideas.*

nuestro, **nuestra**, **nuestros**, **nuestras** *our, of ours*

Ud. tiene una familia grande.	*You have a big family.*
La familia **nuestra** es pequeña.	***Our** family is small.*
Los parientes de Enrique viven en Ecuador.	*Henry's relatives live in Ecuador.*
Los parientes **nuestros** viven en Inglaterra.	***Our** relatives live in England.*

vuestro, **vuestra**, **vuestros**, **vuestras** *your (**vosotros** form), of yours*

Mis amigos son de los Estados Unidos.	*My friends are from the United States.*
Los amigos **vuestros** son de España.	***Your** friends are from Spain.*
Mis primas viven en California.	*My cousins live in California.*
Las primas **vuestras** viven en Madrid.	***Your** cousins live in Madrid.*

Long-form possessive adjectives can also occur with the indefinite article—
un, **uno**, **una**, **unos**, **unas**.

Un estudiante **suyo** recibe buenas notas.	*A student **of yours** receives good marks.*
El maestro explica una idea **nuestra**.	*The teacher explains an idea **of ours**.*
Unos amigos **míos** van de vacaciones.	*Some friends **of mine** are going on vacation.*
Unas amigas **tuyas** prefieren trabajar.	*Some friends **of yours** prefer to work.*

Exercise 22.3

Complete the following sentences with the correct possessive adjective, according to the cue in parentheses.

1. Querido amigo _____, ¿vienes a visitarme? (*of mine*)

2. El libro _____ es más pesado que el libro _____. (*yours/mine*)

3. Tus zapatos son viejos; los zapatos _____ son costosos y nuevos. (*of hers*)

4. A los dos compañeros de cuarto siempre se les pierden las llaves. Afortunadamente, tienen otras llaves _____. (*of theirs*)

5. Unas primas _____ quieren ir a México; la otra no quiere viajar. (*of mine*)

6. La idea de Ofelia es mala; la idea _____ es mejor. (*our*)

7. Favor de venir acá, hijo _____. (*of mine*)

8. Los guantes de Rebeca son de cuero; los guantes _____ son de algodón. (*of theirs*)

Possessive Pronouns

A pronoun takes the place of a noun. A possessive pronoun tells who owns or possesses the noun it is replacing.

Your bicycle is yellow. **Mine** *is red.*

Mine is used instead of *my bicycle,* and it is a possessive pronoun because it replaces the noun, *bicycle,* and tells who owns the noun.

Formation and Uses of Possessive Pronouns

- A possessive pronoun agrees in number and gender with the thing possessed.

- A possessive pronoun is similar to the possessive adjective. In most sentences and questions, it is used with the definite article.

- The definite article is omitted before the possessive pronoun only when the possessive pronoun is followed by a form of **ser**.

el mío, **la mía**, **los míos**, **las mías** *mine*

Tu carro es nuevo; **el mío** es viejo y feo.	*Your car is new;* **mine** *is old and ugly.*
Tu casa es grande; **la mía** tiene cuatro cuartos.	*Your house is big;* **mine** *has four rooms.*
Yo sé que tus amigos están aquí, pero ¿dónde están **los míos**?	*I know that your friends are here, but where are* **mine***?*

Notice how important gender is in the use of possessive pronouns in Spanish. It is clear that **el mío** replaces **tu carro**, because it is masculine. Similarly, **la mía** replaces **su casa** because it is feminine.

el tuyo, **la tuya**, **los tuyos**, **las tuyas** *yours* (**tú** form)

No tengo una pluma. ¿Puedo usar **la tuya**?	*I don't have a pen. May I use **yours**?*
Dejé mis libros en la oficina. ¿Me puedes prestar **los tuyos**?	*I left my books in the office. Can you lend me **yours**?*

el suyo, **la suya**, **los suyos**, **las suyas** *yours* (**Ud./Uds.** forms), *his, hers, theirs*

Compré mi libro ayer. ¿Compró Ud. **el suyo**?	*I bought my book yesterday. Did you buy **yours**?*
La casa de Susana es grande. Mi casa es pequeña. No me gusta la mía. Prefiero **la suya**.	*Susan's house is big. My house is small. I don't like mine. I prefer **hers**.*
Jaime no tiene mis zapatos. Tengo **los suyos**.	*Jim doesn't have my shoes. I have **his**.*
David no sabe dónde están mis llaves. **Las suyas** están en el carro.	*David doesn't know where my keys are. **His** are in the car.*

Remember that the third-person possessive pronouns, both singular and plural, are often ambiguous. **Prefiero la suya** can be translated as *I prefer his, I prefer yours,* or *I prefer theirs,* in addition to *I prefer hers.* It can be clarified in the following manner: **Prefiero la casa de él / de ella / de Ud. / de ellos / de ellas / de Uds.**

el nuestro, **la nuestra**, **los nuestros**, **las nuestras** *ours*

La guitarra de Gloria es vieja. **La nuestra** es nueva y costosa.	*Gloria's guitar is old. **Ours** is new and expensive.*
Elena tiene su propio radio. No quiere **el nuestro**.	*Elena has her own radio. She doesn't want **ours**.*
¿Dónde pusieron Uds. sus libros? Encontramos **los nuestros** en el estudio.	*Where did you put your books? We found **ours** in the study.*

el vuestro, **la vuestra**, **los vuestros**, **las vuestras** *yours* (**vosotros** form)

Mi tren llega de Barcelona el lunes. **El vuestro** llega de Madrid.	*My train arrives from Barcelona on Monday. **Yours** arrives from Madrid.*

Mis revistas están encima del piano.	*My magazines are on top of the piano.*
No puedo ver **las vuestras**.	*I can't see **yours**.*

Exercise 22.4

Complete the following sentences with the correct possessive pronoun, according to the cue in parentheses.

1. El himno nacional de Canadá es más bonito que _____. (*ours*)

2. Nuestros tíos vinieron a vernos ayer. ¿Cuándo vienen _____? (*yours*)

3. Enrique quiere vender su cámara. Me gusta _____, pero voy a

    comprar _____. (*his/yours*)

4. La mujer quería llevar su chaqueta en clase, pero yo tenía calor, y me quité

    _____. (*mine*)

5. Los hijos de Sonia se duermen a las ocho todas las noches; _____
    se duermen a las nueve. (*ours*)

6. Esta alcoba es más pequeña que _____. (*mine*)

7. Este hotel de tres estrellas es menos cómodo que _____. (*ours*)

8. ¿Cuál de los pasteles desea Ud.? El pastel que deseo es más sabroso que

    _____. (*yours*)

Omission of the Article Following *ser* with Possessive Pronouns

When a possessive pronoun follows any form of **ser**, the article (**el**, **la**, **los**, **las**) is omitted.

El gusto es mío.	*The pleasure is mine.*
La casa es mía.	*The house is mine.*

Los zapatos son míos.	*The shoes are mine.*
Estas opiniones son mías.	*These opinions are mine.*

El vestido es tuyo.	*The dress is yours.*
La corbata es tuya.	*The tie is yours.*

Los trajes son tuyos.	*The suits are yours.*
Las faldas son tuyas.	*The skirts are yours.*
El piano es suyo.	*The piano is yours.* (also possible: *is his/her/theirs*)
La guitarra es suya.	*The guitar is his.* (also possible: *is yours/hers/theirs*)
Los tambores son suyos.	*The drums are hers.* (also possible: *are yours/his/theirs*)
Las flautas son suyas.	*The flutes are theirs.* (also possible: *are yours/his/hers*)
El violín es nuestro.	*The violin is ours.*
La computadora es nuestra.	*The computer is ours.*
Los coches son nuestros.	*The cars are ours.*
Las bicicletas son nuestras.	*The bicycles are ours.*

 ## Exercise 22.5

Complete the following sentences with the correct possessive pronoun, according to the cue in parentheses. In these sentences, it appears after a form of **ser**.

1. El libro es _____. (*mine*)

2. Estos espejos son _____. (*yours*)

3. Los mapas son _____. (*ours*)

4. Los gatos son _____. (*his*)

5. La planta es _____. (*hers*)

6. La televisión es _____. (*theirs*)

 ## Exercise 22.6

Complete the following sentences with the correct possessive pronoun, according to the cue in parentheses. In these sentences, it appears after a word other than a form of **ser**.

1. Mi libro está aquí. ¿Dónde está _____? (*yours*)

2. El chaleco guatemalteco cuesta veinte pesos. ¿Cuánto cuesta

   _____? (*his*)

3. El maestro tiene su libro. ¿Quién tiene _____? (*mine*)

4. Los carros de Jaime son costosos; son mejores que _____. (*ours*)

5. No tengo una buena maleta para mi viaje. ¿Me puedes prestar

   _____? (*yours*)

6. ¿Hay platos para la fiesta? ¿Nos pueden Uds. traer _____? (*yours*)

Relative Pronouns

Relative pronouns are related to a noun that has been previously stated.

Que

Que, meaning *that, which,* or *who,* is the most commonly used, all-purpose relative pronoun in Spanish. Referring to persons, places, or things, it comes right after the noun to which it refers.

Este hombre, que habla mucho, es mi amigo.	*This man, who talks a lot, is my friend.*
Tengo la información que necesitas.	*I have the information that you need.*

Que is also used after prepositions. As the object of a preposition, **que** refers to a thing or things only, not to a person or persons.

El edificio en que vivo es viejo.	*The building in which I live is old.*
Tengo la pluma con que él escribe.	*I have the pen with which he writes.*
Los libros de que hablo son interesantes.	*The books of which I am speaking are interesting.*

Quien

Quien means *who* and is used instead of **que** when a form of **ser** is used in the main clause.

Es ella **quien** canta bien.	*It is she who sings well.*
Son ellos **quienes** bailan.	*It is they who dance.*
Soy yo **quien** escribe.	*It is I who is writing.*

Quien and **quienes**, meaning *whom,* are used after prepositions to refer to people.

Ella es la mujer con quien Eduardo vive.	*She is the woman with whom Ed lives.*
El cantante a quien conozco llegó hoy.	*The singer whom I know arrived today.*
Los estudiantes a quienes vi ayer no están aquí hoy.	*The students whom I saw yesterday are not here today.*

Cuyo, cuya, cuyos, cuyas

Cuyo, which means *whose,* can serve as a relative pronoun or relative adjective. It most often acts as an adjective, however, because it typically precedes the noun that it modifies and agrees with it in gender and number.

Los niños **cuya familia** vive lejos se sienten solos.	*The children whose family lives far away feel lonely.*
El hombre **cuyo libro** tengo se fue ayer.	*The man whose book I have left yesterday.*
La doctora **cuyos clientes** son exigentes trabaja duro.	*The doctor whose clients are demanding works hard.*
El guitarrista **cuyas canciones** son originales gana mucho dinero.	*The guitarist whose songs are original earns a lot of money.*

Lo que

Lo que means *that which* and is often translated as *what.* It is a neuter relative pronoun and refers to an abstract idea.

Julia siempre entiende lo que le enseñamos.	*Julia always understands what we teach her. (Julia always understands that which we teach her.)*
Lo que quiero decirles es la verdad.	*What I want to say to you is the truth.*
Lo que Ud. hizo me sorprendió.	*What you did surprised me.*
Fernando tiene lo que necesitas.	*Fernando has what you need.*
¿Oyen Uds. lo que yo oigo?	*Do you hear what I hear?*

When **lo que** is used to mean *whatever*, it is followed by the present subjunctive.

> El día de tu cumpleaños, puedes   *On your birthday, you can do*
>   hacer lo que quieras.   *whatever you want.*

 ## Exercise 22.7

Complete the following sentences with the appropriate relative pronoun. Choose from the list below.

lo que, que, quien, quienes, cuyo

1. Sabemos _____ Luisa sabe.

2. Los hombres, _____ jugaban tenis contra sus esposas, perdían.

3. Este hotel, en _____ pasamos nuestras vacaciones, es maravilloso.

4. Samuel y su hermano, _____ viven en el décimo piso, son carpinteros.

5. Graciela tiene dos nietos con _____ viaja.

6. Ella tiene un bastón con _____ caminar.

7. _____ Raúl hace no le sirve.

8. ¿Eres tú _____ baila bien?

9. Somos nosotros _____ cantan bien.

10. ¿Entendieron Uds. _____ yo les enseñé?

11. ¿Compraste la casa _____ me gustó?

12. No tengo nadie con _____ hablar.

13. A este hombre _____ esposa tiene tres coches no le gusta manejar.

14. Mi mejor amigo, _____ hermanos bailan y cantan, toca bien el violín.

Exercise 22.8

Translate the following sentences into English.

1. Rita vendió la casa que me gustó.

   _____

2. Lo que Ud. dijo era verdad.

   _____

3. No sé si este hombre conocido, que estudia la filosofía, quiere ir a Grecia con sus amigos.

   _____

El que, la que, los que, las que

El que and its related forms are translated as *that, which, who, the one that, the ones that, the one who,* and *the ones who.* They refer to people or things, show gender and number, and can be used instead of **que** for emphasis or clarification. **Que** is used much more in conversation, while the forms of **el que** are used more in written Spanish. This form is not commonly used in speech as a connector. It is good to know these forms, but for conversation, you'll probably use **que**.

Mi hermana, la que es baja, compró tacones.	*My sister, who is short, bought high heels.*
El turista, el que llegó ayer, está cansado.	*The tourist, the one who arrived yesterday, is tired.*
Las mesas, las que son de vidrio, son caras.	*The tables, the ones that are made of glass, are expensive.*
Mis sobrinos, los que estudian la ley, quieren ser abogados.	*My nephews, who study law, want to be lawyers.*

El cual, la cual, los cuales, las cuales

El cual and its related forms also mean *that, which,* or *who.* They are interchangeable with **el que**, **la que**, **los que**, and **las que**. Like the latter forms, these are used more in writing than in speech.

This form replaces **que** when there is some doubt about the reference, or if the relative pronoun is at a distance from the antecedent. These relative pronouns also show gender and number, so they are used to avoid confusion when there is more than one possible noun to which they might refer.

El padre de mi amiga, **el cual** es científico, fue a Alemania a estudiar.	*My friend's father, who is a scientist, went to Germany to study.*
La madre de Federico, **la cual** canta y baila, es actriz.	*Fred's mother, who sings and dances, is an actress.*
Los hermanos de Susana, **los cuales** trabajan en España, hablan español.	*Susan's brothers, who work in Spain, speak Spanish.*
Las hijas de Gabriel, **las cuales** están alegres, viajan mucho.	*Gabriel's daughters, the ones who are happy, travel a lot.*

El cual and its related forms are most frequently used after prepositions other than **a**, **de**, **con** and **en**. They are especially common with compound prepositions.

La razón por la cual Isabel viaja es un misterio.	*The reason why Isabel travels is a mystery.*
Había una guerra durante la cual muchas personas murieron.	*There was a war during which many people died.*
Éste es el edificio enfrente del cual vi el accidente.	*This is the building in front of which I saw the accident.*
Éstas son las calles debajo de las cuales hay varias líneas de metro.	*These are the streets under which there are several subway lines.*
Aquí está la fuente detrás de la cual Lorenzo y Laura se enamoraron.	*Here is the fountain behind which Lorenzo and Laura fell in love.*

NOTE **La razón por la cual** is translated *the reason why* in English. Literally, the translation is *the reason through which*.

Exercise 22.9

Complete the following sentences with the most appropriate relative pronoun.

1. Es ella _____ lo ama.

2. Yo sabía _____ los estudiantes estaban alegres.

3. Muchas personas murieron durante la guerra _____ no era necesaria.

4. La razón por _____ Paulina y Raúl se enamoraron es obvia.

5. Las vacas y los búfalos comen hierba, _____ dan leche.

6. Susana necesita un bastón con _____ andar.

7. Ella necesita una persona con _____ estar.

8. Es un buen barrio en _____ vivir.

9. ¿Cuál es el tema de _____ tú hablas?

10. ¿A _____ buscan Uds.?

11. ¿Es ésta la puerta por _____ entramos?

Demonstrative Adjectives and Pronouns

The demonstrative adjectives and demonstrative pronouns look similar.

Demonstrative Adjectives

Masculine	Feminine	
este	esta	*this*
estos	estas	*these*
ese	esa	*that*
esos	esas	*those*
aquel	aquella	*that (over there)*
aquellos	aquellas	*those (over there)*

Demonstrative Pronouns

Demonstrative pronouns carry a written accent.

The demonstrative pronoun replaces the noun. Whereas **este libro** means *this book*, **éste** (referring to **el libro**) means *this one* and replaces **el libro** (*the book*). The pronunciation is the same for both forms.

	Masculine	Feminine	
NEAR THE SPEAKER	éste	ésta	*this one*
	éstos	éstas	*these (ones)*
NEAR THE LISTENER	ése	ésa	*that one*
	ésos	ésas	*those (ones)*
FAR FROM BOTH	aquél	aquélla	*that one (over there)*
SPEAKER AND LISTENER	aquéllos	aquéllas	*those (over there)*

Los zapatos suyos son más elegantes que **éstos** que están en la ventana.	*Your shoes are more elegant than **these** that are in the window.*
Estos perros feroces ladran mucho, pero **aquéllos** son mansos.	*These wild dogs bark a lot, but **those (over there)** are tame.*
Nos gusta este carro, pero vamos a comprar **ése**.	*We like this car, but we are going to buy **that one**.*
Esta vista de la ciudad es hermosa, pero prefiero **ésa**.	*This view of the city is beautiful, but I prefer **that one**.*

The demonstrative pronoun is also used to express former and latter.

Dos personas, Julia y Ana, se quieren mucho.	*Two people, Julia and Ana, love each other a lot.*
Ésa es alta y delgada; **ésta** es baja y cariñosa.	***The former** is tall and thin; **the latter** is short and affectionate.*

There are three neuter demonstrative pronouns that do not carry written accents. They refer to an object that is not known, a statement, or a general idea.

esto	*this*
eso	*that*
aquello	*that* (farther away in place or time)

¿Qué es **esto**?	*What is **this**?*
¡**Eso** es imposible!	***That** is impossible!*
Aquello me molesta.	***That** annoys me.*

Reading Comprehension

Mi viaje

Estoy preparándome para mis vacaciones en México y se me perdió el pasaporte. ¿Es necesario que yo tenga un pasaporte? Pienso que sí. ¿A quién le pregunto? Debo llamar a mi amigo Juan que viaja mucho. Ojalá que sepa. El año pasado viajó a Oaxaca, una ciudad en México la cual está a seis horas por bus desde la capital. Le gustó mucho o me dijo que le gustó.

Estoy pensando en ir a los Galápagos también donde las tortugas viven más de cien años y los animales y los pájaros actúan como dueños de la isla porque no les tienen miedo a los turistas, los cuales pasean por las islas todo el día, día tras día. Si Juan no está en casa, lo voy a llamar a su celular, el que lleva consigo todo el tiempo. ¿Cuál es su número de teléfono? Se me olvidó.

Verbos

actuar	*to act*
olvidarse	*to forget* (by accident)
pasear	*to take a walk, to stroll*
perderse	*to lose* (by accident)

Preposición

consigo	*with himself*

Preguntas

1. ¿Adónde quiere viajar el protagonista?

   _____

2. ¿Quién es Juan?

   _____

3. ¿Puede Ud. describir los Galápagos?

   _____

4. ¿Cómo son los animales de la isla?

   _____

The Neuter *lo* + Adjective Used as a Noun

The neuter article **lo** followed by the masculine form of an adjective acts as a noun.

Lo difícil es pensar por sí mismo.	*The difficult thing is to think for oneself.*
Lo más importante es preguntar.	*The most important thing is to ask.*
Lo mejor de todo es poder vivir bien.	*The best (thing) of all is to be able to live well.*
Se ve lo bueno y lo malo por todas partes.	*One sees the good and the bad everywhere.*

The neuter article **lo** followed by **de** means *the matter of, the issue of.*

Lo de la mujer le interesa a José.	*The matter of the woman interests Joe.*
Lo de la tecnología le fascina al científico.	*The issue of technology interests the scientist.*

Expressions with *lo*

lo antes posible	*as soon as possible*
lo más posible	*the most possible*
lo más pronto posible	*the fastest possible*
lo menos posible	*the least possible*

Exercise 22.10

Complete the following sentences with the correct form of the article: **el**, **la**, **los**, **las**, *or* **lo**. *In some cases, the article is part of the contraction* **al**. *Remember that the article may also be omitted. If no article is needed, mark an* **X**.

Hoy es (1.) _____ domingo, (2.) _____ 27 de junio. Eduardo fue

(3.) _____ cine ayer. Le gustó (4.) _____ película *María Llena de Gracia*.

(5.) _____ público le gustó mucho también. Me dijo que (6.) _____ bueno

de la película era (7.) _____ de (8.) _____ vida actual en Bogotá,

(9.) _____ capital de Colombia. A Eduardo todo (10.) _____ del cine le interesa. Él va todos (11.) _____ sábados por (12.) _____ noche. Cuando

tiene tiempo, estudia (13.) _____ historia del cine. A veces, (14.) _____

películas que ve son malas, pero no le importa. (15.) _____ importante es que

Eduardo goza mucho de (16.) _____ experiencia. A mí no me gusta ir

(17.) _____ cine. Prefiero (18.) _____ teatro donde (19.) _____ actores

actúan ante nosotros. Cuando yo fui joven, quería ser (20.) _____ actriz,

pero a la edad de cuarenta, decidí hacerme (21.) _____ directora.

Exercise 22.11

Complete the following sentences with **el cual**, **la cual**, **los cuales**, **las cuales**, **cuyo**, **cuya**, **cuyos**, **cuyas**, **quien**, *or* **quienes**. *Use each relative pronoun only one time.*

1. La radio de mi hermano, _____ me gustó, era un regalo
   de mi amigo.

2. Olivia es la persona de _____ hablábamos.

3. La ciudad construyó un nuevo rascacielos desde _____ hay vistas
   maravillosas.

4. Los estudiantes _____ maestro es excelente ganaron todos
   los premios académicos.

5. Conozco a esa mujer _____ madre es de Colombia.

6. Roberto y Jorge vinieron a vernos, _____ son de México.

7. Los muchachos con _____ el jefe hablaba son los mejores
   estudiantes de la clase.

8. Este hombre, _____ opiniones son interesantes, se llama Teodoro.

9. Tengo buenas gafas por _____ puedo ver bien.

10. A Leonardo le molesta su vecino _____ perros ladran toda
    la noche.

Adjectives Used as Nouns

Spanish adjectives can be used as nouns when the noun they modify is omitted.

Me gusta la camisa azul.	*The blue shirt is pleasing to me.*
También me gusta la camisa roja.	*The red shirt is also pleasing to me.*
A Paula le gusta la camisa roja.	*The red shirt is pleasing to Paula.*
Le gusta **la roja**.	***The red one** is pleasing to her.*
Íbamos a comprar un carro viejo, pero cambiamos la decisión y escogimos el carro nuevo.	*We were going to buy an old car, but we changed our mind and we chose the new car.*
Escogimos **el nuevo**.	*We chose **the new one**.*
No nos gustó **el viejo**.	***The old one** wasn't pleasing to us.*
¿Por qué compró Ana la casa azul, si le gusta la casa amarilla?	*Why did Ana buy the blue house, if the yellow house is pleasing to her?*
¿Por qué no compró **la amarilla**?	*Why didn't she buy **the yellow one**?*

Exercise 22.12

Complete the following sentences with the correct adjective used as a noun, according to the cue in parentheses.

EXAMPLE   El hombre viejo no camina bien. La mujer vieja usa un bastón.

_____*Los dos viejos*_____ dan un paseo cada mañana. (*the two old people*)

1. ¿Por qué no te gusta este nuevo restaurante chino?

   ¿Prefieres _____? (*the old one*)

2. Los dos carros son económicos: uno es verde; el otro es blanco.

   Voy a comprar _____. (*the white one*)

3. Al hombre le gustan dos apartamentos: un apartamento grande

   y costoso y otro apartamento mediano y barato. Decide comprar

   _____. (*the big one*)

Pronouns Used as Nouns

Pronouns are words that refer to a noun or take the place of a noun.

El de, la de, los de, las de

The articles **el**, **la**, **los**, **las** followed by **de** can replace a noun when that noun is omitted.

El libro de Olivia y **el** (libro) **de** su hermano son interesantes.	*Olivia's book and **that of** her brother are interesting.*
Tu blusa y la (blusa) de María son hermosas.	*Your blouse and **that of** María are beautiful.*
Los perros feroces viven en el campo.	*The wild dogs live in the countryside.*
Los de mi hermano son animales domesticados.	***My brother's** are pets. (My brother's = Those of my brother = My brother's dogs)*
Estas camisas son caras.	*These shirts are expensive.*
Las de Alicia son baratas.	***Alice's** are cheap. (Alice's = Those of Alice = Alice's shirts)*

El que, la que, los que, las que

The articles **el**, **la**, **los**, **las** followed by **que** can replace a noun when that noun is omitted.

Los dos hombres son amigos.	*The two men are friends.*
El que se llama Alonso juega al baloncesto.	***He who** is called Alonso plays basketball.*
Hay dos mujeres que aman a David.	*There are two women who love David.*
La que está a su lado es su esposa.	***The one who** is at his side is his wife.*
Hay documentos en mi escritorio.	*There are documents on my writing table.*
Los que están en el banco son de mi sobrina.	***Those that** are in the bank are my niece's.*

Pronunciation Practice

Practice the following selection aloud.

Los maderos de San Juan
Un poema por José Asunción Silva

José Asunción Silva nació en 1865 y se murió en 1896 en Bogotá, Colombia. Él comparte con Rubén Darío y otros la estética literaria conocida bajo el nombre de modernismo.

Y aserrín
aserrán
los maderos
de San Juan
piden queso,
piden pan;
los de Roque
Alfandoque;
los de Rique,
Alfeñique;
los de Trique,
Triquitrán.
¡Trique, trique, trique, tran!
¡Trique, trique, trique, tran!

Nombres

aserrán	*nonsense word*
aserrín	*sawdust*
los maderos	*logs*

Reading Comprehension

Lo fatal
Un poema por Rubén Darío

Rubén Darío nació en 1867 en Metapa, Nicaragua, y se murió en su país en 1916. Es considerado como la figura más representativa del modernismo.

Dichoso el árbol que es apenas sensitivo,
y más la piedra dura porque ésa ya no siente,
pues no hay dolor más grande que el dolor de ser vivo,
ni mayor pesadumbre que la vida consciente.

Ser, y no saber nada, y ser sin rumbo cierto,
y el temor de haber sido y un futuro terror…
Y el espanto seguro de estar mañana muerto,
y sufrir por la vida y por la sombra y por

lo que no conocemos y apenas sospechamos,
y la carne que tienta con sus frescos racimos,
y la tumba que aguarda con sus fúnebres ramos,

¡y no saber adónde vamos,
ni de dónde venimos!…

Verbos

aguardar	*to keep*
haber sido	*to have been* (present perfect tense)
sospechar	*to suspect*
tentar	*to tempt*

Nombres

el espanto	*the fright*
la pesadumbre	*the sorrow*
los racimos	*the clusters/bunches*
los ramos	*the bouquets*
el rumbo	*the path*

Expresiones

apenas	*hardly*
sin rumbo	*without direction*

Preguntas

1. Según el poema, ¿por qué son dichosos el árbol y la piedra?

   _____

2. ¿De qué sufre el poeta?

   _____

3. ¿Cuál es el tema del poema?

   _____

4. ¿Cuál es la opinión de Ud. acerca de las ideas del poema?

   _____

23

The Present Perfect Tense

The present perfect tense expresses past action closely related to the present.

The present perfect is a compound tense formed with the present tense of the helping verb **haber** and the past participle of the main verb. The English equivalent of **haber** + past participle is *to have done something*. In the present tense, it corresponds to the present perfect in English: *I have eaten there many times*, for example.

The present perfect tense expresses the following:

* An action that we are waiting for, but that hasn't yet happened
* An action that began in the past and continues to the present
* An action that has happened at various times in the past and may happen again

Formation of the Past Participle

-Ar Verbs

To form the past participle of all **-ar** verbs, drop the ending and add **-ado** to the stem.

alquilar	alquil**ado**	*rented*
apretar	apret**ado**	*squeezed, tightened*
aumentar	aument**ado**	*increased, augmented*
borrar	borr**ado**	*erased*

decepcionar	decepcion**ado**	*disappointed*
empujar	empuj**ado**	*pushed*
estacionar	estacion**ado**	*parked*
estar	est**ado**	*been*
llegar	lleg**ado**	*arrived*
marcar	marc**ado**	*dialed, marked*
tomar	tom**ado**	*taken*
usar	us**ado**	*used*
viajar	viaj**ado**	*traveled*

-*Er* and -*ir* Verbs

To form the past participle of most **-er** and **-ir** verbs, drop the ending and add **-ido** to the stem.

-*Er* Verbs

beber	beb**ido**	*drunk*
comer	com**ido**	*eaten*
entender	entend**ido**	*understood*
perder	perd**ido**	*lost*
ser	s**ido**	*been*
torcer	torc**ido**	*twisted*

-*Ir* Verbs

advertir	advert**ido**	*warned*
añadir	añad**ido**	*added*
convertir	convert**ido**	*converted*
dormir	dorm**ido**	*slept*
hervir	herv**ido**	*boiled*
ir	**ido**	*gone*
oprimir	oprim**ido**	*pressed*
recibir	recib**ido**	*received*

Pronunciation Reminder

In all regular past participles, the Spanish **d** is pronounced like the soft **th** sound in English *other*. Practice the pronunciation of past participles with a **th** sound.

-Er and **-ir** verbs whose stem ends in a vowel have a written accent above the **-i-** in the past participle to maintain the **-ido** sound.

atraer	atra**ído**	*attracted*
caer	ca**ído**	*fallen*
creer	cre**ído**	*believed*
leer	le**ído**	*read*
oír	o**ído**	*heard*
traer	tra**ído**	*brought*

Verbs that end in **-uir** do not carry a written accent in the past participle.

construir	constru**ido**	*constructed*
destruir	destru**ido**	*destroyed*
huir	hu**ido**	*fled*

Irregular Past Participles

Following are the 12 basic irregular past participles in Spanish. Pronounce each of them as you learn them.

abrir	abierto	*opened*
cubrir	cubierto	*covered*
decir	dicho	*told, said*
escribir	escrito	*written*
freír	frito	*fried*
hacer	hecho	*done*
morir	muerto	*died*
poner	puesto	*put*
pudrir	podrido	*rotted*
romper	roto	*broken*
ver	visto	*seen*
volver	vuelto	*returned*

When a prefix is added to any of the irregular verbs above, the past participle shows the same irregularity.

describir	descrito	*described*
descubrir	descubierto	*discovered*
devolver	devuelto	*returned* (an object)
disolver	disuelto	*dissolved*

envolver	envuelto	*wrapped*
oponer	opuesto	*opposed*
resolver	resuelto	*resolved*

Exercise 23.1

Write the past participle of the following verbs. Pronounce each past participle aloud, and make sure you know the meaning of the verb.

1. jugar   _____
2. buscar   _____
3. conocer   _____
4. entrar   _____
5. devolver   _____
6. ser   _____
7. estar   _____
8. dar   _____
9. ver   _____
10. escribir   _____

11. romper   _____
12. tener   _____
13. querer   _____
14. hacer   _____
15. decir   _____
16. ir   _____
17. abrir   _____
18. cerrar   _____
19. morir   _____
20. amar   _____

Formation of the Present Perfect Tense

To form the present perfect tense in Spanish, conjugate the helping verb **haber** (the English auxiliary verb *to have*) in the present tense and follow it with the past participle of the main verb.

yo he comido	*I have eaten*
tú has hablado	*you have spoken*
él ha vuelto	*he has returned*
nosotros hemos sonreído	*we have smiled*
vosotros habéis ido	*you have gone*
ellos han dicho	*they have said*

NOTE The verb **haber** is used as an auxiliary or helping verb to form the perfect tenses. The verb **tener** means *to have* in the sense of possession: **yo tengo dos libros**. **Tener** is never used as an auxiliary verb.

The helping verb **haber** cannot be separated from the past participle. In a question, place the subject after the verb form.

¿Dónde **han estado** Uds.?   *Where have you been?*
¿**Han salido** las mujeres?   *Have the women left?*

 ## Exercise 23.2

Complete the following phrases with the correct past participle of the verb in parentheses. Practice pronouncing each phrase aloud.

1. yo he _____ (ser)

2. tú has _____ (tener)

3. ella ha _____ (poder)

4. nosotros hemos _____ (estar)

5. vosotros habéis _____ (querer)

6. ellas han _____ (saber)

7. yo he _____ (decir)

8. tú has _____ (dar)

9. Ud. ha _____ (volver)

10. nosotros hemos _____ (poner)

11. vosotros habéis _____ (hacer)

12. Uds. han _____ (llegar)

Complete the following phrases with the correct form of the present perfect tense of the verb in parentheses.

13. yo _____ (dormir)

14. tú _____ (romper)

15. ella _____ (abrir)

16. nosotros _____ (estar)

17. vosotros _____ (escribir)

18. ellas _____ (ver)

Uses of the Present Perfect Tense

The present perfect tense expresses an action closely related to the present. Its English equivalent corresponds to the present perfect tense in English. The present perfect tense expresses the following:

- An action that we are waiting for, but that hasn't yet happened

- An action that began in the past and continues to the present

- An action that has happened at various times in the past and may happen again

¿Por qué han apagado Uds. las luces?	*Why have you turned off the lights?*
¿Has comido ya?	*Have you already eaten?*
Los viajeros no han vuelto de México todavía.	*The travelers haven't returned from Mexico yet.*
¿Jamás ha estado en Europa?	*Have you ever been in Europe?*
He andado por este pueblo antes.	*I have walked through this town before.*

NOTE The words **jamás** (meaning *ever* in an affirmative sentence or question), **ya** (meaning *already*), and **todavía** (meaning *still* or *yet*) frequently occur in sentences using the present perfect tense.

Action Waited for or Hoped for

Todavía no he llamado.	*I haven't called yet.* (I might still call.)
Mis invitados no han llegado.	*My guests haven't arrived.*

Compare the following sentences. The first sentence of each pair is in the preterit and the second is in the present perfect.

No llamaron.	*They didn't call.* (The action is complete.)
No han llamado.	*They haven't called.* (There is a possibility that they will call.)
No llegaron.	*They didn't arrive.*
No han llegado.	*They haven't arrived.*

Action That Began in the Past and Continues to the Present

He dormido aquí por cinco horas.	*I have slept here for five hours.*
Hemos vivido en Londres por dos meses.	*We have lived in London for two months.*

Action That Happened in the Past and May Happen Again

Often the actions expressed can be counted.

Eva ha estado en Nueva York tres veces.	*Eva has been in New York three times.*
¿Cuantas veces han comido Uds. en este restaurante?	*How many times have you eaten in this restaurant?*
Hemos comido allí cinco veces.	*We have eaten there five times.*
¿Cuántas veces han visitado México?	*How many times have they visited Mexico?*
Camillo ha visitado México siete veces; Antonio ha ido dos veces.	*Camillo has visited Mexico seven times; Antonio has gone two times.*
Yo he viajado a la ciudad de México cuatro veces. Me he quedado en el mismo hotel dos veces.	*I have traveled to Mexico City four times. I have stayed in the same hotel twice.*

Placement of Object Pronouns with the Present Perfect Tense

The reflexive, indirect, and direct object pronouns are placed directly before the helping verb. This is the only possible position for object pronouns used with the present perfect tense. The object pronouns are never attached to the past participle.

Ellos no **me** han llamado.	*They haven't called me.*
¿Por qué no **le** has hablado a Oscar?	*Why haven't you spoken to Oscar?*
Paula **se lo** ha dicho.	*Paula has said it to you.*
Yo **te** he devuelto el dinero.	*I have returned the money to you.*
Yo **la** he visto antes.	*I have seen her before.*

¿**Te** has duchado hoy?	*Have you showered today?*
El doctor **se** ha lavado las manos tres veces.	*The doctor has washed his hands three times.*
No **nos** hemos levantado todavía.	*We haven't gotten up yet.*

 ## Exercise 23.3

Complete the following sentences with the correct form of the present perfect tense of the verb in parentheses.

1. Laura nos _____ la carta. (traer)

2. Nosotros todavía no la _____. (recibir)

3. Los hoteleros no me _____. (llamar)

4. Sus hermanos nunca le _____ dinero. (prestar)

5. ¿Por qué jamás me _____ tú? (amar)

6. Por fin, mis amigos _____. (volver)

7. El bisabuelo que tenía cien años _____. (morirse)

8. ¿Adónde _____ ellos? (irse)

9. Uds. _____ bien el trabajo. (hacer)

10. Tus colegas siempre _____ bien de ti. (hablar)

11. Irene y su hermano jamás _____. (viajar)

12. Yo la _____ recientemente. (ver)

13. Yo no _____ dormir. (poder)

14. Ellas ya _____. (acostarse)

15. Nosotros _____ a otra casa. (mudarse)

Use of the Infinitive *haber* and the Past Participle

The infinitive form of the helping verb **haber** is used after a preposition.

Me alegro de **haber llegado** a tiempo.	*I am glad to have arrived on time.*
Ella se alegra de **haber hecho** su tarea.	*She is glad to have done her homework.*

Después de **haber encontrado**
sus llaves, el taxista empezó
su trabajo.

After having found his keys,
the cabdriver began his work.

Después de **haber ido** al dentista,
Monica se sintió mejor.

After having gone to the dentist,
Monica felt better.

Because object pronouns can never be attached to the past participle, when
they are needed in an infinitive + past participle construction, they must be
attached to the infinitive, in this case, **haber**.

Me alegro de **haberte** conocido.

I'm glad to have met you.

Los padres de Laura están muy
felices después de **habernos**
visto.

Laura's parents are very happy
after having seen us.

Pedro está contento de haber
cerrado la puerta.

Peter is happy to have closed
the door.

Está contento de **haberla** cerrado.

He is happy to have closed it.

Exercise 23.4

*Complete the following sentences with the correct form of **haber**.*

1. Después de _____ leído el párrafo, los estudiantes están contentos.

2. Nosotros _____ corrido a casa.

3. Sus padres les _____ dado una bienvenida.

4. Después de _____ comido galletas y leche, los niños están listos
   para acostarse.

5. Nosotros ya _____ leído el libro.

6. El muchacho _____ entendido la lección.

7. Sus profesores les _____ enseñado bien.

8. Después de _____ aprobado el examen, ellos se sienten
   satisfechos.

9. ¿_____ hecho bien los niños?

10. Los alumnos _____ empezado a aprender mucho.

Exercise 23.5

Rewrite the following sentences in the present perfect tense. You may include additional words or expressions in the sentence if you wish.

EXAMPLE   Julia no toma mucha cerveza.

   Julia no ha tomado mucha cerveza (todavía).

1. Cruzo la calle a la escuela.

   _____

2. Jamás entro en la clase.

   _____

3. Mis compañeros entran también.

   _____

4. Le decimos "hola" al profesor.

   _____

5. Nos sentamos.

   _____

6. Escribo con lápiz.

   _____

7. Mis amigos usan una computadora.

   _____

8. Contestamos las preguntas.

   _____

9. Almorzamos juntos.

   _____

10. Nos despedimos del profesor.

    _____

11. Vamos en bus a casa.

    _____

12. Les saludamos a nuestros padres al llegar a casa.

    _____

Exercise 23.6

Translate the following sentences into Spanish.

1. *How have you been?*

   _____

2. *Where have all the flowers gone?*

   _____

3. *Who has just called?*

   _____

4. *What have you done?*

   _____

5. *We have sent the document.*

   _____

6. *Have they had breakfast today?*

   _____

7. *I have turned on the oven and have put in the chicken. I have to cook it for an hour.*

   _____

   _____

8. *It is no longer hot, because the students have opened all the windows in the classroom.*

   _____

   _____

9. *The exterminators have killed all the cockroaches.*

   _____

10. *Laura and her daughter have just arrived in Italy.*

    _____

A Word About *acabar de*

Remember: When you want to say *to have just done something*, use the expression **acabar de** in the present tense, not the verb **haber** with the present perfect tense.

Yo **acabo de** llegar.	*I have just arrived.*
Tú **acabas de** cantar.	*You have just sung.*
Él **acaba de** salir.	*He has just left.*
Nosotros **acabamos de** decidir.	*We have just decided.*
Vosotros **acabáis de** pagar.	*You have just paid.*
Ellos **acaban de** volver.	*They have just returned.*

Reading Comprehension

El apartamento

¿Desde cuándo viven los inquilinos en este edificio en la calle cuarenta y seis con la novena avenida? ¿Quién sabe? La gente no se mete en la vida de nadie. Pero yo sí sé porque me gusta observar la ida y vuelta de la muchedumbre. Es verdad que hay muchos inquilinos que ya se han ido o les han alquilado su apartamento a otros. Los apartamentos son pequeños, pero agradables, y bastante baratos en comparación a otros lugares en la ciudad. Por mi parte, sigo firmando el contrato de arrendamiento año de por medio con muchísimas ganas de quedarme. Los porteros son agradables y el superintendente, que vive solo en el primer piso, nos trata bien.

Una pareja del octavo piso ha tenido un bebé hace ocho meses y están viviendo felices. En el décimo piso, dos personas, una mujer que está vieja ya, aunque tiene solamente cuarenta y cinco años, y su compañero (nunca se han casado) se pelean, gritan, y comen mucha comida rápida de restaurantes. (Veo a los mensajeros con pizza o con comida china todo el tiempo). Una mujer muy simpática del tercer piso se ha muerto, y otra mujer del cuarto piso, pelirroja, cuyo perro se ha desaparecido, vive desesperada y triste. En el piso once, un hombre amargado sin amigos sube y baja en el ascensor todos los días. Cuando voy vagando por el edificio, escucho a veces sonidos de amor por la noche en el sexto y el séptimo. En el quinto piso vive un hombre a quien le gusta patinar. Hace muchos años, él tenía una novia bonita e inteligente. Se separaron de repente, y este hombre, tan fuerte y guapo en días pasados, nunca ha tenido otra compañera. Un día voy a escribir un libro, pero por ahora, estoy satisfecha, mirando a la gente, escuchándola ir y venir en la vida cotidiana.

Verbos

estar viejo	*to feel old*
meterse	*to become involved*
patinar	*to skate*
pelear	*to fight*
vagar	*to wander*

Nombres

el contrato de arrendamiento	*the lease*
el inquilino	*the tenant*
la muchedumbre	*the crowd*
el portero	*the doorman*
el superintendente	*the superintendent*

Adjetivos

bonita e inteligente	*pretty and intelligent* (The word **e** is used instead of **y** before words that begin with an emphasized **i-** or **hi-**.)
cotidiano	*daily*
pelirrojo	*red headed*

Expresión

año de por medio	*every other year*

Preguntas

1. ¿Se conoce la gente en este edificio?

   _____

2. ¿Cuántos pisos hay?

   _____

3. ¿Cuántas personas están felices en el edificio?

   _____

4. ¿Cómo sabe tanto de la gente la protagonista?

   _____

24

The Past Perfect Tense

The past perfect tense refers to action that occurred in the past prior to another past action. It is a compound tense. The past perfect tense in Spanish corresponds to the same tense in English: *I had eaten*, for example.

Formation of the Past Perfect Tense

To form the past perfect tense in Spanish, conjugate the helping verb **haber** in the imperfect, and follow it with the past participle of the main verb.

yo había vuelto	*I had returned*
tú habías empezado	*you had begun*
ella había hecho	*she had done*
nosotros habíamos sabido	*we had known*
vosotros habíais dicho	*you had said*
ellas habían comido	*they had eaten*

Uses of the Past Perfect Tense

The past perfect tense occurs in sentences and questions that are directly linked to the past. It expresses an action that precedes another action: A sentence may begin with the imperfect or preterit and continue with the past perfect.

Ud. sabía	que habíamos salido.
You knew (imperfect)	*that we had left.* (past perfect)

Yo creí	que él se había muerto.
I believed (preterit)	*that he had died.* (past perfect)
Ellos vieron a la mujer	que no había dicho nada.
They saw the woman (preterit)	*who hadn't said anything.* (past perfect)

The reflexive, indirect, and direct object pronouns precede the helping verb
haber.

Ella sabía que él no **me** había escrito.	*She knew that he hadn't written to me.*
Me di cuenta de que ellos no **lo** habían hecho.	*I realized that they hadn't done it.*

The infinitive form of the helping verb **haber** is used after a preposition.

Después de **haber llegado** a Perú, los aventureros buscaron un hotel en Cuzco.	*After having arrived in Peru, the adventurers looked for a hotel in Cuzco.*
Después de **haber comido**, fui a la plataforma del tren.	*After having eaten, I went to the train platform.*
El actor aprendió el diálogo sin **haber ensayado** mucho.	*The actor learned the dialogue without having rehearsed much.*

 Exercise 24.1

Translate the following sentences into Spanish.

1. *The children thought that their parents had left.*

   _____

2. *I had already set the table when my family arrived.*

   _____

3. *Roberto went to a country that he had never visited before.*

   _____

4. *My colleagues told me that they had finished their work.*

   _____

Exercise 24.2

Translate the following sentences into English.

1. El profesor sabía que yo había estudiado.

   _____

2. La niña pensaba que su perro había vuelto.

   _____

3. Ellos dijeron que habían devuelto los libros a la biblioteca.

   _____

4. Creíamos que nuestros amigos nos habían escrito.

   _____

5. Estuvimos seguras que los jóvenes habían tenido éxito.

   _____

6. Pensábamos que los ladrones habían estado en el banco.

   _____

7. El policía creía que nosotros los habíamos visto.

   _____

8. Les dijimos a los detectives que no habíamos sido buenos testigos.

   _____

Exercise 24.3

Complete the following sentences with the correct form of the verb in parentheses.

1. Todo el mundo había _____ para el verano. (ir)

2. ¿Habían _____ Uds. mucho tiempo antes de

   _____ al doctor? (esperar/ver)

3. Yo había _____ antes de _____.
   (descansar/cenar)

4. Antes de _____, Anita había _____ sus deudas.
   (jubilarse/pagar)

5. ¿Por qué no le habías _____ al camarero una buena propina

   antes de _____ del restaurante? (dar/salir)

6. Nadie le había _____ a la senadora que ella había

   _____ la elección. (decir/perder)

 # Reading Comprehension

El sueño

Después de haber leído su libro y de haber apagado la tele, Octavio
se acostó. Las noches anteriores él no había podido dormir bien por sus
sueños, digamos, pesadillas, pero esta noche él tenía la determinación
de soñar con buenas cosas. Trató de pensar en algo bueno. ¿Qué será?,
pensaba. El martes, había pensado en el amor y eso le cogió mal, el
miércoles, había pensado en el dinero, pero tampoco le salió bien el sueño.
El jueves pensó en tomar algunas vacaciones en Hawái y muchos tiburones
llenaban sus sueños. Se despertó exhausto, luchando contra los peces.
Hoy siendo viernes, se quedó despierto toda la noche, la única solución
en la cual Octavio podía pensar.

Verbos

cogerle bien/mal a alguien	*to go well/badly for someone*
digamos	*let's say* (the **nosotros** command form of **decir**)
luchar	*to struggle*
salirle bien/mal a alguien	*to go well/badly for someone*
soñar con	*to dream about*
tratar de	*to try to*

Nombres

la pesadilla	*the nightmare*
el pez, los peces	*the fish* (sing. and pl.)
el tiburón	*the shark*

Adjetivos

despierto	*wide-awake*
exhausto	*exhausted*

Expresión

¿qué será?   *What could it be?* (literally, *What will it be?*)

Preguntas

1. ¿En qué trata de pensar Octavio?

   _____

2. ¿Cómo son sus sueños?

   _____

3. ¿Cuál es su solución?

   _____

 # Reading Comprehension

Recordando Nicaragua

En el año 1987 Nicaragua estaba sufriendo los fines de su guerra civil. Los sandinistas luchaban contra el ejército de Somoza, los contras luchaban contra los sandinistas. Daniel Ortega era presidente y líder de los sandinistas, el nombre y el movimiento inspirados por Augusto César Sandino, héroe nacional de Nicaragua que había muerto muchos años atrás.

Era mucho que entender—quien estaba luchando contra quien y por qué.

Fui a Managua, capital de Nicaragua, con un grupo de intérpretes y científicos. Llegamos en agosto a una casa agradable entre gente amable. Desde el principio, nos sentíamos cómodos en nuestra pensión; los dueños nicaragüenses nos trataban bien, nos servían las comidas, y nos mostraban su poesía. (Nos parecía que toda la gente era poeta.)

Después de haber estado en Managua dos días, empezamos nuestro trabajo en la universidad, enseñándoles a los estudiantes avanzados las matemáticas, la ciencia, la medicina, y la astrofísica.

Por la noche volvíamos a la casa y pasábamos muchas noches agradables con amigos; hablábamos de la guerra, de las drogas, de la felicidad. Lo increíble era que a pesar de todo, los nicaragüenses habían mantenido un amor profundo por la vida. Mientras tanto, la guerra continuaba.

Preguntas

1. ¿Por qué estaba sufriendo Nicaragua?

   _____

2. ¿Cómo eran los nicaragüenses?

   _____

3. ¿Quién escribía poesía?

   _____

4. ¿De qué hablaban en las noches?

   _____

The Past Participle as an Adjective

Now that you have learned the past participle, your vocabulary will expand even more, because the past participle is also used as an adjective. As an adjective, the past participle follows the noun it describes, and it agrees with its noun in gender and number.

el restaurante preferido	*the preferred restaurant*
el teléfono perdido	*the lost telephone*
los huevos podridos	*the rotten eggs*
el enemigo conocido	*the known enemy*
la ventana cerrada	*the closed window*
las puertas abiertas	*the open(ed) doors*

 Exercise 24.4

Complete the following phrases with the past participle of the verb in parentheses used as an adjective. Remember that the adjective agrees in gender and number with its noun. Practice pronouncing the phrases aloud.

1. la comida _____ (quemar)

2. la mesa _____ (romper)

3. el pájaro _____ (morir)

4. la tarea bien _____ (hacer)

5. las ideas bien _____ (expresar)

6. el niño _____ (dormir)

7. el amigo _____ (querer)

8. los carros _____ (vender)

9. las blusas _____ (comprar)

10. el año _____ (pasar)

11. los problemas _____ (resolver)

12. el apartamento _____ (alquilar)

13. el tesoro _____ (esconder)

14. las cartas _____ (entregar)

15. la telenovela _____ (grabar)

The Past Participle as an Adjective with *estar*

The past participle as an adjective is usually used with **estar**.

Estoy cansada.	*I am tired.*
¿Estás vestido?	*Are you dressed?*
El baño está ocupado.	*The bathroom is occupied.*
La mesa está puesta.	*The table is set.*
El televisor está prendido.	*The television set is on.*
Estamos enojados.	*We are angry.*
Estamos sentados.	*We are seated.*
Uds. están equivocados.	*You are mistaken.*
Los trabajadores están preocupados.	*The workers are worried.*

When the past participle is used as an adjective with **estar**, it indicates that the idea expressed is the result of an action.

Susana va a escribir un libro. > Ella está escribiendo un libro.
> El libro **está escrito**.

Susana va a escribir un libro.	*Susan is going to write a book.*
Ella está escribiendo un libro.	*She is writing a book.*
El libro **está escrito**.	*The book is written.*

Los músicos van a grabar la canción. > Están grabando la canción.
> La canción **está grabada**.

Los músicos van a grabar la canción.	*The musicians are going to record the song.*
Están grabando la canción.	*They are recording the song.*
La canción **está grabada**.	*The song is recorded.*

La niña va a esconder su muñeca. > Ella está escondiendo su muñeca.
> La muñeca **está escondida**.

La niña va a esconder su muñeca.	*The girl is going to hide her doll.*
Ella está escondiendo su muñeca.	*She is hiding her doll.*
La muñeca **está escondida**.	*The doll is hidden.*

El hombre va a morir. > Él está muriendo. > El hombre **está muerto**.

El hombre va a morir.	*The man is going to die.*
Él está muriendo.	*He is dying.*
El hombre **está muerto**.	*The man is dead.*

NOTE Whether you are aware of this concept or not, you can still use **estar** + past participle with confidence when you are describing someone or something.

 ## Exercise 24.5

*Complete the following sentences with the correct form of **estar** + past participle as an adjective.*

1. El dueño va a cerrar la tienda. Está cerrando la tienda. La tienda

   _____.

2. En la mañana, este hombre va a abrir la tienda. Está abriéndola. La tienda

   _____.

3. Shakira va a escribir una canción. Está escribiéndola. La canción

   _____.

4. Vamos a construir una casa. Estamos construyéndola. La casa

   _____.

5. Los estudiantes van a hacer su tarea. Están haciéndola. La tarea

   _____.

6. Las abejas van a morir. Están muriendo. Las abejas

   _____.

7. Los padres van a freír unos huevos. Están friéndolos. Los huevos

   _____.

8. Vamos a resolver nuestros problemas. Estamos resolviéndolos. Los problemas

   _____.

Exercise 24.6

Write the past participles that appear in the following rhymes. Repeat these rhymes aloud to practice your pronunciation.

1. La mujer está triste
   Triste está la mujer
   La tienda está cerrada
   Y no sabe qué hacer.

   _____

2. El doctor está herido
   Herido está el doctor
   Los médicos preocupados
   Lo cuidan con amor.

   _____

3. El cielo está nublado
   Parece que va a llover
   La gente no quiere mojarse
   Y empieza a correr.

   _____

4. El baúl está arreglado
   Arreglado está el baúl
   La pareja va al Caribe
   A nadar en el agua azul.

   _____

    5. La pareja está separada
        Dividido está el hogar
        Los amantes no se acuerdan
        Cuando se dejaron de amar.

The Past Participle with *ser* and the Passive Voice

The past participle is also used with **ser**. When used with **ser**, the past participle expresses the action itself, in this case, the passive voice, rather than the result of an action. The passive voice consists of **ser** + past participle and is often followed by **por**. The past participle agrees in gender and number with the subject of the sentence.

- In the preterit

El libro *Don Quixote* **fue escrito por** Cervantes.	*The book* Don Quixote *was written by Cervantes.*
La puerta **fue abierta por** el portero.	*The door was opened by the doorman.*
Las casas **fueron robadas por** los ladrones.	*The houses were robbed by the thieves.*
Las iglesias en Guatemala **fueron construidas por** los españoles.	*The churches in Guatemala were constructed by the Spaniards.*
La comida **fue servida por** el camarero.	*The meal was served by the waiter.*

- In the present perfect and past perfect

La carta **ha sido entregada por** el cartero.	*The letter has been delivered by the mailman.*
Los impuestos **han sido preparados por** los contadores.	*The taxes have been prepared by the accountants.*
Los testigos **habían sido advertidos por** el juez.	*The witnesses had been warned by the judge.*
El apartamento **había sido alquilado por** dos amigos.	*The apartment had been rented by two friends.*

In speech, it is generally much better to use the active voice. The passive voice is used infrequently in Spanish. For example, the passive voice is used in this sentence:

El almuerzo **fue preparado por** el cocinero.   *The lunch was prepared by the cook.*

However, it is better to use the active voice you already know.

El cocinero preparó el almuerzo.   *The cook prepared the lunch.*

 Exercise 24.7

Rewrite the following passive sentences as sentences in the active voice.

EXAMPLE   La carta fue escrita por Carla.

Carla escribió la carta.

1. Los vasos fueron hallados por los antropólogos.

    _____

2. El país ha sido gobernado por un dictador.

    _____

3. La clase fue enseñada por el maestro.

    _____

4. El criminal fue reconocido por la víctima.

    _____

5. Los regalos fueron ofrecidos por los padres.

    _____

6. Las camisas habían sido planchadas por Catalina.

    _____

7. Las luces fueron apagadas por los inquilinos.

    _____

8. Se dice que las Américas fueron descubiertas por Colón en 1492.

    _____

Reading Comprehension

El conde Lucanor
por Don Juan Manuel

Don Juan Manuel nació en Escalona, Toledo, y se murió en 1348 en Peñafiel, Valladolid. Él pertenece a la tradición literaria-didáctica de la Edad Media.

Había en la corte de Castilla un hombre de gran inteligencia y virtud llamado don Sancho, el cual era muy estimado por el rey. Una de las expresiones favoritas de don Sancho era la siguiente: "Todo lo que nos pasa es siempre para lo mejor."

Algunos nobles le tenían envidia y lo acusaron de que preparaba una revolución. El rey les creyó y envió un mensajero para que don Sancho viniera inmediatamente a la corte. Al mismo tiempo, el rey daba órdenes para matarlo en camino.

Don Sancho se apresuró a obedecer, pero al bajar de prisa las escaleras de su casa, se cayó y se rompió una pierna. En medio del dolor, repetía: "Todo lo que nos pasa es siempre para lo mejor."

A causa del accidente, no pudo ir a la corte del rey. Mientras tanto, éste descubrió la falsedad de las acusaciones contra don Sancho y castigó a los culpables. Don Sancho se dirigió, por fin, a la corte, donde fue recibido con grandes honores.

Verbos

apresurarse	*to hurry*	enviar	*to send*
caerse	*to fall down*	romperse	*to break*
dirigirse	*to make one's way, to direct oneself*	viniera	*came* (past subjunctive form of **venir**)

Preguntas

1. ¿En qué año nació el autor del cuento?

   _____

2. ¿Por qué lo acusaron a don Sancho de ser revolucionario?

   _____

3. ¿Por qué no lo mataron los mensajeros del rey?

   _____

4. ¿Cuál es la moraleja del cuento?

   _____

VI

Future and Conditional Tenses; Past Subjunctive; Idioms

25

The Future Tense

The future tense is used to express actions that take place in the future. It refers to both the immediate and the remote future. This is a simple tense, in that it has no helping verb in Spanish. In English, the auxiliaries *will* or *shall* are used: *Irene will drink the water*, for example.

Formation of the Future Tense

Most verbs in the future tense are regular. To form the future tense, use the infinitive as the stem and add the following endings to the infinitive: **-é**, **-ás**, **-á**, **-emos**, **-éis**, **-án**. The endings are the same for all **-ar**, **-er**, and **-ir** verbs. Notice that only the **nosotros** form does not carry a written accent. The following list includes new verbs so that you can expand your vocabulary as you practice the pronunciation.

Regular Verbs

-Ar Verbs

cantar *to sing*

yo cantaré	*I will sing*	nosotros cantaremos	*we will sing*
tú cantarás	*you will sing*	vosotros cantaréis	*you will sing*
él cantará	*he will sing*	ellos cantarán	*they will sing*
ella cantará	*she will sing*	ellas cantarán	*they will sing*
Ud. cantará	*you will sing*	Uds. cantarán	*you will sing*

cobrar *to charge* (money)

yo cobraré	nosotros cobraremos
tú cobrarás	vosotros cobraréis
ella cobrará	ellas cobrarán

dar *to give*

yo daré	nosotros daremos
tú darás	vosotros daréis
él dará	ellos darán

estar *to be*

yo estaré	nosotros estaremos
tú estarás	vosotros estaréis
ella estará	ellas estarán

gozar *to enjoy*

yo gozaré	nosotros gozaremos
tú gozarás	vosotros gozaréis
ella gozará	ellas gozarán

marchar *to march*

yo marcharé	nosotros marcharemos
tú marcharás	vosotros marcharéis
él marchará	ellos marcharán

opinar *to opine, to give an opinion*

yo opinaré	nosotros opinaremos
tú opinarás	vosotros opinaréis
Ud. opinará	Uds. opinarán

patinar *to skate*

yo patinaré	nosotros patinaremos
tú patinarás	vosotros patinaréis
él patinará	ellos patinarán

pegar *to hit*

yo pegaré	nosotros pegaremos
tú pegarás	vosotros pegaréis
Ud. pegará	Uds. pegarán

regresar *to return*

yo regresaré	nosotros regresaremos
tú regresarás	vosotros regresaréis
él regresará	ellos regresarán

triunfar *to triumph*

yo triunfaré	nosotros triunfaremos
tú triunfarás	vosotros triunfaréis
Ud. triunfará	Uds. triunfarán

A Word About Pronunciation

When a word carries a written accent, you will stress that syllable: Make sure you pronounce the verbs in this way: **yo cantaré**, **tú cantarás**, **él cantará**, **nosotros cantaremos**, **vosotros cantaréis**, **ellos cantarán**. Practice pronouncing these verb forms aloud with confidence.

-Er Verbs

atender *to attend to, to serve*

yo atenderé	nosotros atenderemos
tú atenderás	vosotros atenderéis
ella atenderá	ellas atenderán

caer *to fall*

yo caeré	nosotros caeremos
tú caerás	vosotros caeréis
Ud. caerá	Uds. caerán

comer *to eat*

yo comeré	nosotros comeremos
tú comerás	vosotros comeréis
Ud. comerá	Uds. comerán

leer *to read*

yo leeré	nosotros leeremos
tú leerás	vosotros leeréis
Ud. leerá	Uds. leerán

merecer *to deserve*

yo mereceré	nosotros mereceremos
tú merecerás	vosotros mereceréis
él merecerá	ellos merecerán

responder *to respond*

yo responderé	nosotros responderemos
tú responderás	vosotros responderéis
ella responderá	ellas responderán

ser *to be*

yo seré	nosotros seremos
tú serás	vosotros seréis
ella será	ellas serán

vencer *to conquer, to vanquish*

yo venceré	nosotros venceremos
tú vencerás	vosotros venceréis
Ud. vencerá	Uds. vencerán

ver *to see*

yo veré	nosotros veremos
tú verás	vosotros veréis
él verá	ellos verán

-*Ir* Verbs

asistir *to attend*

yo asistiré	nosotros asistiremos
tú asistirás	vosotros asistiréis
Ud. asistirá	Uds. asistirán

cumplir *to carry out, to comply, to fulfill, to complete*

yo cumpliré	nosotros cumpliremos
tú cumplirás	vosotros cumpliréis
ella cumplirá	ellas cumplirán

compartir *to share*

yo compartiré	nosotros compartiremos
tú compartirás	vosotros compartiréis
él compartirá	ellos compartirán

corregir *to correct*

yo corregiré	nosotros corregiremos
tú corregirás	vosotros corregiréis
Ud. corregirá	Uds. corregirán

dirigir *to direct*

yo dirigiré	nosotros dirigiremos
tú dirigirás	vosotros dirigiréis
ella dirigirá	ellas dirigirán

inscribirse *to enroll, to register*

yo me inscribiré	nosotros nos inscribiremos
tú te inscribirás	vosotros os inscribiréis
él se inscribirá	ellos se inscribirán

ir *to go*

yo iré	nosotros iremos
tú irás	vosotros iréis
ella irá	ellas irán

vivir *to live*

yo viviré	nosotros viviremos
tú vivirás	vosotros viviréis
él vivirá	ellos vivirán

A Word About *-ir* Verbs with a Written Accent in the Infinitive

-Ir verbs that have a written accent in the infinitive, such as **oír** (*to hear*), **reír** (*to laugh*), and **sonreír** (*to smile*), lose the written accent in the stem in order to form the future: **oiré**, **reiré**, **sonreiré**.

Irregular Verbs

There are only 12 basic irregular verbs in the future tense. These verbs show a change in the stem, but the endings are the same as those you have just learned. Add **-é**, **-ás**, **-á**, **-emos**, **-éis**, **-án** to the irregular stem. Practice saying these verb forms aloud, and learn them so that you will be able to use the future tense freely.

caber *to fit* (one thing inside another)

yo **cabr**é	nosotros **cabr**emos
tú **cabr**ás	vosotros **cabr**éis
ella **cabr**á	ellas **cabr**án

decir *to say*

yo **dir**é	nosotros **dir**emos
tú **dir**ás	vosotros **dir**éis
Ud. **dir**á	Uds. **dir**án

hacer *to do, to make*

yo **har**é	nosotros **har**emos
tú **har**ás	vosotros **har**éis
él **har**á	ellos **har**án

poder *to be able, can*

yo **podr**é	nosotros **podr**emos
tú **podr**ás	vosotros **podr**éis
Ud. **podr**á	Uds. **podr**án

poner *to put*

yo **pondr**é	nosotros **pondr**emos
tú **pondr**ás	vosotros **pondr**éis
él **pondr**á	ellos **pondr**án

querer *to want*

yo **querr**é	nosotros **querr**emos
tú **querr**ás	vosotros **querr**éis
ella **querr**á	ellas **querr**án

saber *to know*

yo **sabré**	nosotros **sabre**mos
tú **sabrás**	vosotros **sabré**is
Ud. **sabrá**	Uds. **sabrán**

salir *to leave, to go out*

yo **saldré**	nosotros **saldre**mos
tú **saldrás**	vosotros **saldré**is
él **saldrá**	ellos **saldrán**

tener *to have*

yo **tendré**	nosotros **tendre**mos
tú **tendrás**	vosotros **tendré**is
ella **tendrá**	ellas **tendrán**

valer *to be worth*

yo **valdré**	nosotros **valdre**mos
tú **valdrás**	vosotros **valdré**is
Ud. **valdrá**	Uds. **valdrán**

Reminder

Valer is most frequently used in the third person.

¿Cuánto vale?	*How much is it worth?*
¿Cuánto valdrá?	*How much will it be worth?*

venir *to come*

yo **vendré**	nosotros **vendre**mos
tú **vendrás**	vosotros **vendré**is
Ud. **vendrá**	Uds. **vendrán**

A Word About *haber*

Habrá means *there will be* and *will there be?* It is the future tense of the verb **haber**.

¿Habrá una fiesta al fin del año?	*Will there be a party at the end of the year?*
¿Habrá clases de literatura el próximo semestre?	*Will there be literature classes next semester?*
¿Habrá mucho que hacer mañana?	*Will there be a lot to do tomorrow?*

Compound forms of verbs are conjugated in the same way as the main verb.

decir
 contradecir *to contradict*   contra**diré**, *etc.*

hacer
 deshacer *to undo*   des**haré**, *etc.*

poner
 componer *to compose*   com**pondré**, *etc.*
 proponer *to propose*   pro**pondré**, *etc.*

tener
 contener *to contain*   con**tendré**, *etc.*
 detener *to detain*   de**tendré**, *etc.*
 mantener *to maintain*   man**tendré**, *etc.*
 retener *to retain*   re**tendré**, *etc.*

venir
 prevenir *to prevent*   pre**vendré**, *etc.*

Uses of the Future Tense

The future tense is used in both Spanish and English to express a future time. The simple future transmits more of a commitment or a strong decision than does the future periphrastic (**ir** + **a** + *infinitive*). The difference also exists in English: *I will arrive at 7 P.M.* is a little stronger in terms of commitment than *I am going to arrive at 7 P.M.*

¿A qué hora estarás en casa?	*At what time will you be home?*
Paula llegará más rápido por avión.	*Paula will arrive faster by plane.*
Yo haré la tarea para la semana que viene.	*I will do the homework for the coming week.*
Carlos vendrá a verme cuando quiera.	*Carlos will come to see me when he wants.*
El cantante cantará si le gusta la música.	*The singer will sing if he likes the music.*
¿Quién será el próximo presidente de los Estados Unidos?	*Who will be the next president of the United States?*

Exercise 25.1

Complete the following sentences with the correct future form of the verb in parentheses. All verbs in this exercise are regular.

1. Si Isabel va a Italia, yo _____ también. (ir)

2. Sara dice que _____ el martes. (llegar)

3. Yo te _____ mañana, si quieres. (ver)

4. El profesor sabe que nosotros _____ durante las vacaciones. (estudiar)

5. El amigo no _____ la pronunciación de Manuel. (corregir)

6. Los artistas piensan que la gente _____ sus pinturas. (comprar)

7. El hombre nos promete que _____ de fumar. (dejar)

8. Nadie me _____ a México; yo _____ solo. (acompañar/viajar)

9. ¿Dónde _____ tú más tarde? (estar)

10. Los periodistas izquierdistas dicen que _____. (triunfar)

11. Después de la escuela secundaria, los estudiantes _____ a la universidad. (asistir)

12. ¿Cuánto me _____ Ud. por este chaleco? (cobrar)

13. Nosotros _____. (vencer)

14. Si yo te hago una pregunta, ¿me _____? (responder)

Exercise 25.2

Complete the following sentences with the correct future form of the verb in parentheses. All verbs in this exercise are irregular.

1. Yo lo _____. (hacer)

2. El novio piensa que ella _____ a verlo. (venir)

3. Él no _____. (salir)

4. Nosotros no le _____ nada a nadie. (decir)

5. ¿_____ tú ir de vacaciones en julio? (poder)

6. Si los padres no los vigilan, sus hijos _____ la ropa en el piso.
(poner)

7. ¿Cuánto _____ esta chaqueta? (valer)

8. ¿Quién _____ las llaves? (tener)

9. El espía no sabe nada hoy, pero _____ mucho mañana. (saber)

10. ¿_____ mucha gente en el gimnasio el primero de enero?
(haber)

Exercise 25.3

Translate the following sentences into Spanish, using verbs from the list below. Use each verb only one time.

aprender, comprar, decir, fijarse, gustar, perderse, poder, practicar, quejarse, reírse, repetir, ser, tener cuidado

1. *If she is not careful, she will get lost.*

   _____

2. *If Jorge tells it to me, I will not repeat it to anyone.*

   _____

3. *If we practice, we will be able to learn a new language.*

   _____

4. *They will buy the house if they like the garden and the balcony.*

   _____

5. *If the play is funny, the audience will laugh.*

   _____

6. *He will never notice anything. He will never complain.*

   _____

Exercise 25.4

Rewrite the following sentences in the future tense. This exercise includes both regular and irregular verbs.

EXAMPLE   Como mucho el día de acción de gracias.

       Comeré mucho el día de acción de gracias.

1. Él viene a verme. _____

2. Tengo una cita con el dentista en febrero.

   _____

3. ¿Cuánto vale el carro? _____

4. ¿Qué me dices? _____

5. Salimos para México en julio. _____

6. Trabajo en un teatro. _____

7. Hay once estudiantes aquí. _____

8. Empezamos a estudiar. _____

9. El muchacho tiene éxito. _____

10. Los deportistas tienen sed. _____

11. ¿Cuánto me cobra Ud.? _____

12. Yo patino porque me gusta. _____

13. Ella no se mete en la vida de los otros.

    _____

14. El pueblo vence. _____

15. Triunfamos. _____

16. La muchacha cumple diez años el miércoles.

    _____

17. Olivia vive en Perú. _____

18. La maestra corrige la tarea. _____

19. Yo asisto a la universidad. _____

20. Elena sueña que te vio. _____

Exercise 25.5

Translate the following sentences into English.

1. Sabré más mañana de lo que sé hoy.

   _____

2. Tres sillas y ocho estudiantes no cabrán en el salón.

   _____

3. Los médicos no dormirán hasta las cuatro de la mañana.

   _____

4. Pronto volveré.

   _____

5. De vez en cuando, te visitaré en Brasil.

   _____

6. Si Uds. quieren ir de compras, yo los llevaré.

   _____

7. Si él se pone nervioso, hablará en voz baja.

   _____

8. Si corres mucho, podrás perder peso.

   _____

9. Si Ud. pierde sus llaves, ¿qué hará?

   _____

10. Ellos me dicen que Uds. se casarán el año que viene.

    _____

Expressing Doubt or Probability in the Present

The equivalent in English can be *I wonder* or *it is probably* to indicate doubt or probability. You will know from context whether the sentence or question expresses the simple future or probability in the present.

¿Qué hora será?	*I wonder what time it is.*
Serán las diez.	*It's probably ten o'clock.*

¿Dónde estará Enrique?	*I wonder where Henry is.*
Estará en casa.	*He's probably at home.*
¿Quién será?	*I wonder who that is. /*
	Who can that be?
¿Cuántos años tendrán ellas?	*I wonder how old they are. /*
	How old might they be?
No vendrá hoy.	*He probably won't come today.*

Expressing the Future Using the Present Tense

- The present indicative is often used when there is another element in the sentence that indicates future time.

Ella canta mañana.	*She'll sing tomorrow.*
Bailamos el viernes.	*We'll dance on Friday.*

- The present tense, not the future, is used when asking for instructions.

¿Doblo aquí?	*Shall I turn here?*
¿Camino a la derecha?	*Shall I walk to the right?*

- The present tense, not the future, is used when you're asking for things. These are not actions that take place in the future; in these cases, *will* is a helping verb expressing a voluntary mood.

¿Me da el bolígrafo, por favor?	*Will you give me the pen, please?* (literally, *Do you give me the pen, please?*)
¿Me prestas tu carro?	*Will you lend me your car?* (literally, *Do you lend me your car?*)
¿Me llamas cuando llegues?	*Will you call me when you arrive?* (literally, *Do you call me when you arrive?*)
¿Le traes flores?	*Will you bring him flowers?* (literally, *Do you bring him flowers?*)
¿Nos dan Uds. regalos?	*Will you give us presents?* (literally, *Do you give us presents?*)

Exercise 25.6

Rewrite the following sentences to indicate probability.

EXAMPLE   El libro no cabe en mi bolsa.

El libro no cabrá en mi bolsa.

1. ¿Tiene hambre el niño? _____

2. ¿Qué hace la mujer? _____

3. ¿Quién pone la mesa? _____

4. Ella sabe las direcciones. _____

5. ¿Cuánto vale este apartamento lujoso?

_____

Placement of Reflexive, Indirect, and Direct Object Pronouns

Review object pronouns as you continue adding to your knowledge of tenses. The reflexive, indirect, and direct object pronouns have two possible positions when used with the future tense.

- Object pronouns can be placed directly before the conjugated verb.

- Object pronouns can be attached to an infinitive if one is used in the phrase or sentence.

Paula le dará direcciones.   *Paula will give you directions.*
Esta noche leeré un libro y   *Tonight, I will read a book*
   después me acostaré.   *and then I'll go to bed.*
¿Quién me podrá contestar?   }
¿Quién podrá contestarme?   }   *Who will be able to answer me?*

¿Lo podrás llamar más tarde?   }
¿Podrás llamarlo más tarde?   }   *Will you be able to call him later?*

The Future Progressive Tense

The future progressive tense emphasizes action that will be in progress in the future. When you don't need to express action that will be in progress in the future, use the simple future tense.

Formation of the Future Progressive Tense

The future progressive is a compound tense. To form this tense, conjugate **estar** in the future and follow it with the gerund of the main verb.

yo estaré comiendo	*I will be eating*
tú estarás jugando	*you will be playing*
Ud. estará festejando	*you will be celebrating*
nosotros estaremos bebiendo	*we will be drinking*
vosotros estaréis bailando	*you will be dancing*
Uds. estarán celebrando	*you will be celebrating*

Uses of the Future Progressive Tense

The future progressive tense emphasizes action that will take place in the future: *I will be arriving by 10 o'clock,* for example. If you don't need to emphasize the action, use the simple future: *I will arrive by 10 o'clock.*

Estaré llegando a medianoche.	*I will be arriving at midnight.*
¿Cuándo estarás saliendo para el Canadá?	*When will you be leaving for Canada?*
Mi amigo estará escuchando música toda la mañana.	*My friend will be listening to music all morning.*
Estaremos leyendo su libro esta noche.	*We will be reading your book tonight.*
Los muchachos estarán jugando al tenis hasta las cinco cuando oscurezca.	*The children will be playing tennis until five o'clock when it gets dark.*

The Future Perfect Tense

In Spanish, as in English, the future perfect tense refers to an action that will be completed in the future before another action occurs or before some point of time in the future.

Formation of the Future Perfect Tense

The future perfect is a compound tense. To form this tense, conjugate **haber** in the future and follow it with the past participle of the main verb.

yo habré comido	*I will have eaten*
tú habrás cocinado	*you will have cooked*
Ud. habrá visto	*you will have seen*
nosotros habremos limpiado	*we will have cleaned*
vosotros habréis vuelto	*you will have returned*
Uds. habrán ido	*you will have gone*

Uses of the Future Perfect Tense

The future perfect tense expresses action that will have taken place by a specific time in the future.

La muchacha habrá leído el artículo para el viernes.	*The girl will have read the article by Friday.*
Yo habré visto esta película antes de que el grupo se reúna.	*I will have seen this film before the group meets.*
Las mujeres habrán terminado su conversación antes de preparar la cena.	*The women will have finished their conversation before preparing supper.*
Julia habrá bailado con este hombre tres veces antes de salir de la fiesta.	*Julia will have danced with this man three times before leaving the party.*
En agosto, la camarera habrá trabajado en el restaurante un año.	*In August, the waitress will have worked in the restaurant for a year.*

Exercise 25.7

Translate the following sentences into English.

1. ¿Adónde habrás ido después de salir de tu casa?

   _____

2. Habremos comprado nuestros tiquetes para el sábado.

   _____

3. Habré visto a los estudiantes antes de que viajen a México.

   _____

4. En un mes, habré vivido aquí por diez años.

   _____

5. ¿Habrás terminado tu trabajo para la semana que viene?

   _____

Reading Comprehension

El porvenir

"Volveré," dice el amante,
"comeré," dice el glotón,
"bailaré," dice el cojo,
"trabajaré," dice él sin profesión.

"Votaré," dice el ciudadano,
"me reiré," dice el juglar,
"dormiré," dice el insomne,
"te cuidaré," dice su mamá.

"Prometeré," dice el político,
"curaré" dice el doctor,
"recordaré" dice el amnésico,
"enseñaré" dice el profesor.

Y todos se encontrarán
Y todos se hablarán
Todos dirán la verdad y mentiras
Y todos se morirán.

Verbos

cuidar	*to take care of, to care for*
encontrarse	*to meet*
votar	*to vote*

Nombres

el amante	*the lover*
el amnésico	*the amnesiac*
el cojo	*the cripple, the lame person*
el glotón	*the glutton*
el insomne	*the insomniac*
el juglar	*the juggler*
el porvenir	*the future*

Preguntas

1. ¿Cuáles personas dicen la verdad?

   _____

2. ¿Cuáles mienten?

   _____

3. ¿Con quiénes se identifica Ud.?

   _____

26

The Conditional Tense

The conditional tense is used to describe actions that are uncertain in the future. Unlike the future tense, which expresses future certainty, the conditional expresses an action that would happen if another condition were met. This is a simple tense, in that it uses no helping verb in Spanish. It corresponds to the conditional tense in English, which uses *would* as an auxiliary verb: *I would go, but I don't have time,* for example.

Formation of the Conditional Tense

Most verbs are regular in the conditional tense. To form the conditional, use the infinitive as the stem and add the following endings to the infinitive: **-ía**, **-ías**, **-ía**, **-íamos**, **-íais**, **-ían**. These endings are used for all verbs, both regular and irregular, in the conditional tense. Practice pronouncing the following conditional verb forms aloud and be sure to stress the accented syllable.

 Pronunciation Reminder
Practice pronouncing the **d** with a soft **th** sound.

Regular Verbs

-*Ar* Verbs

ayudar *to help*

yo ayudaría	nosotros ayudaríamos
tú ayudarías	vosotros ayudaríais
Ud. ayudaría	Uds. ayudarían

disfrutar *to enjoy*

yo disfrutaría	nosotros disfrutaríamos
tú disfrutarías	vosotros disfrutaríais
él disfrutaría	ellos disfrutarían

estar *to be*

yo estaría	nosotros estaríamos
tú estarías	vosotros estaríais
ella estaría	ellas estarían

felicitar *to congratulate*

yo felicitaría	nosotros felicitaríamos
tú felicitarías	vosotros felicitaríais
Ud. felicitaría	Uds. felicitarían

festejar *to feast, to celebrate*

yo festejaría	nosotros festejaríamos
tú festejarías	vosotros festejaríais
él festejaría	ellos festejarían

fracasar *to fail*

yo fracasaría	nosotros fracasaríamos
tú fracasarías	vosotros fracasaríais
Ud. fracasaría	Uds. fracasarían

llenar *to fill*

yo llenaría	nosotros llenaríamos
tú llenarías	vosotros llenaríais
ella llenaría	ellas llenarían

recordar *to remember*

yo recordaría	nosotros recordaríamos
tú recordarías	vosotros recordaríais
él recordaría	ellos recordarían

 Pronunciation Reminder

The **r** at the beginning of a breath group is pronounced as an **rr** trill. Practice pronouncing these forms of **recordar** with the trilled **r**.

-*Er* Verbs

beber *to drink*

yo bebería	nosotros beberíamos
tú beberías	vosotros beberíais
Ud. bebería	Uds. beberían

conocer *to know, to be acquainted with*

yo conocería	nosotros conoceríamos
tú conocerías	vosotros conoceríais
él conocería	ellos conocerían

proteger *to protect*

yo protegería	nosotros protegeríamos
tú protegerías	vosotros protegeríais
ella protegería	ellas protegerían

ser *to be*

yo sería	nosotros seríamos
tú serías	vosotros seríais
él sería	ellos serían

traer *to bring*

yo traería	nosotros traeríamos
tú traerías	vosotros traeríais
ella traería	ellas traerían

volver *to return*

yo volvería	nosotros volveríamos
tú volverías	vosotros volveríais
Ud. volvería	Uds. volverían

-*Ir* Verbs

admitir *to admit*

yo admitiría	nosotros admitiríamos
tú admitirías	vosotros admitiríais
ella admitiría	ellas admitirían

dormir *to sleep*

yo dormiría	nosotros dormiríamos
tú dormirías	vosotros dormiríais
él dormiría	ellos dormirían

exigir *to demand*

yo exigiría	nosotros exigiríamos
tú exigirías	vosotros exigiríais
él exigiría	ellos exigirían

fingir *to pretend*

yo fingiría	nosotros fingiríamos
tú fingirías	vosotros fingiríais
Ud. fingiría	Uds. fingirían

Pronunciation Reminder

The **g** before an **i** is pronounced like the English **h** as in *hot*.

ir *to go*

yo iría	nosotros iríamos
tú irías	vosotros iríais
ella iría	ellas irían

medir *to measure*

yo mediría	nosotros mediríamos
tú medirías	vosotros mediríais
Ud. mediría	Uds. medirían

Irregular Verbs

There are 12 basic irregular verbs in the conditional tense. The conditional and future tenses have the same stems in their irregular verbs. Add **-ía**, **-ías**, **-ía**, **-íamos**, **-íais**, **-ían** to the irregular stem. Practice pronouncing these verb forms aloud, and learn them so that you will be able to use the conditional tense freely.

caber *to fit* (one thing inside another)

yo **cabría**	nosotros **cabríamos**
tú **cabrías**	vosotros **cabríais**
ella **cabría**	ellas **cabrían**

decir *to say, to tell*

yo **diría**	nosotros **diríamos**
tú **dirías**	vosotros **diríais**
Ud. **diría**	Uds. **dirían**

hacer *to do, to make*

yo **haría**	nosotros **haríamos**
tú **harías**	vosotros **haríais**
él **haría**	ellos **harían**

poder *to be able, can*

yo **podría**	nosotros **podríamos**
tú **podrías**	vosotros **podríais**
Ud. **podría**	Uds. **podrían**

poner *to put*

yo **pondría**	nosotros **pondríamos**
tú **pondrías**	vosotros **pondríais**
él **pondría**	ellos **pondrían**

querer *to want*

yo **querría**	nosotros **querríamos**
tú **querrías**	vosotros **querríais**
ella **querría**	ellas **querrían**

saber *to know*

yo **sabría**	nosotros **sabríamos**
tú **sabrías**	vosotros **sabríais**
Ud. **sabría**	Uds. **sabrían**

salir *to leave, to go out*

yo **saldría**	nosotros **saldríamos**
tú **saldrías**	vosotros **saldríais**
él **saldría**	ellos **saldrían**

tener *to have*

yo **tendría**	nosotros **tendríamos**
tú **tendrías**	vosotros **tendríais**
ella **tendría**	ellas **tendrían**

valer *to be worth*

yo **valdría**	nosotros **valdríamos**
tú **valdrías**	vosotros **valdríais**
Ud. **valdría**	Uds. **valdrían**

Reminder

As noted, **valer** is most often used in the third person:

¿Cuánto vale?	*How much is it worth?*
¿Cuánto valdría?	*How much would it be worth?*
Valdría la pena.	*It would be worth the trouble.*

venir *to come*

yo **vendría**	nosotros **vendríamos**
tú **vendrías**	vosotros **vendríais**
Ud. **vendría**	Uds. **vendrían**

A Word About *haber*

Habría means *there would be* and *would there be?* It is the conditional tense of the verb **haber**.

Sin estudiantes, no habría universidades.	*Without students, there would be no universities.*
¿Habría luz sin sol?	*Would there be light without the sun?*
¿Habría comida sin plantas?	*Would there be food without plants?*

Compound forms of verbs are conjugated in the same way as the main verb.

decir

contradecir *to contradict*   contra**diría**, *etc.*

hacer

deshacer *to undo*   des**haría**, *etc.*

poner

    componer *to compose*   com**pondr**ía, *etc.*

    proponer *to propose*   pro**pondr**ía, *etc.*

tener

    contener *to contain*   con**tendr**ía, *etc.*

    detener *to detain*   de**tendr**ía, *etc.*

    mantener *to maintain*   man**tendr**ía, *etc.*

    retener *to retain*   re**tendr**ía, *etc.*

venir

    prevenir *to prevent*   pre**vendr**ía, *etc.*

Uses of the Conditional Tense

The conditional tense expresses action that is uncertain in the future. This tense corresponds to the English conditional tense: *I would go*, for example.

Nadie comería en este restaurante.	*No one would eat in this restaurant.*
Me gustaría ir al cine con mi amigo.	*I would like to go to the movies with my friend.*
¿Te gustaría ir conmigo?	*Would you like to go with me?*
Nos encantaría viajar a Perú.	*We would love to travel to Peru.*
Elena dijo que cerraría la maleta.	*Elena said that she would close the suitcase.*
Yo sabía que el mago no me diría nada.	*I knew that the magician wouldn't tell me anything.*
¿Gastarías todo en un día?	*Would you spend everything in one day?*

A Word About English *would*

In English, the translation of the Spanish imperfect tense sometimes uses the word *would* as a helping verb when expressing repeated action in the past. Following are examples of the imperfect tense:

Cuando Madeleine era niña, ella practicaba el piano cada día.	*When Madeleine was a child, she would practice the piano every day.*
El hombre viejo ponía sus dientes en agua cada noche antes de dormirse.	*The old man would put his teeth in water every night before falling asleep.*

Exercise 26.1

Complete the following sentences with the correct conditional form of the verb in parentheses.

1. Yo _____. (producir)

2. Nosotros lo _____. (hacer)

3. ¿Qué _____ Uds.? (decir)

4. Él _____ pero no quiere. (venir)

5. ¿Cuánto me _____ Ud. por mi libro? (dar)

6. Ellos _____ temprano. (acostarse)

7. Los niños y sus padres _____ pronto. (regresar)

8. ¿Por qué _____ Ud. tacones? (llevar)

9. ¿A Uds. les _____ salir esta noche? (gustar)

10. ¿_____ luz sin electricidad? (haber)

11. Yo _____ esa película. (ver)

12. Nosotros no _____ esta noche. (salir)

13. Laura dijo que _____ mañana. (llegar)

14. Yo sabía que ella _____. (entender)

15. ¿Quién _____ hacer tal cosa? (poder)

16. ¿Por qué _____ Samuel al teatro si siempre se duerme? (ir)

Placement of Reflexive, Indirect, and Direct Object Pronouns

The reflexive, indirect, and direct object pronouns have two possible positions when used with the conditional tense.

- Object pronouns can be placed directly before the conjugated verb.

- Object pronouns can be attached to an infinitive if one is used in the phrase or sentence.

Yo te prestaría mi carro, pero está en el taller de mecánico.	*I would lend my car to you, but it is in the shop.*
¿Te interesaría comprarlo?	*Would it interest you to buy it?*

¿Cuánto me cobraría por la flor?

Enrique le daría las flores a su novia, pero no tiene bastante dinero para comprárselas.

How much would you charge me for the flower?

Henry would give flowers to his girlfriend, but he doesn't have enough money to buy them for her.

 ## Exercise 26.2

Rewrite the following sentences in the conditional tense. Be sure to include all necessary written accents. Pronounce your answers aloud.

EXAMPLE   Nadie duerme aquí. *Nadie dormiría aquí.*

1. Yo la ayudo. _____

2. Ella va de compras. _____

3. ¿Miras tú televisión? _____

4. Ellos venden la comida. _____

5. Los mozos les dan la comida a los clientes.

   _____

6. Tenemos mucho que hacer. _____

7. El conductor maneja rápidamente. _____

8. ¿Cantas? _____

9. ¿Vienen Uds. a mi casa? _____

10. Yo lo hago. _____

11. No le digo nada. _____

12. Te cobro cien dólares. _____

13. Los niños no leen mucho. _____

14. Sé nadar. _____

15. Hay mucha gente en los trenes. _____

16. No caben más. _____

17. Le traigo las flores a su hermana. _____

18. Nos ponemos los zapatos. _____

19. ¿Puede Ud. acompañarme al bus? _____

20. ¿A Uds. les gusta ir al cine? _____

Exercise 26.3

Complete the following sentences with the correct conditional form of the verb in parentheses.

1. Ella _____ tocar el piano, pero nunca practica. (poder)

2. La enfermera le prometió al paciente que él _____. (mejorarse)

3. Yo no _____ de la situación. (quejarse)

4. Nosotros no le _____ nada. (decir)

5. Enrique y su esposa sabían que sus hijos _____ en sus vacaciones. (divertirse)

6. Emanuel y su hermano nos aseguraron que todo _____ bien. (estar)

7. Los gemelos _____ una fiesta pero no es su cumpleaños. (tener)

8. La terapeuta física me dijo que no me _____ más los pies. (doler)

Exercise 26.4

Translate the following sentences into Spanish.

1. *José would like to learn to swim, but he is afraid of the water.*

   _____

2. *I would not say anything to him, because I do not know him well.*

   _____

3. *Our Mexican friends would come to California to visit their family, but they prefer to travel to Europe this year.*

   _____

   _____

4. *Juan told me that he would give the book to you if you want to study it.*

_____

5. *We would go to Julia's party, but we don't know where she lives.*

_____

The conditional tense may be used to express speculation or conjecture in the past. The translation *I wonder or It was probably* indicates doubt or conjecture. You will know from context whether the sentence or question expresses the simple conditional or probability in the past.

¿Qué hora sería?	*I wonder what time it was.*
¿Dónde estaría el doctor?	*I wonder where the doctor was. / Where could the doctor have been?*
Estaría en el hospital.	*He was probably at the hospital.*
¿Cuántos años tendrían estas mujeres?	*I wonder how old these women were.*
¿Quién sería?	*Who could that have been? / I wonder who that was.*

The Conditional Progressive Tense

The conditional progressive tense expresses doubt about action in the future.

Formation of the Conditional Progressive Tense

The conditional progressive is a compound tense. To form this tense, conjugate **estar** in the conditional and follow it with the gerund of the main verb.

yo estaría limpiando	*I would be cleaning*
tú estarías pintando	*you would be painting*
Ud. estaría bailando	*you would be dancing*
nosotros estaríamos durmiendo	*we would be sleeping*
vosotros estaríais dibujando	*you would be drawing*
Uds. estarían escribiendo	*you would be writing*

Uses of the Conditional Progressive Tense

The conditional progressive tense expresses doubt in the future and emphasizes the action. When you don't need to emphasize the action, use the simple conditional. You'll find that the simple conditional is used more frequently in everyday speech.

¿Quién estaría haciendo ruido?	*Who would be making noise?*
Yo estaría tocando el piano,	*I would be playing the piano,*
pero me lesioné las manos.	*but I hurt my hands.*
Las parejas estarían bailando,	*The couples would be dancing,*
pero se cansaron.	*but they got tired.*

The Conditional Perfect Tense

The conditional perfect tense is used to express an action that would have taken place, but did not: *I would have paid you, but I left my money at home,* for example.

Formation of the Conditional Perfect Tense

The conditional perfect is a compound tense. To form this tense, conjugate the helping verb **haber** in the conditional tense and follow it with the past participle of the main verb.

yo habría ido	*I would have gone*
tú habrías salido	*you would have gone out*
él habría sonreído	*he would have smiled*
nosotros habríamos escrito	*we would have written*
vosotros habríais entrado	*you would have entered*
ellos habrían llamado	*they would have called*

Uses of the Conditional Perfect Tense

The conditional perfect tense, which is used to refer to an action that would have occurred but did not, is often followed by English *but.*

Nos habríamos quedado, pero	*We would have stayed, but*
no nos gustó la situación.	*we didn't like the situation.*

Ella habría ido a España este mes, pero no tenía tiempo.	*She would have gone to Spain this month, but she didn't have time.*
Tú lo habrías podido hacer, pero se te pasó el deseo.	*You would have been able to do it, but you lost the desire.*

Remember that reflexive, indirect, and direct object pronouns precede the verb form. The object pronouns are never attached to the past participle.

Yo **te** habría llamado, pero me dormí temprano.	*I would have called you, but I fell asleep early.*
El doctor **lo** habría ayudado, pero tenía miedo de un pleito.	*The doctor would have helped him, but he was afraid of a lawsuit.*
Los actores **le** habrían dado flores a su directora, pero costaban demasiado.	*The actors would have given flowers to their director, but they cost too much.*

The conditional perfect tense may also express speculation or conjecture in the past.

La gente honesta habría devuelto la cartera y el dinero.	*The honest people had probably returned the wallet and the money.*
Habrían sido las once cuando los muchachos llegaron.	*It must have been eleven o'clock when the children arrived.*
Habría sido noviembre cuando nos reunimos.	*It must have been November when we met.*

 ## Exercise 26.5

Translate the following sentences into Spanish.

1. *He would have arrived on time, but he lost the directions.*

   _____

2. *We would not have told our secret to anyone.*

   _____

3. Juan and his companion would have gone to Mexico, but they decided to save their money for the following year.

   _____

   _____

4. Antonio and I would have traveled to Colombia, but the flight cost too much.

   _____

5. Enrique would have been a good president, but he wanted to have more time to spend with his family.

   _____

   _____

6. Elvira would have returned the money that she found, but she gave it to her son.

   _____

   _____

 # Reading Comprehension

¿Qué haría Ud. en las siguientes situaciones?

Answer the following questions orally.

1. ¿Diría Ud. una mentira para proteger a su amigo?

2. ¿Compraría Ud. algo antes de verlo?

3. Si vas a un casino, ¿cuánto dinero apostarías antes de irte?

4. Ud. está en una clase de veinte estudiantes y todos están copiando excepto Ud. (Ellos reciben el examen de antemano y aprenden de memoria las respuestas sin saber nada. Ud. está estudiando.) ¿Le diría Ud. al maestro lo que está pasando en la clase?

5. Su hijo tiene catorce años y quiere jugar al fútbol americano para su escuela. Ud. sabe que es peligroso y que muchos niños se lesionan. ¿Lo dejaría jugar o firmaría el documento prohibiéndole que juegue?

6. Su mejor amigo está para casarse. Ud. está en un restaurante y ve a su prometida besar a otro hombre. ¿Se lo diría a su amigo?

7. Ud. encuentra una cantidad de dinero en las montañas con la identificación de una persona que se había muerto en un accidente. ¿Le devolvería Ud. el dinero a la familia?

8. ¿Viajaría Ud. solo?

9. ¿Tomaría Ud. crédito por un libro que no había escrito?

10. Su mejor amigo es pintor. ¿Le diría Ud. la verdad si a Ud. no le gusta su pintura?

Verbos

aprender de memoria	*to learn by heart, to memorize*
copiar	*to copy*
firmar	*to sign*
lesionarse	*to get hurt*

27

The Present Perfect Subjunctive

The present perfect subjunctive mood refers to the recent past and is translated as the present perfect in English: *the train has arrived,* for example.

Like all subjunctive moods, the present perfect subjunctive must be caused. The main clause must have a verb or expression that calls for the use of the subjunctive mood in the dependent clause. The present or future tense of certain verbs in the main clause will cause the present perfect subjunctive in the dependent clause.

Formation of the Present Perfect Subjunctive

The present perfect subjunctive is a compound verb form. To form the present perfect subjunctive, conjugate the present subjunctive of the helping verb **haber** and follow it with the past participle of the main verb.

yo haya hablado	*I have spoken*
tú hayas llegado	*you have arrived*
ella haya huido	*she has fled*
nosotros hayamos vendido	*we have sold*
vosotros hayáis leído	*you have read*
ellas hayan votado	*they have voted*

Uses of the Present Perfect Subjunctive

The present perfect subjunctive can be used to express a past action if the main clause is in the present or future tense. The main clause must contain a verb or expression that causes the subjunctive in the dependent clause. The most common use is the present indicative in the main clause and the present perfect subjunctive in the dependent clause.

Yo sé	que el tren ha llegado.
I know (present indicative)	*that the train has arrived.* (present perfect)
Yo **dudo**	que el tren **haya** llegado.
I doubt (present indicative)	*that the train has arrived.* (present perfect subjunctive)
El maestro sabe	que los estudiantes han estudiado.
The teacher knows	*that the students have studied.*
El maestro **espera**	que los estudiantes **hayan** estudiado.
The teacher hopes	*that the students have studied.*

NOTE The English translation of the dependent clause is the same, whether the Spanish verb is in the indicative or the subjunctive mood.

- Main clause in the present, dependent clause in present perfect subjunctive

Me alegro de que Fernando **haya estado** bien.	*I am glad that Fernando has been well.*
Enrique duda que su amigo le **haya escrito**.	*Henry doubts that his friend has written to him.*
Yo lo siento que Uds. no **hayan ido** a España.	*I regret it that you have not gone to Spain.*
Irene no piensa que su vecino **se haya quejado** de ella.	*Irene doesn't think that her neighbor has complained about her.*
¿Esperas que le **hayamos dado** el dinero al dueño?	*Do you hope that we have given the money to the owner?*
Es probable que la mujer **haya parqueado** el carro.	*It is probable that the woman has parked the car.*
¿Conocen Uds. a alguien que **haya vivido** en Japón?	*Do you know anyone who has lived in Japan?*
Nos gusta que tú **hayas tenido** éxito.	*It pleases us that you have been successful.*
Me alegro de que Uds. **se hayan divertido**.	*I am glad that you have had a good time.*

Exercise 27.1

Translate the following sentences into Spanish.

1. *Is it possible that they have fallen asleep?*

   _____

2. *It is probable that we have had a lot of opportunities.*

   _____

3. *We are glad that our two friends have met each other.*

   _____

4. *I'm sad that the hotel hasn't called to confirm my reservation.*

   _____

5. *José hopes that we have felt well.*

   _____

6. *The lawyer is glad that his clients have read the contract.*

   _____

7. *The engineers regret that the buildings have had problems.*

   _____

8. *The worker is sad that his boss has not called to find out where he is.*

   _____

Exercise 27.2

Complete the following sentences with the correct present perfect subjunctive form of the verb in parentheses.

EXAMPLE   El hombre está triste de que su familia no lo _*haya visitado*_. (visitar)

1. Espero que Uds. _____ bien. (estar)

2. Nos alegramos mucho de que el bañero le _____ la vida
   a la nadadora. (salvar)

3. Miguel duda que nosotros _____ a subir la montaña. (atreverse)

4. ¿Conoces a alguien que _____ todas las obras de Shakespeare? (leer)

5. La rey quiere que su reina _____ feliz. (ser)

6. Los viajantes esperan que los trenes no _____. (demorarse)

7. Son las seis de la mañana. La mamá no piensa que sus hijos

   _____. (levantarse)

8. Son las once de la noche el sábado. Patricia espera que sus amigos

   _____ mucho en la fiesta. (divertirse)

9. Me alegro mucho de que Uds. _____ a la clase. (venir)

10. Es una lástima que el vaso _____. (romperse)

- Main clause in the future, dependent clause in the present perfect subjunctive

  If the verb in the main clause is either the future periphrastic (**ir** + **a** + *infinitive*) or the simple future, the present perfect subjunctive can be used in the dependent clause. This structure is used infrequently in everyday speech.

Será fantástico que todo el mundo **haya** leído este libro.	*It will be fantastic that everyone has read this book.*
Será importante que los chóferes **hayan aprendido** a manejar.	*It will be important that the drivers have learned to drive.*
El director esperará que los actores **hayan aprendido** el argumento.	*The director will hope that the actors have learned the script.*
Susana no irá a menos que su mejor amiga **haya ido**.	*Susan will not go unless her best friend has gone.*

Reading Comprehension

La isla en el Caribe

Me alegro mucho de que mis amigos se hayan puesto tan contentos antes de mi gran viaje a verlos. Se llaman Samuel y Teresa y viven en una isla que se llama Saba.

Nos encontramos por primera vez en el Yucatán donde viajamos juntos.

Según ellos, Saba es el mejor sitio del mundo. Estoy muy emocionada de que ellos me hayan invitado a su hogar tan especial. Ella es francesa y él es de Inglaterra. Han pasado más de veinte años fuera de sus países. No sé por qué han escogido esta isla en el medio del Caribe. Nunca me han dado la razón y nadie sabe el porqué, excepto ellos.

Estoy contenta de que hayamos podido estar en contacto por tanto tiempo, comunicándonos por correo electrónico.

Arreglo mi maleta, pensando en lo que mis amigos me han dicho. Con cuidado, meto en ella bloqueador, anteojos de sol y camisas de algodón. Me dicen que llueve mucho, así que incluyo un paraguas pequeño y un impermeable. En caso de que haya sol, y esperándolo, traigo dos trajes de baño, una bata, sandalias y gafas para nadar. A ellos les gusta bucear, y a mí también. Dejo en casa mi abrigo, y escojo una chaqueta y un chaleco que compré en Guatemala. Me gusta llevar pantalones, pero voy a traer una falda también. No sé si necesitaré calcetines o botas, pero los traeré de todos modos.

Será mi primer viaje a la isla y mis amigos la describen como un paraíso, pero un paraíso sin muchas provisiones. Me piden que les lleve muchos víveres como nueces, queso, cereal y chocolate. Mi pobre maleta, cambiada a maletón, pesa mucho con toda la comida, pero llevaré todo, y con muchas ganas.

Me recogieron en el aeropuerto y fuimos a Saba a su hogar. Ellos se sentaron en el sofá. Samuel empezó a trabajar en la computadora; ella no hizo nada aquella primera noche.

Esta pareja que siempre hablaba, dejó de hablar.

Dormí bastante bien la primera noche a pesar de los insectos, reyes de la casa que andaban por toda la casa, y el sonido de la ranas más allá de mi ventana.

Samuel y Teresa, mis queridos amigos, no sé lo que les había pasado. Pasé mis vacaciones a solas. Ellos no se atrevían a salir de la casa, hasta sacar la basura. Samuel llegaba al lindero de la casa, suspiraba y volvía a la sala mientras Teresa cocinaba.

Por fin, me llevaron al aeropuerto, me dejaron allí, nos despedimos y nos separamos. Fue la última vez que los vi.

Verbos

atreverse (a)	*to dare (to)*
bucear	*to snorkel, to skin dive*
recoger	*to pick up*
suspirar	*to sigh*

Nombres

el abrigo	*the coat*
la bata	*the robe*
las botas	*the boots*
los calcetines	*the socks*
el chaleco	*the vest*
la chaqueta	*the jacket*
la falda	*the skirt*
el impermeable	*the raincoat*
el lindero	*the edge, the border*
el maletón	*the big suitcase*
la nuez, las nueces	*the nut, the nuts*
los pantalones	*the pants*
el paraguas	*the umbrella*
la rana	*the frog*
el rey	*the king*
el traje de baño	*the bathing suit*
la última vez	*the last time*

Expresiones

de todos modos	*anyway*
en caso de	*in case*
fuera de	*outside (of)*
más allá de (mi ventana)	*outside (my window)*
por fin	*at last*
por primera vez	*for the first time*

Preguntas

1. ¿Dónde está Saba?

   _____

2. ¿Cómo es la isla?

   _____

3. ¿Qué pone la persona en su maleta? ¿Por qué pesa tanto?

   _____

4. ¿Se llevaron bien?

   _____

5. ¿Van a verse de nuevo?

   _____

6. ¿La persona que viaja, es mujer u hombre?

   _____

28

The Imperfect Subjunctive

The imperfect subjunctive mood expresses past action. So far, you have studied the present subjunctive and the present perfect subjunctive. Next is the imperfect subjunctive. If the main clause begins in the past, it can cause the subjunctive in the past.

Remember that the subjunctive mood cannot exist alone. Another element in the sentence always causes it to be used. The imperfect subjunctive is used after the following elements:

- Certain impersonal expressions
- Certain verbs
- Certain conjunctions
- Certain dependent adjective clauses
- Certain expressions

Formation of the Imperfect Subjunctive

To form the imperfect subjunctive for all verbs, first drop the ending of the third-person singular of the preterit. What remains is the stem of the imperfect subjunctive for all forms.

Any irregularity in the stem of the preterit tense will have the same irregularity in the imperfect subjunctive.

Imperfect Subjunctive of -*ar* Verbs

To conjugate all but three **-ar** verbs in the imperfect subjunctive, begin with the third-person singular (**él**, **ella**, **Ud.**) of the preterit tense. Drop the preterit ending and add **-ara**, **-aras**, **-ara**, **-áramos**, **-arais**, **-aran** to the stem.

Infinitive	Third-Person Preterit	Imperfect Subjunctive	
bailar	bailó	yo bailara tú bailaras ella bailara	nosotros bailáramos vosotros bailarais ellas bailaran
cantar	cantó	yo cantara tú cantaras él cantara	nosotros cantáramos vosotros cantarais ellos cantaran
cerrar	cerró	yo cerrara tú cerraras Ud. cerrara	nosotros cerráramos vosotros cerrarais Uds. cerraran
recordar	recordó	yo recordara tú recordaras él recordara	nosotros recordáramos vosotros recordarais ellos recordaran

The only **-ar** verbs with different endings in the imperfect subjunctive are verbs that are irregular in the preterit: **andar**, **estar**, **dar**.

Imperfect Subjunctive of -*er* and -*ir* Verbs

To conjugate both **-er** and **-ir** verbs in the imperfect subjunctive, drop the ending from the third-person singular of the preterit to get the stem. Then add **-iera**, **-ieras**, **-iera**, **-iéramos**, **-ierais**, **-ieran** to the stem.

-*Er* Verbs

Infinitive	Third-Person Preterit	Imperfect Subjunctive	
beber	bebió	yo bebiera tú bebieras él bebiera	nosotros bebiéramos vosotros bebierais ellos bebieran
comer	comió	yo comiera tú comieras ella comiera	nosotros comiéramos vosotros comierais ellas comieran

Infinitive	Third-Person Preterit	Imperfect Subjunctive	
conocer	conoció	yo conociera	nosotros conociéramos
		tú conocieras	vosotros conocierais
		Ud. conociera	Uds. conocieran
entender	entendió	yo entendiera	nosotros entendiéramos
		tú entendieras	vosotros entendierais
		él entendiera	ellos entendieran
ver	vio	yo viera	nosotros viéramos
		tú vieras	vosotros vierais
		ella viera	ellas vieran
volver	volvió	yo volviera	nosotros volviéramos
		tú volvieras	vosotros volvierais
		él volviera	ellos volvieran

-Ir Verbs

Infinitive	Third-Person Preterit	Imperfect Subjunctive	
abrir	abrió	yo abriera	nosotros abriéramos
		tú abrieras	vosotros abrierais
		él abriera	ellos abrieran
escribir	escribió	yo escribiera	nosotros escribiéramos
		tú escribieras	vosotros escribierais
		ella escribiera	ellas escribieran
salir	salió	yo saliera	nosotros saliéramos
		tú salieras	vosotros salierais
		Ud. saliera	Uds. salieran
vivir	vivió	yo viviera	nosotros viviéramos
		tú vivieras	vosotros vivierais
		Ud. viviera	Uds. vivieran

-Ir verbs that are irregular in the third-person singular of the preterit show the same irregularity in the stem of the imperfect subjunctive.

Infinitive	Third-Person Preterit	Imperfect Subjunctive	
mentir	mintió	yo mintiera	nosotros mintiéramos
		tú mintieras	vosotros mintierais
		él mintiera	ellos mintieran
pedir	pidió	yo pidiera	nosotros pidiéramos
		tú pidieras	vosotros pidierais
		ella pidiera	ellas pidieran
seguir	siguió	yo siguiera	nosotros siguiéramos
		tú siguieras	vosotros siguierais
		ella siguiera	ellas siguieran
dormir	durmió	yo durmiera	nosotros durmiéramos
		tú durmieras	vosotros durmierais
		Ud. durmiera	Uds. durmieran
morirse	se murió	me muriera	nos muriéramos
		te murieras	os murierais
		él se muriera	ellos se murieran

A Word About Pronunciation

The stress in the imperfect subjunctive is on the second-to-last, or penulti-mate, syllable. As you practice, make sure you pronounce the verbs in this way: **yo cant̲a̲ra, tú cant̲a̲ras, él cant̲a̲ra, nosotros cant̲á̲ramos, vosotros can-t̲a̲rais, ellos cant̲a̲ran**. If a word carries a written accent, stress the accented syllable: **nosotros cant̲á̲ramos**. The more you practice, the more natural this sound becomes.

Irregular Stems in the Preterit

Verbs with irregular stems in the preterit have the same irregularity in the imperfect subjunctive. Drop the ending from the third-person singular and add **-iera**, **-ieras**, **-iera**, **-iéramos**, **-ierais**, **-ieran** to the stem.

Infinitive	Third-Person Preterit	Imperfect Subjunctive	
andar	anduvo	yo anduviera	nosotros anduviéramos
		tú anduvieras	vosotros anduvierais
		él anduviera	ellos anduvieran

Infinitive	Third-Person Preterit	Imperfect Subjunctive	
caber	cupo	yo cupiera	nosotros cupiéramos
		tú cupieras	vosotros cupierais
		ella cupiera	ellas cupieran
dar	dio	yo diera	nosotros diéramos
		tú dieras	vosotros dierais
		Ud. diera	Uds. dieran
estar	estuvo	yo estuviera	nosotros estuviéramos
		tú estuvieras	vosotros estuvierais
		Ud. estuviera	Uds. estuvieran
hacer	hizo	yo hiciera	nosotros hiciéramos
		tú hicieras	vosotros hicierais
		él hiciera	ellos hicieran
poder	pudo	yo pudiera	nosotros pudiéramos
		tú pudieras	vosotros pudierais
		ella pudiera	ellas pudieran
poner	puso	yo pusiera	nosotros pusiéramos
		tú pusieras	vosotros pusierais
		Ud. pusiera	Uds. pusieran
querer	quiso	yo quisiera	nosotros quisiéramos
		tú quisieras	vosotros quisierais
		él quisiera	ellos quisieran
saber	supo	yo supiera	nosotros supiéramos
		tú supieras	vosotros supierais
		ella supiera	ellas supieran
tener	tuvo	yo tuviera	nosotros tuviéramos
		tú tuvieras	vosotros tuvierais
		Ud. tuviera	Uds. tuvieran
venir	vino	yo viniera	nosotros viniéramos
		tú vinieras	vosotros vinierais
		él viniera	ellos vinieran

Irregular preterits whose stem ends in **-j** have **-eran**, not **-ieran**, in the third-person plural. Take a look at **decir**, **producir**, and **traer**.

Infinitive	Third-Person Preterit	Imperfect Subjunctive	
decir	dijo	yo dijera	nosotros dijéramos
		tú dijeras	vosotros dijerais
		ella dijera	ellas dijeran
producir	produjo	yo produjera	nosotros produjéramos
		tú produjeras	vosotros produjerais
		Ud. produjera	Uds. produjeran
traer	trajo	yo trajera	nosotros trajéramos
		tú trajeras	vosotros trajerais
		él trajera	ellos trajeran

The conjugations for **ir** and **ser** are identical in the imperfect subjunctive. The meaning will be clarified in context.

Infinitive	Third-Person Preterit	Imperfect Subjunctive	
ser	fue	yo fuera	nosotros fuéramos
		tú fueras	vosotros fuerais
		Ud. fuera	Uds. fueran
ir	fue	yo fuera	nosotros fuéramos
		tú fueras	vosotros fuerais
		él fuera	ellos fueran

A Word About *haber*

Hubiera is the imperfect subjunctive form of **haber**, formed from the third-person singular of the preterit, **hubo**, meaning *there was, there were*.

Compound forms of verbs are conjugated in the same way as the main verb.

decir
    contradecir *to contradict*   yo contradijera, *etc.*

hacer
    deshacer *to undo*   yo deshiciera, *etc.*

poner

componer *to compose*	yo compusiera, *etc.*
proponer *to propose*	yo propusiera, *etc.*

tener

contener *to contain*	yo contuviera, *etc.*
detener *to detain*	yo detuviera, *etc.*
mantener *to maintain*	yo mantuviera, *etc.*

producir

conducir *to conduct*	yo condujera, *etc.*
traducir *to translate*	yo tradujera, *etc.*

traer

atraer *to attract*	yo atrajera, *etc.*
distraer *to distract*	yo distrajera, *etc.*

venir

prevenir *to prevent*	yo previniera, *etc.*

Uses of the Imperfect Subjunctive

When the main clause contains a verb or expression that causes the subjunctive in a dependent clause, the presence of an element in the main clause that begins in the past makes it mandatory to use the imperfect subjunctive in the dependent clause. You do not have to make any decisions, nor do you have a choice about whether or not to use it. The conditional can also cause the imperfect subjunctive in the dependent clause.

After Certain Impersonal Expressions

Certain impersonal expressions in the main clause will cause the subjunctive in the dependent clause.

If the impersonal expressions are in the preterit, the imperfect, or the conditional tense, they will cause the imperfect subjunctive in the dependent clause. Note the differences in the English translations for the dependent clauses below, depending on what is expressed by the verb in the main clause.

- Preterit

Fue una lástima que no **pudiéramos** ir a la fiesta.	*It was a shame that we were not able to go to the party.*
Fue importante que ella no **se enojara**.	*It was important that she not get angry.*
Fue posible que el hombre **colgara** el teléfono.	*It was possible that the man hung up the telephone.*

- Imperfect

Era probable que ella no **quisiera** ir al dentista.	*It was probable that she didn't want to go to the dentist.*
Era posible que el estudiante **supiera** la respuesta.	*It was possible that the student knew the answer.*
Era posible que Octavio la **conociera** en Madrid.	*It was possible that Octavio met her in Madrid.*

- Conditional

¿**Sería** posible que su esposo **tuviera** razón?	*Would it be possible that her husband was right?*
¿**Sería** posible que Isabel **se fuera**?	*Would it be possible that Isabel went away?*
¿**Sería** posible que **cocinaras** esta noche?	*Would it be possible for you to cook tonight?*
Sería necesario que la policía **capturara** el criminal.	*It would be necessary that the police force capture the criminal.*

Exercise 28.1

Complete the following sentences with the correct imperfect subjunctive form of the verb in parentheses, then translate the sentence.

EXAMPLES   Fue fantástico que nosotros <u>tuviéramos</u> éxito. (tener)
It was fantastic that we were successful.

Era imposible que Octavio <u>durmiera</u> bien anoche. (dormir)
It was impossible that Octavio slept well last night.

¿Sería posible que ellos me <u>vieran</u> en el teatro? (ver)
Would it be possible that they saw me in the theater?

1. Fue importante que Jaime me _____. (hablar)

2. Era una lástima que ella no _____ bien anoche. (sentirse)

3. ¿Fue posible que Uds. _____ a mi hermana? (conocer)

4. Fue necesario que nosotros _____ ejercicios. (hacer)

5. Era imposible que no _____ tráfico hoy. (haber)

6. Fue urgente que la ambulancia _____ dentro de cinco minutos. (llegar)

7. Era posible que nosotros le _____ un regalo a la maestra. (dar)

8. Fue dudoso que mi sobrina me _____ la verdad; fue posible que me _____. (decir/mentir)

9. Sería bueno que Uds. _____. (mejorarse)

10. Era probable que toda la clase _____. (graduarse)

11. Sería imposible que Sara _____ sin decirnos nada. (irse)

12. Fue bueno que nosotros la _____. (llamar)

13. Sería necesario que los turistas _____ mucha agua en las montañas. (tomar)

14. Sería dudoso que nosotros _____ a México este año. (viajar)

15. Fue posible que Beatriz e Isabel _____ en Italia. (quedarse)

After Certain Verbs

Review the verbs that cause the subjunctive mood in a dependent clause, namely, verbs that express wishes and preferences; verbs that express hope, regret and emotion; verbs that express orders; and verbs that express uncertainty. These verbs in the main clause will cause the subjunctive mood in the dependent clause. If the main clause is in the preterit, the imperfect, or the conditional, the dependent clause will be in the imperfect subjunctive.

- Preterit

  Yo **quise** que Ud. **cantara**.

  Mi suegra **se alegró** de que yo la **visitara**.

  Tu amigo te **pidió** que lo **llamaras**.

  I wanted you to sing. (literally, *I wanted that you sang.*)

  My mother-in-law was happy that I visited her.

  Your friend asked you to call him.

| Los padres de Paula le **exigieron** que ella **compartiera** sus juguetes. | *Paula's parents demanded that she share her toys.* |

- Imperfect

Yo **esperaba** que él **tuviera** tiempo.	*I hoped that he had time.*
Julieta **esperaba** que Romeo **viniera** a verla.	*Juliet hoped that Romeo would come to see her.*
Esperábamos que Uds. **pudieran** pasar sus vacaciones con nosotros.	*We were hoping that you would be able to spend your vacation with us.*

- Conditional

Los padres **desearían** que sus hijos **jugaran** en el parque.	*The parents would want their children to play in the park.*
¿A Ud. le **molestaría** que yo **fumara**?	*Would it bother you that I smoke?*
Yo **preferiría** que él no **viniera**.	*I would prefer that he not come.*

A Word About the English Translations

You can see that English translations of the imperfect subjunctive are not exact. Just remember that if you start out in either the past (preterit or imperfect) or the conditional in the main clause, the verb or impersonal expression will cause the imperfect subjunctive in the dependent clause.

Exercise 28.2

Translate the following sentences into English. In these sentences, the verb in the main clause is in the preterit and the verb in the dependent clause is in the imperfect subjunctive.

1. Quise que ellas me escribieran.

   _____

2. Mi vecino prefirió que yo no le trajera nada.

   _____

3. Nos alegramos de que él llegara temprano.

    _____

4. Ella nos rogó que no nos fuéramos.

    _____

5. Me alegré de que te mudaras a una casa.

    _____

6. El dueño insistió en que pagáramos la renta.

    _____

7. Yo le dije a mi amigo que me llamara.

    _____

8. El turista le sugirió al taxista que no condujera tan rápido.

    _____

 ## Exercise 28.3

Complete the following sentences with the correct imperfect subjunctive form of the verb in parentheses. In these sentences, the verb in the main clause is in the preterit.

EXAMPLE   El abogado insistió en que la mujer _*fuera*_ a la corte. (ser)

1. Yo quise que Julio me _____ en español. (hablar)

2. Julio me aconsejó que yo _____ más. (estudiar)

3. Susana insistió en que su primo _____ con su hermano. (bailar)

4. Manuel no quiso que su esposa _____ en el cabaret. (cantar)

5. Me alegré de que Uds. _____ a la clase. (venir)

Exercise 28.4

Complete the following sentences with the correct imperfect subjunctive form of the verb in parentheses. In these sentences, the verb in the main clause is in the imperfect.

1. Ella quería que sus padres _____ en Nueva York. (quedarse)

2. La madre no quería que nosotros le _____ flores. (traer)

3. La doctora le aconsejaba al paciente que _____ menos. (comer)

4. El hombre le sugería que Ud. me _____ el libro. (prestar)

5. La mujer esperaba que nosotros la _____. (ayudar)

6. Los candidatos nos rogaban que _____ por ellos. (votar)

Exercise 28.5

Complete the following sentences with the correct imperfect subjunctive form of the verb in parentheses. In these sentences, the verb in the main clause is in the conditional.

1. El dentista esperaría que sus pacientes _____ en su oficina a las nueve de la mañana. (estar)

2. Me gustaría que tú _____. (callarse)

3. Ella se alegraría de que nosotros lo _____. (hacer)

4. Te gustaría que yo te _____ al tren esta noche? (acompañar)

Exercise 28.6

Translate the following sentences into English.

1. El muchacho quería que sus padres le trajeran un regalo.

   _____

2. Los amigos de Miguel querían que él perdiera peso.

   _____

3. ¿Para qué querían Uds. que yo les prestara dinero?

   _____

4. Federico esperaba que Linda se casara con él.

_____

5. La estudiante en España se alegró de que sus padres estuvieran orgullosos de ella.

_____

6. Yo quise que ellos se quedaran conmigo.

_____

7. Esperábamos que no fuera nada grave.

_____

8. El marido no quería que su esposa se jubilara.

_____

 ## Exercise 28.7

Complete the following sentences with either the infinitive or the correct imperfect subjunctive form of the verb in parentheses. Read the sentences and questions carefully.

EXAMPLE   El hombre flaco no quería _comer_ el helado. (comer)

1. Yo no quería _____ en el tren. Me gusta _____ en la ducha. (cantar/cantar)

2. Es importante _____ bien para _____ bien. (comer/vivir)

3. Fue importante que los doctores _____ a los pacientes. (cuidar)

4. El hombre esperaba que sus vecinos _____ de escuchar música en alto volumen. (dejar)

5. ¿Por qué me dijiste que yo te _____? (esperar)

6. Susana le pidió a su hijo que _____. (acostarse)

7. La mujer no quiso _____ en el ascensor. (bajar)

8. Antes de _____ a México, Antonio llamó a sus amigos. (viajar)

9. Yo no creía que _____ la verdad. (ser)

10. ¿Qué querías tú que yo te _____? (decir)

Reading Comprehension

El barco económico

Lucía siempre tenía ganas de ir a las Islas Galápagos y quería que su buen amigo la acompañara, pero no quiso. Después de haberlo pensado bien, decidió ir sola, primero a Quito, capital de Ecuador. Ella conoció a mucha gente en la ciudad, exploró los vecindarios durante el día; por la noche volvía a su hotel que le costaba cinco dólares. Ella comía el desayuno en una cafetería, el almuerzo en otra, y cenaba en un buen restaurante en el centro. Esperaba que alguien pasara por allí, que la viera sentada, que entrara en el restaurante, y que hablara con ella. Esperaba que los dos se llevaran bien y que él quisiera ir con ella a la isla.

Al fin y al cabo, Lucía viajó a Guayaquil, la entrada de las islas, y la salida de los barcos y cruceros. En la agencia de viajes, le sugirieron que fuera en barco económico con un grupo pequeño de aventureros. "Costaría menos," dijo la agente, "y sería más divertido el viaje." La agente la convenció.

La mujer tomó la decisión, compró su pasaje de ida y vuelta para el próximo día, y después de una noche inquieta e indecisa, abordó el barco chiquito. Aquella primera noche, el barco salió, y entre las olas, la tormenta, y el huracán, los ocho pasajeros pasaron la noche mareados bajo las estrellas centelleantes del cielo.

Verbos

abordar	*to board*
convencer	*to convince*
llevarse (bien)	*to get along (well)*
tener ganas	*to desire*

Nombres

el huracán	*the hurricane*
las olas	*the waves*
la tormenta	*the storm*
el vecindario	*the neighborhood*

Adjetivos

centelleante	*twinkling*
inquieto	*unquiet, agitated*
mareado	*seasick*

Expresiones

al fin y al cabo	*after all*
e indecisa	*and indecisive* (When expressing *and* in Spanish, **e** replaces **y** before a word that begins with an emphasized **i-** or **hi-**.)
el pasaje de ida y vuelta	*round-trip ticket*

Preguntas

1. ¿Cuántos pasajeros hay en el barco económico?

   _____

2. ¿Adónde fue Lucía?

   _____

3. ¿A ella le gustó Quito?

   _____

4. ¿Quién habló con ella en el restaurante?

   _____

5. ¿Qué decidió hacer?

   _____

6. ¿Piensa Ud. que los pasajeros se van a divertir?

   _____

After Certain Conjunctions

The subjunctive form follows certain conjunctions if the main clause has a different subject from the dependent clause.

Ella les enseñó a sus estudiantes **para que** ellos **aprendieran**.	*The professor taught her students so that they learned.*
Antes de que él **fuera** a España, le vendimos su boleto.	*Before he went to Spain, we sold him his ticket.*
En caso de que ellos te **llamaran**, ¿qué les dirías?	*In case they called you, what would you say to them?*
A pesar de que Emil le **diera** flores, la mujer no aceptó su invitación.	*In spite of the fact that Emil gave her flowers, the woman didn't accept his invitation.*

Yo no lo haría **sin que** Uds. me **ayudaran**.	*I wouldn't do it without your helping me.*
Yo te iba a esperar **hasta que llegaras**.	*I was going to wait for you until you arrived.*

After Certain Dependent Adjective Clauses

The subjunctive mood is used in a dependent clause if the object or person described in the main clause of a sentence is indefinite or nonexistent. In the following examples, the objects and persons described in the main clause are not known.

¿Conoció Ud. a **alguien** que **supiera** hablar chino?	*Did you meet anyone who knew how to speak Chinese?*
Yo había buscado una **piscina** que **quedara** cerca de mi casa.	*I had looked for a pool that was located near my house.*
Nunca encontramos a **nadie** que siempre **tuviera** razón.	*We never found anyone who was always right.*

After Certain Expressions

- **ojalá**

  An interjection of Arabic origin, **ojalá** means *would to God that* or *may God grant that* and expresses great desire. It can also be translated as *I hope.*

Ojalá que fuera verdad.	*Would to God that it were true.*
Ojalá que Uds. vivieran aquí conmigo.	*Would to God that you lived here with me.*
Ojalá que pudiera hacerlo.	*I hope that you were able to do it.*

- **como si**

  A verb that follows **como si** (*as if*) will be in the imperfect subjunctive. The verb in the main clause can be in the present, the past, or the conditional.

Ud. le trata como si **fuera** niño.	*You treat him as if he were a child.*
El hombre lo describe como si **estuviera** allí.	*The man describes it as if he were there.*

Carla nos dio las direcciones
como si **supiéramos** el camino.

*Carla gave us directions as if we
knew the way.*

Los hombres nos saludaron como
si nos **conocieran**.

*The men greeted us as if they
knew us.*

Los hombres nos hablaban como
si los **conociéramos**.

*The men spoke to us as if we knew
them.*

Pietro hablaría como si **tuviera**
razón.

*Pietro would speak as if he were
right.*

- **quisiera**

The verb **querer** can be used in the imperfect subjunctive in a main
clause, where it is used to soften statements and questions. This form
changes the translation of *I want*, for example, to *I would like*.

yo quisiera   nosotros quisiéramos
tú quisieras   vosotros quisierais
Ud. quisiera   Uds. quisieran

Compare the meanings of the following pairs of sentences:

Quiero más café, por favor.

I want more coffee, please.

Quisiera más café, por favor.

I would like more coffee, please.

Queremos ir contigo al
aeropuerto.

*We want to go with you to the
airport.*

Quisiéramos ir contigo.

We would like to go with you.

¿Quieres pedir prestado mi libro?

Do you want to borrow my book?

¿Quisieras pedirlo prestado?

Would you like to borrow it?

- **pudiera**

The imperfect subjunctive form of **poder** can be used independently in
a main clause. It is used to soften statements, for example, **puedo** (*I can,
I am able*) to **yo pudiera** (*I could, I would be able*).

yo pudiera   nosotros pudiéramos
tú pudieras   vosotros pudierais
ella pudiera   ellas pudieran

Compare the meanings of the following pairs of sentences:

¿Puedes prestarme diez dólares?

Can you lend me ten dollars?

¿Pudieras prestarme diez dólares?

Could you lend me ten dollars?

| ¿Nos puede dar mil dólares? | *Can you give us a thousand dollars?* |
| ¿Nos pudiera Ud. dar mil dólares? | *Could you give us a thousand dollars?* |

 Exercise 28.8

Complete the following sentences with either the infinitive or the correct imperfect subjunctive form of the verb in parentheses.

1. Sara habla sin _____ nada. (saber)

2. La mamá prendió las luces para que sus hijos _____ ver. (poder)

3. Él baila como si _____ un bailarín profesional. (ser)

4. Ojalá que ella _____ hoy. (venir)

5. ¿Había alguien que _____ todas las capitales de los Estados Unidos? (saber)

6. Dolores preparó la comida antes de _____. (ducharse)

7. Ella preparó la comida antes de que su hijo _____ para la escuela. (salir)

8. El niño no quiere _____ las manos antes de _____. (lavarse/comer)

9. Elena y su hermana viajan como si _____ mucho dinero. (tener)

10. Ojalá que Fernando nos _____ la verdad. (decir)

11. Isabel nos contó todo como si ella _____ allí. (estar)

12. Antes de _____ a España, él estudió por dos años. (ir)

13. Íbamos a jugar tenis hasta que _____ a llover. (empezar)

14. La enfermera no le daría medicina a la paciente a menos que ella la _____. (necesitar)

Exercise 28.9

Rewrite the following sentences in the past tense. Make sure you read the main clause carefully to see whether the subjunctive is necessary in the dependent clause.

EXAMPLES   Yo sé que el tren viene. <u>*Yo sabía que el tren venía.*</u>

                  Yo dudo que el tren venga. <u>*Yo dudaba que el tren viniera.*</u>

1. Laura quiere que su esposo la acompañe a Chile.

   _____

2. Es necesario que la gente no fume en los edificios.

   _____

3. Julia está contenta de que Uds. estén aquí.

   _____

4. Yo sé que su nieta quiere ir a la universidad.

   _____

5. Me alegro de que puedas correr en el maratón.

   _____

6. ¿Qué quieres que yo haga?

   _____

7. Raúl y yo esperamos que Uds. se encuentren bien.

   _____

8. ¿Es importante que el carpintero sepa lo que está haciendo?

   _____

9. Espero que el vuelo de mis amigos llegue a tiempo.

   _____

10. Los deportistas dudan que ganemos el partido.

    _____

11. Nuestros amigos nos ruegan que no subamos a la cumbre de la montaña.

    _____

12. Los entrenadores insisten en que la gente haga más ejercicio.

    _____

Exercise 28.10

Translate the following sentences into Spanish.

1. *It was necessary that she begin the lessons on time.*

   _____

2. *It was a pity that he didn't know how to express himself.*

   _____

3. *Would it be possible that they had already left the reunion?*

   _____

4. *Joann's children begged her not to smoke.*

   _____

5. *Would you like me to speak with your boss?*

   _____

6. *My brother doubted that I sang well yesterday.*

   _____

7. *My daughter's teacher suggested that I call her.*

   _____

8. *I wanted them to stay with me. They wanted me to go with them.*

   _____

9. *I would like to make a documentary that is about the Incas.*

   _____

10. *I want to take your photo, if you don't mind.*

    _____

After *si* in a Contrary-to-Fact *si*-clause

When you express the idea that an action would happen (conditional tense) *if* another action occurred in the past, the imperfect subjunctive is used in the clause that begins with **si**.

Si él tuviera más tiempo,
   me traería flores.

*If he had more time, he would
   bring me flowers.*

Si Ud. anduviera más rápido, llegaría a tiempo.	*If you walked more quickly, you would arrive on time.*
¿**Si yo** te **diera** un regalo, lo aceptarías?	*If I gave you a present, would you accept it?*
Si Ricardo bailara mejor, su compañera estaría contenta.	*If Richard danced better, his companion would be happy.*

A Word About the *si*-clause in the Present

A **si**-clause used with a present tense verb never causes the subjunctive. When you express the idea that an action will happen (future tense) *if* another action occurs in the present, the imperfect subjunctive is not used.

Si tú vas, yo iré también.	*If you go, I will go too.*
Si ellos vienen a verme, estaré contenta.	*If they come to see me, I will be happy.*
Si Lola quiere asistir a una universidad, sus padres pagarán el primer año.	*If Lola wants to attend a university, her parents will pay the first year.*

In the following examples, a clause whose verb is in the conditional tense begins the sentence. Note that the imperfect subjunctive follows the word **si**. It doesn't matter whether the sentence begins with the conditional tense or the **si**-clause, the subjunctive always follows **si**.

Yo iría a la fiesta **si tú fueras** también.	*I would go to the party if you were going also.*
Mi hermano me vería más, **si viviera** cerca.	*My brother would see me more if he lived close by.*
Podríamos hacer la tarea **si tuviéramos** más tiempo.	*We would be able to do the homework if we had more time.*
Habría más gente en la playa **si hiciera** calor.	*There would be more people at the beach if it were hot.*
Iríamos a verla **si** nos **invitara**.	*We would go to see her if she invited us.*
¿Me harías un préstamo **si yo prometiera** devolvértelo?	*Would you give me a loan if I promised to return it to you?*

Exercise 28.11

Complete the following sentences with the correct form of the verbs in parentheses. Each sentence requires both the conditional and the imperfect subjunctive verb forms. Remember that the imperfect subjunctive follows the si-clause.

EXAMPLES   ¿Qué _haría_ Ud. si sus amigos le _dijeran_ una mentira? (hacer/decir)

            Si no _hubiera_ tráfico, _podríamos_ salir más tarde. (haber/poder)

1. Si Fernando _____ más alto, _____ deportista. (ser/ser)

2. Si a María le _____ bailar, _____ a fiestas. (gustar/ir)

3. Si nosotros le _____ cartas, nuestro amigo nos

   _____. (escribir/responder)

4. Si yo _____ mejor, yo _____ reírme. (sentirse/poder)

5. Los artistas _____ más dinero, si _____ sus pinturas. (ganar/vender)

6. Los médicos dicen que los insomnes _____ mejor

   si _____ a la misma hora cada noche. (dormir/acostarse).

7. Nosotros _____ con soltura si _____ todos los verbos. (hablar/saber)

8. La muchacha no _____ frío si _____ la chaqueta. (tener/ponerse)

9. El niño no _____ tanto si no le _____ el estómago. (llorar/doler)

10. Yo no _____ si Ud. _____ que yo

    _____. (irse/querer/quedarse)

If the sentence or question includes the word **si** in a sentence that is not contrary-to-fact, but rather is simply a statement, the subjunctive is not used.

     Si yo **he dicho** algo indiscreto,   *If I have said something*
        lo siento.   *indiscreet, I am sorry.*

Si ellos **han completado** el curso, los felicito.	*If they have completed the course, I congratulate them.*
Si Jaime **estaba** aquí, no lo vimos.	*If James was here, we didn't see him.*

 ## Reading Comprehension

Xochicalco
(The place of the flowers)

Si Leonora pudiera viajar al pasado, ella viajaría al décimo siglo para averiguar por qué casi todos los centros de los mayas se habían desaparecido acerca del año 900 A.D. Nadie sabe la causa, según ella. Pienso que ella habría sido una buena arqueóloga por su curiosidad, pero me dijo que jamás le gustaba la idea de excavar la tierra, ni con máquinas, ni con las manos. Prefiere andar por las ruinas, sintiendo como era la vida en la edad de los mayas.

¿Has oído de Xochicalco, cerca de Cuernavaca, México? Supongo que no. Es poco conocido, pero magnífico, dice ella. La estructura principal se llama 'la serpiente emplumada' y ella se quedaba horas mirándola, tratando de entender lo que significa el arte del templo.

Me contó que quería subir la pirámide de Quetzalcóatl, pero no pudo. Un guía la vio intentar y la mostró como se hace. En vez de ascender recto, como hace casi toda la gente, él le dijo que subiera y bajara zigzagueando. De esta manera, escaló rápida y fácilmente.

¿Has oído de Ceibal en Guatemala? Por fin, Leonora fue con otro fanático de los mayas y estaba muy feliz con su compañero. Viajaron por barco por el Río Pasión. Me habría gustado acompañarla también, pero ella no pensaba en mí. De todos modos, ella y su amigo se enteraron que Ceibal, poblado en 900 B.C. y abandonado en 900 A.D., habría podido ser el centro de la civilización maya. En un sitio bien escondido, vieron estatuas de hombres negros y otras que parecían ser judíos. Estoy seguro que se divirtieron mucho.

Leonora quería que yo te recomendara otros sitios fantásticos para explorar. En el Yucatán, sería una maravilla que visitaras las ruinas de Tulum en la costa de México, o Chitzén Itzá entre Cancún y Mérida, Uxmal donde se ve estatuas de Chac, el dios de la lluvia, o Tikal, en Guatemala, una de las más grandes de todas. Y si vas, no te olvides de mí y el secreto del zigzag.

Verbos

averiguar	*to find out, to verify*
enterarse	*to become informed*
escalar	*to climb*
excavar	*to excavate, to dig*
suponer	*to suppose*
zigzaguear	*to zigzag*

Preguntas

1. ¿Es hombre o mujer el narrador/la narradora?

   _____

2. ¿Cuántas personas hay en el cuento?

   _____

3. ¿Cuántas ruinas menciona la persona principal?

   _____

4. De las ruinas mencionadas en esta narración, ¿cuál es la más antigua?

   _____

29

The Past Perfect Subjunctive

The past perfect subjunctive, also called the pluperfect subjunctive, is often translated the same as the indicative past perfect tense in English, for example, *I had eaten*. Like all subjunctives, this form must be caused by a verb or expression that causes the use of the subjunctive mood in the dependent clause.

Formation of the Past Perfect Subjunctive

The past perfect subjunctive is a compound verb form. To form the past perfect subjunctive, use the imperfect subjunctive of the helping verb **haber** and follow it with the past participle of the main verb.

yo hubiera contestado	*I had answered*
tú hubieras hablado	*you had spoken*
ella hubiera escrito	*she had written*
nosotros hubiéramos ido	*we had gone*
vosotros hubierais estudiado	*you had studied*
ellas hubieran votado	*they had voted*

Uses of the Past Perfect Subjunctive

The past perfect subjunctive expresses action that happened before another action occurred. As you know, the subjunctive mood cannot exist alone. An element in the main clause causes the subjunctive in the dependent clause.

After Certain Verbs

Certain verbs cause the subjunctive in a dependent clause. If the verb in the main clause is in the past (imperfect or preterit), these verbs can cause the past perfect subjunctive in the dependent clause.

Yo **esperaba**   que el avión **hubiera** llegado.
I hoped (imperfect)   *that the plane had arrived.*
                         (past perfect subjunctive)

Rosario **quería**   que hubiéramos pagado la cuenta.
Rosario wanted   *that we had paid the bill.*
   (imperfect)   (past perfect subjunctive)

Me **alegré**   de que ella **hubiera** vuelto.
I was glad (preterit) *that she had returned.* (past perfect subjunctive)

Ella dudaba que sus amigos hubieran tenido razón.	*She doubted that her friends had been right.*
Yo no creía que el alcalde te hubiera reconocido.	*I didn't believe that the mayor had recognized you.*
El niño temía que su madre se hubiera ido.	*The child feared that his mother had gone.*
Lo sentimos que Uds. no se hubieran sentido bien.	*We were sorry that you had not felt well.*

After Certain Impersonal Expressions

Certain impersonal expressions in the main clause cause the subjunctive in a dependent clause. If these expressions are in the past, they can cause the past perfect subjunctive in the dependent clause.

Fue **posible** que los niños se **hubieran** dormido.	*It was possible that the children had fallen asleep.*
Era importante que yo hubiera asistido a la conferencia en México.	*It was important that I had attended the conference in Mexico.*

- After **ojalá**

The past perfect subjunctive is used to express a contrary-to-fact wish in the past with **ojalá**.

Ojalá que yo hubiera sabido.	*I wish that I had known. / Would to God that I had known.*

Ojalá que la hubiéramos encontrado.	*Would to God that we had found her.*
Ojalá que ellos se hubieran quedado.	*Would to God that they had stayed.*

- **quisiera**

The use of the imperfect subjunctive of **querer**, most often **quisiera**, in the main clause can cause the past perfect subjunctive in the dependent clause.

La niña quisiera que su mamá le hubiera dado un caballo para su cumpleaños.	*The child wished that her mother had given her a horse for her birthday.*
Ellos quisieran que el hotel hubiera tenido una piscina.	*They wished that the hotel had had a swimming pool.*
¿Quisieras tú que yo te hubiera dicho la verdad?	*Did you wish that I had told you the truth?*

Exercise 29.1

Complete the following sentences with the correct past perfect subjunctive form of the verb in parentheses. In these sentences, the main clause is in the imperfect or preterit. Note the element that causes the use of this mood.

EXAMPLE   Era importante que nosotros ___*hubiéramos recibido*___ el cheque. (recibir)

1. Jorge no estaba seguro que nosotros _____ la cuenta. (pagar)

2. Ella esperaba que nosotros _____ una cita con su hija. (hacer)

3. Yo no podía creer que mi amigo _____ tal cosa. (decir)

4. No había nadie en la fiesta que _____ por todo el mundo. (viajar)

5. La princesa nunca creía que su príncipe _____. (venir)

6. Deseábamos que no _____ tanto. (llover)

7. Elena se alegró mucho de que Uds. _____. (mejorarse)

8. Sus parientes sintieron mucho que Irene y Gustavo no

   _____. (casarse)

9. Roberto dudaba que nosotros _____ todo el dinero.
   (gastar)

10. Yo no pensaba que las flores _____. (vivir)

Exercise 29.2

Translate the following sentences into English.

1. Ojalá que no se lo hubiéramos dicho.

   _____

2. Ojalá que Uds. hubieran estado bien.

   _____

3. Ojalá que hubiéramos ido de vacaciones.

   _____

4. Fue necesario que el carpintero lo hubiera construido.

   _____

5. Fue urgente que nosotros hubiéramos llevado al hombre enfermo al hospital.

   _____

6. Era una lástima que nadie hubiera estado en el teatro.

   _____

7. Esperábamos que todo el mundo se hubiera aprovechado de la situación.

   _____

8. Los porteros dudaban que los inquilinos nuevos hubieran pintado las paredes.

   _____

9. El abogado no pensaba que sus clientes hubieran ganado.

   _____

10. Fue posible que los ladrones hubieran robado el banco.

   _____

The Contrary-to-Fact Conditional *si*-clause in the Past

When you express the idea that an action would have happened (conditional perfect tense) *if* another action had occurred in the past, the past perfect subjunctive follows the clause that begins with **si**.

Review the conditional perfect tense:

yo habría hecho	*I would have done*
tú habrías comido	*you would have eaten*
ella habría hablado	*she would have spoken*
nosotros habríamos escrito	*we would have written*
vosotros habríais cocinado	*you would have cooked*
ellas habrían contestado	*they would have answered*

The **si**-clause expresses the idea that something would have happened if something else had happened. Remember that the subjunctive form follows **si**.

Si yo **hubiera** tenido más tiempo, yo habría ido a verlo.	*If I had had more time, I would have gone to see him.*
Si Paulo **hubiera seguido** las direcciones, él habría llegado a tiempo.	*If Paul had followed the directions, he would have arrived on time.*
Ella habría sabido la respuesta **si hubiera leído** el cuento.	*She would have known the answer if she had read the short story.*
Habríamos mirado la película **si hubiéramos podido** hallar la grabación.	*We would have watched the movie if we had been able to find the tape.*

A Word About the *si*-clause

In everyday speech, the perfect conditional (for example, **habría hecho**) is sometimes replaced by the past perfect subjunctive (**hubiera hecho**). In these sentences, when a **si**-clause is present, both clauses will contain the same tense—the past perfect subjunctive.

Compare the following sentences to the ones you have just studied. Note that the English translations are the same. Both forms are correct.

Si él **hubiera tenido** más tiempo, yo **habría ido** a verlo.	*If he had had more time, I would have gone to see him.*
Si él **hubiera tenido** más tiempo, yo **hubiera ido** a verlo.	*If he had had more time, I would have gone to see him.*

Si Paulo **hubiera seguido** las direcciones, él **habría llegado** a tiempo.	*If Paul had followed the directions, he would have arrived on time.*
Si Paulo **hubiera seguido** las direcciones, él **hubiera llegado** a tiempo.	*If Paul had followed the directions, he would have arrived on time.*
Carmen **habría sabido** la respuesta si **hubiera leído** el cuento.	*Carmen would have known the answer if she had read the story.*
Carmen **hubiera sabido** la respuesta si **hubiera leído** el cuento.	*Carmen would have known the answer if she had read the story.*
Si Ana **hubiera puesto** las gafas en la mesa, ella las **habría encontrado**.	*If Ana had put the eyeglasses on the table, she would have found them.*
Si Ana **hubiera puesto** las gafas en la mesa, ella las **hubiera encontrado**.	*If Ana had put the eyeglasses on the table, she would have found them.*

 Exercise 29.3

Review the conditional perfect tense, then translate the following sentences into Spanish. Remember that object pronouns are placed directly before the verb form and are never attached to the past participle.

EXAMPLE　　*We would have eaten.* ___Habríamos comido.___

1. *I would have gone.* _____

2. *You would have eaten.* _____

3. *We would have laughed.* _____

4. *They would have told you.* _____

5. *The teachers would have taught.* _____

6. *Marisa would have been happy.* _____

7. *Hillary would have been president.* _____

8. *It would have been possible.* _____

9. *The women would have learned it.* _____

10. *The men would have left.* _____

Exercise 29.4

Translate the following sentences into Spanish. These sentences include a contrary-to-fact **si**-*clause.*

EXAMPLE   *We would have eaten in the restaurant if we had gone there before.*

Habríamos comido en el restaurante si hubiéramos ido

allá antes.

1. *I would have gone to the party if I had not been afraid.*

   _____

2. *You (Ud.) would have eaten the fish if we had cooked it at home.*

   _____

3. *We would have laughed if the movie had been funny.*

   _____

4. *They would have told you the truth if you (tú) had wanted to know it.*

   _____

5. *The teachers would have taught if the students had arrived.*

   _____

6. *Marisa would have been happy if she had known how to skate.*

   _____

7. *Hillary would have been president if more people had voted for her.*

   _____

8. *It would have been possible that they had seen me.*

   _____

9. *The women would have learned it if they had bought the book.*

   _____

10. *The men would have left the house if they had had somewhere to go.*

    _____

Reference Chart:
Sequence of Tenses with the Subjunctive Mood

If the verb in the main clause is in the present or future, the verb in the dependent clause can be in the present subjunctive.

Present and Future		Present Subjunctive
PRESENT INDICATIVE	Ud. espera	que su amiga llame.
PRESENT PERFECT	Ud. ha esperado	que su amiga llame.
PRESENT PROGRESSIVE	Ud. está esperando	que su amiga llame.
SIMPLE FUTURE	Ud. esperará	que su amiga llame.
FUTURE PERIPHRASTIC	Ud. va a esperar	que su amiga llame.
IMPERATIVE	Espere (Ud.)	que su amiga llame.

If the verb in the main clause is in the present or future, the verb in the dependent clause can be in the present perfect subjunctive, depending on the meaning you want to express.

Present and Future		Present Perfect Subjunctive
PRESENT INDICATIVE	Yo espero	que Sara haya llamado.
PRESENT PERFECT	He esperado	que ella haya llamado.
PRESENT PROGRESSIVE	Estoy esperando	que Juan haya llamado.
SIMPLE FUTURE	Esperaré	que ellos hayan llamado.
FUTURE PERIPHRASTIC	Voy a esperar	que tú hayas llamado.
IMPERATIVE	Espere (Ud.)	que él haya llamado.

If the verb in the main clause is in the past (imperfect or preterit) or conditional, the verb in the dependent clause can be in the imperfect subjunctive.

Past and Conditional		Imperfect Subjunctive
IMPERFECT	Ud. insistía	que él cantara.
PRETERIT	Ud. insistió	que el cantante cantara.
PAST PERFECT	Ud. había insistido	que el cantante cantara.
PAST PROGRESSIVE	Ud. estaba insistiendo	que ellos cantaran.
	Ud. estuvo insistiendo	que ellos cantaran.
CONDITIONAL	Ud. insistiría	que cantáramos.
PERFECT CONDITIONAL	Ud. habría insistido	que la cantante cantara.

If the verb in the main clause is in the past (imperfect or preterit) or conditional, the verb in the dependent clause can be in the past perfect subjunctive.

Past and Conditional		Past Perfect Subjunctive
IMPERFECT	Ud. insistía	que la bailarina hubiera bailado.
PRETERIT	Ud. insistió	que el bailarín hubiera bailado.
PAST PERFECT	Ud. había insistido	que ellos hubieran bailado.
PAST PROGRESSIVE	Ud. estaba insistiendo	que todos hubieran bailado.
	Ud. estuvo insistiendo	que todos hubieran bailado.
CONDITIONAL	Ud. insistiría	que hubiéramos bailado.
PERFECT CONDITIONAL	Ud. habría insistido	que yo hubiera bailado.

 ## Exercise 29.5

Complete the following sentences with the correct present subjunctive form of the verb in parentheses. The verb in the main clause is in the present tense.

EXAMPLE   Te digo que _te cuides_. (cuidarse)

1. Espero que Uds. _____ bien. (estar)

2. Nos alegramos mucho de que el hombre _____ en el maratón. (correr)

3. El cocinero espera que te _____ su comida. (gustar)

4. Te digo que no _____. (quejarse)

5. Es imposible que nosotros _____ todo. (saber)

6. Dudamos que los inquilinos le _____ al dueño. (ganar)

7. Ojalá que los huéspedes _____. (venir)

8. ¿Hay alguien aquí que _____ cien dólares? (tener)

9. Espero que Uds. _____ bien. (sentirse)

10. La pareja sugiere que los invitados _____ bien. (vestirse)

Exercise 29.6

Complete the following sentences with the correct present subjunctive form of the verb in parentheses. The verb in the main clause is in the imperative.

1. Dile al niño que _____. (acostarse)

2. Dígale al taxista que nos _____ a nuestro destino. (llevar)

3. Pídele al hombre malo que _____. (irse)

4. Aconséjenles a los acusados que _____ un buen abogado. (conseguir)

5. Deja que ellos _____. (entrar)

6. No permitas que los niños _____. (caerse)

Exercise 29.7

*Complete the following sentences with the correct present subjunctive form of the verb in parentheses. The verb in the main clause is in the simple future or future periphrastic (**ir** + **a** + infinitive).*

1. ¿Será imposible que los adolescentes _____ a sus padres? (escuchar)

2. Susana no irá a menos que su mejor amigo _____. (ir)

3. Voy a pedir que la gente no _____ más. (fumar)

4. Margarita insistirá que su compañero _____ el oficio de la casa. (hacer)

5. El juego no se acabará hasta que la mujer gorda _____. (cantar)

Exercise 29.8

Complete the following sentences with the correct present subjunctive form of the verb in parentheses. The verb in the main clause is in the present perfect.

1. Yo he querido que Uds. _____ a mi novio. (conocer)

2. ¿Has deseado que tu familia _____ viajar contigo? (poder)

3. Le hemos dicho a la juventud que _____ ocho horas cada noche. (dormir)

4. Juana les ha sugerido a sus padres que no _____ tanto. (trabajar)

5. Las dos familias han esperado siempre que sus hijos _____ felices. (ser)

6. ¿Quién se ha alegrado de que sus enemigos _____ éxito? (tener)

7. Ha sido difícil que la gente _____ construir una casa nueva. (lograr)

8. Ha sido bueno que nosotros _____ todo. (aprender)

Exercise 29.9

Complete the following sentences with the correct imperfect subjunctive form of the verb in parentheses. The verb in the main clause is in the preterit.

1. Fue necesario que los bomberos _____ en la casa quemada. (entrar)

2. El soldado dudó que _____ mucho peligro. (haber)

3. Mandé que el camarero me _____ la cuenta. (traer)

4. Ella salió sin que nosotros _____. (fijarse)

5. Yo te rogué que _____ a mi lado. (sentarse)

6. El dueño mandó que nosotros _____ del edificio en seguida. (salir)

Exercise 29.10

Complete the following sentences with the correct imperfect subjunctive form of the verb in parentheses. The verb in the main clause is in the imperfect.

1. Julia esperaba que su amigo _____. (mejorarse)

2. Ellos temían que Ud. no _____. (regresar)

3. Los profesores se alegraban de que a sus alumnos les _____ su clase. (encantar)

4. Estábamos contentos de que Miguel le _____ el anillo. (dar)

5. José lo sentía que nosotros no _____. (animarse)

6. Yo no creía que tú me _____. (ver)

Exercise 29.11

Complete the following sentences with the correct imperfect subjunctive form of the verb in parentheses. The verb in the main clause is in the conditional.

1. ¿Sería posible que la guerra no _____? (empezar)

2. ¿Sería posible que la gente poderosa _____ de la guerra? (desistir)

3. Sería probable que los turistas de la ciudad _____ en el campo. (perderse)

4. Ella lo haría si _____ necesario. (ser)

5. La mujer viajaría si _____ caminar. (poder)

6. El hombre tocaría el violín como si _____ en el concierto. (estar)

7. ¿Te gustaría que nosotros _____ con tu jefe? (hablar)

8. Yo iría a Bolivia si yo _____ bien el español. (saber)

9. ¿Qué haría Ud. si su mejor amigo no le _____ nada? (decir)

10. ¿Cambiarías tu manera de vivir si tú _____ mucho dinero? (ganar)

Exercise 29.12

Translate the following sentences into English.

1. El autor leyó el artículo para que pudiéramos entenderlo.

   _____

2. Antes de que su novia fuera a España, Federico estudió el español por dos años.

   _____

3. Íbamos a jugar al tenis hasta que empezara a llover.

_____

4. El doctor sabía que al paciente se le había hinchado la rodilla.

_____

5. Elena aprendería a hablar español, pero no le gusta estudiar.

_____

6. Fue necesario que el mejor arquitecto diseñara el museo.

_____

7. No sería posible que sucediera tal desastre.

_____

8. El juez esperó que los testigos hubieran visto todo.

_____

9. Los turistas llegarían a las dos si los trenes no se demoraran tanto.

_____

10. Yo hubiera ido de vacaciones con ella si ella me hubiera invitado.

_____

11. ¿Le habrías hecho el favor si Andrés te hubiera pedido?

_____

12. ¿Sería posible que Uds. aprendieran y entendieran todas las lecciones?

_____

 # Reading Comprehension

Su punto de vista

Lo confieso: no pienso mucho en la comida. Si yo hubiera sido mejor cocinera, si hubiera tenido el talento para combinar ingredientes, tal vez yo hubiera podido disfrutar más las celebraciones de glotonería.

Era un día nublado de noviembre. Lo recuerdo bien. Yo vivía con cuatro mujeres en un apartamento grande y alegre, de colores exuberantes. Cada noviembre hacíamos planes para el día de acción de gracias. Mi compañera de cuarto cocinaba un pavo de dieciocho libras y se despertaba durante la noche para lardearlo. Otra amiga horneaba un pastel de calabaza. Un amigo que vivía cerca traía verduras, frutas y queso. Para la gente a quien no le gustaba el pavo, cocinábamos jamón, chuletas, pescado, pollo asado y pato. Invitábamos a todos nuestros amigos. A las cinco de la tarde, empezábamos nuestra cena con la bebida tradicional—el ponche de huevo. Aquella noche, dejé mi plato de cebollas y judías verdes y me fui.

Huí a un restaurante y cené sola, pero no me importó. Por lo menos, no me tocó comer pavo. Hubo muchas tentaciones como mejillones en vino blanco, camarones y langosta en salsa verde y calamares fritos. Ofrecieron una ensalada con manzanas, nueces y pasas, aceitunas y tomates. Para el plato fuerte, ordené la paella para dos porque lleva mariscos, guisantes y chorizo. Después de descansar un rato, comí el flan de España y el helado de fresas. Bebí agua mineral; no tomé ni vino, ni cerveza, ni champaña, ni licor y no me emborraché. Volví a casa; mis amigos estuvieron contentos de verme, les había gustado mi plato de verduras y todos se acostaron agradecidos.

Verbos

combinar	*to combine*
emborracharse	*to get drunk*
hornear	*to bake*
lardear	*to baste*
ordenar	*to order*
tocarle (a uno)	*to have to*

Nombres

la aceituna	*the olive*
los calamares	*the squid*
los camarones	*the shrimp*
la cebolla	*the onion*
el chorizo	*the sausage*
la chuleta	*the pork chop*
la glotonería	*gluttony*
los guisantes	*the peas*
el jamón	*the ham*
la judía verde	*the string bean*
la langosta	*the lobster*
la libra	*the pound*
la manzana	*the apple*
el marisco	*the shellfish*

el mejillón	the mussel
la nuez, las nueces	the nut, the nuts
la paella	the traditional rice dish of Spain
la pasa	the raisin
el pastel de calabaza	the pumpkin pie
el pato	the duck
el pavo	the turkey
el pescado	the fish
el plato fuerte	the main course
el pollo asado	the roast chicken
el ponche de huevo	the eggnog
el queso	the cheese
las verduras	the vegetables

Adjetivo

| nublado | cloudy |

Expresiones

| tal vez | perhaps |
| un rato | a little while |

Preguntas

Answer the following questions orally.

1. ¿Es hombre o mujer la persona principal del cuento?

2. ¿Están enfadadas con ella sus compañeras de cuarto?

3. ¿Te gusta celebrar el día de acción de gracias?

4. ¿Cuál es tu comida favorita?

5. ¿Te molesta comer solo/sola?

6. ¿Cocinas bien?

30

Idioms

A **modismo** is a word or phrase that does not translate exactly into English. **Modismos** are idioms; they are not slang.

Idioms with Prepositions

a fuerza de	*by dint of*
a la derecha	*to the right*
a la izquierda	*to the left*
a la vez	*at the same time*
a lo lejos	*in the distance*
a lo mejor	*probably*
a pie	*on foot*
a principios de	*at the beginning of*
a solas	*alone*
a través de	*across*
al aire libre	*in the open air*
al mismo tiempo	*at the same time*
al principio	*at the beginning, early on*
al revés	*inside out*
de buen humor	*in a good mood*
de buena gana	*willingly*
de día	*by day*
de esta manera	*in this way*
de hoy en adelante	*from now on*
de mal humor	*in a bad mood*
de mala gana	*unwillingly*

de ninguna manera	*by no means*
de noche	*by night*
de nuevo	*again*
de pie	*standing*
de pronto	*suddenly*
de repente	*suddenly*
de todos modos	*anyway*
¿de veras?	*really?*
derecho	*straight ahead*
día/semana/mes/año de por medio	*every other day/week/month/year*
en cambio	*on the other hand*
en cuanto a	*in regard to*
en efecto	*in fact, as a matter of fact*
en seguida	*right away*
por ninguna parte	*nowhere, not anywhere*
por todas partes	*everywhere*
recto	*straight ahead*

 Exercise 30.1

Translate the following sentences into English.

1. Al principio, todo era maravilloso.

   _____

2. Te pusiste la camisa al revés.

   _____

3. A fuerza del estudio, ella aprendió bien la historia.

   _____

4. Fuimos a Madrid a pie.

   _____

5. No me hables ahora; estoy de mal genio.

   _____

6. Ellos no encontraron sus llaves por ninguna parte.

   _____

7. No sé qué hacer en cuanto a sus problemas.

   _____

8. De día trabajo, de noche duermo.

   _____

9. Si queremos llegar a tiempo, tenemos que ir a la derecha.

   _____

10. La muchacha puede escuchar música y estudiar a la vez.

    _____

11. Pienso estar en México a principios de julio.

    _____

12. Él me prestó su carro de mala gana.

    _____

13. Les gusta cenar al aire libre.

    _____

14. En efecto, Pablo lo supo ayer pero no me dijo nada.

    _____

15. Un barco nos llevó a través del río.

    _____

16. Estoy de muy buen humor hoy.

    _____

17. Ud. debe caminar a la izquierda.

    _____

18. A lo mejor, Enrique y Salomé vendrán la semana que viene.

    _____

19. Lo hacemos de buena gana.

    _____

20. El hombre prefiere caminar derecho.

    _____

21. A lo lejos, la veo venir.

    _____

22. Me gusta descansar. A mi amiga en cambio le gusta trabajar.

    _____

23. Les digo que lo hagan de esta manera.

   _____

24. Escribo guiones para la televisión. ¿De veras?

   _____

25. Miguel no tiene mucho dinero, pero decidió viajar de todos modos.

   _____

26. Tú no tuviste éxito la primera vez, pero trataste de nuevo.

   _____

27. De hoy en adelante, vamos a correr cada día.

   _____

28. Asistimos a las clases día de por medio.

   _____

29. De repente, empezó a llover.

   _____

30. Se ve lo bueno y lo malo por todas partes.

   _____

Idioms with Verbs

With *tener*

tener _____ años	to be _____ years old
tener calor	to be hot
tener celos	to be jealous
tener cuidado	to be careful
tener dolor de (cabeza)	to have a (head)ache
tener envidia	to be envious
tener éxito	to be successful, to have success
tener frío	to be cold
tener ganas de	to want, to desire
tener hambre	to be hungry
tener la culpa	to take the blame, to be at fault
tener la palabra	to have the floor
tener lugar	to take place
tener mala cara	to look bad
tener miedo de	to be afraid of, to have fear of

tener mucho/poco/algo/ nada que hacer	*to have a lot/a little/something/ nothing to do*
tener por	*to take someone for, to consider someone to be*
tener prisa	*to be in a hurry*
tener que ver con	*to have to do with*
tener rabia	*to be in a rage, to be very angry*
tener razón	*to be right*
tener sed	*to be thirsty*
tener sueño	*to be sleepy*
tener suerte	*to be lucky*
tener vergüenza	*to be ashamed*

With *dar*

dar a	*to lead to* (places)
dar con	*to run into*
dar de comer	*to feed*
dar gritos	*to shout*
dar la cara	*to face*
dar la hora	*to strike the hour*
dar las gracias	*to give thanks*
dar un abrazo	*to give a hug, to embrace*
dar un paseo	*to take a walk*
dar una vuelta	*to take a walk*
darse cuenta de	*to realize*
darse la mano	*to shake hands*
darse por vencido	*to give up*
darse prisa	*to hurry*

With *echar*

echar de menos	*to miss* (a person or place)
echar flores	*to flatter*
echar la culpa	*to blame*
echarse a llorar	*to burst out crying*

With *hacer*

hace buen/mal tiempo	*it's good/bad weather*
hace calor	*it's hot/warm*
hace frío	*it's cold*
hace viento	*it's windy*

hacer caso a	*to pay attention to*
hacer daño a	*to harm*
hacer el bien/el mal	*to do good/bad*
hacer falta	*to be lacking*
hacer un papel	*to play a part*
hacer un viaje	*to take a trip*
hacerse + *profession*	*to become*
hacerse daño	*to hurt oneself*
hacerse tarde	*to become late*

With *hay*

| hay cupo | *there is space* |
| hay que | *it is necessary* |

With *llevar*

llevar a cabo	*to carry out* (a project, for example)
llevar la contraria	*to take the opposite point of view*
llevarse (algo)	*to carry (something) away*
llevarse bien/mal con	*to get along well/badly with*

With *meter*

meter la pata	*to put one's foot in one's mouth*
meter las narices	*to snoop around*
meterse en donde no le llaman	*to meddle*

With *poner*

poner a alguien por las nubes	*to heap praise on someone*
poner en claro	*to make clear*
poner en duda	*to put in doubt*
poner en ridículo	*to make look ridiculous*
poner las cartas sobre la mesa	*to put the cards on the table*
poner pleito	*to sue*
ponerse a	*to start to*

With *quedar*

quedar boquiabierto	*to be left astonished*
quedar en	*to agree on*
quedarse con	*to keep*
quedarse con el día y la noche	*to be left penniless*

With *tomar*

tomar en serio	*to take seriously*
tomarle el pelo	*to pull someone's leg*
tomárselo con calma	*to take it easy*

Exercise 30.2

Match each of the following sentences with the idiom that best describes it.

1. _____ Es agosto en Nueva York.
2. _____ Estamos cansados.
3. _____ Él no se equivoca.
4. _____ No hay agua en el desierto.
5. _____ No hice nada malo.
6. _____ A mi amigo le gusta apostar.

a. No tiene mucha suerte.
b. No tengo la culpa.
c. Tenemos calor.
d. Siempre tiene razón.
e. Los animales tienen sed.
f. Tenemos sueño.

Exercise 30.3

Translate the following sentences into English.

1. Cristina le hace caso a su maestro porque le agrada.

   _____

2. Elisa se lleva bien con su suegra.

   _____

3. Al niño le gustaba dar de comer a los pájaros en el parque.

   _____

4. El hotel da a la plaza.

   _____

5. Guillermo se hizo abogado.

   _____

6. Hace mucho tiempo que la visitante no ve a su patria. La extraña mucho y quiere darles un abrazo a todos sus amigos.

   _____

   _____

7. Me gustó el chaleco guatemalteco; le di doscientos pesos al vendedor y me lo llevé.

   _____

8. Me di cuenta de que todo no estaba bien.

   _____

9. La niña se echó a llorar.

   _____

10. Los mariscos me hacen daño.

   _____

Time Expressions

Present

The idea of how long someone has been doing something can be expressed by three different Spanish constructions, all using the simple present tense. The English translation is expressed best by the present perfect tense. The action begins in the past and continues into the present.

All three constructions below, shown with their literal translations, express the following question in the present:

How long has your professor been writing her book?

1. ¿Cuánto tiempo lleva su profesora escribiendo su libro?
   How much time does the professor carry writing her book?

2. ¿Desde cuándo escribe ella su libro?
   Since when does she write her book?

3. ¿Cuánto tiempo hace que ella escribe su libro?
   How much time does it make that she writes her book?

The same three constructions, shown with their literal translations, express the following statement in the present:

She has been writing her book for four years.

1. La autora lleva cuatro años escribiendo su libro.
    The author carries four years writing her book.

2. Ella escribe su libro desde hace cuatro años.
    She writes her book since it makes four years.

3. Hace cuatro años que ella escribe su libro.
    It makes four years that she writes her book.

Past

To express how long someone had been doing something, Spanish uses the imperfect tense. The English translation of this construction is expressed best by the past perfect tense. The action was continuing in the past when something else happened.

The constructions below, shown with their literal translations, express the following question in the past:

How long had Lorena been waiting for the bus when it arrived?

1. ¿Cuánto tiempo llevaba Lorena esperando el bus cuando llegó?
    How much time was Lorena carrying waiting for the bus when it arrived?

2. ¿Desde cuándo esperaba ella el bus cuando llegó?
    Since when was she waiting for the bus when it arrived?

3. ¿Cuánto tiempo hacía que ella esperaba el bus cuando llegó?
    How much time did it make that she was waiting for the bus when it arrived?

The constructions below, shown with their literal translations, express the following statement in the past:

She had been waiting for 30 minutes when the bus arrived.

1. Lorena llevaba media hora esperando cuando el bus llegó.
    Lorena carried a half hour waiting when the bus arrived.

2. Ella esperaba desde hacía media hora cuando el bus llegó.
    She was waiting since it made a half hour when the bus arrived.

3. Hacía media hora que ella   *It made a half hour that she*
   esperaba cuando el bus llegó.   *was waiting when the bus*
                                         arrived.

 Exercise 30.4

Translate the following sentences into Spanish, using the present tense and one of the forms of expressing "how long." Try to practice all three possible forms as you complete the exercise.

EXAMPLES   How long has Jaime lived in the United States?

   ¿Cuánto tiempo hace que Jaime vive en los Estados Unidos?

OR   *¿Desde cuándo vive Jaime en los Estados Unidos?*

OR   *¿Cuánto tiempo lleva Jaime viviendo en los Estados Unidos?*

1. *How long has the child been watching television?*

   _____

2. *How long has Adam been sleeping?*

   _____

3. *How long have you been wearing glasses?*

   _____

4. *How long have Isabel and Carlos been waiting?*

   _____

5. *How long have they been friends?*

   _____

6. *He has been sleeping for eight hours.*

   _____

7. *I've been wearing glasses for two years.*

   _____

8. *They have been waiting for 15 minutes.*

   _____

Exercise 30.5

Translate the following sentences into English.

1. ¿Cuánto tiempo hacía que Ud. estaba en Chile cuando tuvo que salir?

   _____

2. ¿Desde cuándo nadaban los niños cuando el bañero llegó?

   _____

3. ¿Cuánto tiempo llevaba Antonio leyendo cuando se durmió?

   _____

4. Hacía dos meses que yo estaba en Paraguay cuando decidí volver a casa.

   _____

5. El hombre frustrado esperaba el tren desde hace veinte minutos.

   _____

6. Llevábamos quince meses viviendo en Paris.

   _____

Reading Comprehension

El fin del juego

Queridos lectores,

    Espero que a Uds. les haya gustado el libro. Ha sido un buen viaje y me alegro de que Uds. hayan llegado hasta el fin. Les dejo con una parte interesante de la historia de Sócrates en la cual él explica por qué no le va a molestar el fin de su vida.

    Ahora, me despido de Uds. y les deseo todo lo mejor.

Hasta el próximo,

La autora

La defensa de Sócrates
escrito por Platón

La asamblea vota por la inocencia o la culpabilidad de Sócrates. Lo condena a la pena de muerte. Lo siguiente es la respuesta de Sócrates ante la asamblea, antes de que se lo lleve a la cárcel.

SÓCRATES La gente dirá que Uds. condenan a muerte a Sócrates, un hombre sabio. Dirán que soy sabio si lo soy o no. Si Uds. hubieran esperado por un rato, sus deseos hubieran sido realizados en el camino de la naturaleza. Pueden ver que soy un hombre viejo.

Me gustaría discutir con Uds., los cuales me han absuelto, lo que ha pasado. Concédanme, les suplico, un momento de atención, porque nada impide que conversemos juntos, puesto que queda tiempo. Quiero decirles, como amigos, lo que acaba de sucederme, y explicarles lo que significa. Sí, jueces míos, me ha sucedido hoy una cosa maravillosa.

Nos engañamos todos sin duda si creemos que la muerte es un mal. Una prueba evidente de ello es que si yo hubiera de realizar hoy algún bien, el dios* no hubiera dejado de advertírmelo como acostumbra.

La muerte es un tránsito del alma de un lugar a otro. ¿Qué mayor ventaja puede presentar la muerte? Si la muerte es una cosa semejante, la llamo con razón un bien; porque entonces el tiempo todo entero, no es más que una larga noche.

Pero si la muerte es un tránsito de un lugar a otro, y si, según se dice, allá en un lugar está el paradero de todos los que han vivido, ¿qué mayor bien se puede imaginar, jueces míos? ¿Qué transporte de alegría no tendría yo cuando me encontrara con los héroes de la antigüedad, que han sido las víctimas de la injusticia? ¿Qué placer el poder comparar mis aventuras con las suyas? Pero aún sería un placer más grande para mí pasar allí los días, interrogando y examinando a todos estos personajes, para distinguir los que son verdaderamente sabios de los que creen serlo y no lo son. ¿Hay alguno, jueces míos, que no diera todo lo que tiene en el mundo por examinar al que condujo un ejército contra Troya, u Odiseo o Sísifo, y tantos otros, hombres y mujeres, cuya conversación y examen serían una felicidad inexplicable?

Ésta es la razón, jueces míos, para que nunca pierdan las esperanzas aún después de la tumba, fundadas en esta verdad: que no hay ningún mal para el hombre de bien, ni durante la vida, ni después de su muerte; y que los dioses tienen siempre cuidado de cuanto tiene relación con él; porque lo que en este momento me sucede a mí no es obra de azar, y estoy convencido de que el mejor partido para mí es morir ahora y liberarme de todos los disgustos de esta vida.

La hora de partir ha llegado, y nos vamos cada cual por su camino— yo, a morir, y Uds. a vivir. Solo dios sabe cual es mejor.

---

*Sócrates siempre decía que tenía un dios familiar, un dios personal y divino que le hacía advertencias desde su niñez. En cuanto a su juicio, esta voz no le había dicho nada.

Verbos

absolver	*to absolve*
acabar de + *infinitive*	*to have just* (+ infinitive)
acostumbrar	*to be accustomed*
advertir	*to warn*
conceder	*to concede*
engañarse	*to deceive oneself*
fundar	*to found*
impedir	*to impede*
realizar	*to fulfill*
significar	*to mean, to signify*
suplicar	*to beg*

Nombres

el azar	*chance*
el ejército	*the army*
la esperanza	*the hope*
el héroe	*the hero*
el paradero	*the place, the destination*
la tumba	*the tomb, the grave*

Expresiones

en cuanto a	*in regard to*
puesto que	*since*

Preguntas

1. ¿Cuál es la actitud de Sócrates ante la muerte?

   _____

2. ¿Cuál es la diferencia entre su dios personal y los dioses del estado?

   _____

3. ¿Qué espera hacer después de la muerte?

   _____

4. ¿Por qué quiere hablar con los jueces?

   _____

5. ¿Qué significa "no hay ningún mal para un hombre de bien, ni durante la vida, ni después de la muerte"? ¿Está Ud. de acuerdo con esta filosofía de Sócrates?

   _____

Appendix
List of Verbs

A

abordar *to board*
abrazar *to embrace*
abrir *to open*
absolver *to absolve*
acabar de (hacer algo) *to have just (done something)*
acabarse *to use up*
acercarse *to approach, to near*
aclarar *to clarify*
acompañar *to accompany*
aconsejar *to advise*
acordarse *to remember*
acostarse *to go to bed*
acostumbrar *to be accustomed*
actuar *to act*
acusar *to accuse*
adivinar *to guess*
admitir *to admit*
advertir *to warn*
agotar *to exhaust, to use up*
agradar *to be pleasing*
agradecer *to thank*
aguantar *to tolerate*
ahorrar *to save* (money)
alcanzar *to reach, to overtake*
almorzar *to have lunch*
alquilar *to rent*
alzar *to lift*

amar *to love*
amenazar *to threaten*
añadir *to add*
andar *to stroll, to walk*
animarse *to cheer up*
añorar *to yearn, to miss*
anular *to annul*
anunciar *to announce*
apagar *to turn off*
aparecer *to appear*
apartarse *to separate*
apostar *to bet*
apoyar *to support*
apreciar *to appreciate*
aprender *to learn*
apresurarse *to hurry*
apretar *to squeeze, to tighten*
aprobar *to pass* (a test)
arrancar *to pull out, to root out*
arreglar *to arrange, to fix*
arreglarse *to get dressed up, to get ready*
arriesgar *to risk*
asegurar *to assure*
asistir (a) *to attend, to be present at*
asustarse *to become scared*
atender *to attend to, to serve*
aterrizar *to land*
atraer *to attract*
atravesar *to cross*

atreverse (a) *to dare to*
averiguar *to check out, to find out*
ayudar *to help*

B

bailar *to dance*
bajar *to descend*
bajarse de *to get off* (a bus)
barrer *to sweep*
basar *to base*
beber *to drink*
bendecir *to bless*
besar *to kiss*
borrar *to erase*
bostezar *to yawn*
botar *to throw away*
brillar *to shine*
brindar *to drink a toast*
broncear *to tan*
bucear *to dive, to snorkel*
buscar *to look for*

C

caber *to fit* (one thing inside another)
caer *to fall*
caerse *to fall down*
calentar *to warm*
callarse *to be quiet*
calmarse *to calm down*
cambiar *to change*
cambiar de idea *to change one's mind*
cantar *to sing*
captar *to grasp the meaning of* (a word)
capturar *to capture*
cargar *to load*
casarse *to get married*
castigar *to punish*
celebrar *to celebrate*
cenar *to dine*
cepillarse *to brush* (one's teeth)
cerrar *to close*
charlar *to chat*
cobrar *to charge* (money)

cocinar *to cook*
coger *to catch, to grab*
colgar *to hang up* (a picture)
colocar *to put, to place*
combinar *to combine*
comenzar *to begin*
comer *to eat*
comparar *to compare*
compartir *to share*
competir *to compete*
componer *to compose*
comprar *to buy*
comunicar *to communicate*
conceder *to concede*
condenar *to condemn*
conducir *to drive*
confesar *to confess*
confirmar *to confirm*
conocer *to know, to be acquainted*
conseguir *to obtain*
construir *to build*
contar *to count, to tell a story*
contar con *to rely on*
contener *to contain*
contestar *to answer*
continuar *to continue*
contradecir *to contradict*
contribuir *to contribute*
convertir *to convert*
copiar *to copy*
corregir *to correct*
correr *to run*
corromper *to corrupt*
coser *to sew*
costar *to cost*
crear *to create*
crecer *to grow*
creer *to believe*
cruzar *to cross*
cubrir *to cover*
cuidar *to take care of*
cuidarse *to take of oneself*
cumplir *to complete, to comply*

D

dar *to give*
dar una vuelta *to take a walk*
darse cuenta (de) *to realize*
decepcionar *to disappoint*
decidir *to decide*
decir *to say, to tell*
defenderse *to defend oneself*
dejar *to allow, to leave* (something behind)
dejar de (hacer algo) *to stop (doing something)*
demorarse *to delay*
depender (de) *to depend (on)*
desaparecer *to disappear*
desayunarse *to have breakfast*
descansar *to rest*
describir *to describe*
descubrir *to discover*
desear *to desire*
desesperarse *to despair*
deshacer *to undo*
desistir *to desist*
despedirse (de) *to take one's leave (of)*
despertarse *to wake up*
destruir *to destroy*
detener *to detain*
detenerse *to stop*
devolver *to return* (an object)
dibujar *to draw*
dirigir *to direct*
disculparse *to apologize, to excuse oneself*
diseñar *to design*
disfrutar *to enjoy*
disolver *to dissolve*
distinguir *to distinguish*
distraer *to distract*
divertirse *to have a good time*
dividir *to divide*
divorciarse *to divorce*
doblar *to turn*
doler *to hurt*

dormir *to sleep*
dormirse *to fall asleep*
ducharse *to take a shower*
dudar *to doubt*
durar *to last*

E

echar *to give off, to throw* (multiple meanings)
elegir *to elect*
emborracharse *to get drunk*
empezar *to begin*
empujar *to push*
enamorarse *to fall in love*
encantar *to enchant*
encontrar *to find*
encontrarse (con) *to meet*
enfadarse *to get angry*
enfermarse *to become sick*
engañarse *to deceive oneself*
engordarse *to get fat*
enojarse *to get angry*
ensayar *to rehearse*
enseñar *to teach*
entender *to understand*
enterarse *to become informed*
entrar (en) *to enter*
entregar *to deliver, to hand in*
envejecer *to grow old*
enviar *to send*
envolver *to wrap*
equivocarse *to make a mistake*
escalar *to climb, to scale*
escapar *to escape*
escoger *to choose*
esconderse *to hide oneself*
escribir *to write*
escuchar *to listen to*
espantar *to scare, to frighten*
esperar *to wait for, to hope*
esquiar *to ski*
establecer *to establish*
estacionar *to park*

estar *to be*
estornudar *to sneeze*
exagerar *to exaggerate*
examinar *to examine*
excavar *to excavate, to dig*
exigir *to demand*
explicar *to explain*
explicarse *to explain oneself*
explorar *to explore*
expresarse *to express oneself*
extrañar *to miss* (a person or place)

F

felicitar *to congratulate*
festejar *to feast, to celebrate*
fijarse *to notice*
fingir *to pretend*
firmar *to sign*
fracasar *to fail*
fregar *to wash up* (plates), *to scrub, to scour*
freír *to fry*
fumar *to smoke*
fundar *to found*

G

ganar *to win*
gastar *to spend money*
gemir *to groan*
girar *to turn, to rotate*
gobernar *to govern*
gozar *to enjoy*
grabar *to record, to tape*
graduarse *to graduate*
gritar *to yell*
gustar *to be pleasing*

H

hacer *to do, to make*
hallar *to find*
hervir *to boil*
hinchar *to swell*
hincharse *to swell up*

hornear *to bake*
huir *to flee*

I

ignorar *not to know, not to pay attention*
imaginar *to imagine*
imaginarse *to imagine*
impedir *to impede*
implorar *to implore*
importar *to be important to*
inscribirse *to enroll, to register*
insistir *to insist*
inspirar *to inspire*
intentar *to intend*
interrumpir *to interrupt*
introducir *to insert*
investigar *to investigate*
ir *to go*
irse *to go away*

J

jubilarse *to retire*
jugar *to play* (a game)
juntar *to unite, to join*
jurar *to swear*

L

ladrar *to bark*
lastimarse *to hurt oneself*
lavarse *to wash oneself*
leer *to read*
lesionarse *to injure oneself*
levantarse *to get up*
liberar *to liberate*
limpiar *to clean*
llamar *to call*
llamarse *to call oneself, to be called*
llegar *to arrive*
llenar *to fill*
llevar *to carry, to wear*
llevarse (bien) *to get along (well)*
llorar *to cry*
llover *to rain*

lloviznar *to drizzle*
lograr *to attain*
luchar *to struggle, to fight*
lucir *to light up*

M

madrugar *to get up early*
maltratar *to mistreat*
mandar *to order, to send*
manejar *to drive*
mantener *to maintain*
maquillarse *to put on makeup*
marcar *to dial, to mark*
marchar *to march*
mascar *to chew*
masticar *to chew*
matar *to kill*
medir *to measure*
mejorarse *to get better*
mencionar *to mention*
mentir *to lie*
merecer *to deserve*
meter *to put inside*
meterse *to meddle, to interfere*
mezclar *to mix*
mirar *to look at, to watch*
mojarse *to get wet*
molestar *to annoy, to bother*
morder *to bite*
morir *to die*
morirse *to die*
mostrar *to show*
mover *to move*
moverse *to move oneself*
mudarse *to move* (from one place to
   another)
murmurar *to mumble*

N

nacer *to be born*
nadar *to swim*
necesitar *to need*
negar *to deny*

nevar *to snow*
notar *to note*

O

obedecer *to obey*
observar *to observe*
ocurrir *to occur*
ocurrirse *to get an idea, to occur to*
ofrecer *to offer*
oír *to hear*
oler *to smell*
olvidar *to forget*
olvidarse *to forget*
operar *to operate*
opinar *to opine, to have an opinion*
oponer *to oppose*
optar *to opt*
ordenar *to order*
oscurecer *to grow dark*

P

pagar *to pay*
parar *to stop*
pararse *to stand up*
parecer *to seem*
parquear *to park*
partir *to leave*
pasar *to pass, to spend* (time)
pasear *to take a walk, to stroll*
patinar *to skate*
pedir *to request*
pegar *to hit*
peinarse *to brush* (one's hair)
pelear *to fight*
pensar *to think*
pensar de *to think of, to opine*
pensar en *to think about*
perder *to lose*
perderse *to become lost, to lose*
perdonar *to pardon*
permitir *to permit*
pertenecer *to belong to*
picar *to sting*

pintar *to paint*
pisar *to step on, to tread on*
planchar *to iron*
poder *to be able, can*
poner *to put*
ponerse *to put on* (clothes), *to become* (emotion)
ponerse a *to begin*
portarse *to behave*
poseer *to possess*
preferir *to prefer*
preguntar *to ask a question*
preguntarse *to wonder*
prender *to turn on*
preocuparse (por) *to worry (about)*
preparar *to prepare*
presentar *to introduce, to present*
prestar *to lend*
prevenir *to prevent*
probar *to taste, to test*
probarse *to try on*
producir *to produce*
prohibir *to prohibit, to forbid*
prometer *to promise*
proponer *to propose*
proteger *to protect*
publicar *to publish*
pudrir *to rot*
pulir *to polish*

Q

quedarse *to stay, to remain*
quejarse *to complain*
quemar *to burn*
quemarse *to burn oneself*
querer *to want*
quitarse *to take off* (clothes)

R

realizar *to fulfill*
rebajar *to lower, to reduce*
recibir *to receive*
recoger *to pick up*

reconocer *to recognize*
recordar *to remember*
recuperarse *to recuperate*
reducir *to reduce*
referir *to refer*
regalar *to give a gift*
regresar *to return*
reírse *to laugh*
relatar *to relate a story*
renunciar *to renounce*
repetir *to repeat*
reportar *to report*
rescatar *to save, to rescue*
resolver *to resolve*
respirar *to breathe*
responder *to respond*
resultar *to result*
retener *to retain*
retirarse *to retire*
reunirse *to meet*
rezar *to pray*
robar *to rob*
rogar *to beg*
romper *to break*

S

saber *to know, to know how*
sacar *to take out*
salir *to leave, to exit, to go out*
salirle (bien) *to come out (well)*
saltar *to jump*
saludar *to greet*
salvar *to save* (a life)
satisfacer *to satisfy*
secar *to dry*
seguir *to follow, to continue*
sembrar *to sow*
sentarse *to sit down*
sentir *to regret*
sentirse *to feel* (an emotion)
separarse *to separate*
servir *to serve*
significar *to mean, to signify*

sollozar *to sob*
soltar *to loosen, to let go*
sonar *to sound*
soñar (con) *to dream (about)*
sonreír *to smile*
sorprender *to surprise*
sospechar *to suspect*
subir *to go up, to ascend*
subrayar *to underline*
suceder *to happen, to occur*
sufrir *to suffer*
sugerir *to suggest*
suplicar *to beg*
suponer *to suppose*
suspirar *to sigh*

T

tapar *to cover up, to plug up*
temblar *to tremble*
temer *to fear*
tener *to have*
tentar *to tempt*
terminar *to finish*
tirar *to throw*
tocar *to touch, to play* (an instrument)
tocarle a alguien *to be someone's turn*
tomar *to take*
torcer *to twist*
trabajar *to work*
traducir *to translate*
traer *to bring*
tragar *to swallow*
tranquilizarse *to calm down*
tratar *to treat*

tratar de (hacer algo) *to try to (do something)*
tratarse (de) *to be about*
triunfar *to triumph*
tronar *to thunder*
trotar *to trot*

U

usar *to use*

V

vacilar *to hesitate*
vagar *to wander*
valer *to be worth*
velar *to watch over, to stay awake*
vencer *to conquer, to vanquish*
vender *to sell*
venir *to come*
ver *to see*
vestirse *to get dressed*
viajar *to travel*
vigilar *to watch over, to guard*
visitar *to visit*
vivir *to live*
volar *to fly*
volver *to return*
votar *to vote*

Y

yacer *to lie down*

Z

zigzaguear *to zigzag*
zumbar *to buzz*

Answer Key

Chapter 1
Nouns, Articles, and Adjectives

1.1   1. el   2. el   3. la   4. la   5. el   6. el   7. la   8. el   9. el   10. la   11. la   12. la
13. el   14. el   15. la   16. la   17. el   18. el   19. la   20. la

1.2   1. los animales   2. las amistades   3. los teléfonos   4. los trenes   5. las ventanas
6. los doctores   7. las ciudades   8. las bolsas   9. las mesas   10. los idiomas
11. las plantas   12. las flores   13. los perros   14. las ilusiones   15. las clases
16. las lecciones   17. los taxistas   18. las lámparas   19. las sillas   20. las luces

1.3   1. the book   2. the page   3. the house   4. the flowers   5. the bathroom
6. the wine   7. the boy   8. the brother   9. the library   10. the coffee   11. the train
12. the planet   13. the (male) dentist   14. the garden   15. the flower   16. the beer
17. the plant   18. the friendship   19. the truth   20. the luck   21. the (male)
manager   22. the store   23. the window   24. a museum   25. a mirror
26. a bookstore   27. a pen   28. a lesson   29. an idea   30. a suitcase
31. the armchair   32. the friends

1.4   1. viejo   2. difícil   3. maravilloso   4. simpática   5. amarilla   6. hermoso
7. delgada OR flaca   8. blanco   9. caro   10. barato   11. pequeño   12. fantástico
13. inteligente   14. interesante   15. grande   16. rico   17. joven   18. roja
19. azul   20. verde

1.5   1. las lámparas azules   2. los amigos fantásticos   3. los perros grises   4. las cervezas
negras   5. los vinos rosados   6. las personas fuertes   7. los días maravillosos
8. las luces verdes   9. las ciudades pequeñas   10. los muchachos jóvenes

1.6   1. los tomates rojos   2. los hombres fuertes   3. las mujeres delgadas   4. las blusas
amarillas   5. las canciones interesantes   6. los planetas verdes   7. las ventanas azules
8. los hoteles viejos

Chapter 2
Estar, Ser, and Subject Pronouns

2.1　　1. está (changing condition)　2. están (location)　3. está, está (health)
4. están (health)　5. están (location)　6. está (location)　7. está, está (changing mood)
8. están (changing mood)　9. estoy (changing mood)　10. está (location)

2.2　　1. Yo estoy en la casa amarilla. ¿Dónde está Ud.? OR ¿Dónde estás tú? OR ¿Dónde están Uds.?　2. Las blusas rojas están en la tienda grande.　3. La flor blanca está en la ventana.　4. Estamos en el tren.　5. ¿Cómo está Ud.? Estoy bien, gracias. OR ¿Cómo están Uds.? OR ¿Cómo estás tú?　6. Estamos cansados y estamos contentos.

2.3　　1. es (point of origin)　2. son, es (profession)　3. son (point of origin)
4. son (description)　5. es (description)　6. somos (identification)　7. son (material)
8. son (point of origin)　9. soy, es (point of origin)　10. es (possession)
11. Eres (identification)　12. son (description)　13. es (profession)

2.4A　　1. es (point of origin)　2. es (identification)　3. son (profession)　4. son (description)
5. somos (profession)

　　B　　1. está (location)　2. está, estoy (health)　3. está (health)　4. estamos (location)
5. Estás (changing mood)　6. están (location)

　　C　　1. están (health)　2. eres (profession)　3. es (description)　4. están (location)
5. están (health), estamos (health)　6. son (description)　7. están (location)
8. está (changing mood)　9. son (description)　10. están (location), es (description)
11. está (health), está (changing mood)　12. son (description)　13. están (location),
son (point of origin), son (point of origin)　14. es (point of origin)
15. están (location), están (changing mood), son (identification)　16. está (location)
17. está (location)　18. estamos (changing mood), somos (identification)
19. Es (point of origin), son (point of origin)　20. está (changing mood), es (description)

2.5　　*Answers will vary.*　1. Estoy bien, gracias.　2. Ella está en la casa.
3. Soy de Nueva York.　4. El hombre está en el carro.　5. El concierto es en el parque.　6. Estoy alegre.　7. La lección es difícil.　8. Las flores están en el piso. Son de Florida.　9. El apartamento de Tomás es pequeño.　10. Sí, estoy muy cansado.　11. No, los periódicos no están en la casa de Alicia.　12. Está en la calle once.　13. No, soy de Chicago.　14. Yo soy profesor.

2.6　　1. están　2. estoy　3. es　4. está　5. es　6. es　7. es

Chapter 3
Hay, Interrogative Words, Days, and Months

3.1A　　1. Is there an easy lesson in the book?　2. There are no cockroaches in the restaurant.
3. Are there red blouses in the store?　4. There are flowers on the balcony of the apartment.　5. Is there class today?　6. Are there more questions from the students?

　　B　　1. Hay muchas plumas en la mesa del maestro.　2. ¿Hay un doctor en el hospital?
3. Hay dos mujeres en la clase.　4. No hay cerveza en la casa de Lisa.

3.2　　1. Cuál　2. Qué　3. Cómo OR Dónde　4. Por qué　5. Quién　6. Por qué
7. Cuántos　8. Cómo OR Dónde

3.3　　1. En　2. De　3. De　4. Con　5. En　6. De

3.4A 1. the beautiful room   2. the pleasant person   3. the sweet friendship
4. the exciting play   5. the beautiful day   6. the low building   7. the strange dream
8. the long war   9. the wide avenue   10. the new year

B 1. el niño cariñoso   2. la tarea fácil   3. la ciudad peligrosa   4. la persona baja
5. el mes corto   6. la playa hermosa   7. la mujer amistosa   8. el hombre amable
9. la avenida estrecha   10. las personas orgullosas

3.5 *Answers will vary.*

3.6 1. es   2. está   3. es   4. es   5. Hay   6. está, está, está   7. Hay   8. están, hay
9. Hay, Es   10. hay   11. son, son   12. somos, son   13. Es, está   14. estoy, está
15. Es   16. Hay   17. es, es   18. son, están   19. están, está   20. es   21. es, son

3.7 1. Where are the students on Sundays?   2. Saturday and Sunday are holidays.
3. In the spring, there are beautiful flowers in the parks.   4. In the autumn, there are
yellow and red leaves on the trees.   5. What day is today? Today is Wednesday. What
month is it? It is September.   6. How many days are there in June? How many days
are there in a year?   7. The streets of Mexico are narrow. The houses are low and
pretty.   8. Why are the newspapers and the magazines on the floor?   9. There is
class, but the students are at the beach where there is a swimming pool also.
The professor is angry but the students are happy.   10. The buildings of the big cities
are tall.   11. The children are at the beach because it is summer.   12. A lot of people
are in the restaurants because it is winter.

Chapter 4
Numbers, Dates, and Time

4.1 1. veintiocho, cuatro, veintinueve   2. treinta y un   3. siete, cincuenta y dos
4. setenta y seis, sesenta y siete   5. veintiuna, un   6. ciento treinta y cinco
7. dos mil cuatrocientos cincuenta y seis   8. Noventa y uno, quinientos cuarenta
y dos, seiscientos treinta y tres   9. Ochocientos sesenta, cincuenta, ochocientos diez
10. cien, cien   11. quince, doscientas cincuenta y cuatro   12. doscientos treinta
y cinco

4.2 1. la calle setenta y dos   2. el piso cuarenta   3. la calle ciento treinta y cinco
4. El tercer capítulo   5. La cuarta lección   6. el quinto mes

4.3 1. jueves, once   2. los sábados   3. cien   4. el dieciocho de octubre mil novecientos
setenta y tres   5. catorce, dos mil seis   6. primer, primera

4.4A 1. a las seis de la tarde   2. A las ocho de la mañana   3. A la una de la tarde
4. A las siete y quince de la noche   5. Son las diez de la noche.

B 1. Son las dos y veinte de la tarde.   2. Son las cuatro y media de la mañana.
3. Son las nueve y cuarto de la noche.   4. Son las seis en punto.   5. Son las cuatro
menos veinticinco de la tarde.   6. Son las siete y diez de la mañana.   7. A eso de las
dos de la tarde.   8. A las nueve de la mañana exactamente.

4.5 1. It is two o'clock in the afternoon and the students are in class.   2. The kitchen
is dirty, but the bathroom is clean.   3. Where are the restaurant's 13 waiters?
4. There is class on Mondays and Thursdays.   5. At eight thirty, the soup is cold
and the dishes are dirty.   6. How many glasses are there on the table at seven in
the morning in Richard's house?

4.6   *Answers will vary.*   1. Hay cincuenta y dos semanas en un año.   2. Hay trescientos sesenta y cinco días en un año.   3. Son cincuenta y seis.   4. Son ciento noventa y siete.   5. Es grande.   6. Porque hay muchas flores.   7. Sí, es deliciosa. 8. El desayuno es a las siete de la mañana.

Chapter 5
Regular Verbs

5.1   1. nada   2. estudia   3. descansamos   4. llega   5. cantan, bailan   6. hablan 7. compra   8. trabaja, cocina   9. entran   10. escucho   11. mira   12. practican 13. limpian   14. viajo, bajo   15. contesta

5.2   *Answers will vary.*

5.3   1. corre   2. bebe   3. comemos   4. aprenden   5. leo, leen   6. comprendemos 7. venden   8. rompen

5.4   1. comparte   2. abre   3. vive   4. discutimos   5. Escribes   6. deciden   7. recibe 8. suben

5.5   1. toman   2. lleva   3. debe   4. toca   5. debemos   6. llevo   7. pasa   8. toca 9. gana   10. Toma

Chapter 6
Irregular Verbs

6.1   1. cierro   2. piensa   3. juegan   4. almorzamos   5. Recuerdas   6. empieza

6.2   1. sabe, saben   2. perdemos   3. hace   4. tengo, tiene, tenemos   5. vuelve 6. entienden   7. puedo   8. vemos   9. devuelve   10. pongo   11. quiere

6.3   1. Yo sé donde hay un restaurante barato en la quinta avenida.   2. Carlos no quiere hacer una cita con el dentista.   3. No queremos limpiar el apartamento hoy. 4. Veo un gato gris y un pájaro azul.   5. Ella entiende las ideas pero no quiere hablar. 6. ¿Quién puede cantar y bailar en la fiesta?   7. Hago la tarea a las ocho los lunes. 8. Queremos volver al trabajo el martes.

6.4   1. repite   2. miente   3. salir   4. dormimos   5. seguir   6. vienen   7. oír 8. prefiere   9. sirven

6.5   *Answers will vary.*

6.6   1. cierran, salen   2. juegan   3. almorzamos   4. empieza   5. sabe   6. entiende, recuerda   7. prefiero   8. tengo   9. ser   10. seguimos   11. duermen   12. encontrar 13. viene   14. estamos   15. Puede   16. veo, veo   17. hay   18. volver   19. pongo, sirve   20. hacer, hago

6.7   1. What floor do Pablo's friends live on? Are they from Peru? Do they speak English? 2. What are you talking about? With whom are you speaking?   3. Sebastián leaves Carla's house at eight o'clock in the morning. He arrives at the office at nine o'clock. He works eight hours. At what hour can he arrive at Carla's house?   4. Why is there a tree in the house?   5. To be or not to be.   6. At noon, we enter the building and go up to the third floor; at three o'clock in the afternoon, we go down to the first floor and we leave.

Chapter 7
Ir and the Future

7.1 1. van 2. vamos 3. ir 4. va 5. ir 6. voy 7. Vas 8. ir, ir

7.2 1. van a estar 2. va a firmar 3. voy a terminar 4. va a comprar 5. vamos a celebrar 6. va a aceptar 7. vamos a disfrutar, vamos 8. voy a cocinar, ir 9. va a apagar 10. van a pasar

7.3 *Answers will vary.*

7.4 1. tienen hambre 2. tiene sed 3. tengo suerte 4. tienen sueño 5. tenemos frío, tenemos calor 6. tiene la palabra 7. Tienes (tú) miedo 8. tengo prisa 9. tiene éxito 10. tiene dolor 11. tener cuidado 12. tiene razón 13. tiene lugar 14. tenemos ganas 15. años tiene 16. tiene que ver con

7.5 1. acabo de 2. tengo que 3. tratar de 4. dejar de

7.6 1. para aprender 2. que ella está aquí 3. que vive aquí 4. que yo debo ir 5. para tocar 6. Para quién 7. que necesito 8. para dos personas

7.7 1. ser 2. correr 3. cocinar 4. está 5. cerramos 6. abro, salen 7. trata 8. tienen 9. hace, Bebe 10. ir, vive 11. empieza, debemos 12. trabajo 13. duerme, come, nada, juega 14. sabe 15. pierde

7.8 1. ir, va 2. vas 3. vamos 4. van 5. voy, voy

7.9 1. tiene sueño, tiene hambre 2. venir 3. hacer, tiene miedo 4. salen, vuelven OR regresan 5. lee, saber 6. hay 7. toma, prefiere 8. ganar 9. llegar 10. son, está 11. subo, bajo 12. regresa OR vuelve, cocinar 13. tengo frío 14. tiene calor 15. tiene sed 16. perdemos 17. tiene razón

7.10 1. el pelo, los ojos 2. la cara 3. pie OR tobillo 4. la boca, los dientes 5. el oído 6. el hígado 7. los pulmones 8. rodilla 9. estómago 10. los labios

7.11 1. está 2. son 3. estar 4. es 5. Ser, ser 6. está 7. estar 8. somos 9. es 10. es 11. es, es 12. soy, son

7.12 1. hijos 2. hermanos 3. esposa 4. esposo 5. nietos 6. abuela 7. tío 8. tía 9. cuñado 10. cuñada 11. suegro 12. suegra 13. abuelo 14. parientes

Chapter 8
Adjectives and Adverbs

8.1 1. mis 2. sus 3. sus 4. nuestros 5. su 6. su 7. sus 8. sus 9. nuestra 10. nuestra 11. su 12. su

8.2 1. Esta, ese 2. estas, esas 3. aquel, aquella 4. Esta, esos 5. Aquellas 6. esos 7. Este

8.3 1. francesa 2. japonesa 3. los guatemaltecos 4. canadiense 5. Los nicaragüenses 6. Los costarricenses 7. hindú, hindú 8. portugués

8.4 1. todos 2. única 3. mucha 4. bastante, ambos 5. último 6. cada 7. buen 8. mala 9. algunas, algunos 10. pocos 11. próximo 12. otro 13. varias

8.5 1. misma clase 2. ciudades antiguas 3. hombre pobre 4. pobre niña 5. gran mujer 6. viejas amigas

8.6   1. la mejor   2. tan caro   3. el más grande   4. más interesante   5. tantos
6. más pequeña   7. más alta, más alto   8. más emocionantes   9. menor,
más contenta, mayor   10. menos anchas   11. tan inteligentes   12. más vieja
13. más que   14. menos que   15. más bello   16. la mejor   17. mayor   18. la menor
19. más picante   20. más limpio   21. más cariñosos   22. el mejor, el peor
23. más importante, más importante   24. más triste   25. más cansados
26. tanta   27. tantos   28. mejor   29. menos   30. más

8.7   1. sinceramente   2. locamente   3. totalmente   4. verdaderamente
5. inocentemente   6. cariñosamente   7. completamente   8. normalmente

8.8   1. siempre, temprano   2. bien, claramente   3. lentamente   4. felizmente
5. frecuentemente   6. Todavía no   7. Ya no   8. arriba, abajo   9. rápida, alegremente
10. siempre, cariñosamente   11. mucho   12. Derecho   13. allá   14. honesta,
sinceramente

8.9   1. Mi hermano menor tiene diez años.   2. Él entiende este capítulo, pero no quiere
aprender todas las palabras.   3. Yo sé porque su hermana quiere ir a España. Sus
parientes están allí.   4. Cada año, el día de acción de gracias, cocinamos demasiado.
5. Juan siempre pierde sus guantes.   6. Su abuela es mayor que su abuelo.   7. El
último mes del año es diciembre; el primer mes es enero.   8. Tenemos una buena
clase; aprendemos mucho.   9. Su libro acaba de llegar.   10. Yo sé que mi gato es más
inteligente que su perro.   11. Estos árboles son más viejos que aquellos árboles.
12. Escuchamos las mismas canciones tristes todos los días.   13. Piensas que el
presidente de los Estados Unidos es un gran hombre?   14. ¿Viene Ud. a nuestra fiesta
el viernes? Empieza a las nueve de la noche.   15. Carolina es tan alta como Enrique;
su hermana es la más alta de todos.   16. Este libro es el libro más interesante de la
biblioteca.   17. ¿Cuál es el animal más peligroso del mundo?   18. Soy la única
persona de la familia que sabe jugar al tenis. A veces, yo gano; a veces, pierdo.

8.10   1. Mr. Gomez does his work with difficulty.   2. She speaks sincerely and her friend
answers humbly (with humility).   3. This woman always explains everything clearly.
4. Frankly, I don't want to go out tonight. I prefer to read and to write calmly.
5. Bernard always goes to the same restaurant. He thinks that it is the best restaurant
in the city.

Chapter 9
Negatives and Prepositions

9.1   1. no aprendemos nada.   2. Nadie va a la fiesta. / Ninguna persona va a la fiesta.
3. no escucho nunca (jamás).   4. no tienen ningún enemigo.   5. no hay ningún
hospital por aquí.   6. nunca viajo.   7. no es nada cómica.   8. no bailo nunca.

9.2   1. No tengo más que treinta dólares en mi cartera.   2. Nunca estamos contentos.
3. No hago nada hoy.   4. No quiero ir tampoco.   5. Este programa no es nada
interesante.   6. ¿No quieres tomar nada?   7. No hay ninguna farmacia por aquí.
8. Ella no tiene ninguna amiga.   9. El novio nunca limpia el apartamento.
10. Ella no estudia jamás.   11. Ninguna mujer quiere bailar con él.
12. Nadie vive en la casa blanca.

9.3   *Answers will vary.*   1. No quiero ir tampoco.   2. Nadie cocina para mí.
3. No es nada interesante.   4. Yo nunca voy de vacaciones.   5. No hablo con nadie
tan temprano a las seis de la mañana.   6. No corro nunca al tren.

9.4   1. conmigo   2. sin ti   3. en él   4. consigo   5. para ellos   6. Entre él y ella
7. Entre tú y yo   8. hacia nosotros   9. conmigo, con él   10. cerca de él
11. delante de ellos / ante ellos   12. delante de nosotros / ante nosotros
13. detrás de ella   14. lejos de él, cerca de mí

9.5   1. Antes del almuerzo   2. Después de la cena   3. Después de comer   4. Antes de ir
5. A pesar de salir   6. sin escuchar   7. para aprender   8. debajo de, encima de
9. cerca de   10. hacia   11. para   12. detrás de   13. sobre   14. por
15. delante de / ante   16. por   17. por, por   18. lejos de   19. por   20. para

9.6   1. She never speaks against her friends.   2. Sara's shoes are underneath her bed.
3. Australia is far from the United States.   4. The school is between the church and
the bank.   5. I can see the river from my window.   6. She sleeps eight hours every night.
She sleeps from 11:00 until 7:00.   7. Under the law, who has protection?   8. I put one
book on top of the other.   9. Anthony never sings without us.   10. The witness has to
appear before the judge.   11. The children talk a lot about the film.   12. The author
writes about history and human rights.   13. The movie theater is far from the market.

9.7   1. Entro en la tienda por la puerta.   2. Todo el mundo quiere ir, excepto Samuel.
3. Todos los hombres bailan salvo Pablo.   4. Mi jardín está pegado al jardín de mi vecino.
5. Caminamos hacia el parque.   6. Hay una parada de buses enfrente de la casa de Laura.
7. Según las noticias, mucha gente no va a votar.   8. Hay sillas cómodas alrededor de la
piscina.   9. Día tras día, ellos trabajan mucho.   10. La casa de Jaime está detrás de la
escuela.   11. ¿Vas a estudiar para el examen?   12. Ella no quiere viajar por miedo.

9.8   *Answers will vary.*

9.9   1. bebe, toma/bebe   2. toca, practica   3. hay   4. Van   5. sé, ser   6. quiere ir, viven
7. limpio, tengo que   8. dejar   9. es   10. sabemos, está   11. empieza, salimos
12. entendemos   13. están   14. puede   15. trata de cocinar, tiene éxito   16. hace
17. viaja   18. toca, toca, juegan   19. va a pagar   20. volver/regresar   21. tiene,
debe ir   22. comprar   23. Vienes, tomar   24. nadar   25. corren

9.10   1. Antes de cantar   2. Después de descansar   3. Para llegar   4. Después de comer
5. después de estar   6. sin escuchar   7. A pesar de trabajar   8. antes de ir   9. Antes
de tomar   10. En vez de hacer   11. por   12. por   13. para, por   14. para, por

9.11   1. sexta, séptima   2. rápidamente, a la izquierda   3. octavo   4. A las once menos
quince, tercer   5. treinta y cuatro, tercera   6. A veces, debajo de, Frecuentemente,
en   7. mayor   8. menor   9. séptima, a la derecha, a la izquierda, recto/derecho
10. hasta las once de la mañana   11. a las ocho de la mañana   12. a las ocho menos
cuarto/quince   13. la primera   14. más estrechas   15. más alta que, mayor que
16. mejor   17. más triste que   18. menores   19. más fuerte que, mejor   20. peor

9.12   1. Mi sobrina va a tener trece años la próxima semana.   2. Las muchachas tienen
hambre y sed y nadie sabe cocinar.   3. Ningún niño quiere ir al dentista. No sé porque
todo el mundo tiene miedo de ir.   4. La película empieza a las ocho. Tenemos que
llegar a las siete y media.   5. Ella piensa que él debe tratar de correr todos los días
para ser más fuerte.   6. Ella va siempre a Las Vegas en el invierno. Pierde
frecuentemente. Pero hoy tiene suerte y gana cien dólares.   7. Esa iglesia es vieja.
Es mucho más vieja que este templo.   8. Trato de hablar con mis amigos en español.
Tengo mucho que aprender. Debo estudiar cada mañana.   9. Carla pasa mucho
tiempo en la tienda. Mira la ropa, pero sale sin comprar nada.   10. ¿Cuántos
terremotos hay en California cada año?   11. ¿Quién está aquí? Soy yo.   12. Jorge es
un buen hombre.   13. Elena y sus amigos son inteligentes.   14. Su abuela y su abuelo
están contentos porque sus nietos están bien.

9.13   1. to open   2. to have just   3. to accept   4. to save (money)   5. to have lunch
6. to turn off   7. to appear   8. to learn   9. to arrange, to fix   10. to dance
11. to go down, to descend   12. to drink   13. to change   14. to walk   15. to sing
16. to celebrate   17. to close   18. to cook   19. to eat   20. to share   21. to buy
22. to understand   23. to answer   24. to run   25. to cross   26. to owe, should, must,
ought to   27. to decide   28. to stop (doing something)   29. to rest   30. to describe
31. to return (an object)   32. to draw   33. to enjoy   34. to turn, to fold
35. to sleep   36. to begin   37. to find   38. to understand   39. to enter   40. to write
41. to listen to   42. to be   43. to study   44. to explain   45. to sign   46. to smoke
47. to win   48. to enjoy   49. to speak   50. to do, to make   51. to go   52. to play
53. to read   54. to clean   55. to arrive   56. to fill   57. to wear, to carry   58. to cry
59. to drive   60. to dial, to mark   61. to lie   62. to put in   63. to look at, to watch
64. to swim   65. to need   66. to hear   67. to stop   68. to pass, to spend (time)
69. to think   70. to lose   71. to paint   72. to be able   73. to put   74. to practice
75. to prefer   76. to turn on   77. to prepare   78. to want   79. to receive
80. to remember   81. to return   82. to review   83. to repeat   84. to break
85. to know, to know how   86. to leave, to exit   87. to follow, to continue   88. to be
89. to serve   90. to smile   91. to go up, to ascend   92. to have   93. to have to (do
something)   94. to finish   95. to throw   96. to touch, to play (an instrument)
97. to take   98. to work   99. to try to (do something)   100. to use   101. to sell
102. to come   103. to see   104. to travel   105. to live   106. to return   107. to vote

Chapter 10
The Indirect Object

10.1   *Pronunciation exercise only.*

10.2   1. me gusta   2. le gusta   3. le gusta   4. me gusta   5. les gusta   6. les gusta
7. les gusta   8. me gusta   9. te gusta   10. nos gusta   11. le gustan   12. le gustan
13. les gustan   14. me gustan   15. te gustan   16. le gusta   17. le gusta
18. nos gusta   19. les gusta   20. les gusta   21. les gusta   22. les gusta

10.3   1. A ella   2. A Ud.   3. A mí   4. a ti, a ellos   5. a nadie   6. A quién

10.4   1. Les encantan esos carros rojos.   2. Te agradan los programas.   3. Me gustan las
sillas.   4. Nos importan nuestros amigos.   5. Le fascinan esas computadoras.

10.5   1. Susan's head hurts.   2. I lack a pencil with which to write.   3. Why isn't dancing
pleasing to you?   4. Exotic trips enchant us.   5. News of the day is interesting to her.
6. Does her perfume bother you?   7. Are the lessons important to you?   8. Is it
convenient for you to continue your studies this year?   9. To drive in the rain is not
pleasing to him.   10. Hot weather is not pleasing to her.

10.6   *Answers will vary.*

10.7   1. me escribe   2. nos escriben   3. me da   4. te pregunto   5. me dice   6. le presta
a él   7. les enseñamos a Ana y José   8. nos traen   9. le digo a él   10. le pregunto
al taxista, me cobra

10.8   1. me quiere dar   2. les quiere enseñar a sus estudiantes   3. me van a comprar
4. le quiero vender / te quiero vender   5. te puedo traer   6. le debe decir
7. nos puede enseñar   8. Me puede hacer   9. le quiero dar   10. me preguntan

10.9   1. quiere contarme   2. va a prestarle   3. va a escribirle   4. vamos a venderles
5. quiero prestarles

10.10   1. te doy   2. le trae   3. nos quiere enseñar / quiere enseñarnos   4. les vamos
a escribir / vamos a escribirles   5. me prestas

10.11   1. Can you tell me, why doesn't Sandra like to play the guitar?   2. Elena's friend
lends her books to you.   3. Elena gives her brother the pens that he needs.
4. The music lessons are not expensive. The teacher charges his students $15 per hour.
5. Playing tennis is fascinating to me, but it suits me more to swim.   6. The doctor is
not in his office. I don't know if he wants to speak with me.   7. Between you and me,
we have to decide who is going to tell the children a story.   8. Why does the lawyer
ask the witnesses questions, if he already knows the answers?   9. Can you sell me
two suitcases quickly? I am going to travel tomorrow.   10. She wants to call us
on Thanksgiving Day.   11. Celebrating St. Valentine's Day is pleasing to her.
12. Does it suit you to have chicken soup when you are sick?   13. I tell her that her
idea is good.   14. Coffee is not pleasing to her; her colleague always brings her tea.
15. The waiter brings a glass of water to the man. He brings a glass of milk to the
youngsters.

10.12   1. Do you want to travel with me next year? Do you have a vacation? Where do you
want to go?   2. Where do you like to eat? Do you prefer to eat in a restaurant or at
home?   3. Does the pollution of the big cities bother you?   4. Is dancing pleasing
to you? Who likes to dance with you?   5. The restaurant on 42nd Street and Ninth
Avenue is not pleasing to them. Do you know the reason?   6. It is Susan's birthday.
Should I bring her flowers?   7. We tell the children that it is important to study.
Why don't they pay attention to us?   8. I lend money to Mary because she is a good
friend and she always returns the money to me. Do you lend money to your friends?
9. What do you answer the child if he tells you that he is afraid to swim?
10. They want to give you a car in order to celebrate the New Year, but they only have
$500. What should they do?   11. We are hungry. Who is going to teach us to cook?
12. Where am I? Can you give me good directions?   13. Your best friend wants to give
you a good gift. He wants to do you the favor of cleaning your apartment. How many
rooms do you have?   14. The child asks you, "Why are there clouds in the sky?"
Do you know the reason?

10.13   1. Cada año él le da un regalo a su novia.   2. Carla nunca me dice sus secretos.
3. Enrique no nos quiere prestar dinero. / Enrique no quiere prestarnos dinero.
4. ¿Quién les va a comprar libros a los niños? / ¿Quién va a comprarles libros a los
niños?   5. Después de escribirles a sus amigos, él va al cine.   6. Ellos nos cobran
demasiado. Les cobramos poco.   7. ¿Por qué no les contesta Ud. a los estudiantes?
Le hacen muchas preguntas.   8. Les vamos a dar un perro a Pedro y a Rosa. /
Vamos a darles un perro a Pedro y a Rosa.   9. Te traigo café si me traes té.
10. Le digo a Ud. que el tren viene.   11. ¿Por qué nos enseña Ud. el alemán si
queremos aprender el francés?   12. Ella escucha todo, pero no te dice nada.
13. La tía de Susana le dice que quiere ir a México para sus vacaciones. Ella me dice
a mí que quiere ir a París.   14. Después de estudiar mucho, ¿le duelen los ojos?
15. Todo el mundo quiere ir al partido de fútbol, salvo yo.

Chapter 11
The Direct Object

11.1 1. besa a su esposo 2. llamar a sus amigos 3. acompaño a mi abuela
4. hallar a mi hermano menor 5. extraña a su familia 6. miramos a la maestra
7. ayudar a los pacientes 8. conozco a Pedro 9. ven a sus estudiantes
10. cuidan a sus hijos 11. lleva a los turistas 12. escucha al maestro 13. encontrar a
su hermana 14. grita a su jefe 15. invitar a Ramona 16. esperar a su amiga

11.2 1. me espera 2. te conoce 3. van a ayudarnos / nos van a ayudar 4. extrañarlas
5. lo busco, lo encuentro 6. lo ama 7. visitarla 8. Las ven 9. los saludamos
10. lo va a dejar / va a dejarlo 11. los cuida 12. Después de llamarlo
13. la conocemos 14. la escucha 15. Antes de invitarla

11.3 1. If a man accompanies a beautiful woman to the reunion, is he going to kiss her?
2. It seems to us that the boy is sick and cannot do his homework. We decide to
help him. 3. Sara always arrives late and we don't want to wait for her any longer.
4. Do you miss your family who lives far away? Do you want to visit them?
5. The English people are going to arrive in the United States this afternoon.
We are going to take them from the airport to a good hotel.

11.4 1. Veo a José pero no me ve. 2. No sabemos donde están los turistas que nos visitan
de España. 3. Ellos van a visitar a sus amigos en el Canadá despúes de vender su
barco.

11.5 1. lo tengo, quiero leerlo 2. la quiere limpiar / quiere limpiarla 3. los tenemos,
los vemos 4. no los puede usar, los quiere vender 5. comprarlos 6. los encuentra /
los halla 7. estudiarla 8. encontrarlas/hallarlas 9. los aman 10. tenerlo

11.6 1. la 2. Lo 3. la 4. le 5. me, te 6. les 7. Los 8. nos 9. Les 10. les 11. me
12. les 13. la 14. los 15. lo 16. la 17. las 18. las 19. las, las 20. Me, me

11.7 *Answers will vary.*

11.8 1. Veo a mis amigos todos los sábados. Nos gusta ir al cine. 2. Ella mira a la
profesora, escucha bien, pero todavía no entiende nada. 3. Lisa espera a su hermana
que siempre llega tarde. 4. Viajamos a Ecuador para estar con nuestros parientes.
5. La lección es difícil y él la quiere estudiar para el examen. 6. ¿Puede Ud.
ir al correo por mí? Tengo una carta para mi amiga y la quiere mandar hoy.
7. ¿Quieres acompañarlo a la fiesta? Él es tímido y no quiere ir solo. 8. ¿De dónde
la conoce Ud.? ¿La ve todo el tiempo? 9. Ella tiene zapatos nuevos pero no los lleva
nunca. 10. Casi nunca te veo.

Chapter 12
Reflexive Verbs

12.1 1. despertarme 2. me levanto 3. me baño, me ducho 4. me siento 5. se llaman
6. se dedican 7. nos divertimos 8. expresarnos 9. acostarse 10. Me duermo

12.2 1. caerse 2. se afeita, se pinta 3. te enojas 4. nos quitamos 5. se ponen
6. quedarme 7. se preocupa 8. mudarme 9. tranquilizarse 10. nos alegramos
11. me cepillo 12. se peinan

12.3 1. se desayunan 2. se encuentran con 3. se ponen 4. se ríe 5. se equivoca 6. me acuerdo 7. Se aprovecha 8. se queja de 9. se fija en 10. burlarse de 11. Se parecen 12. meterme en 13. se demoran 14. se enamora 15. nos callamos 16. se atreve a 17. se portan 18. se fía en

12.4 1. se despierta 2. se ducha 3. vestirse 4. desayunarse 5. se encuentra con / se reúne con 6. se dedican 7. Se ayudan 8. Se dice 9. se atreven 10. preocuparse 11. tranquilizarse/calmarse 12. sentirse 13. se demoran 14. se quema 15. se queda 16. se baña 17. se acuesta 18. se duerme

Chapter 13
The Present Subjunctive

13.1 1. diga 2. haga 3. conozcan 4. durmamos 5. sepa 6. tomemos 7. se levanten 8. llegue 9. me quede 10. esté 11. dé 12. vayas 13. sean 14. lean 15. tenga 16. traigamos 17. se sientan

13.2 1. diga 2. pague 3. se sientan 4. deje de llorar 5. expliquemos 6. tenga 7. dé 8. sepa 9. haya 10. vayan 11. sea 12. hagamos 13. esté 14. vean

13.3 *Answers will vary.* 1. Lo siento que mi amigo tenga malos sueños. 2. Es posible que ella no se divierta mucho. 3. Él duda que seamos buenos estudiantes. 4. Ella teme que no volvamos a los Estados Unidos. 5. Yo le pido que Sara me traiga flores a mi casa. 6. Dudo que Ud. conozca a mi tío. 7. Es una lástima que no nos veamos mucho. 8. ¿Es posible que no haya clase los lunes? 9. No creo que Carla sea de Polonia.

13.4 1. visite 2. traigamos 3. ame 4. vea/veamos 5. están 6. se queja 7. entienda 8. puedas 9. se acuerde 10. estén

13.5 1. se levanta 2. ir 3. se desayunen 4. salir 5. se diviertan 6. viene 7. se pongan 8. sea

13.6 1. Después de que, me bañe 2. a menos que, vayan 3. luego que, tenga 4. para que, sepan 5. luego que, terminen 6. Antes de que, venga 7. para que, puedas 8. hasta que, lleguen 9. En caso de que, tengan 10. para que, estén 11. A pesar de que, tengan 12. sin que, invite 13. después de que, se vayan 14. pueda 15. nos reunamos / nos encontremos 16. vuelvan/regresen 17. aprenda

13.7 1. se enfermen 2. descansemos 3. llegue 4. se quejen 5. cocine 6. duermas 7. haya 8. tenga 9. esté 10. quiera 11. acompañe 12. sea 13. venga 14. hable

13.8 1. me acueste 2. se mejore 3. son 4. estudie 5. toque 6. gusta 7. vayan 8. haya 9. estén, llegue 10. va 11. conozca 12. nade 13. vuelvan 14. visites 15. pueda 16. pongan 17. hagan 18. se sientan, estén 19. se casen 20. vayas 21. debes 22. necesita

13.9 1. quieren 2. dé 3. ser 4. dormir 5. entiendan 6. leer 7. se ríe 8. hagas 9. está, escoja 10. podamos 11. salgan 12. comer, vivir 13. gusta 14. son 15. busquemos 16. se pone, hace 17. estar, estén 18. viajar, aprender 19. lleguen 20. sea 21. dormir, se despierte 22. digan, llegar, sepa 23. compartir 24. coma 25. tengan 26. te quedes 27. regreses

13.10   1. No me gusta que se vaya.   2. Él se alegra de que ella le dé flores a su esposo.
3. Es importante que ella sepa la fecha.   4. Me alegro de que mis amigos estén bien.
5. Es dudoso que Paula conozca a Raúl.   6. Es posible que yo sea una buena
estudiante.   7. Esperamos que la película empiece a las dos.   8. Ojalá que haga
buen tiempo hoy.   9. Tal vez el tren llegue a tiempo.   10. Quiero que Rosa tenga
mucha suerte.   11. Me alegro de que nos veamos mucho.

13.11   1. Pedro no piensa que el viaje sea bueno.   2. Me alegro de conocerle.
3. Esperamos que te sientas mejor.   4. ¿Me puede llamar cuando llegue a casa?
5. Laura insiste en que los niños se pongan la chaqueta.   6. Roberto espera que Julia
baile con él esta noche.

13.12   1. to embrace   2. to accompany   3. to advise   4. to remember   5. to go to bed
6. to shave   7. to be agreeable   8. to thank   9. to become happy   10. to love
11. to walk   12. to cheer up   13. to rush   14. to take advantage of
15. to fix oneself up   16. to attend (an event)   17. to get frightened   18. to dare
19. to help   20. to get off   21. to bathe oneself   22. to kiss   23. to make fun of
24. to look for   25. to fall down   26. to become quiet   27. to calm down
28. to carry   29. to brush (one's hair/teeth)   30. to chat   31. to charge   32. to begin
33. to be acquainted with, to know   34. to tell a story   35. to be convenient to
36. to converse   37. to take care of   38. to give   39. to realize   40. to say, to tell
41. to dedicate oneself   42. to defend oneself   43. to leave (something or someone)
44. to delay   45. to have breakfast   46. to desire, to want   47. to take one's leave
48. to wake up   49. to have a good time   50. to be painful, to hurt   51. to fall asleep
52. to take a shower   53. to doubt   54. to fall in love   55. to be enchanting
56. to meet   57. to get angry   58. to get sick   59. to get angry   60. to teach
61. to send   62. to make a mistake   63. to choose   64. to wait for
65. to express oneself   66. to miss (a person or place)   67. to lack
68. to be fascinating   69. to trust   70. to notice   71. to yell at   72. to have (helping
verb)   73. to become (a profession)   74. to find   75. to be important   76. to insist
77. to interest   78. to invite   79. to go away, to leave quickly   80. to hurt oneself
81. to wash oneself   82. to get up   83. to call   84. to call oneself   85. to send
86. to put makeup on   87. to kill   88. to get better   89. to meddle, to get involved in
90. to be annoying, to bother   91. to die   92. to move   93. to move (from one place
to another)   94. to stand up   95. to seem   96. to resemble   97. to ask for, to request
98. to comb (one's hair)   99. to permit   100. to put makeup on, to put nail polish on
101. to put on (clothing), to become (an emotion)   102. to behave oneself
103. to ask, to question   104. to wonder   105. to worry   106. to lend
107. to prohibit   108. to remain   109. to complain   110. to burn oneself
111. to take off (clothing)   112. to pick up   113. to laugh   114. to meet
115. to jump   116. to greet   117. to sit down   118. to feel (health or emotion)
119. to suggest   120. to delay   121. to bring   122. to calm down   123. to see
124. to get dressed   125. to visit   126. to become (an emotion)

Chapter 14
The Preterit Tense

14.1   1. abrió   2. cerré   3. viajamos   4. miró   5. visité, invité   6. empezó, llovió
7. regresaron, escucharon   8. gustó   9. se acostó   10. sonó   11. soñó
12. vi   13. nos divertimos   14. ofreció   15. ayudaron

14.2   1. Me gustó viajar.   2. leí un periódico.   3. cerraron la puerta.   4. Les ofrecí ayuda.
5. volviste tarde?   6. no se callaron.   7. se acordó de la idea.   8. empezó a las ocho.

14.3   1. dijo, dije   2. hicimos, hicieron   3. diste, darte   4. Hubo   5. traje, trajeron
6. pusieron, puso   7. estuve, estuvieron   8. tuvo, tuve   9. fueron, fuimos
10. fue, fui   11. vinieron, vino   12. anduvimos, anduvieron   13. produje
14. cupieron

14.4   1. cupieron   2. trajo/dio   3. fue   4. pudieron   5. quiso   6. fuimos   7. anduvimos
8. estuvo   9. puse   10. dijo, tuve   11. hiciste   12. supimos   13. dio/trajo
14. produjo   15. vinieron   16. hubo

14.5   1. fue   2. fui   3. estuvimos   4. te fuiste   5. fueron   6. estuvo   7. estuvieron
8. Fue   9. estuvo   10. fue

14.6   *Answers will vary.*

14.7   1. durmió   2. siguieron   3. preferí, prefirió, prefirió   4. se despidió
5. nos divertimos, se divirtieron   6. se sintió, se vistió   7. se murió   8. sirvieron
9. mentí, mintieron   10. sonrió   11. se rió   12. repitió   13. corrigieron
14. me sentí, se sintieron

14.8   1. me tropecé   2. pagué   3. entregó   4. vagamos   5. colgué   6. castigó

14.9   1. contribuyó   2. se cayó   3. influyó   4. huyeron   5. construyeron   6. destruiste

14.10   1. Trabajé mucho ayer. Anoche, descansé.   2. Anoche, miramos televisión en vez
de estudiar.   3. Yo le di a él mi perro; él no me dio nada.   4. Ella leyó la carta de su
amigo hace un mes.   5. Recibimos el paquete hace una semana.   6. ¿Qué le dijiste
a ella? Te dije que él se murió el año pasado. / ¿Qué le dijo Ud. a ella? Le dije que
él se murió.   7. Los niños se acostaron a las nueve anoche.   8. Vi a su hermana ayer.

14.11   1. entré   2. tomamos   3. se durmieron, me dormí   4. vieron, vi   5. Empezó
6. Hizo   7. cobró, cobró   8. escribimos, recibieron   9. se despertó   10. Encontraste
11. quise   12. fue, fue   13. dijo   14. pudieron

Chapter 15
The Imperfect Tense

15.1   1. comía (repeated action)   2. era (description)   3. iban (repeated action)
4. eran (point of origin)   5. nos veíamos (repeated action)   6. eran (point of origin)
7. llegaba (repeated action)   8. volvíamos (repeated action)   9. Había (situation)
10. practicaba (continuous action)   11. ibas (continuous action)   12. iba (continuous
action)   13. tenía (age)   14. comían, comían (continuous action, continuous action)
15. visitaban (repeated action)   16. bebían (repeated action)   17. era (description)
18. tenía, tenía (description, description)   19. Eran, brillaba (time, situation)
20. leía (continuous action)   21. hacía (continuous action)   22. estábamos (condition)
23. era, se reía (description, continuous action)   24. decía/decías/decían (continuous
action)   25. hacían (continuous action)   26. venía (continuous action)
27. Hacía, Hacía, estaban, estaba (narration, narration, narration, narration)
28. cocinaba (repeated action)

15.2 1. Ellos eran de España. 2. ¿Qué hora era? 3. Nosotros estábamos bien.
4. Mi jardín era el más hermoso de la ciudad. 5. Los tres amigos estaban aquí.
6. No estaba cansada. 7. Éramos cantantes. 8. ¿Dónde estabas?
9. Yo estaba en la casa con mi perro.

15.3 1. Era la una y llovía. 2. Yo lo sabía. 3. Él lo podía hacer bien. 4. Los niños
querían comer hamburguesas. 5. Estudiábamos cuando el maestro entró.
6. El hombre huía cuando el policía lo cogió. 7. Todas las noches por muchos años,
ella tenía el mismo sueño. 8. ¿Qué me decía/decías? 9. ¿Qué te iba a decir? /
¿Qué le iba a decir? 10. ¿Por qué la llamó él? 11. ¿Qué hora era cuando te
dormiste (se durmió) anoche? 12. ¿Quién se enfermó ayer? 13. Íbamos a viajar a
Cuba, pero no teníamos dinero. 14. Conocí a tu/su amigo en México. 15. Se fue sin
decirnos nada. 16. ¿Quién le dio las buenas noticias hoy? 17. El hombre estaba en
el banco cuando el ladrón entró. Todo el mundo tenía miedo. 18. El año pasado,
fuimos a España. Nos divertimos.

15.4 1. fue 2. fue 3. iba 4. íbamos 5. fuimos 6. iban 7. iba, iba 8. Ibas 9. fue
10. fueron

15.5 1. The child's mother told him that everything was going to be fine. 2. Did your
feet hurt you during your trip? 3. There was a time when I visited museums.
4. I came, I saw, I conquered. 5. Between the second and third floor, I realized
that I was going to fall down. 6. A long time ago, we used to have a very good time.
7. I didn't know what to do. 8. They had a good relationship. He always cooked
and she always washed the dishes.

15.6 1. compraste 2. traje 3. Era, tenía 4. Empezó, cerré 5. cruzaba, llamó
6. estuvieron 7. andábamos, vimos 8. cobró, cobró 9. escribimos, recibieron
10. caminaba, me di cuenta de, sabía, estaba 11. conoció 12. se divertían
13. iba 14. llegaron, se quedaron

15.7 1. I wanted to have coffee this morning. My colleague brought it to me.
2. The children have a lot of gifts. Their grandparents want them to give them to me.
3. She bought me a jacket. After buying it for me, she became happy.
4. My father refused to give me his car. Instead of giving it to me, he sold it to me.
5. I learned the directions well because my relatives gave them to me carefully.
6. She wants to give me three suitcases for my trip. I prefer that she lend them to me.
7. Each morning, the vendors used to sell me vegetables. Today they didn't sell me
anything. 8. I need two good books. I have to buy them because my friend doesn't
want to lend them to me.

15.8 1. She doesn't give you water; she sells it to you. 2. We ought to give you the ring that
you want this year. We ought to give it to you. 3. Last night my older brother brought
me an apple. He brought it to me because I was hungry. 4. You still have my compact
discs. I want you to return them to me. 5. I like the lobster in this restaurant. I hope
that the waiter serves it to me quickly. 6. I gave you the money because you are a
good friend. I gave it to you because I have confidence in you. 7. I don't know why
she didn't want (refused) to show you her lamps. She showed them to me yesterday.
8. At the beginning, we didn't want to give you a bicycle, but finally we gave it to you.

15.9 1. te lo 2. se lo 3. Me lo 4. se la 5. se los 6. se la 7. hacérselas 8. Me los
9. Te la 10. Se lo 11. Se la 12. Se la 13. contárselo 14. se los

15.10 1. Yo le dije todo. Ud. no me dijo nada. / Yo te dije todo. Tú no me dijiste nada. 2. Íbamos a darles dos cuadernos a los estudiantes. 3. Lisa no tiene nada con que escribir. Tengo dos bolígrafos y decido dárselos. 4. Le di a mi sobrino un violín. Se lo di. 5. Él le iba a dar la guitarra a Héctor. Decidió dármela. 6. ¿Quién nos puede mostrar los abrigos nuevos? ¿Quién nos los quiere mostrar? 7. Los pájaros cantaban y los niños jugaban. 8. Carmen leyó un buen libro hace dos semanas. Ella me lo dio ayer. 9. Le devolví el libro hoy. Se lo devolví a las diez de la mañana. 10. Elena tuvo malos sueños anoche. Me los contó esta mañana. 11. Nos gusta compartir todo. 12. Su abuela quiere que Ud. le lea el artículo. / Tu abuela quiere que le leas el artículo. 13. Esperamos que él sepa nadar para que nos pueda enseñar. 14. José le prestó a Miguel el dinero. Se lo prestó ayer. 15. Tu primo te hizo un favor. Él te lo hizo porque es un buen amigo. / Su primo le hizo un favor. Él se lo hizo porque es un buen amigo. 16. Después de traerle café, fui a mi oficina. Ella me llamó más tarde. 17. Ella compraba una guitarra cuando su amigo le ofreció un piano. 18. Vimos el sofá que ella tenía en su casa. Nos lo dio.

15.11 1. te lo secas 2. quitárnoslo 3. se los cepillaron 4. se las puso 5. me lo corté 6. se las van a lavar 7. se lo peina

15.12 1. He liked the chicken and ate it up. 2. Michael couldn't enter his house because he lost his keys. 3. The spoon fell (I dropped the spoon) on the table and I became furious. 4. They realized that their friends were not coming to see them. 5. How did it occur to you to write a book together? 6. I forgot to do my homework. My patience ran out. 7. Watch out! You are going to drop the glasses. We broke two already. 8. After putting on their socks, they put on their shoes and left.

15.13 1. to approach 2. to drown 3. to reach, to overtake 4. to threaten 5. to pull out, to root out 6. to attract 7. to fit 8. to punish 9. to hang 10. to put in place, to place 11. to compose 12. to conclude 13. to drive 14. to build, to construct 15. to contain 16. to contradict 17. to contribute 18. to correct 19. to believe 20. to undo 21. to stick out 22. to destroy 23. to detain 24. to distract 25. to distribute 26. to hand in, to deliver 27. to flow 28. to flee 29. to include 30. to influence 31. to justify 32. to throw, to shoot 33. to get up early 34. to maintain 35. to chew 36. to hit, to glue 37. to fish 38. to possess 39. to prevent 40. to produce 41. to propose 42. to publish 43. to fulfill 44. to pray 45. to take out 46. to beg 47. to translate 48. to swallow 49. to bump into 50. to wander

Chapter 16
Ser and *Estar* and the Present Tense

16.1 1. están (location) 2. está, está (health, health) 3. están (health) 4. están (location) 5. está (location) 6. está, está (changing mood, changing mood) 7. están (changing mood) 8. estoy (changing mood) 9. está (location) 10. está (location)

16.2 1. El rió está cerca de mi casa. 2. Australia está lejos de los Estados Unidos. 3. La flor blanca está encima de la mesa. 4. Los niños están juntos a sus padres. 5. La escuela está entre la iglesia y el banco. 6. La casa de Julia está detrás del correo. 7. Paula está aquí con sus hermanos. 8. Sus/Tus zapatos están debajo de mi silla. 9. Nuestro problema está bajo control. 10. Los parientes de Elena están en España. Sus maletas están en los Estados Unidos.

16.3 1. es, es (profession, point of origin) 2. son, es (profession, profession) 3. son (point of origin) 4. son (description) 5. es (description) 6. somos (identification) 7. son (material) 8. son (point of origin) 9. soy, es (point of origin, point of origin) 10. es (possession) 11. Eres (profession) 12. son (description) 13. es (point of origin) 14. es (profession) 15. Es (impersonal expression)

16.4 1. es 2. es 3. son 4. son 5. somos 6. está 7. estoy 8. está 9. estamos 10. Estás 11. están

16.5 1. soy 2. están 3. están 4. eres 5. es 6. están 7. están, estamos 8. es, están 9. está 10. son 11. están, es 12. está, está 13. es 14. están, están, son 15. está 16. está 17. es 18. Son 19. es 20. es

16.6 1. Los dentistas están en sus oficinas. 2. Todo el mundo está enfermo. Hasta los doctores están enfermos. 3. La sopa está caliente. La comida está deliciosa/sabrosa. 4. Es necesario estudiar. 5. ¿Es posible aprender todo?

16.7 1. está 2. Ser, ser 3. es 4. están 5. estoy 6. eres 7. es, Son 8. es 9. Son, es 10. Es 11. es 12. ser 13. estar 14. está 15. está 16. está 17. es 18. está 19. están 20. es 21. está 22. estar 23. está, está 24. están 25. soy 26. es 27. está, está 28. está 29. estamos 30. es

Chapter 17
Ser and *Estar* in the Preterit and Imperfect Tenses

17.1 1. fue 2. fui 3. estuvimos 4. estuvo 5. estuvieron 6. estuvo 7. estuvieron 8. Fue 9. estuvo 10. estuvieron 11. estuve 12. estuvimos

17.2 1. Yo era de Venezuela. 2. Ellos eran de España. 3. ¿Qué hora era? 4. Nosotros estábamos bien. 5. Mi jardín era el más hermoso de la ciudad. 6. Los tres amigos estaban aquí. 7. Yo no estaba cansada. 8. Éramos cantantes. 9. ¿Dónde estabas? 10. Yo estaba en la casa con mi hermana.

17.3 1. fui 2. estuvimos 3. era 4. estuvo 5. fue 6. fue, fui 7. era 8. era 9. Eran 10. era 11. era 12. estuvo/fue 13. estuvimos 14. Era/Fue 15. Era/Fue

17.4 1. compraste 2. traje 3. Era, tenía 4. Empezó, cerré / Empezaba, cerraba 5. cruzaba, llamó 6. estuvieron 7. andábamos, vimos 8. cobró, cobró 9. escribimos, recibieron 10. caminaba, me di cuenta de, sabía, estaba. 11. conoció 12. se divertían 13. iba 14. llegaron, se quedaron

Chapter 18
The Present Progressive Tense

18.1 1. hablando 2. besando 3. andando 4. viajando 5. limpiando 6. cenando 7. sacando 8. bebiendo 9. comiendo 10. aprendiendo 11. agradeciendo 12. escogiendo 13. viendo 14. abriendo 15. asistiendo 16. insistiendo 17. permitiendo 18. prohibiendo 19. creyendo 20. leyendo 21. trayendo 22. huyendo 23. oyendo 24. sirviendo 25. pidiendo 26. corrigiendo 27. repitiendo 28. siguiendo 29. durmiendo 30. muriendo 31. diciendo 32. haciendo

18.2   1. está corrigiendo   2. estamos sacando   3. estoy estudiando   4. estamos haciendo
5. están preparando   6. estás diciendo   7. está nevando   8. están durmiendo
9. están escribiendo   10. están hablando   11. estás friendo   12. está comiendo

18.3   1. leyendo   2. sabe   3. tocando   4. conocer   5. tener, quiere   6. almuerzan, salen
7. devolver   8. graduarse, hacer

18.4   1. está repitiendo   2. están siguiendo   3. estamos leyendo   4. están haciendo
5. están almorzando   6. estoy hirviendo   7. está siguiendo   8. están esperando

18.5   1. ¿Les están hablando las mujeres a los hombres?   2. ¿Qué me estás diciendo (tú)? /
¿Qué estás diciéndome? / ¿Qué me está diciendo (Ud.)?   3. ¿Puede Ud. repetir
la pregunta? Los estudiantes no le está prestando atención. / Los estudiantes no está
haciéndole caso.   4. Sabemos que él está buscando una idea. La necesita para escribir
un cuento.   5. ¿Qué está pasando?   6. El abogado fantástico está soñando con un viaje
a Italia.

18.6   *Answers will vary.*

18.7   1. quiere   2. viene   3. sabe, sabe   4. estoy pensando   5. podemos   6. llamando
7. sonríe   8. juegan   9. está confesando   10. despertarse   11. van   12. haciendo

18.8   1. We are going to María's house because she is preparing chicken with rice.   2. The waiter
is serving us our meal.   3. The nannies are taking care of a lot of children in the park.
4. It is 8 o'clock at night and it is already late, but the man keeps reading his favorite book.
He keeps reading it until 11 o'clock.   5. The girl is swimming in the pool, because her
parents think that it is dangerous to swim in the ocean.   6. The children are putting the
plates in the oven. They are putting them in the oven to annoy their parents.   7. Why are
you lying to her/him?   8. Who is laughing?   9. The elephant has been living in the zoo
for five years.   10. We keep learning Spanish.

18.9   1. ¿Por qué está llorando la gente?   2. Está lloviendo.   3. ¿Estás mirando televisión
ahora? / ¿Está (Ud.) mirando televisión ahora?   4. ¿Por qué están riéndose las
muchachas? / ¿Por qué se están riendo las muchachas?   5. Nos toca a nosotros. Estamos
usando las computadoras ahora.   6. Teresa está esperando el tren, pero está perdiendo
paciencia.   7. ¿En qué estás pensando? / ¿En qué está pensando?   8. Estamos tratando
de dormirnos.

Chapter 19
The Past Progressive Tenses

19.1   1. Yo estaba limpiando la casa.   2. Rosa seguía comiendo.   3. Pablo les estaba vendiendo
medicina a sus amigos.   4. Estábamos aprendiendo a bailar.   5. ¿Por qué me estaba
mintiendo ella? / ¿Por qué estaba mintiéndome?   6. ¿Qué estaba Ud. haciendo? /
¿Qué estaba haciendo Ud.?   7. ¿Quién estaba durmiendo en el tren?   8. Todo el mundo
estaba saliendo para las salidas.   9. Los muchachos y las muchachas estaban tirando
la pelota.   10. Los políticos estaban empezando su campaña electoral.

19.2 1. We were having a good time until the play began.   2. Did you want to feed the birds in the park?   3. We knew that we were going to be successful.   4. The women were celebrating their retirement until 11 o'clock at night.   5. I was getting acquainted with Mexico, little by little.   6. Our professor was teaching for an hour yesterday.   7. We were working when our friends arrived.   8. What were you talking about?   9. She wasn't listening to me.   10. The waiter wasn't serving us the meal.   11. The teachers were repeating the instructions until we understood.   12. Why were you looking for them for so long when you knew that your friends were hiding?   13. We were dancing last night until midnight.   14. Nobody was walking around here.

19.3 1. esperaron   2. dijo   3. trajeron   4. se cayeron   5. di   6. pudo   7. fuimos   8. gustó   9. viste   10. conoció

19.4 1. era   2. tenían   3. quería   4. estudiaba   5. jugaba   6. escribía   7. estaba, se quejaba   8. ponía

19.5 1. le/les/te   2. les   3. le   4. me   5. te/le/les   6. nos

19.6 1. Julia looks for her sister. She is looking for her.   2. We take care of the babies. We take care of them.   3. The two brothers/siblings help their family. The family appreciates their help.   4. The gardener looks at the birds. He looks at them fly.   5. The students greet their teacher. They greet her every day.   6. Why are you calling me today? Why are you calling me at home?   7. Manuel visits the woman in Peru. He wants to marry her in the spring.   8. All the tourists are waiting for the train. It doesn't bother them to wait for it because it is cool out.

19.7 1. I swear it to you.   2. I put on my gloves. I put them on.   3. The indigenous woman doesn't sell water to us; she gives it to us.   4. I like the shellfish in this restaurant. The waiter serves them to me with pleasure.   5. Ana brings dessert to her friends. She brings it to them.

19.8 1. ¿Les dice la verdad a sus amigos? Se la decimos. / ¿Les dices la verdad a tus amigos? Te la decimos.   2. Siempre le escribo cartas. Se las estoy escribiendo ahora. / Siempre le escribo cartas. Estoy escribiéndoselas ahora.   3. Irene le da regalos a su hijo cada Navidad. Este año, va a dárselos el día de su cumpleaños. / Irene le da regalos a su hijo cada Navidad. Este año, se los va a dar el día de su cumpleaños.   4. Le mostramos la nueva zapatería a mi amiga. Ella mira los tacones, pero no se los compra.   5. A veces, la gente no entiende lo que decimos. A veces tenemos que explicárselo.   6. Enrique les lee un cuento a sus hijos cada noche a las ocho. Se lo está leyendo ahora. / Enrique les lee un cuento a sus hijos cada noche a las ocho. Está leyéndoselo ahora.

19.9 1. Michael couldn't enter his house because he lost his keys.   2. The spoon fell and I got angry.   3. Careful! The glasses are going to fall. We broke two already.   4. It didn't occur to me to work yesterday.   5. You couldn't prepare the garlic soup last night. You ran out of garlic.   6. I forgot to do my homework.

Chapter 20
The Present Subjunctive

20.1 1. vengan   2. diga   3. haga   4. conozcan   5. durmamos   6. sepa   7. tomemos   8. se levanten   9. llegue   10. me quede   11. esté   12. dé   13. vayas   14. sean   15. lean   16. tenga   17. traigamos   18. se sienten

20.2 1. diga   2. pague   3. se sientan   4. deje de llorar   5. expliquemos   6. tenga   7. dé   8. sepa   9. haya   10. vayan   11. sea   12. hagamos   13. esté   14. bese

20.3 *Answers will vary. Some possible answers are shown.*   1. Yo dudo que a mis padres les guste viajar.   2. Lo siento que mi amigo tenga malos sueños.   3. Es posible que ella no se divierta mucho.   4. Él duda que seamos buenos estudiantes.   5. Ella teme que no volvamos a los Estados Unidos.   6. Yo le pido que Sara me traiga flores a mi casa.   7. Dudo que Ud. conozca a mi tío.   8. Es una lástima que mi hermano y yo no nos veamos mucho.   9. ¿Es posible que no haya clase los lunes?   10. No creo que Carla sea de Polonia.

20.4 1. tengan   2. tienen   3. visite   4. traigamos   5. ame   6. corrijamos   7. están   8. se queja   9. se quede   10. se van   11. baile   12. vea   13. estén   14. sepan   15. es   16. haga

20.5 1. antes de que, visite   2. Después de que, me bañe   3. a menos que, vayan   4. luego que, tenga   5. para que, sepan   6. luego que, terminen   7. Antes de que, venga   8. para que, puedas   9. hasta que, lleguen   10. En caso de que, tengan   11. para que, estén   12. a pesar de que, tengan   13. sin que, invite   14. después de que, se vayan   15. Cuando, pueda   16. cuando, nos reunamos / cuando, nos encontremos   17. Cuando, vuelvan / Cuando, regresen   18. cuando, aprenda

20.6 1. se enfermen   2. descansemos   3. llegue   4. se quejen   5. cocine   6. duermas   7. haya   8. tenga   9. esté   10. quiera   11. acompañe   12. sea   13. venga   14. hable

20.7 1. estén   2. pique   3. obtenga   4. conozca   5. sepa   6. ganen   7. vengan   8. preste   9. aprendan   10. ensayen

20.8 1. abramos   2. te vayas   3. perdone   4. nade   5. llegue

20.9 1. escuchen   2. fume   3. se pierda   4. diga, tome   5. cante

Chapter 21
Commands

21.1 1. Take your medicine and call the doctor in the morning.   2. Continue to the right, please.   3. Close the door, please, and open the window.   4. Run to the store and buy milk.   5. Prepare the meal tonight and afterward, take out the garbage, please.   6. Read *Don Quixote* for the class and write your opinion about the main theme.   7. Eat more fruits and vegetables.   8. Count on me.

21.2 1. apaga   2. comparte   3. decide   4. devuelve   5. dobla   6. mira   7. oye   8. regresa   9. termina   10. tira

21.3 1. Di   2. Sé   3. Lee   4. Escribe   5. Ten   6. Pon   7. Ven   8. Haz   9. Trae   10. Espera

21.4 1. fíjate   2. anímate   3. cállate   4. arréglate   5. muévete   6. vete   7. quédate   8. párate   9. cepíllate   10. vístete   11. diviértete   12. duérmete

21.5 1. Do me a favor.   2. Tell us the truth.   3. Go away.   4. Put on your socks.   5. Leave now.   6. Be a good dog.   7. Be careful.   8. Come here.

21.6 1. corre, no corras   2. camina, no camines   3. bebe, no bebas   4. sigue, no sigas   5. repite, no repitas   6. habla, no hables   7. mira, no mires   8. rompe, no rompas   9. vende, no vendas   10. abre, no abras   11. sube, no subas   12. empieza, no empieces   13. miente, no mientas   14. sal, no salgas   15. pon, no pongas   16. toca, no toques

21.7   1. No comas la ensalada en Guatemala. No la comas.   2. No corras; otro tren viene.
3. No me digas el secreto. No me lo digas.   4. No lo hagas.   5. No lo toques.
6. No tengas miedo.   7. No le prestes dinero a ella. No se lo prestes.   8. No vengas tarde
al desfile.   9. No nos des malas noticias.   10. No le traigas dulces al niño. No se los
traigas.   11. No te vayas.   12. No te preocupes.   13. No me esperes.   14. No tengas
envidia.

21.8   1. Don't swim in this lake.   2. Don't walk in the mud.   3. Don't go to bed late.
4. Don't give it to us.   5. Don't leave the dirty plates on the table.   6. Don't work so much.
7. Don't come to class on Monday.   8. Don't arrive late.

21.9   1. diga, no diga   2. haga, no haga   3. trabaje, no trabaje   4. entre, no entre
5. lea, no lea   6. espere, no espere   7. beba, no beba

21.10   1. quédense, no se queden   2. siéntense, no se sienten   3. levántense, no se levanten
4. acuéstense, no se acuesten   5. duérmanse, no se duerman

21.11   1. digamos   2. empecemos   3. sigamos   4. vámonos   5. despertémonos   6. juguemos
7. esperemos   8. entremos   9. tomemos   10. crucemos   11. durmámonos
12. almorcemos   13. comamos   14. descansemos   15. volvamos

21.12   1. No lo toques.   2. No me lo digas.   3. No lo hagas.   4. Ayúdeme.   5. Dele el libro.
6. Déselo.   7. No se lo dé.   8. Bésame.   9. Siéntense Uds., por favor.   10. Empecemos.
11. Espérennos.   12. Vayan a la derecha.   13. Ten cuidado.   14. Llene este formulario,
por favor.   15. No bebas tanto.   16. Saca la basura.   17. No se vaya.   18. No se
preocupen.   19. Sigamos las direcciones.   20. Maneje más despacio, por favor.
21. Quédense por favor.   22. Llámame.   23. No compre nada.   24. No se rían.
25. Vamos.

21.13   1. se quede   2. diga   3. comer   4. se mejoren   5. busco   6. gusta   7. venga   8. sea
9. quiere   10. visite   11. llega   12. hagan   13. compremos   14. estar, estés   15. ir
16. gusta   17. guste   18. llame   19. esté   20. sepa   21. eres   22. vaya   23. tenga
24. haya

Chapter 22
Nouns, Articles, Adjectives, and Pronouns

22.1   1. el, X   2. X, la   3. los, la   4. el   5. las   6. las   7. X, la   8. la, las   9. la

22.2   1. mis   2. sus   3. sus   4. sus   5. su   6. su   7. su   8. nuestra   9. nuestra   10. su

22.3   1. mío   2. suyo/tuyo, mío   3. suyos   4. suyas   5. mías   6. nuestra   7. mío   8. suyos

22.4   1. el nuestro   2. los suyos / los tuyos   3. la suya, la suya / la tuya   4. la mía
5. los nuestros   6. la mía   7. el nuestro   8. el suyo

22.5   1. mío   2. suyos/tuyos   3. nuestros   4. suyos   5. suya   6. suya

22.6   1. el suyo / el tuyo   2. el suyo   3. el mío   4. los nuestros   5. la tuya   6. los suyos

22.7   1. lo que   2. que   3. que   4. que   5. quienes   6. que   7. Lo que   8. quien
9. quienes   10. lo que   11. que   12. quien   13. cuya   14. cuyos

22.8   1. Rita sold the house that I liked.   2. What you said was true.   3. I don't know if this
well-known man, who studies philosophy, wants to go to Greece with his friends.

22.9   1. quien   2. que   3. que / la que / la cual   4. la cual   5. las que / las cuales   6. que
7. quien   8. que   9. que   10. quien / quienes   11. la cual

22.10   1. X   2. el   3. al   4. la   5. Al   6. lo   7. lo   8. la   9. X   10. lo   11. los   12. la
13. la   14. las   15. Lo   16. la   17. al   18. el   19. los   20. X   21. X

22.11   1. la cual   2. quien   3. el cual   4. cuyo   5. cuya   6. los cuales   7. quienes   8. cuyas
9. las cuales   10. cuyos

22.12   1. el viejo   2. el blanco   3. el grande

Chapter 23
The Present Perfect Tense

23.1   1. jugado   2. buscado   3. conocido   4. entrado   5. devuelto   6. sido   7. estado
8. dado   9. visto   10. escrito   11. roto   12. tenido   13. querido   14. hecho
15. dicho   16. ido   17. abierto   18. cerrado   19. muerto   20. amado

23.2   1. sido   2. tenido   3. podido   4. estado   5. querido   6. sabido   7. dicho   8. dado
9. vuelto   10. puesto   11. hecho   12. llegado   13. he dormido   14. has roto
15. ha abierto   16. hemos estado   17. habéis escrito   18. han visto

23.3   1. ha traído   2. hemos recibido   3. han llamado   4. han prestado   5. has amado
6. han vuelto   7. se ha muerto   8. se han ido   9. han hecho   10. han hablado
11. han viajado   12. he visto   13. he podido   14. se han acostado   15. nos hemos mudado

23.4   1. haber   2. hemos   3. han   4. haber   5. hemos   6. ha   7. han   8. haber   9. Han
10. han

23.5   1. He cruzado la calle a la escuela.   2. Jamás he entrado en la clase.   3. Mis compañeros
han entrado también.   4. Le hemos dicho "hola" al profesor.   5. Nos hemos sentado.
6. He escrito con lápiz.   7. Mis amigos han usado una computadora antes.   8. Hemos
contestado las preguntas.   9. Hemos almorzado juntos.   10. Nos hemos despedido
del profesor.   11. Hemos ido en bus a casa.   12. Les hemos saludado a nuestros padres
al llegar a casa.

23.6   1. ¿Cómo has estado? / ¿Cómo ha estado? / ¿Cómo han estado?   2. ¿Adónde han ido todas
las flores?   3. ¿Quién acaba de llamar?   4. ¿Qué has hecho? / ¿Qué ha hecho?   5. Hemos
mandado/enviado el documento.   6. ¿Se han desayunado ellos hoy?   7. He prendido el
horno, y he metido el pollo. Tengo que cocinarlo por una hora.   8. Ya no hace calor porque
los estudiantes han abierto todas las ventanas en el salón.   9. Los exterminadores han
matado todas las cucarachas.   10. Laura y su hija acaba de llegar a Italia.

Chapter 24
The Past Perfect Tense

24.1   1. Los niños pensaban/pensaron que sus padres habían salido.   2. Ya había puesto la mesa
cuando mi familia llegó.   3. Roberto fue a un país que él nunca había visitado antes.
4. Mis colegas me dijeron que ellos habían terminado su trabajo.

24.2   1. The professor knew that I had studied.   2. The child thought that her dog had
returned.   3. They said that they had returned the books to the library.   4. We believed
that our friends had written to us.   5. We were sure that the young people had been
successful / had had success.   6. We thought that the thieves had been in the bank.
7. The police believed that we had seen them.   8. We told the detectives that we had
not been good witnesses.

24.3 1. ido 2. esperado, ver 3. descansado, cenar 4. jubilarse, pagado 5. dado, salir 6. dicho, perdido

24.4 1. quemada 2. rota 3. muerto 4. hecha 5. expresadas 6. dormido 7. querido 8. vendidos 9. compradas 10. pasado 11. resueltos 12. alquilado 13. escondido 14. entregadas 15. grabada

24.5 1. está cerrada 2. está abierta 3. está escrita 4. está construida 5. está hecha 6. están muertas 7. están fritos 8. están resueltos

24.6 1. Cerrada 2. herido, preocupados 3. nublado 4. arreglado 5. separada, dividido

24.7 1. Los antropólogos hallaron los vasos. 2. Un dictador ha gobernado el país. 3. El maestro enseñó la clase. 4. La víctima reconoció al criminal. 5. Los padres ofrecieron los regalos. 6. Catarina había planchado las camisas. 7. Los inquilinos apagaron las luces. 8. Se dice que Colón descubrió las Américas en 1492.

Chapter 25
The Future Tense

25.1 1. iré 2. llegará 3. veré 4. estudiaremos 5. corregirá 6. comprará 7. dejará 8. acompañará, viajaré 9. estarás 10. triunfarán 11. asistirán 12. cobrará 13. venceremos 14. responderás

25.2 1. haré 2. vendrá 3. saldrá 4. diremos 5. podrás 6. pondrán 7. valdrá 8. tendrá 9. sabrá 10. Habrá

25.3 1. Si ella no tiene cuidado, se perderá. 2. Si Jorge me lo dice, yo no se lo repetiré a nadie. 3. Si practicamos, podremos aprender un idioma nuevo. 4. Ellos comprarán la casa si les gustan el jardín y el balcón. 5. Si la obra de teatro es chistosa/divertida, el público se reirá. 6. Él nunca se fijará en nada. No se quejará jamás.

25.4 1. Él vendrá a verme. 2. Tendré una cita con el dentista en febrero. 3. ¿Cuánto valdrá el carro? 4. ¿Qué me dirás? 5. Saldremos para México en julio. 6. Trabajaré en un teatro. 7. Habrá once estudiantes aquí. 8. Empezaremos a estudiar. 9. El muchacho tendrá éxito. 10. Los deportistas tendrán sed. 11. ¿Cuánto me cobrará Ud.? 12. Yo patinaré porque me gusta. 13. Ella no se meterá en la vida de los otros. 14. El pueblo vencerá. 15. Triunfaremos. 16. La muchacha cumplirá diez años el miércoles. 17. Olivia vivirá en Perú. 18. La maestra corregirá la tarea. 19. Yo asistiré a la universidad. 20. Elena soñará que te vio. / Elena sueña que te verá.

25.5 1. I will know more tomorrow than what I know today. 2. Three chairs and eight students will not fit in the classroom. 3. The doctors will not sleep until four o'clock in the morning. 4. I will return soon. 5. From time to time, I will visit you in Brazil. 6. If you want to go shopping, I will take you. 7. If he becomes nervous, he will speak softly. 8. If you run a lot, you will be able to lose weight. 9. If you lose your keys, what will you do? 10. They tell me that you will get married next year.

25.6 1. ¿Tendrá hambre el niño? 2. ¿Qué hará la mujer? 3. ¿Quién pondrá la mesa? 4. Ella sabrá las direcciones. 5. ¿Cuánto valdrá este apartamento lujoso?

25.7 1. Where will you have gone after leaving your house? 2. We will have bought our tickets for Saturday. 3. I will have seen the students before they travel to Mexico. 4. In one month, I will have lived here for 10 years. 5. Will you have finished your work for the coming week?

Chapter 26
The Conditional Tense

26.1 1. produciría 2. haríamos 3. dirían 4. vendría 5. daría 6. se acostarían
7. regresarían 8. llevaría 9. gustaría 10. Habría 11. vería 12. saldríamos
13. llegaría 14. entendería 15. podría 16. iría

26.2 1. Yo la ayudaría. 2. Ella iría de compras. 3. ¿Mirarías tú televisión? 4. Ellos venderían
la comida. 5. Los mozos les darían la comida a los clientes. 6. Tendríamos mucho que
hacer. 7. El conductor manejaría rápidamente. 8. ¿Cantarías? 9. ¿Vendrían Uds.
a mi casa? 10. Yo lo haría. 11. No le diría nada. 12. Te cobraría cien dólares.
13. Los niños no leerían mucho. 14. Sabría nadar. 15. Habría mucha gente en los trenes.
16. No cabrían más. 17. Le traería las flores a su hermana. 18. Nos pondríamos los
zapatos. 19. Podría Ud. acompañarme al bus? 20. ¿A Uds. les gustaría ir al cine?

26.3 1. podría 2. se mejoraría 3. me quejaría 4. diríamos 5. se divertirían 6. estaría
7. tendrían 8. dolerían

26.4 1. A José le gustaría nadar, pero tiene miedo del agua. 2. Yo no le diría nada porque no
lo conozco bien. 3. Nuestros amigos mexicanos vendrían a California a visitar a su familia,
pero prefieren viajar a Europa este año. 4. Juan me dijo que le daría el libro si quiere
estudiarlo. / Juan me dijo que le daría el libro si lo quiere estudiar. / Juan me dijo que te
daría el libro si quieres estudiarlo. / Juan me dijo que te daría el libro si lo quieres estudiar.
5. Iríamos a la fiesta de Julia, pero no sabemos dónde vive.

26.5 1. Él habría llegado a tiempo, pero se le perdieron las direcciones. 2. No le habríamos
dicho nuestro secreto a nadie. 3. Juan y su compañero habrían ido a México, pero
decidieron ahorrar su dinero para el año entrante. 4. Antonio y yo habríamos viajado
a Colombia, pero el vuelo costó demasiado. 5. Enrique habría sido un buen presidente,
pero quería tener más tiempo para pasar con su familia. 6. Elvira habría devuelto el
dinero que halló, pero se lo dio a su hijo.

Chapter 27
The Present Perfect Subjunctive

27.1 1. ¿Es posible que ellos se hayan dormido? 2. Es probable que hayamos tenido muchas
oportunidades. 3. Estamos alegres de que nuestros dos amigos se hayan conocido.
4. Estoy triste de que el hotel no me haya llamado para confirmar mi reservación.
5. José espera que nosotros nos hayamos sentido bien. 6. El abogado se alegra de que
sus clientes hayan leído el contrato. 7. Los ingenieros lo sienten que los edificios hayan
tenido problemas. 8. El trabajador está triste de que su jefe no lo haya llamado para
averiguar donde está.

27.2 1. hayan estado 2. haya salvado 3. nos hayamos atrevido 4. haya leído 5. haya sido
6. se hayan demorado 7. se hayan levantado 8. se hayan divertido 9. hayan venido
10. se haya roto

Chapter 28
The Imperfect Subjunctive

28.1   1. hablara: It was important that James speak to me.   2. se sintiera: It was a shame that she didn't feel well last night.   3. conocieran: Was it possible that you knew my sister? 4. hiciéramos: It was necessary that we do exercises.   5. hubiera: It was impossible that there was no traffic today.   6. llegara: It was urgent that the ambulance arrive within five minutes.   7. diéramos: It was possible that we gave a present to the teacher. 8. dijera, mintiera: It was doubtful that my niece told me the truth; it was possible that she lied to me.   9. se mejoraran: It would be good that you get better.   10. se graduara: It was probable that the whole class graduated.   11. se fuera: It would be impossible that Sara left without saying anything to us.   12. llamáramos: It was good that we called her. 13. tomaran: It would be necessary that the tourists drink a lot of water in the mountains. 14. viajáramos: It would be doubtful that we travel to Mexico this year.   15. se quedaran: It was possible that Beatriz and Isabel stayed in Italy.

28.2   1. I wanted them to write to me.   2. My neighbor preferred that I bring nothing to him. 3. We were glad that he arrived early.   4. She begged us not to go.   5. I was glad that you moved to a house.   6. The owner insisted that we pay the rent.   7. I told my friend to call me.   8. The tourist suggested to the cab driver that he not drive so fast.

28.3   1. hablara   2. estudiara   3. bailara   4. cantara   5. vinieran

28.4   1. se quedaran   2. trajéramos   3. comiera   4. prestara   5. ayudáramos   6. votáramos

28.5   1. estuvieran   2. te callaras   3. hiciéramos   4. acompañara

28.6   1. The child wanted his parents to bring him a present.   2. Michael's friends wanted him to lose weight.   3. Why did you want me to lend you money?   4. Fred hoped that Linda would marry him.   5. The student in Spain was glad that her parents were proud of her. 6. I wanted them to stay with me.   7. We hoped that it was nothing serious. 8. The husband did not want his wife to retire.

28.7   1. cantar, cantar   2. comer, vivir   3. cuidaran   4. dejaran   5. esperara   6. se acostara 7. bajar   8. viajar   9. fuera   10. dijera

28.8   1. saber   2. pudieran   3. fuera   4. viniera   5. supiera   6. ducharse   7. saliera 8. lavarse, comer   9. tuvieran   10. dijera   11. estuviera   12. ir   13. empezara 14. necesitara

28.9   1. Laura quería/quiso que su esposo la acompañara a Chile.   2. Era/Fue necesario que la gente no fumara en los restaurantes.   3. Julia estaba/estuvo contenta de que Uds. estuvieran aquí.   4. Yo sabía que su nieta quería ir a la universidad.   5. Me alegré de que pudieras correr en el maratón.   6. ¿Qué querías que yo hiciera?   7. Raúl y yo esperábamos/esperamos que Uds. se encontraran bien.   8. Era/Fue importante que el carpintero supiera lo que estaba haciendo.   9. Esperaba/Esperé que el vuelo de mis amigos llegara a tiempo.   10. Los deportistas dudaban/dudaron que ganáramos el partido. 11. Nuestros amigos nos rogaban/rogaron que no subiéramos a la cumbre de la montaña. 12. Los entrenadores insistían/insistieron que la gente hiciera más ejercicio.

28.10   1. Era/Fue necesario que ella empezara las lecciones a tiempo.   2. Era/Fue una lástima que él no supiera expresarse.   3. ¿Sería posible que ellos ya hubieran salido de la reunión? 4. Los hijos de Juana le rogaban/rogaron que no fumara.   5. ¿Quisieras que yo hablara con tu jefe?   6. Mi hermano dudó que yo cantara bien ayer.   7. La maestra de mi hija sugirió que yo la llamara.   8. Yo quería que ellos se quedaran conmigo. Ellos querían que yo fuera con ellos.   9. Me gustaría hacer un documental que se trata de los inca.   10. Yo quiero tomar su foto, si no le molesta.

28.11   1. fuera, sería   2. gustara, iría   3. escribiéramos, respondería   4. me sintiera, podría 5. ganarían, vendieran   6. dormirían, se acostaran   7. hablaríamos, supiéramos 8. tendría, se pusiera   9. lloraría, doliera   10. me iría, quisiera, me quedara

Chapter 29
The Past Perfect Subjunctive

29.1   1. hubiéramos pagado   2. hubiéramos hecho   3. hubiera dicho   4. hubiera viajado 5. hubiera venido   6. hubiera llovido   7. se hubieran mejorado   8. se hubieran casado 9. hubiéramos gastado   10. hubieran vivido

29.2   1. I wish / Would to God that we had not said it to him/you/her.   2. I wish that you had been well.   3. I wish that we had gone on vacation.   4. It was necessary that the carpenter construct it. / It was necessary for the carpenter to have constructed it.   5. It was urgent that we take the sick man to the hospital.   6. It was a pity that no one had been in the theater.   7. We hoped that everyone had taken advantage of the situation. 8. The doormen doubted that the new tenants had painted the walls.   9. The lawyer didn't think that his clients had won.   10. It was possible that the thieves had robbed the bank.

29.3   1. Yo habría ido.   2. Tú habrías comido. / Ud. habría comido. / Uds. habrían comido. 3. Nos habríamos reído.   4. Ellos le habrían dicho.   5. Los maestros habrían enseñado. 6. Marisa habría estado contenta.   7. Hillary habría sido presidente.   8. Habría sido posible.   9. Las mujeres lo habrían aprendido.   10. Los hombres habrían salido.

29.4   1. Yo habría ido a la fiesta si yo no hubiera tenido miedo.   2. Ud. habría comido el pescado si lo hubiéramos cocinado en casa.   3. Nos habríamos reído si la película hubiera sido chistosa/divertida.   4. Ellos te habrían dicho la verdad si tú la hubieras querido saber. / Ellos te habrían dicho la verdad si tú hubieras querido saberla.   5. Los maestros habrían enseñado si los estudiantes hubieran llegado.   6. Marisa habría estado contenta si hubiera sabido patinar.   7. Hillary habría sido presidente si más gente hubiera votado por ella. 8. Habría sido posible que me hubieran visto.   9. Las mujeres lo habrían aprendido si hubieran comprado el libro.   10. Los hombres habrían salido de la casa si hubieran tenido adonde ir.

29.5   1. estén   2. corra   3. guste   4. te quejes   5. sepamos   6. ganen   7. vengan 8. tenga   9. se sientan   10. se vistan

29.6   1. se acueste   2. lleve   3. se vaya   4. consigan   5. entren   6. se caigan

29.7   1. escuchen   2. vaya   3. fume   4. haga   5. cante

29.8   1. conozcan   2. pueda   3. duerma   4. trabajen   5. sean   6. tengan   7. logre 8. aprendamos

29.9   1. entraran   2. hubiera   3. trajera   4. nos fijáramos   5. te sentaras   6. saliéramos

29.10   1. se mejorara   2. regresara   3. encantara   4. diera   5. nos animáramos   6. vieras

29.11   1. empezara   2. desistiera   3. se perdieran   4. fuera   5. pudiera   6. estuviera
7. habláramos   8. supiera   9. dijera   10. ganaras

29.12   1. The author read the article so that we could understand it.   2. Before his girlfriend
went to Spain, Fred studied Spanish for two years.   3. We were going to play tennis until
it began to rain.   4. The doctor knew that his patient's knee had swollen.   5. Elena would
learn to speak Spanish, but she doesn't like to study.   6. It was necessary for the best
architect to design the museum.   7. It wouldn't be possible for such a disaster to occur.
8. The judge hoped that the witnesses had seen everything.   9. The tourists would arrive
a two o'clock if the trains weren't so delayed.   10. I would have gone on vacation with her
if she had invited me.   11. Would you have done him the favor if Andrew had asked you?
12. Would it be possible that you learned and understood all the lessons?

Chapter 30
Idioms

30.1   1. At the beginning, everything was wonderful.   2. You put on your blouse inside out.
3. By dint of study, she learned history well.   4. We went to Madrid on foot.
5. Don't speak to me now; I'm in a bad mood.   6. They didn't find their keys anywhere.
7. I don't know what to do in regard to your/his/her/their problems.   8. By day, I work;
by night, I sleep.   9. If we want to arrive on time, we have to go to the right.   10. The girl
can / is able to listen to music and study at the same time.   11. I think I'll be in Mexico
at the beginning of July.   12. He lent me his car unwillingly.   13. They like to dine in the
open air.   14. In fact, Paul found out yesterday but said nothing to me.   15. A boat carried
us across the river.   16. I am in a very good mood today.   17. You should walk to the left.
18. Probably Henry and Salome will come next week.   19. We do it willingly.
20. The man prefers to walk straight ahead.   21. In the distance, I see her coming.
22. I like to rest. On the other hand, my friend likes to work.   23. I tell them to do it
in this way.   24. I write scripts for television. Really?   25. Michael doesn't have a lot
of money, but he decided to travel anyway.   26. You weren't successful the first time,
but you tried again.   27. From now on, we are going to run every day.   28. We attend class
every other day.   29. Suddenly, it began to rain.   30. One sees the good and the bad
everywhere.

30.2   1. c   2. f   3. d   4. e   5. b   6. a

30.3   1. The girl pays attention to her teacher because she likes him.   2. Elisa gets along well
with her mother-in-law.   3. The boy liked to feed the birds in the park.   4. The hotel faces
the plaza.   5. Bill became a lawyer.   6. The visitor hasn't seen her homeland for a long
time. She misses it a lot and wants to give all her friends a hug.   7. I liked the Guatemalan
vest; I gave 200 pesos to the seller and carried it away.   8. I realized that everything was
not all right.   9. The child burst out crying.   10. Shellfish harms me.

30.4   *Answers will vary. Some possible answers are shown.*   1. ¿Cuánto tiempo hace que
el muchacho mira televisión?   2. ¿Desde cuándo duerme Adam?   3. ¿Cuánto tiempo
lleva Ud. llevando gafas?   4. ¿Cuánto tiempo hace que Isabel y Carlos esperan?
5. ¿Desde cuándo son amigos ellos?   6. Hace ocho horas que él duerme.
7. Llevo dos años llevando gafas.   8. Hace quince minutos que ellos esperan.

30.5 1. How long had you been in Chile when you had to leave? 2. How long had the children been swimming when the lifeguard arrived? 3. How long had Tony been reading when he fell asleep? 4. I had been in Paraguay for two months when I decided to return home. 5. The frustrated man had been waiting for the train for 20 minutes. 6. We had been living in Paris for 15 months.

Index